Selfless Revolutionaries

Selfless Revolutionaries

Biko, Black Consciousness, Black Theology,
and a Global Ethic of Solidarity and Resistance

Allan Aubrey Boesak

CASCADE Books • Eugene, Oregon

SELFLESS REVOLUTIONARIES
Biko, Black Consciousness, Black Theology, and a Global Ethic of Solidarity and Resistance

Copyright © 2021 Allan Aubrey Boesak. All rights reserved. Except for brief quotations in critical publications or reviews, no part of this book may be reproduced in any manner without prior written permission from the publisher. Write: Permissions, Wipf and Stock Publishers, 199 W. 8th Ave., Suite 3, Eugene, OR 97401.

Cascade Books
An Imprint of Wipf and Stock Publishers
199 W. 8th Ave., Suite 3
Eugene, OR 97401

www.wipfandstock.com

PAPERBACK ISBN: 978-1-7252-8592-7
HARDCOVER ISBN: 978-1-7252-8591-0
EBOOK ISBN: 978-1-7252-8593-4

Cataloguing-in-Publication data:

Names: Boesak, Allan Aubrey, author.

Title: Selfless revolutionaries : Biko, black consciousness, black theology, and a global ethic of solidarity and resistance / Allan Aubrey Boesak.

Description: Eugene, OR : Cascade Books, 2021 | Includes bibliographical references and index.

Identifiers: ISBN 978-1-7252-8592-7 (paperback) | ISBN 978-1-7252-8591-0 (hardcover) | ISBN 978-1-7252-8593-4 (ebook)

Subjects: LCSH: Biko, Steve.| Black theology | Black Consciousness Movement of South Africa. | Black nationalism.

Classification: DT1949.B55 B64 2021 (paperback) | DT1949.B55 B64 (ebook)

07/21/21

For Jeremiah A. Wright

Fearless prophet, fiery preacher, unapologetically black scholar, unashamedly Christian witness for justice, and above all, beloved older brother and friend.

What shoulders to stand on!

With great admiration and deep gratitude.

At a time such as this, it is not light that is needed, but fire; it is not the gentle shower, but thunder. We need the storm, the whirlwind, and the earthquake.

−FREDERICK DOUGLASS, JULY 4, 1852

The whites . . . have occupied the country forcibly and appropriated it to themselves. That, of course, does not prove their right to it. A large number even from among them believe that they will have to fight again to defend their occupation. But we shall say no more about this. One will reap as one sows.

−MAHATMA GHANDI, OCTOBER 22, 1910

There is a fire no water can put out.

−MARTIN LUTHER KING JR., APRIL 3, 1968

At some stage one can foresee a situation where black people will feel they have nothing to live for and will shout to their God: "Thy will be done!" . . . If the white God had been doing the talking all along, at some stage the Black God will have to raise His voice and make Himself heard . . .

−STEVE BIKO, SEPTEMBER 1970

Contents

Acknowledgments		ix
Preface: "Where Do We Go from Here?"		xi
	Introduction: "Biko Lives!" *Black Consciousness, Black Theology, and the Politics of Manufactured Contentment*	1
1	"Selfless Revolutionaries" *Black Consciousness, Black Theology, and the Validity of the Ethics of Global Solidarity and Resistance*	27
2	Rebels at the Lectern and in the Pulpit *Hegemony, Harmony, and the Critical Dimensions of Intellectual and Theological Integrity*	62
3	"Who Will Rescue Me from This Body of Death?" *Black Theology, Black Consciousness, and the Quest for Meaningful, Humanized Consciousness*	90
4	"A Restless Presence" *Black Theology, the Prophetic Church, and "Post-apartheid," "Post-racial" Challenges*	124
5	Testing the Inescapable Network of Mutuality *Luthuli, King, and Biko—Global Challenge, Global Solidarity, Global Resistance*	152

6	In Search of Our Human Face	187
	Black Consciousness, Indivisible Justice, Inclusive Humanity, and the Politics of Vulgarity	
7	The Need for "a Fighting God"	225
	Black Theology, Black Singularity, and the Essence of Revolutionary Authenticity	
8	When Tomorrow Is Yesterday	254
	Black Theology, Black Consciousness, and Our Incomplete Revolution	
Bibliography		285
Index		305

Acknowledgments

Although somewhat longer in the making, this book was completed while South Africa was in complete lockdown due to COVID-19. I have, of course, experienced curfews, house arrest, and isolation in prison under apartheid, but we have never known a complete lockdown of the whole country before. The coronavirus brought with it anxieties and fears we have not experienced since the influenza pandemic of 1918, of which I had only heard stories of terrible devastation among our communities from my mother. So this experience came with unforeseen challenges. My wife and I were mostly alone throughout this time, and I am inexpressibly grateful for the space she gave me to finish this project within the confines of isolation and amidst these strange, disconcerting, and demanding circumstances.

Some say writing is a lonesome business. In a sense I suppose that is true, though I must confess that for me, a large part of the joy of writing is the constant conversation in one's head and heart with others as one wrestles with their work and the challenges and stimulation their thoughts represent, earnestly hoping that none of them are misrepresented in my own work. Seclusion works best for that, in my experience. But that sometimes calls for extraordinary sacrifices from others close to the one who is doing the writing, and only love can make those. So once again, thank you, Elna.

I have been writing for some years now, and I find myself constantly in conversation with myself in my earlier works. Reading and re-reading, re-valuating and engaging in self-critical reflection, I am amazed at what I have learned from others over the years, and I am deeply appreciative of what I have been able to unlearn, always hoping that this process contributes to a better product. That said, the pestilence that brought the lockdown is a terrifying thing, and I am filled with gratitude to God that I could find such comfort in writing during so extraordinary a time.

Something I have said before, but which now has taken on added significance, is my discussions with my children as they grow older and have more interest in what their father is writing. Sarah is close by, and I could bounce ideas off her on a regular basis with sometimes surprising results. Andrea is all the way across the ocean, now a senior at the University of San Francisco, and she has taken a class in liberation theology, which, she confessed, she has found fascinating. The profit for me has been prolonged Skype sessions of extraordinarily stimulating conversation. It is such a joy and encouragement when one's children show genuine interest in one's work, and can direct you to articles and books they were reading, and share the sometimes surprisingly relevant conversations with friends on social media. Thank you.

Something else I have never experienced to this extent before: in lieu of libraries all being closed by the lockdown throughout this process of writing, and with my own books not always in reach, it was a blessing to be able to do some research online and to find much that stimulated new thinking. So I owe a huge debt of gratitude to all those unseen colleagues, in academia and other spheres so crucial to my thinking and development, who have posted articles of such high academic and journalistic standards online. I thank those colleagues who were willing to take some time reading and commenting on some of these chapters. They have been immensely helpful, but my friend and esteemed colleague, Professor Tinyiko Maluleke, deserves a special word of thanks for his critical and encouraging engagement. Some of the matters discussed in this work are topics of great contention, and I hope they can sense where their help has kept me from going completely off the rails. Without access to all this, I honestly do not know what I would have done to finish this work.

Portions of some of these chapters have been published elsewhere over the past year or so. Chapter 2 first appeared as a tribute in memory of James Cone in a special edition of *Journal of Theology for South Africa* (March 2019). Originally, chapter 4 was a contribution to *Contesting Post-racialism: Conflicted Churches in the United States and South Africa*, published by the University Press of Mississippi (2015). Earlier forms of chapters 5, 6, and 7 appeared in *Hervormde Theological Studies* 75.4 (2019), *Hervormde Theological Studies* 76.3 (2020), and in *Black Theology: An International Journal* 18.3 (2020), respectively. My sincere gratitude to all for their permission to use them here. Some, or sections of them, have been presented as papers at conferences and on invitation in classes before the coronavirus forced us into isolation, and I am grateful for the opportunity for face-to-face conversation—now no longer to be taken for granted—that helped to shape their final form. Needless to say, all of them have of course been expanded and substantially reworked for this publication.

I was a preacher before I was a writer, and I still am. That means that besides an extra dose of discipline, one needs the sobering and steady guiding hand of a good editor. At Cascade, I have had that in abundance, and I am deeply grateful to my publisher and their dedicated team of colleagues with whom I have enjoyed such a fruitful relationship for the last few years. I am deeply grateful to Blake Adams, my copyeditor, who has been extraordinarily helpful and admirably patient in his work with me. Special thanks is also due to my editor on this one, Dr. Charlie Collier, a kindred spirit in the global struggle for freedom. It was a special privilege having minds of such great wisdom, patience, and sensitivity guiding me in this effort. In important ways, they have helped to make this book a better one.

Preface

"Where Do We Go from Here?"

"Every truth, it seems, has its time," wrote influential and respected South African intellectual Njabulo Ndebele in his Foreword to the fortieth edition of Steve Biko's enduring classic, *I Write What I Like*. "Before that time arrives, the truth may be seen, perhaps even intuited, but never really grasped."[1] That is true, not only for the one truth that Ndebele (re)discovered and meditates on, as we shall see, but for the many truths Biko had tried to teach us. They are being discovered anew for this generation, and Biko has remained alive because of the inescapable, prophetic truthfulness not just of his words, but of his life and death.

The rediscovery of Biko and the movement he was father to, Black Consciousness is, it seems, a sweeping phenomenon. The relevance of the man and his work is so clear, so powerful, so disrupting, that it cannot be ignored; not by politics and not by academia. This is so because Biko and Black Consciousness have continued to captivate the minds of generation after generation, and so has, for the last decade or so, its inseparable twin, Black liberation theology. This reemerged phenomenon has stubbornly insisted on calling our attention to what the struggle for liberation really was fought for, and in doing that, simultaneously calling us all to account.

As one of those from the first generation who embraced Black Consciousness and Black theology, I am a participant in this development with grateful enthusiasm, and this book is an expression of my hope that something of the selfless revolutionary spirit that had driven Steve Biko will take a new hold on us.

The reason why the truth of Steve Biko's life, work, and death remains so utterly moving, so deeply compelling, so immeasurably powerful, is because Biko's original intention, to liberate his people, is still so acutely present. "The source of that intention," writes Ndebele, "is the prevailing conditions of un-freedom and their effects on people."[2] Ndebele wrote this in 2017, but the relevance of those words hold even now, if not more so, than then. Unless these conditions are ended soon, they "are

---

1. Biko, *I Write What I Like*, viii.
2. Biko, *I Write What I Like*, viii.

transferred from one generation to another."³ However, it is not only the conditions of un-freedom that are transferred. Also carried from one generation to another is the longing to rediscover the meaning of the work, life, and death of this man.

> Each generation may find something to emphasise; and the next, something else, such that there is change and yet continuity in witness.⁴

It is that change and yet continuity in witness that are my concerns in what follows. I can only pray that the continuity is clearly seen, and the authenticity of the witness is recognized as some of those truths are grappled with, albeit perhaps not yet fully grasped. Rediscovering those truths have taken me on a journey of renewed thinking and commitment that I hope the reader will sense, and share. So, from chapter to chapter, we will reflect on the meaning and impact of South Africa's politics of contentment on our political processes, the workings of our democracy, and our self-understanding since 1994. We will try to unpack what it means to be a "selfless revolutionary" at a time when it seems that everything that we have fought for, everything that is sacred, everything that is precious, and every sacrifice made with so much love is for sale, and not even to the highest bidder. What does it mean to be a "selfless revolutionary" at a time when selfishness and self-centeredness, greed and instant gratification, entitlement and self-aggrandizement, have become the hallmarks of our political life? What is political discourse when the people's first reaction to the very word "politician" is distrust, derision, and cynicism? When solidarity has become a word from a foreign lexicon; and when the once hope-filled slogan "A Better Life for All!" has been exchanged for the cynical "It's my time to eat!"; and when "An injury to one is an injury to all" has now become "I have not joined the struggle in order to be poor"—what have we become? When the haunting struggle song, expressing our black togetherness, "Senzina" ("What have we done?"), mourning the inexpressibly cruel reality that apartheid has made our very blackness the cause of our oppression, has been exchanged for the embittered cry, "Colored, you are on your own!"—Black Consciousness turned on its head—where do we go from here? What shall we say to Biko?

In these pages, we will grapple with what Biko called that "first truth, bitter as it may seem," and explore whether we, too, possess the character that will embrace, for our own times and challenges, Black Consciousness as a critical, self-critical, liberating, empowering, and humanizing consciousness. We will acknowledge Biko's chastising words when he told us that we blacks, theologians and preachers, have "connived" at keeping Christianity "the ideal religion for the maintenance of the subjugation of our people."⁵ We will try to respond to Biko's blistering critique of the church and join him in his belief that "no nation can win a battle without faith," and ask, recalling Albert John Mvumbi Luthuli, whether the prophetic church in South Africa can be

3. Biko, *I Write What I Like*, ix.
4. Biko, *I Write What I Like*, viii–ix.
5. Biko, *I Write What Like*, 61.

revived, even though Biko did not have much faith in the church. Can we once again, as in the late 1970s and 1980s, convince him that we indeed are the "restless presence" in church and in society that will not give up on justice?

Biko demanded that intellectuals must be a "living part of Africa and of her thought."[6] That "being a part" is a struggle, however, and "there is no place outside that fight for the artists or for the intellectual" who themselves are not "concerned with, and completely at one with the people in the great battle of Africa and of suffering humanity."[7] That "fight" is a fight against the ongoing consequences of colonization and imperialism, against coloniality and Eurocentric hegemony. Can black intellectuals be those rebels at the lectern and in the pulpit that this fight calls for? And can our desire and struggle for an authentic Afro-plurality simultaneously be a fight for "suffering humanity"? Can we heed Martin Luther King Jr.'s and Biko's call for us to "join the world revolution"? For our solidarity to rise above race and tribe, to embrace "the wider loyalties" of the human community, rather than just the narrow loyalties of nationalism and ethnocentricity, so that, in these times especially, we find ourselves on the "right side" of the revolution? Biko set before us a task we still have not completed—that of giving South Africa, and the world, "the greatest gift, a human face."[8] What does that mean for us, and for the revolutions of the "shirtless and barefoot peoples of the earth rising up as never before," as Martin Luther King Jr. spoke of them?[9] And can we make this a revolution of enduring, nonviolent militancy, as Albert Luthuli pleaded for?

Biko thought that our own black revolution is a "microcosm of the revolution in the black world."[10] We will test this truth as we test King's belief in a worldwide revolution, one in which we are all caught up "in a single garment of destiny, an inescapable network of mutuality."[11] In "the quest for our true humanity," can we, in these times of self-obsessed ethnicisms, narrow nationalisms, unrepentant racism, and rising fascism, with Biko, hope to work not just for ourselves, but for "all suffering humanity"? On this journey, we shall discover, with Biko, that Black theology is not just a "contextual" or "situational" theology. If it is to be a true liberation theology, Biko argued, it will search for Jesus as "a fighting God" who will "not let the lie rest unchallenged"; a theology which refuses to be bound by "absolutes."[12] We will probe what that means, as we dare to ask what Biko would have said had he been confronted with women and LGBTQI persons in their struggles for the recognition of their humanity, their dignity, and their rights.

6. Biko, *I Write What I Like*, 35.
7. Biko, *I Write What I Like*, 35.
8. Biko, *I Write What I Like*, 51.
9. King, "Beyond Vietnam," 216.
10. Biko, *I Write What I Like*, 78.
11. King, "Remaining Awake," 269.
12. Biko, *I Write What I Like*, 104.

If we don't achieve a society with "an entirely new economic policy," Biko warned, we will remain captive to neo-liberal capitalist structures and strictures that will not bring the "open, non-racial, non-sexist, egalitarian society" Black Consciousness was striving for.[13] If we do not do that, there will be no real future, and our colonialist-apartheid structures of disparities and inequalities will be exacerbated, so that "tomorrow will be like yesterday."[14]

These are the truths (though perhaps not all) that Biko's work, life, and death have confronted us with. Ndebele saw it rightly: Biko was, indeed, "as the gospels speak of Jesus, 'a prophet powerful in speech and action before God and the whole people.'"[15] I speak of a "prophet" not as one who sees the future, but rather one who sees what *God* sees, and *as* God sees: through the eyes of the oppressed, the despised, the outcasts, the ravaged, the powerless, and those whose imaginations and dreams of justice and peace are transformed by the imagination of God. I propose that we start here with one such truth Biko reveals on the very first pages of his book.

"Where do we go from here?" is a question Biko posed very early on, as he reflects on the future role of the just-established black South African Students Organization (SASO). He does so in a very short piece titled, "Black Campuses and Current Feelings."[16] We have heard this question before and see here already signs of the "inescapable network" and "single garment of destiny" we shall discuss in chapter 4. In 1967, Martin Luther King Jr. made this question the title of his book—a book that began to reveal in systematic fashion and unquestionable clarity not only the "global King" but also the "radical King."[17] It was a book in which King addressed, clearly and powerfully, the "evil triplets" of global war, global poverty, and global capitalism. But for James Cone, too, this became a question, paraphrased into the title of his 1984 work.[18]

The question demanded King's attention as he pondered the civil rights struggle and its victories of the immediate past, the Civil Rights Act and the Voting Rights Act. Rather than crowing over those victories, King knew that these were only the first phase. This was no time for the movement to rest on its laurels. With these legal victories, he knew, "[only] one phase of the civil rights revolution came to an end."[19] Those who thought that for King the end goal was the right to sit anywhere on buses and trains, to eat at lunch counters with whites, or even "integration" as a social normality, were wrong. There would be a "next phase." That next phase would bring new challenges as the demands of the black masses, going far beyond mere integration, would grow. As a result, the road ahead would not be easier: "The persistence

---

13. Biko, *I Write What I Like*, 169.
14. Biko, *I Write What I Like*, 169.
15. Biko, *I Write What I Like*, vii–viii.
16. See Biko, *I Write What I Like*, 18–19.
17. See King, *Where Do We Go From Here*.
18. See Cone, *For My People*.
19. King, *Where Do We Go From Here*, 3.

of *racism in depth* and the dawning awareness that Negro demands will *necessitate structural changes in society* have generated a new phase of white resistance *in North and South*."[20]

Note the growing radicalization in King's perspectives. He knows that racism is neither a shallow stain on the surface of society that can be washed away easily by the mere existence of a law, nor an attitudinal affliction that can be cured by the rhetoric of superficial reconciliation. King did not dismiss the importance of just and legitimate laws—far from it, as we can see from the painstaking discussion in his "Letter from a Birmingham Jail." That same letter also makes clear that King was extremely realistic about whites, liberal, moderate, or conservative, and not open to cheap reconciliation. American racism and white supremacy are cankers of a depth that will demand deep and radical surgery. Neither is racism simply a thing "of the South." The experience in Chicago had taught him irrevocably that racism, whether blatantly practiced or subtly employed, is everywhere. Neither is it a mere matter of attitudes. It is structural and systemic and it dare not be seen as an isolated phenomenon: inextricably bound with militarism and capitalism, these comprise the "triple evils" embedded deeply into American society. Hence, its eradication would need, as he would explain in his "Beyond Vietnam" speech that same year, in a reference to the parable of the Good Samaritan, more than just symbols of charity:

> On the one hand, we are called to play the Good Samaritan on life's roadside, but that will be only an initial act. One day we must come to see that the whole Jericho Road must be transformed so that men and women will not be constantly beaten and robbed as they make their journey on life's highway. True compassion is more than flinging a coin to a beggar. It comes to see that an edifice which produces beggars needs restructuring.[21]

King himself was facing new challenges. Malcolm X's persuasive message of black power, black nationalism, and black separatism had captured a whole new generation. King would readily accept black power and what it entailed, knowing that was exactly what he was employing, and urging the masses to embrace, even though he did not name it in those terms. But he would remain resolute against black separatism and black nationalism.[22]

So for King, the question "Where do we go from here?" would lead to a far more radical engagement with racism, militarism, and capitalism, a far more aggressive stance toward war, a far deeper commitment not just to the civil rights struggle, but the struggle for human rights. It would become an altogether far greater reach into the struggles of the oppressed peoples of the world.

---

20. King, *Where Do We Go From Here,* 12. Emphasis added.
21. King, "Beyond Vietnam," 177.
22. King, *Where Do We Go From Here,* 33, 46.

> The shirtless and barefoot people of the land are rising up as never before. The people who sit in darkness have seen a great light. We in the West must support these revolutions.[23]

As indicated above, and as we will further explore in chapter 2, James Cone's use of this question leads him to a new program for Black theology and the Black Church. As did Martin King, Cone sees the only viable future for Black theology and the Black Church in a global reach of solidarity, an ethic and practice of genuine inclusivity, for "a truly liberated social order cannot have men dominating women."[24] Following Martin Luther King Jr. and Steve Biko, Cone envisioned "a new order" that would be "democratic and socialist, including a Marxist critique of monopoly capitalism."[25] Cone saw that "the new black perspective must be a global vision that includes the struggles of the poor in the Third World . . . There will be no freedom for anybody until all are set free."[26]

Perhaps it is wise to pause here to note that, originally, the term "Third World" did not have a negative connotation. For those of us within the Ecumenical Association of Third World Theologians established in the early 70s, for example, brought together by the desire and necessity to reflect theologically on our participation in the freedom struggles of our own people and the oppressed around the world, journalist Vincent Bevin's description of the term captures precisely how we saw it:

> It was used in the sense of the "Third Estate" during the French Revolution, the revolutionary common people who would overthrow the First and the Second Estates of the monarchy and the clergy. "Third" did not mean third-rate, but something more like the third and final act: the first group of rich, white countries had their crack at creating the world; so did the second, and this was the new movement, full of energy and potential, just waiting to be unleashed. It was not just a category; it was a movement.[27]

Between these two came Biko. At the time, his concerns centered mostly on SASO, but whether intentionally or not, it was already a question for the wider black world. The question intrigued Biko, who found it asked repeatedly "everywhere he went." It showed, he thought, "a lack of insight as to what can be done."[28] Perhaps it seemed to him a sign of resignation: it was not a lack of insight into "what is to be done"; it was a lack of insight into what *can be done*. We should note, even visualize, the phrasing. "What is to be done" is a phrase that goes along with a shrug of helplessness, with up-turned palms, with the expression on the face that admits to having given up. In

23. King, "Beyond Vietnam," 216.
24. Cone, *For My People*, 203.
25. Cone, *For My People*, 204. See the discussion in the footnote in ch. 3.
26. Cone, *For My People*, 204.
27. See Bevins, *Jakarta Method*, 19–20.
28. Biko, *I Write What I Like*, 19.

his own mind, Biko was no longer wondering whether anything should be done. He knew that, despite the matrix of power of the history of colonization, the erasure of just about everything meaningful from African life, and relentless attempts to capture the African mind, something *could* be done. He saw it, retrospectively, as part of a problem caused by colonization and apartheid.

> This again is the tragic result of the old approach, where blacks were made to fit into a pattern largely and often wholly, determined by white students. Hence our originality and imagination have been dulled to the point where it takes a supreme effort to act logically even in order to follow one's beliefs and convictions.[29]

But not all is lost, it seems. Biko finds hope in the quality of leadership he discovered among the black students, despite what Frantz Fanon would call "the Apocalypse"[30] of colonization and apartheid visited upon them. Clearly encouraged, Biko observes, "One would have thought that by now everybody has been cowed down to the point of dogged acceptance of all that comes from authority."[31] He has in mind the white authorities at black university colleges, but as surely, his vision would have already included the white power structures of apartheid South Africa as a whole. So, turning potential into reality, Biko and his comrades set about building SASO, the start of radical black student politics, the seeds of a new revolution, the birth of a movement that would change history and the face of South Africa.

It is within this visionary context that he speaks words that, as he himself, would become lived reality and living legacy, radiate lasting inspirational power, gain the authenticity of martyrdom, the solidity of truthful substance, and the unconquerable presence of immortality. He speaks to the student generation of his time, of course, but his words have the power to reach over time, space, and generations. The history of South Africa's youth-led revolution would be the incontrovertible evidence of this truth. He claims this not for himself, but for all of us who heard and did what was required of us, and for all who are ready to hear anew, and once again do what is required. And precisely in this lies his greatness.

> But some things are common to all—to bear witness to the unity of the black students, to give proper direction, and depth to the movement and to make themselves worthy of the claim that they are the leaders of tomorrow.[32]

Now, of course, we know that in the revolution of 1976 and the 80s all those young people and students transcended the "leaders of tomorrow" designation and became the leaders of the day. But in this ongoing revolution, post-1994, finding

---

29. Biko, *I Write What I Like*, 19.
30. See Fanon, *Wretched of the Earth*, 249.
31. Biko, *I Write What I Like*, 61.
32. Biko, *I Write What I Like*, 19.

ourselves on battlefields we thought we had conquered, and fighting pharaohs "who look like us,"[33] we still, perhaps more than ever, have to prove ourselves "worthy." Do we give that "depth" to the freedom movement when the very freedom we fought for turns out, in the hands of *faux* liberators, to be a new state of un-freedom?

It is this message this book is trying to convey. The last fifteen years or so, particularly, have seen a powerful resurgence of interest in Black Consciousness and Black theology in South Africa. Calls on Biko and Fanon rang out with more and more frequency in the #Rhodesmustfall and #Feesmustfall student movements of 2015 and 2016. It is also a recurring theme in new and fierce debates on nonracialism and South Africa's reconciliation project. Politicians, especially in the debates on "white monopoly capital" and land reform, have also made Biko and Black Consciousness their departure point and fall-back position. Not every call on Biko has done him justice, however. Black theologian and public commentator Tinyiko Maluleke's cry in his reflections on Biko's legacy, "Will the Real Black God Stand, Please!?"[34] says as much.

When Biko asked that question, he knew "from here" would lead to struggle and confrontation with powers he would himself accurately describe as "evil." It would lead to pain and suffering and doubt. Although he was not afraid of it, he could not foresee that that "from here?" would end in his torture and brutal murder, and that so soon. He knew "from here" would lead to struggle, but did he think that after almost a quarter century we would still draw on him for inspiration for an ongoing struggle, so much of it against our own? It is my fervent hope that this book will help in bringing some unity in the plurality of Biko's rich and inspiring life. And perhaps, as Archbishop Desmond Tutu has said reflecting on Biko's life, work, and untimely death, Black Consciousness and the memory and legacy of that indestructible "martyr of hope," as Fr. Aeldred Stubbs called him, might once again lead us to a new black renaissance.

SOWETO DAY/YOUTH DAY, JUNE 16, 2020

---

33. See Boesak, *Pharaohs on Both Sides*.
34. See Maluleke, "Will the Real Black God Stand, Please!"

Introduction

"Biko Lives!"
Black Consciousness, Black Theology, and the Politics of Manufactured Contentment

"No Serious-Minded Freedom Fighters"

Spray-painted on a wall in a black South African township, the cry *Biko Lives!* is almost shocking in its bold simplicity. It is just as powerful, prophetic, and true as the words I saw painted on a section of the Apartheid Wall in Bethlehem, Palestine: "*This Wall May Take Care of the Present, But It Has No Future!*"[1] *Biko Lives!* is not a mournful sigh; it is a revolutionary cry, and the editors of the publication about the life and legacy of Steve Biko who made this the title of their valuable compilation of essays, who had taken these words from a 1984 edition of the publication *Frank Talk,* were right in making this the lead epigraph of their book:

> Biko Lives! Two words slashed across a ghetto wall. A phrase that haunts the nights of South Africa's rulers. Reactionaries and opportunists of every stripe hope and pray that it will disappear under a rain of blood and white-wash reform. But it remains, bold and powerful; not a tired and worn-out slogan, but a battle cry of a generation whose hopes and aspirations are for revolution, an end to all exploitation and oppression.[2]

In this, too, they were right: the cry is not about mournfulness or nostalgia. It is a cry of a generation "whose hopes are for revolution." Against the grain of the dominant narrative in South Africa, the words "exploitation" and "oppression" are not considered inappropriate, impolite, or too daring. Neither is that pointed finger at the "haunted

---

1. The picture of those words on the Apartheid Wall near Bethlehem, taken by a friend on my first and only trip to Palestine, remains a treasured and singularly inspiring possession.
2. See Mngxitama et al., *Biko Lives!*, 1.

nights" of South Africa's rulers. They are the reality for the vast majority of South Africa's people. That is why their "hopes" and "aspirations" are not for "reform" or for "incremental improvement," patiently waiting upon the "better life for all" our rulers promised. They are for "revolution." These words are from 1984, but the editors use them to frame their important book in 2007, already more than a decade into South Africa's democratic dawn and thirty years after the murder of Steve Biko.

Elsewhere, I have entered into a much more detailed and extended discussion on the question of a new understanding of "revolution." That discussion pertains here as well, and for the purposes of the conversation in this Introduction, we need to return to the gist of that argument as presented there.[3] There, I recalled the enormously influential Indian lay theologian M. M. Thomas, who wrote frequently and passionately about the revolutions going on in the Global South world throughout the 1950s and 1960s. India's militant, nonviolent revolution led by Mahatma Gandhi against the British colonialist presence was the dominant force to help Thomas shape a new concept of revolution, though not to the exclusion of those situations where military action was deemed necessary for the resistance. Thomas's concern was not only the political and social meaning of these revolutions. Central for him was the question: Even though forces of evil might be present in these revolutions, can Christians discern God at work in these revolutions, and should Christians become involved in these revolutions themselves? It is a question Biko, too, would have asked. Reading Thomas has influenced my thinking ever since.[4]

Thomas argued that Christ, as Lord of history, is at work in all nations of the world in spite of and indeed *through* the ambiguous political, economic, and social actions in any given country. These upheavals, insofar as they represent the search for what he called "the new humanity" (an important term we shall return to below) for freedom and a new dimension of humane life, fulfill the promises of Christ and must be seen as commensurate with the work of God in Christ in the world.

This does not mean that these revolutions determine the work of God, much less that the gospel can be identified with all that happens in such revolutions. Rather, that God is in control of the revolutions of history; not that the divine power is subordinate to the revolutionary purposes of human beings, but that the "pressures of God are at work in them."[5] In other words, whatever pressures there are towards violence, self-centeredness, selfishness, and self-aggrandizement, "the pressures of God," toward selflessness, nonviolence, and revolutionary love are there, "at work in them." Wherever human beings rise above themselves, find the courage to work for genuine justice, dignity, and humanity, resist the forces of evil by overcoming evil with good,

---

3. See "Introduction" in Boesak, *Pharaohs on Both Sides*.

4. See Boesak, *Farewell to Innocence* (1977); Boesak, *Black and Reformed* (1984); and the majority of my work since, especially the most recent, *Pharaohs on Both Sides* (2017) and *Children of the Waters of Meribah* (2019).

5. Thomas and McCaughey, *Christian in World Struggle*, 15.

and seek to create room for the flourishing of justice and humanity, there God is at work, for that is the will of God for humanity.[6]

Importantly, Thomas asserts that "basic" to the revolution is "the new sense of dignity and historical mission"[7] embraced by the people. This assertion touches on two crucial aspects: on the people's right to, and ownership of, their agency as subjects of history, and the people's right to the power to *be* those agents of change in their own history. He means the people's right to claim ownership of their own revolution. As a result, "the demand of the people is for *power as the bearer of dignity* and for significant and *responsible participation in society and social history.*"[8] The importance of this insight cannot be overestimated. The breadth and depth of the revolutionary waves engulfing the world this very moment is testimony to this truth. So is the unexpected ways in which it manifests itself. As the revolution in the United States spreads from the urban centers to small, more remote towns that have until now considered themselves untouched by, and immune to, the "mayhem" and "chaos" caused by the Black Lives Matter movement in the cities, this truth "is marching on." In Selah, in eastern Washington state, the revolution has struck, wildly disrupting the conservative hold over the town and its people. Young people, led by twenty-year-old Fabio Perez, journalist Mike Baker reports, have started chalking sidewalks and the street with Black Lives Matter graffiti. City officials profess to be perplexed about the sudden activism. The city administrator, Don Wayman, said he did not see any racial issues to address, calling the Black Lives Matter movement "devoid of intellect and reason" and characterizing the activists as a "mob."[9]

In early June, Baker writes, Fabio, after watching those history-changing eight minutes forty-nine seconds of George Floyd's death, began drawing the words "Black Lives Matter" on the street outside his home, which lies on a dead end. He included references to black people whose deaths in recent years around the country have sparked protests over racial injustice. By the end of the week, a city crew came by with a street sweeper to clean it off. Some friends joined him to draw more, and a cleaning crew again washed them off. "First came the warning. Then the pressure washer." Some friends came by to draw more, and a cleaning crew again washed them off. "They did it again. Then again." The youths who did the chalk writing stood their ground, tried to protect their writings, and then, dripping wet, stood in silent protest, holding up signs that said, "Hate has no home in Selah."[10] Now some residents in the overwhelmingly white neighborhood have invited the young men to write those Black Lives Matter messages on their driveways. Together, they have "disarmed" the city leaders, the "rulers and authorities" with all their power and self-importance,

---

6. Thomas, "Issues."
7. Thomas and McCaughey, *Christian in World Struggle*, 19.
8. Thomas and McCaughey, *Christian in the World Struggle*, 19.
9. See Baker, "Writing 'Black Lives Matter' in Chalk a Crime."
10. Baker, "Writing 'Black Lives Matter' in Chalk a Crime."

disempowered them, "and made a public spectacle of them, triumphing over them" (Col 2:15). Their surrender is only a matter of time. All because one twenty-year-old said enough is enough. This is power as the bearer of dignity in the hands of the people for significant and responsible participation in society and social history. M. M. Thomas would have been delighted.

In this book, I will argue throughout that this is more true today than ever before. In James Cone's *Black Theology and Black Power*, he makes clear that Black theology has made its choice.[11] The question for Black liberation theology here is threefold: First, what is the nature of this worldwide revolution? Second, can we as Christians see God's purposes at work in this revolution? Third, should Christians join in this struggle for the sake of God's purposes, which M. M. Thomas identifies as justice, a new humanity, and the humanization of the world? Here, within the new historical context we are presently facing, I will attempt to respond to these questions, and they are bound to return in some form or another throughout this work.

There is no indication that Steve Biko had ever read M. M. Thomas. But in 1971, he, too, and this time not within the context of the anti-colonialist struggles of the 1950s and 1960s, expressed the reality of worldwide struggles of oppressed people, connected through a global sense of solidarity and inspired by a shared ethic of resistance. He speaks of "the black people of the world" who, in "choosing to reject the legacy of colonialism and white domination and to build around themselves their own values, standards and outlook on life,"[12] have arrived at a common, hence better, understanding of their task in the world. This was an understanding that elevated oppressed people above the ambitions of mere nationalism. Hence, Black Consciousness, he argues in agreement with Fanon, is a "national consciousness, which is not nationalism"[13] which tends to bind one to the aspirations of one nation only. The global solidarity that comes through the new-found consciousness "is the only thing which will give us an international dimension."[14]

Fanon and Biko had illustrious forebears. In 1955, at the now-famous Bandung Conference, where the seeds for the formation of the Non-Aligned Movement were sown, a movement of Third World countries determined not to bow either to the will of the United States or the Soviet Union, but to work for self-determination as defined by themselves, and for an independent stance in international affairs. They sought an

---

11. It might be argued that James Cone represented the more radical wing of Black theology, while someone like Deotis Roberts in the United States, and Bishop Alpheus Zulu in South Africa, for example, were more cautious on this point. As Cone would later, in 1974 I argued that it was not necessary for the "Black revolution" to choose between Martin Luther King Jr. and Malcolm X; that both represented a black ethic of resistance. I did, however, find the nonviolent, militant ethic of Martin King, and as expressed first by Albert Luthuli, and following his example, by Black Consciousness in South Africa, more persuasive. See Boesak, *Coming In Out of the Wilderness*.

12. Biko, *I Write What I Like*, 78.

13. Biko, *I Write What I Like*, 78.

14. Biko, *I Write What I Like*, 78.

independent way for themselves and their relationship to the rest of the world. They spoke of nationalism, but it was "a nationalism not based on race or language but constructed by the anti-colonial struggle and drive for social justice."[15] That historic conference, wrote Richard Wright, celebrated African American author of the immensely important novel *Native Son*, in language echoed by Frantz Fanon not much later, was "the conference of the despised, the insulted, the hurt, the dispossessed—in short, the underdogs of the human race."[16]

So Biko can argue that "the black-white struggle in South Africa is but a microcosm of the global confrontation between the Third World and the rich white nations of the world which is manifesting itself in an ever more real manner as the years go by."[17] Most importantly, for Biko, the revolution is all about restoring a revolutionary consciousness about black people's humanity and personhood, their dignity and right to restoration of their full humanity, their agency to take responsibility for history. To that end, they claim the power of their black personhood to make themselves the subjects of that revolutionary process. For Black Consciousness, that was a power not only to restore black personhood; it was a power to give humanity the "human face" it longs for and deserves. For Black Consciousness, too, the revolution is not about power for power's sake, but as Thomas put it, as "the demand of the people ... for *power as the bearer of dignity* and for significant and *responsible participation in society and social history.*" As the multi-racial, intergenerational, international, inter-gender Black Lives Matter crowds flood the streets of the world's cities today, this should be uppermost in all our minds.

The worldwide revolution that Black Consciousness joined was most recently best described by Iranian scholar Hamid Dabashi as he writes about the Arab Spring in the Middle East and North Africa. It is an understanding of the concept of revolution with which I am in complete agreement. Dabashi writes,

> Revolution in the sense of a radical and sudden shift of political power with an accompanying social and economic restructuring of society—one defiant class violently and conclusively overcoming another—is not what we are witnessing here, or not quite yet. There is a deep-rooted economic and social malaise in all these societies ... No single angle of vision—economic, social, political, or cultural—would reveal the totality (and yet inconclusive disposition) of these massive social uprisings. Instead of denying these insurgencies the term "revolution," we are now forced to reconsider the concept and understand it anew ... The longer these revolutions take to unfold, the more enduring, grassroots-based, and definitive will be their emotive, symbolic, and institutional consequences.[18]

15. See Bevins, *Jakarta Method*, 56.
16. See Wright, *Color Curtain*, 16.
17. Biko, *I Write What I Like*, 78.
18. See Dabashi, *Arab Spring*, 5, 6.

Dabashi's argument opens new ways of understanding revolution. Revolution should no longer be defined solely by the presence or degree of violence, but by the depth and longevity of permanent and fundamental change. It is not so much a matter of one class overcoming and removing another class, in one violent, historic moment. There will be a series of historic moments, perhaps over several years, revealing a "grass-roots-based" enduring surge towards fundamental change of society. We must also, I think, keep in mind what M. M. Thomas and Martin Luther King Jr. understood about this kind of revolution. Dr. King, as did Albert Luthuli, not only spoke of a revolution of nonviolent militancy, he also spoke of a revolution that represented a "revolution of values."[19] We will return to this concept in chapter 4, but for now it is important to understand that King had in mind a revolution that not only changed our social and political circumstances, but also our minds, our ways of life. The test is not just the placing of power in different hands, the test is the character of the new society, its humanness and inclusivity, its responsiveness to what one can call its continuing ubuntufication. It changes our relationships with each other as global neighbors, bound together with bonds that "no document from human hands"[20] can undo, and with the earth. For Thomas, as we have seen above, it is a revolution with the people at its center, driven by the people's demand "for power as the bearer of dignity and for significant and responsible participation in society and social history."[21]

These revolutions, including the revolution that ended formal and legal apartheid in South Africa, as well as the Black Lives Matter and Standing Rock resistance movements in the United States, have not yet run their course. What we are witnessing in the Middle East and North Africa, in Palestine and South Africa, and in the US is, in the words of Hamid Dabashi, "the unfolding of an open-ended revolt, the conjugation of a new revolutionary language and practice, predicated on a reading of reality that is an *opera aperta*—an 'open work' . . . a self-propelling hermeneutics that mobilizes a constellation of suggestions yet to be fully assayed."[22] But they will continue, because they are grounded in the will for genuine freedom and justice anchored in the hearts of the people, the active participants and agents in changing their own history.

As far as Christians are concerned, Black liberation theology, with Thomas, would consistently argue they are "in the grip of an essential truth"[23] and that is the truth about God's own struggle for justice, peace, and human fulfilment, or as Thomas would frame it, "the creation of a new humanity."[24] Such Christians understand the prophetic pathos, essential to every revolution and prophetic presence in it as seen in the lives of Christians who were not afraid to be obedient to the voice of God they

19. King, "Beyond Vietnam," 216.
20. King, "Beyond Vietnam," 206.
21. Thomas and McCaughey, *Christian in the World Struggle*, 19.
22. Dabashi, *Arab Spring*, 230. See also Boesak, *Kairos, Crisis, and Global Apartheid*, 19–20.
23. Thomas and McCaughey, *Christian in the World Struggle*, 39, 40.
24. Thomas, "Issues," 89–98.

heard in the cries of the poor and the oppressed. They exhibit the passion that M. M. Thomas proclaimed to be "the essential truth of the struggle,"[25] compelling Christians to join struggles for justice, making it impossible for them to stand by in feigned neutrality and spiritualized unconcern. These are all issues this book will return to in greater detail.

In 2005, referring to the 1970s, I wrote that Black Consciousness, Black power, and Black theology have

> merged and emerged as the key which unlocked the door to the future for the oppressed people of South Africa at a time when most of us thought that all was lost. It rekindled the almost decayed hope in the hearts of the downtrodden, reasserted the faith of the people in the liberation God of the Exodus, the prophets, and of Jesus of Nazareth. It reclaimed the gospel for the poor and the oppressed; rediscovered, rewrote the vision and ran with it, as the prophet Habakkuk enjoins us to do; unleashed the tremendous energies of a people who, long before Thabo Mbeki discovered it, knew that they were born of a people who would not tolerate oppression. It came at a most opportune time, a *Kairos* moment, to put it biblically, and it paved the way for the decisive phase of the struggle during the eighties as it found expression in the United Democratic Front. It became a spiritual force without which resistance to apartheid would have remained singularly ineffectual.[26]

In writing this then, I was engaging the views of former president Nelson Mandela, articulated in an article he wrote while still in prison on Robben Island, but which the African National Congress (ANC) saw fit to publish in 2001, presumably when it became clear that their efforts to erase both the legacy and memory of Black Consciousness and its impact upon the people were failing.[27] Mandela raises many interesting points in that piece, some of which I discussed in *The Tenderness of Conscience*. One of the things that struck me most forcefully, however, was Nelson Mandela's disdain for Black Consciousness thinkers and advocates, whom he dismissed as "fanatics" for arguing that "race" was a social and political construct; and as "romantic" because of the slogan, "Black is beautiful." Most disturbing of all, though, was his opinion that Black Consciousness adherents were "not serious" as "freedom fighters" because of their critique of Marxism.[28] I do not intend to repeat those arguments here. I will

25. See Thomas and McCaughey, *Christian in the World Struggle*, 38–41.

26. See Boesak, *Tenderness of Conscience*, 10–17.

27. See Mandela, "Whither the Black Consciousness Movement?," 21–64. Mandela delivered an historic address from the balcony of Cape Town City Hall after his release from prison on February 11, 1990. The broader South African public saw and heard him for the first time since his imprisonment for twenty-seven years. Mandela thanked a long list of political formations, including, and "with pride," white organizations like the Black Sash and the National Union of South African Students, for their contribution to the struggle. The Black Consciousness movement, however, was not mentioned. Neither was the name of Steve Biko.

28. Mandela, "Whither the Black Consciousness Movement?," 43.

simply refer to the "three fundamental mistakes" I read in Mandela's argumentation. In summary then:

- Mandela places all emphasis on the political groupings that came about as a result of the Black Consciousness philosophy and then proceeds to contrast them with the ANC and its historical role in South Africa's struggle and judge them accordingly. No other movement can compare with the ANC's history, of course, so it becomes a bit of a straw man argument. The unsuccessful political ventures of these groups then become "proof" that the Black Conscious Movement has not only failed miserably, it has no future. Hence the "Whither" in Mandela's title.

- Mandela shows no cognizance of the fact that Black Consciousness served as unmissable preparation for a whole new generation of political activists, not only to become politically active, but to become an essential part of the historical movement of the oppressed in South Africa, and that in ways and numbers never seen before. I described it then as a "flaw" that will have all sorts of consequences for "the way in which the ANC conceived itself, the people, and the struggle after 1994."[29]

- There is no acknowledgement in the discussion of the *philosophy* of Black Consciousness—its meaning politically, socially, and psychologically—and therefore no need to respond to the philosophical challenges that philosophy continued to pose to both the regime, the freedom movement itself, and the people of South Africa, then as well as now.

However, Mandela and the ANC had to concede that the erasure tactics did not work. In 2004, Mandela delivered the annual Steve Biko Lecture in Cape Town. He did not explicitly renounce his previous views, but he did have to admit to a recognition of, and an appreciation for, Black Consciousness that he had not shown before:

> As we now increasingly speak of and work for an African Renaissance, the life, work, thoughts, and example of Steve Biko assume a relevance and resonance as in the time that he lived. His revolution had a simple but overwhelmingly powerful dimension in which it played itself out—that of radically changing the consciousness of people. The African Renaissance calls for and is situated in exactly such a fundamental change of consciousness: consciousness of ourselves, our place in the world, our capacity to shape history, and our relationship with each other and the rest of humanity.[30]

29. Boesak, *Tenderness of Conscience*, 11.

30. See Nelson Mandela, "Fifth Steve Biko Memorial Lecture." It also meant that President Thabo Mbeki, succeeding Mandela in 1999, when he embarked in earnest upon his most ambitious project, the "African Renaissance," realized that he could no longer sustain his denialism regarding the role and contribution of Black Consciousness to the struggle. Neither could he maintain any credible and sustainable argument for an African renaissance if he refused to give full credit to the relevance and necessity of the Black Consciousness philosophy. As a result, Mbeki's speeches, as evidenced abundantly in the compilation of his addresses, *Africa: The Time Has Come*, are replete with terms, ideas, and arguments taken from Black Consciousness. Perhaps the speech that Mbeki seemed most proud

It is noteworthy that Mandela had to acknowledge that the Black Consciousness movement was nothing less than a "revolution," by that admission inadvertently retracting his early judgment that Black Consciousness adherents were not "serious-minded revolutionaries." Perhaps, though we will never know, especially in light of the haste with which the ANC abandoned Marxist ideology and embraced neoliberal capitalist ideology and policies, he had also revised this judgment, which at the time was based on their rejection of Marxist theory.[31] In his argument, Mandela claimed that Marxism "had led to the removal of all kinds of oppression for a third of mankind, and the removal of all sources of national and international friction."[32] And he could not but pay tribute to the great goal Biko and Black Consciousness strove towards, that of giving Africa and the world the "greatest gift possible, a human face."[33]

Black Consciousness has outlived that criticism, and its re-emergence, and the direction it is giving as a point of reference in our current debates and struggles, are evidenced in the fact that Biko is alive in ways no one has imagined. It is indeed a reality that "haunts the nights of South Africa's rulers," and it is a rallying cry for South Africa's new revolutionary generation. If it were up to them, the "hopes and prayers" of the "reactionaries and opportunists" would go unanswered. By 2007, the contributors to *Biko Lives!* are saying with the epigraph, it could no longer be disputed that the manufactured contentment that marked the first years of the post-1994 euphoria had lost its grip.

The Politics of Manufactured Contentment

The expression "manufactured contentment" is deduced from the hugely influential work of Edward Herman and Noam Chomsky in their contested, but still unsurpassed, treatise on the real role of the mass media in our societies. It today stands as a classic work on the subject.[34] Far from serving as instruments of information and furthering open, democratic, and informed public debate on vital issues, Herman and Chomsky argue the media offer us "a propaganda model."[35] Arguably, one crucial sentence from the first pages of their book sums up their argument. Edwards and Chomsky write,

---

of and that endeared him to the hearts of many South Africans in ways his policies never could, "I Am an African," is, even though unintended perhaps, his most humble and unadorned homage to Black Consciousness. It is also, in my view, his most beautiful piece of writing. To experience the true power and beauty of it, one should watch the video online, where it can be found.

31. It might be argued that while the ANC discarded Marxist ideology in favor of neoliberal capitalist ideology, it has not divested itself of its dictatorial instincts.

32. Mandela, "Whither the Black Consciousness movement?," 43. For one who called Black Consciousness adherents "romantic" for proclaiming that "Black Is Beautiful," this was a singularly romantic view of Marxism.

33. See Mandela, "5th Steve Biko Lecture."

34. See Herman and Chomsky, *Manufacturing Consent*.

35. Herman and Chomsky, *Manufacturing Consent*, xi.

"The media serve, and propagandize on behalf of, the powerful societal interests that control and finance them."[36] In other words, the real role of the media, through the projection of dominant narratives, is to further, protect, and justify the hegemony of the ruling elites.

Scott Lovaas has written an enlightening dissertation on the principle of "manufactured consent" as it applies to the post-1994 situation in South Africa.[37] Lovaas argues that the South African media play the same role Herman and Chomsky uncovered in the United States. He is right. Across the board, South African media are no exception. Scrutinizing three aspects of media attention as examples—viz. forestry, terrorism, and former president Thabo Mbeki's pet project under the broad umbrella of the African Renaissance, the "New Partnership for African Development" (NEPAD)—he investigates the media's role as a propaganda model and comes to the same conclusion. South African media, too, serve the interests of the dominant class.

> South Africans, however familiar with [the practices of propaganda, mind control, indoctrination and "the duping of the masses"], view them as tactics of the apartheid regime, and any remains are vestiges of days gone by. However, the quest to influence, manipulate, peddle, and ultimately win over "the hearts and minds" of fellow citizens has been with humanity from the beginning of time and does not require a repressive regime.[38]

That is undoubtedly true. Here I will not speak of manufactured consent. Instead, tipping my hat in grateful acknowledgement to Edward Herman and Noam Chomsky, I will discuss what I shall call the politics of manufactured contentment. I will do so in special reference to one of the most important processes within the development of our young democracy; namely, our efforts toward national reconciliation. I will not spend much time on the role of the media in that regard however. Others have more than adequately done so. Annelies Verdoolaege, for example, has scrupulously scrutinized the ways in which South African media, and in her study of one specific but widely watched TV channel in its coverage of the TRC proceedings, could not completely avoid "the pitfalls of partiality and sensationalism."[39] Its discourse was ideologically loaded, leaning into the dominant narrative "that favoured national reconciliation as a successful project."[40] There seems, she concludes, "to be a link between the reconciliation-oriented discourse of this TV programme and the Commission's objective of promoting national reconciliation."[41]

---

36. Herman and Chomsky, *Manufacturing Consent*, xi.
37. See Lovaas, "Manufacturing Consent in Democratic South Africa."
38. Lovaas, "Manufacturing Consent in Democratic South Africa," 9.
39. Verdoolaege, "Media Representations."
40. Verdoolaege, "Media Representations."
41. See Verdoolaege, "Media Representations." See also Krabill, "Symbiosis."

Tinyiko Maluleke saw it right. "We must," he argues, "recognise the national (continental?) psychological, and spiritual implications of the TRC as a *national process,* and as *a national ritual*—its symbolic intentions to *promote national unity and reconciliation.*"[42] Maluleke, too, makes note of the number of prominent religious figures involved in the TRC processes and workings, prompting the question whether *the church* was thus well presented in the TRC, to which, for him, the answer is "no."

South Africa's reconciliation project, as a way of dealing with its particularly vicious colonialist and apartheid past, would take center stage for the better part of the 1990s and into the new millennium. It is not saying too much to suggest that it is the racial aspect—and the fact that South Africa, as a settler colonialist society, had become a particularly important point of reference in world politics—that made it different from, if not to say unique, with regard to other situations. After 1994, South Africa's white people would remain in the country with the vast black majority as their neighbors, compatriots, and rulers, albeit not their equals. Economic power would remain firmly in white hands, reinforcing apartheid's vast socio-economic inequalities. The dynamics and paradigms of South Africa as a settler colony would change dramatically. But however dramatic, the real question was: How substantial would those changes be, and how could these be managed best? There was an even more urgent question, however, and it has legal, political, and moral implications. Apartheid was a crime against humanity. How would the black majority deal with the criminals, especially when the Western world (in unvarnished white solidarity) had made its position clear: South Africa was to be "a good news story"?[43] Would we even be allowed to call them criminals? It was vital that, beyond free and fair elections, South Africa's reconciliation project, more so than any other, should be deemed "successful." More than anything else, I think, it was the permanent presence of white people that demanded it. That powerful presence, undergirded by that global white solidarity, would also determine, define, and judge the measure of that success.

It is against this background that I will discuss the concept of manufactured contentment, not in connection with the role of the media, but in regard to the utterances and writings of powerful public figures and revered religious personalities to create not just manufactured consent, but "manufactured contentment" around reconciliation as a "national project."[44] For the Truth and Reconciliation Commission (TRC) to be accepted and applauded by the black oppressed majority in South Africa, with apartheid so fresh in their minds and the wounds so far from healed, the media,

42. See Maluleke, "Truth, National Unity, and Reconciliation," 324.

43. In the aftermath of the first democratic elections in 1994, one of the key international observers (from Germany) explained to me why it was so important for the Western world that South Africa be a "good news story." It was a very enlightening, if at times disturbing, conversation.

44. Apart from the books from the pen of Archbishop Tutu, of which *No Future without Forgiveness* was by far the most widely influential, deputy Chair of the TRC and Methodist cleric Alex Boraine had published three books on the topic. The international speaker's circuit was a well-traveled road for the well-known TRC figures.

though much needed, were never going to be enough. That was, after all, a media that had served the interests and *only* the interests of the white dominant classes for as long as anyone could remember. The (black) public trust for the propaganda model to work was simply not there.

At first, the ANC had wanted the establishment of a truth commission, similar to those in Chile and Argentina, for example. It was former president F. W. De Klerk who persuaded the ANC that it would be better to have a truth *and* reconciliation commission.[45] In the discussions, as I recalled in my reflections in *Tenderness of Conscience*, I thought two points were important here. First, that we should keep in mind that De Klerk's and his National Party's motivations here were at once political, religious, and theological. Better than the ANC, just returned from thirty years in exile, De Klerk understood the deeply religious nature of our people, and being an Afrikaner, he knew just how powerful a tool of manipulation religious appeal could be. The National Party needed the added word "reconciliation," which served as a biblical cover for their political motivations. It was a word, they knew, and better than the fresh-from-exile ANC, that would resonate powerfully with South Africa's black population, for whom faith is a serious matter. Desperately desired biblical notions of "forgiveness" flow much more naturally from reconciliation than from a concept such as "truth seeking."

Second, whatever "truth" would be allowed to come out—and not much did, in the end[46]—would be "softened" and managed by framing it within reconciliation with its gospel imperatives, which our people, as a deeply spiritual people, would understand and accept much easier.[47] And that is exactly what happened. So from the start, "reconciliation" would become, politically, a national project framed and infused by a decidedly Christian spirituality that would make the political not only acceptable, but imperative. Forgiveness, rather than remorse, repentance, restoration, and justice, became by far the most dominant and natural notion, inextricably bound to the process the TRC presided over. It would be years before we remembered what Aeldred Stubbs reminded us of in his reflections on the life of Steve Biko so long ago: "The real miracle of the Gospel is not forgiveness but repentance."[48]

There is a reason why President Nelson Mandela asked a venerated spiritual figure like Archbishop Desmond Tutu to chair the TRC. That was never an innocent request. Desmond Tutu was highly respected not only as a leader in the struggle against apartheid; he was a revered spiritual leader, one that could place his *imprimatur* of both

---

45. I recount the discussion and decision in the National Executive Committee in September 1993 at which I was present. See Boesak, *Tenderness of Conscience*, 182.

46. See Bell and Ntsebeza, *Unfinished Business*. The authors reveal that in the six months before the TRC started, national intelligence agencies destroyed more than forty-four metric tons of documents, paper, discs, and microfilm. They speak about "a paper Auschwitz." Bell and Ntsebeza, *Unfinished Business*, 7.

47. See Boesak, *Tenderness of Conscience*, 181–83.

48. See Stubbs, "Memoir," in Biko, *I Write What I Like*, 242.

religious authority and struggle credentials on the proceedings and the whole process that politicians on their own could never provide. "While other commissions were just truth commissions," theologian John De Gruchy correctly observed, "ours was chaired not by a judge or a lawyer but an archbishop, a pastor and father confessor."[49] An "eminent person," like a retired politician (from the hated and discredited apartheid era?) or a judge, for the same reason, would never do. But for South Africa's black people, deeply spiritual as we are, the combination of the iconic, even deified Nelson Mandela[50] (the one who asked) and the revered spiritual leader and outspoken Christian, Desmond Tutu (the one who graciously accepted), both of whom we honored with the title "Father," would be irresistible.

And even though noted figures like Jakes Gerwel, at the time director in the Office of President Mandela, would later complain that the TRC suffered from "excessive spirituality" because of the presence of so many religious personalities in the commission,[51] they served an absolutely vital role. They were necessary to provide the spiritual, but manufactured contentment, so much more than the media's manufactured consent, or the politicians' rhetoric, on their own, could ever accomplish. Desmond Tutu was not just the chairperson of the commission. He indeed, and effortlessly because it was so natural for him, became the nation's father confessor. There was no deceit or pretentiousness there, and the people felt it. It was not the political message of the TRC—even though the *goals* set for it were decidedly political—but the *spiritual* aura of the proceedings that made the victims of oppression, torture, and abuse so willing to accept the reconciliation on offer. It was not the speeches so much as the candles and the prayers in the name of Jesus; Tutu in his purple bishop's garb, the cross resting on his breast, calling upon the guidance of the Holy Spirit in what was supposed to be secular proceedings, that persuaded our people. It was the Archbishop's embodied spirituality, the moments of emotional, respectful silence; the reverence surrounding all of it that made the oppressed be so *content* with it, even though the TRC proved incapable of providing the restoration of justice so sorely needed.[52] It would be years before there was any meaningful critique of the TRC from black theological circles in South Africa.

I suggest that it was within this indispensable framework that the politicians could spread their message that served the real, intended political goals and simultaneously protect the interests of the dominant political and economic aristocracy. I have always found it rather striking that even though the messaging of these political figures was thoroughly political, the language they employed was one of intentional moral righteousness, a tone sure to resonate heavily with our people. For a while, they all sounded like preachers.

49. De Gruchy, *Reconciliation*, 41.
50. See Boesak, *Pharoahs on Both Sides*, ch. 6.
51. See Gerwel, "Reconciliation."
52. See the discussion in Boesak, *Tenderness of Conscience*, ch. 6.

So we hear then-Deputy Minister of Justice Johnny De Lange speaking about the "uniqueness" of our reconciliation process.[53] This uniqueness, he says, stems "from our morality as a people," the "unique epilogue" of our Constitution, where it makes reconciliation a requirement for the reconstruction of our society.[54] He stresses how we can achieve "both justice and reconciliation, not just one or the other."[55] By that he actually means that the egregious human rights violators would not all be held to account. Perhaps some foot soldiers would pay some price. The top brass who gave the orders and oversaw it all, however, the politicians who made the laws, created the climate, and gave political protection; the judiciary who closed their eyes to injustice, torture, and the most horrific violence; the media who covered it up and propagandized it all as righteous, logical, and natural; the religious leaders who justified it all as God's will and the perpetrators' duty for God and country, would all remain unnamed, untouched, and unblemished.

It would be what De Lange called "restorative justice in its essence."[56] It is not perfect justice, he concedes, but "justice in its perfect state" in any case does not exist anywhere.[57] But South Africans are called "to rise above narrow, party-political interests to a higher, nobler goal, for our divided country as a whole to emerge from a shameful past as the winner."[58]

De Lange goes to some length to demonstrate the morality of this stance. It is justice, he says, "that focuses on the future rather than the past; on understanding rather than vengeance; on reparation rather than retaliation, on *Ubuntu* rather than victimization."[59] This is almost church language, spoken to persuade and convince. The truth, though, is that black South Africans never called for vengeance; that reparation, let alone restoration, for the victims never happened; that there was so much more concern for the victimization of the perpetrators than there was for the re-victimization of the victims, and that Ubuntu became such a shamelessly abused concept to lull the victims into contentment.[60] We did not insist on "victor's justice," though our victory over formal apartheid was thorough. Neither did we insist on "victim's justice," though after 350 years of colonialist and apartheid brutality, dispossession,

---

53. See De Lange, "Historical Context," 14–15.

54. De Lange, "Historical Context," 23.

55. De Lange, "Historical Context," 24.

56. I have dealt extensively on the question of the TRC and justice; see Boesak, *Pharaohs on Both Sides*, ch. 4. There is of course room for restorative justice, but I argued there that the TRC's use of it was not wholly appropriate, conflated with what is also called "transitional justice," which in many cases, certainly in South Africa's case, became a form of impunity for apartheid human rights violators.

57. De Lange, "Historical Context," 25.

58. De Lange, "Historical Context," 23.

59. De Lange, "Historical Context," 24.

60. TRC observer Richard Wilson has reminded us of how the word Ubuntu, as often as the phrase "Christian forgiveness," was used to persuade the victims of apartheid to once again make the sacrifices that were never demanded of white people; see Graybill, *Truth and Reconciliation in South Africa*, 35.

and genocide, we could have. Instead, we settled for what Mahmood Mamdani called "survivor's justice."[61] That means the black oppressed accepted that colonialism and apartheid, albeit in very different ways, made victims of us all—of the blacks by violently depriving us of our humanity, and of the whites by making them lose theirs. Such impossible magnanimity cries out for real, radical justice, which never came. Nevertheless, we did not rise up in anger. We did not clog the streets with our protests because, in our minds, reconciliation required our forgiveness, even if it was not asked for, nor deserved, for without it there would be no future.

In the same vein, we hear Cabinet Minister Kader Asmal:

> So often it appears that history teaches only despair; cynicism can seem to sweep all before it, as it did in the old South African governance. But in a new environment, one that takes unflinchingly the full measure of the past, South Africa can become a safe place for the idealism, the sort of place and time where hope and history rhyme.[62]

Then-Deputy President Thabo Mbeki spoke of the "miracles" South Africans (read: black South Africans) were now called to achieve as we took on the challenges of reconciliation. In Mbeki's language, the focused concentration on reconciliation between whites (the perpetrators and beneficiaries of apartheid) and blacks (the victims of apartheid) is both faded and broadened. In Mbeki's logic, blacks could no longer think of themselves as victims of colonialism and apartheid that lasted for more than 350 years, since the victims now include so many more. And we have not only "common goals" but a "shared destiny."[63] The aspirations of blacks to right the wrongs of the past no longer have standing on their own. These are all conflated with, and embedded in, the common goals shared with whites, which in fact might be vastly different, in fact quite opposite, but will nonetheless, in the context of whites' economic dominance, become the definitive frame of the "shared future." By 1998, too, oppression no longer existed. Oppressor and oppressed alike were relics of the past, both "former":

> The challenge ahead of us is to achieve reconciliation between the former oppressor and the formerly oppressed, between black and white, between rich and poor (who in our conditions, are also described by colour), between men and women, the young and the old, the able and the disabled ... South Africans seeking to reconcile ourselves with one another ... moved to act together in pursuit of common goals, understanding that we cannot escape a shared destiny.[64]

---

61. See the detailed discussion in Boesak, *Pharaohs on Both Sides*, ch. 4.
62. See Asmal et al., *Reconciliation through Truth*, 216.
63. Mbeki, *Africa*, 41.
64. See Mbeki, *Africa*, 41.

The language sounds as if Mbeki is talking about the inclusiveness of God's love, or the love we are exhorted to exhibit to one another, but he isn't. He is in fact far from convinced that we can "approach the matter of reconciliation purely on the basis of the biblical injunction 'to love thy neighbour as thyself' as a voluntary outpouring of goodwill by a multitude of individuals who happened to be moved by the spirit."[65] Apparently, this love is a mere spiritual, romantic, sentimentality that cannot help us, because "reconciliation has and had to be based on the removal of injustice."[66] It is an old, long-discredited Marxian idea that does not hold water when one reads the Bible correctly.

Here, according to Mbeki's reasoning, Christian love is an impediment to justice because the two are incompatible. Christians will vigorously dispute this, and I have done so.[67] Another problem here is that if one, in the context of South Africa's past, present, and future, and the real challenges for reconciliation, de-emphasizes the reality of the intensely racialized nature of South Africa's political economy, one risks missing the point. Mbeki's reasoning does not so much signal a racial inclusion as it effects a color-blind leveling. Of course, South Africans should indeed "all" be reconciled to one another. But black South Africans were not discriminated against and oppressed because they were disabled, or elderly, or poor, but because they were *black*. And it need not be repeated that the white economically challenged, the white disabled, and the white elderly were always privileged *because* they were white. The point Mbeki wants to bring across is that since we are all South Africans, black South Africans should not raise their expectations too high. Doing that, he tells them, will jeopardize "our common goals" and "our shared destiny." But the spiritual language is not meant to be helpful; it is meant to defuse dissatisfaction and political dissent through the pre-emptive inculcation of guilt. Black South Africans who could not accept this state of affairs would be seen as unpatriotic, selfish, and self-serving, in a way denying their own Christian calling to embrace all God's children. The sentence is repeated. They would be the New South Africa's malcontents, the spoilers of the good news. And here Mbeki's politics of contentment dovetails neatly with the politics of concealment.

In his speech in parliament in 1999, President Mandela, in line with ANC ideology, also emphasized reconciliation as a "national," that is, political, project. But Mandela had an added dimension other politicians lacked. When I first reflected on these matters back in 2005, I read President Mandela's understanding of reconciliation as in contrast with that of his ANC comrades. "The quest for reconciliation," Mandela said in 1999, "was the fundamental objective of the people's struggle, to set up a government based on the will of the people, and build a South Africa which indeed belongs to

---

65. Mbeki, *Africa*, 55.

66. Mbeki, *Africa*, 55.

67. I have engaged Mbeki on this issue; see Boesak, *Tenderness of Conscience*, 175, and in an exposition of 1 Cor 13, on 235–37.

all."[68] The quest for reconciliation, in his words then, was not a political objective, the *outcome* of pre-1994 secret talks. No, it was the opposite, indeed, "the spur that gave life to our difficult negotiation process and the agreements that emerged from it."[69]

Tinyiko Maluleke saw it earlier,[70] but I thought then that Mandela's interpretation was one "that leaves more room for the spiritual inspiration for our reconciliation process."[71] In a sense, that was true. However, rereading it through the lens of manufactured contentment, it takes on a different hue. While resituating the reconciliation process as a "spur towards" rather than a result of negotiations, Mandela also makes reconciliation "the fundamental objective of the people's struggle."[72] In other words, *all along!* The secret talks have been heavily critiqued, and the negotiation processes and the "outcomes" have become much more scrutinized. But Mandela sought a reversal of the critique, and hence offered a *post facto* absolution. In this speech, reconciliation is now offered as intimately connected to the people's centuries-old struggle against colonialism and apartheid, and even more intimately to the people's sacrifices for their freedom. Mandela struck a chord: We have always believed, and I have preached, that a revolution which does not leave room for reconciliation would be incomplete. The president did not lie when he said this. But within the contemporary context, the reconciliation process is elevated above the debates and questions about reconciliation, justice, and restoration (of land, for example); of reconciliation and an amnesty process that at times looked more like impunity freely granted. The pre-negotiation secret talks and their outcomes, which robbed South Africa's oppressed not of revenge (which we did not seek), but of justice and equity (which we desired), are now sanctified by Mandela as "the spur" towards reconciliation. By doing this, Mandela added a secular sacramental element to the spiritual sacredness the TRC had already acquired for itself. As a result, the forgiveness that was relentlessly demanded from blacks as a Christian duty became, linked to the struggle, what Kader Asmal called "a civic sacrament *for the victims* to fulfil."[73]

In that same address, however, Mandela did another thing. He harshly castigated critics of the regime who dared to speak up publicly. One should remember that this is during a time when the ANC government was being criticized severely for its disastrous and corrupt arms deal, its abandonment of the "Reconstruction and Development Programme" (RDP) aimed specifically at the eradication of poverty and socio-economic inequality, and its more and more blatant embrace of neoliberal capitalism. Keeping this in mind gives context to Mandela's ire.

68. See Mandela, "Address in Special Debate."

69. See Mandela, "Address at the Opening of Parliament."

70. See Maluleke, "Truth, National Unity and Reconciliation," 325: "TRC developed from 'the negotiated settlement' to the 'interim constitution' and finally to the new constitution."

71. See Boesak, *Tenderness of Conscience*, 176–77.

72. Mandela, "Address in Special Debate."

73. See Asmal et al., *Reconciliation through Truth*, 49. Emphasis mine.

Moreover, in 1996, influential Ugandan social scientist, Mahmood Mamdani, published one of the first critical analyses, a devastating critique of the TRC he titled, "Reconciliation without Justice," revealing a flaw in the TRC's philosophy that ran like a fault line right through the whole process. The TRC has created what he called "fractured elites." "If reconciliation is to be durable," Mamdani wrote, "would it not need to be aimed at society (beneficiaries and victims) and not simply at the fractured elite (perpetrators and victims)?"[74] And does not justice become the demand for *systemic reform of society as a whole*, so that the "target" is *all* who benefited, rather than just the personal conversion of the "perpetrator"?[75] It was a thoughtful, well-reasoned, thoroughly justified critique; from Uganda, no less, and from a respected academic who had a global reach, and it stung.

Mandela did not spare the rod. The persons in the president's cross hairs were not just criticizing, the president said, they were "slaughtering" the country by their words and deeds. As with all ruling elites, here too is that fatal conflation: Their decisions and actions become those of the country as a whole; and their credibility becomes the credibility of the country. So while the decisions are unilateral, the people should share responsibility for the mistakes. Criticism of the government becomes criticism of the country. Despite the irritation, Mandela, rather diplomatically, always used the inclusive form of speech, "We are slaughtering each other," but it is clear that he was not really speaking in collective self-examination or in Bikoesque self-critique. The language is particularly strong. "We are slaughtering one another in the words we spew from our lips. We slaughter one another and our country by the manner in which we exaggerate its weaknesses to the wider world." Turning somewhat snide, and in a reminder of how the apartheid regime always pointed to "outside agitation" as the real reason for discontent at home, the president called the critics "heroes of the gab," persons who sought recognition and approval from abroad, "who astound their foreign associates by their self-flaggelation." Then came the authoritarian warning: "This must come to an end."[76]

There are some who speculated that Mandela was actually addressing white critics of the black government, because white people can travel abroad more easily, finding a more welcoming ear in the West eager to hear of blacks failing in government. This is a spurious, not to mention racist, argument. Black struggle activists, including those in the churches, were highly critical of some of the policy decisions the ANC were taking. The scrapping of the RDP ministry and the simultaneous plans for neoliberal programs such as GEAR (Growth, Employment, and Redistribution) were causes of deep anger. The stunning depth of the corruption that was beginning to surface after the arms-deal scandal, the slow pace of service delivery to the poor at every level, the deliberate reinstatement of apartheid's hated racial categorizations,

---

74. Mamdani, "Reconciliation without Justice," 4.
75. See Mamdani, "Reconciliation without Justice."
76. See Mandela, "Address at the Opening of Parliament."

were all things that caused great concern and led to constant upheaval. I suggest that the ANC leadership and Mandela, at the behest of the deracialized economic elite and the new black political aristocracy, was putting the masses in their place, reasserting the old Leninist maxim that real leadership is in the hands of the "vanguard of the revolution," the elite who were the only ones qualified to lead the struggle. The masses, who cannot be trusted with the process, had only to listen and obey. Criticism of the vanguard collective was out of place and not permissible.[77] For such a strategy to work in a non-communist, open democracy longing for recognition and support from the West, manufactured contentment is the way, since manufactured consent works so well in those Western societies.

Is it working though? In recent years, the debate whether Mandela himself was a "sell-out" reached such a fevered pitch among black youth that a liberal weekly newspaper felt compelled to publish a rather desperate editorial piece trying to douse the fires. "Mandela didn't sell out," it argued, "the post-94 ANC did."[78] In other words, that there was a "sell out" cannot really be disputed anymore. Only, it was not Mandela's doing. It was the "post-1994 ANC." But if the secret talks were the cradle of the accommodation of white, neoliberal, capitalist capture of South Africa's future, and Mandela was included in those talks from at least 1985, where does one draw the line? And wasn't Nelson Mandela our first 1994 president? And if not his, whose leadership was it that steered the "post-1994 ANC"? These are disturbing questions, though no longer sacrosanct, it seems.

My guess is that the angry, disillusioned youth who have seen no gains from the new democracy, scoured raw by the grinding, ongoing impoverishment, and mocked by the ostentatious displays of wealth of the new black elite—those who feel betrayed by a reconciliation process that was little more than what I called "political pietism"[79] because it was indeed "without justice" as Mahmood Mamdani found—are not appeased. In the townships, sunk into the mire by poverty that has no end, frustrated by the lack of meaningful education, and even when they do have some, the lack of opportunities and jobs, would not have been impressed. They would have no reason to be persuaded into consent or contentment by privileged persons writing in the pages of the white-controlled media.

As I was writing this, a young friend of mine from the 1980s activist generation wrote on his Facebook page as he was pondering the death of George Floyd and the protests that followed. He apologizes for its length, but he feels it now has to be said. His series of questions, relentlessly piercing and brutally honest as they are, need to be heard, pondered, and responded to, even as he fears that this might be too uncomfortable a conversation to have.[80] Rudy Oosterwyk writes,

77. See my detailed discussion of these matters in Boesak, *Tenderness of Conscience*, 159–67.
78. See Claassens, "Mandela didn't sell out."
79. See Boesak and DeYoung, *Radical Reconciliation*.
80. Excerpted from the Facebook post of Rudy Oosterwyk as communicated to the author, June 3, 2020.

> Is it possible that we may never overcome apartheid? That it was never really possible to forgive the horrendousness that was apartheid? That the latent effects of apartheid and by extension, racism, white supremacy, and white privilege will remain with us forever, socially, politically, and economically? That the history of the degradation of black South Africans will remain as part of the structural make-up of our national psyche for many centuries to come still? Is it possible that apartheid was so successful that any attempt at genuine reconciliation remains an ongoing national failure? . . . Was forgiveness not just the lowest hanging political fruit to give and take at the time? Never mind the Freedom Charter. Never mind the spirit of the UDF. Never mind the heroic battles in the streets fought by the student movements against the army and the police . . . We were going to forgive white people never mind all of this, all our offerings, all our sacrifices, all our losses. Forgiveness was offered as an essential ingredient for the creation of a non-racial and democratic South Africa . . . Forgiveness was the ultimate offering with no specific return or benefit for black South Africans . . . I think it's time we unburden ourselves from this language of forgiveness because the conditions for it were never there to begin with, and it will never be there to enable it. What we need now is a different language, a language that speaks of accountability . . . We must have this conversation as equals, as peers and co-owners of all that this land has to offer.

This is the language of the younger black generation who have been force-fed the fruits of manufactured contentment, and they are finding it too bitter to swallow. Are we—again, and so soon!—facing James Baldwin's chilling warning, taken from the old black spiritual?

> God gave Noah the rainbow sign,
> No more water, the fire next time![81]

"Perhaps a Black Renaissance"

In just about every edition since the first publication of Biko's classic *I Write What I Like,* contributors express the hope that Biko's legacy would continue to be valued in South Africa and worldwide. The latest 2017 edition, published to celebrate the 40th anniversary of the first publication, and which will be our reference throughout this book, is no different. By this time though, not just Biko's legacy, as something to cherish and ponder upon, but the powerful relevance of his thinking has become clear, and not just to those of us who were adherents of the Black Consciousness movement.

In this edition, Ames Dhai, director of the Steve Biko Center for Bioethics at the University of the Witwatersrand, states about Biko's work,

---

81. See Baldwin, *Fire Next Time*, 11–106.

> Forty years later, while much has been achieved, there is so much more still to be done. Pigmentation differences have re-emerged to erode the black solidarity and freedom that Steve Biko died for. It is clear that the task of Black Consciousness is incomplete. A re-awakening of the energy and drive toward the work of Black Consciousness is an ethical imperative. After all, is that not what Steve would want?[82]

In an excellent essay on Biko's "challenge to religion," black theologian Tinyiko Maluleke observes that the Biko legacy is (still) the object of fierce debate. "Biko more than thirty years ago framed a theological agenda that, in all honesty, we have yet to exhaust. None of the challenges [to religion and theology] have been met. Much work remains to be done."[83] The challenge Biko poses specifically to Black liberation theology is undisputed, and this book is an effort to respond seriously to that challenge. As a challenge to religion in general, that is true as well as important. We have to pause here to make another observation. Maluleke frames his remarks by reminding us of Biko's belief that "no nation can win a battle without faith."[84] With Biko and Maluleke, I believe that religion can play a decisive role in helping to shape societies in their struggles for freedom and for the establishing of an open, inclusive, responsive, responsible democracy, where justice for the people is central to all decision making, and the dignity of the people comes before expediency in politics.

In his book, *The Great Terror War*, international law scholar Richard Falk is hopeful of the positive role of religion in society today, despite the distressing signs of religion "wrecking world order," as Falk titled this chapter in his book. He argues for this, even while acknowledging that religion is part of the dangers threatening to wreck global order. Falk nonetheless concludes that in the realm of global politics and in the face of an American "counterapocalyptic reading of September 11 . . . taking the unprecedented form of a nonterritorial, counterterrorist crusade" that wields its interventionary authority throughout the world through the exercise of "monopoly control over the militarization of space and oceans, only the great world religions have the credibility, legitimacy, and depth of understanding to identify and reject the idolatry that seems to lie at the core of this American project of planetary domination."[85]

One hopes that this might be true, but we must not ignore the issues raised by those who believe religion as such is so fundamentally corrupt, so fundamentally irredeemable, that it has nothing to say, nothing to contribute because of our history of violence, divisionism, hypocrisy, and cruelty. The so-called New Atheists have found an eloquent spokesperson in Richard Dawkins who does not mince words in his blistering critique of religion:

---

82. Biko, *I Write What I Like*, xvii.
83. Mngxitama et al., *Biko Lives!*, 115–28.
84. Biko, *I Write What I Like*, 64.
85. Falk, *Great Terror War*, 82–128.

> The God of the Old Testament is arguably the most unpleasant character in all fiction: jealous and proud of it; a petty, unjust, unforgiving control freak; a vindictive, bloodthirsty ethnic cleanser; a misogynistic, homophobic, racist, infanticidal, genocidal, filicidal, pestilential, megalomaniacal, sadomasochistic, capriciously malevolent bully.[86]

Dawkins uses this picture of the "God of the Old Testament" to write off religion as a whole. Such a god is indeed a menace to human life and the life of the earth. We know of course that Dawkins's picture of God is much too simplistic. The issue is much more complex.[87] Still, he has a point, as far as it goes. However, this is what Biko would denounce as "the appalling irrelevance of the interpretation given to the Scriptures," something he would accuse black preachers of.[88] So it is crucial to be honest and begin with the question: What kind of religion are we talking about? And we must, with Biko in mind, begin with that unforgettable nineteenth-century African American freedom fighter and abolitionist Frederick Douglass's persistent and fine distinction between "the two religions" and by the same token the two different readings of the Bible. It is a distinction of such timelessness and enduring relevance that one shall have reason to return to again and again:

> I love the religion of our blessed Savior . . . which comes from above, in the wisdom of God which is first pure, then peaceable, gentle . . . without partiality and without hypocrisy . . . which makes it the duty of its disciples to visit the fatherless and the widow in their affliction. I love that religion . . . It is because I love this religion that I hate the slave-holding, the woman-whipping, the mind-darkening, the soul-destroying religion that exists in America . . . loving the one I must hate the other; holding to one I must reject the other.[89]

Douglass was not finished:

> I assert most unhesitatingly, that the religion of the south is a mere covering for the most horrid crimes—a justifier of the most appalling barbarity—a sanctifier of the most hateful frauds—and a dark shelter under which the darkest, foulest, grossest, and most infernal deeds of slaveholders find the strongest protection.[90]

Yet we must not confuse Douglass with Dawkins:

> What I have said respecting and against religion, I mean strictly to apply to the *slave-holding religion* of this land, and with no possible reference to

---

86. Dawkins, *God Delusion*, 51.

87. I have discussed the matter of our reading and interpretation of scripture in Boesak, *Children of the Waters of Meribah*, ch. 1.

88. Biko, *I Write What I Like*, 60.

89. See Douglass, *My Bondage and My Freedom*.

90. See Douglass, *Narrative*, 77.

Christianity proper; for, between the Christianity of this land, and the Christianity of Christ, I recognize the widest possible difference . . . I can see no reason, but for the most deceitful one, for calling the religion of this land Christianity.[91]

Following the lead of famed Swiss theologian Karl Barth, however, I too make the distinction between religion and faith. Religion, devoid from a relationship with God, and a mere refuge for cultural and political ideology, is idolatry. It is, Barth said, "the enemy of faith."[92] The distinction is necessary, and as we have learned from Frederick Douglass, vital.

Where religiosity is satisfied with form, faith is concerned with substance. Where religion seeks a place of comfort within the world and its rules, structures, and systems, faith seeks to disrupt those systems and structures, challenging those rules and exposing them as unjust rules that favor only the rich and powerful.

When war is at its most profitable, and religion is at its most complacent because it is complicit, faith is most combative in its work for peace. When religion betrays the poor and is craven before the powerful, faith stands with the poor in combative love and seeks to empower the powerless. When religion worships false gods as all-powerful, runs to them for protection and salvation, and threatens those who speak the truth, faith remembers Jeremiah:

> Their gods are like scarecrows in a cucumber patch.
> They cannot speak, and they have to be carried, for they cannot walk.
> Do not be afraid of them, for they can neither do you harm
> Nor can they do you any good. (Jer 10:5)

When religion worships at the altar of greed and avarice, faith reminds us that we cannot serve God and Mammon. When religion joins Mammon on "those beds of ivory, lounges on their couches, and eat lambs from their flocks . . ."; when religion and Mammon "sing idle songs to the sound of the harp . . . drink wine from bowls, and anoint themselves with the finest oils, but are not grieved over the ruin of Joseph," then faith will say with Amos,

> Let justice roll down like waters,
> And righteousness like an everflowing stream. (Amos 6:4–6; 5:24)

When religion bows before Mammon, to "tear the skin off" God's people "and the flesh off their bones"; to "eat the flesh" of God's people, "flay their skin off them," all for the sake of profit; when Mammon proceeds to "break their bones in pieces, and chop them up like meat in a kettle," and when the false prophets of the false gods of religion

---

91. Douglass, *Narrative*, 118.

92. See Barth, *Epistle to the Romans*, especially the section on 1:18–32; see also Barth, *Doctrine of the Word of God*, loc. 18.

"make war against those who put nothing into their mouths," faith remembers Micah, and takes prophetic courage:

> But as for me, I am filled with power,
> with the Spirit of the LORD,
> and with justice and might. (Mic 3:8)

When religion dons the robes of cowardice and covers up the lie, faith clothes itself in righteousness and stands for the truth. When religion embraces political pietism, calculated forgetfulness and hardheartedness and calls it reconciliation, faith calls for repentance that translates into justice, restitution, and the restoration of dignity.

When religion beats the drums of hatred, revilement, and extremism, faith sings the songs of justice, love, and freedom. When religion preaches exclusivist dogma, faith rejoices in the inclusive love of God. When religion justifies hypocrisy and bigotry in the name of God, faith, with the prophet Isaiah, exposes the truth: "This people honor me with their lips, but their hearts are far from me" (Isa 29:13; Matt 15:8). Faith stands with Jesus as he says, "And as I am lifted up, I will draw *all* unto me" (John 12:32). No exceptions, no excuses; no ifs, no buts, no howevers.

This, I suggest, is how we should understand Biko when he said that this is the faith we cannot do without, that we need in our struggles for justice, dignity, and freedom. It is this faith, he would say elsewhere, that is "the righteousness of our strength."[93] This is the faith through which we will win. But if our faith in God "is spoilt by our having to see Him through the eyes of the same people we are fighting against, then there obviously begins to be something wrong in that relationship."[94] That, Biko would argue here, is not the faith he is speaking of. That is religiosity.

Biko knew only too well that the religion brought by colonialism, that religion that justified land theft, oppression, slavery, and genocide, was not the faith we needed. It was not simply and generally "a religion" that served the God of liberation, justice, and dignity. It was rather, one that offered "an appalling irrelevance in the interpretation to the Scriptures," "the ideal religion for the colonization of our people."[95] That was not the "faith" Biko talked about. His warning to black preachers that "nowadays it was *our* interpretation of the Bible that still makes Christianity the ideal religion for the subjugation of the people," still stands.[96] He was searching for the religion of Jesus, the selfless revolutionary because of Jesus's love for God, God's people, and God's justice. And later Biko would say that Black liberation theology is the kind of faith that gave him hope.

This is the thinking we should learn to embrace, or re-embrace, as the case may be. The necessity to re-embrace these two legacies, that of Biko and Black Consciousness

---

93. Biko, *I Write What I Like*, 135–56.
94. Biko, *I Write What I Like*, 64.
95. Biko, *I Write What I Like*, 61.
96. Biko, *I Write What I Like*, 61.

for our times indeed seems to be the calling of our times. Clearly, as the editors of *Biko Lives!* point out, Biko was not the only exponent of the Black Consciousness philosophy. It is true, however, that his thinking had an extraordinary impact on the whole movement. It was not only influential; it was formative. No one else has formulated that thinking with such clarity, such force, such enduring power.

However, rereading Biko inevitably means reinterpreting Biko for situations he did not live to see, experience, think about, or discuss, as one has to do when rereading Martin Luther King Jr. It is never straightforward. The risks of such rereading and re- (or new) interpretation are clear. In doing this, however, I reminded myself of the words of caution expressed by historian Thomas Bates as he writes about new understandings of Gramsci's concept of hegemony. He talks about the task of the historian, but it is applicable to any interpreter:

> The historian, placed in the uncomfortable role of archaeologist, risks creating the illusion of a theory which wasn't there, or arbitrarily emphasizing a casual idea. What justifies a post-mortem reconstruction of the theory is the fact that the concept of hegemony is the unifying thread of Gramsci's prison notes, and appears to be the logical conclusion to his political experience.[97]

Thus cautioned, we shall try to find the "unifying thread" in Biko's thought as expressed in his *I Write What I Like,* which may lead us to draw appropriate and logical conclusions from his political experience, always trying to follow the logic of his thinking. Nkosinathi Biko considers *I Write What I Like* the "authoritative point of reference on the depth and breadth of political insight that built the Black Consciousness movement into the most powerful force of the seventies."[98] Even though he wrote this in 2017, his observation that we live in a time in which "our nation is taking stock of the road we have walked"[99] from 1994, it is without doubt still true in 2020, and we now know that that road is much rockier than we have been prepared for. Now, more than ever, we should be "reviewing some of the political actions we have adopted."[100] Indeed, writes Steve Biko's son,

> almost without fail, we can take each of the top challenges still facing us as a nation, and find a substantive and relevant reference in the writings of Biko.[101]

That is true. This book is an effort to ensure that Biko's thinking, as his son hopes, "continue[s] to be a part of the national dialogue as we continue to define ourselves."[102] Here again, it is not unwise to remind ourselves of yet another word of caution, and to

---

97. See Bates, "Gramsci," 35.
98. Biko, *I Write What I Like*, xxxii.
99. Biko, *I Write What I Like*, xxxiii.
100. Biko, *I Write What I Like*, xxxiii.
101. Biko, *I Write What I Like*, xxxiii.
102. Biko, *I Write What I Like*, xxxiii.

consider the very pertinent questions Puerto Rican scholar at U. C. Berkeley, Ramón Grosfogel, poses in regard to decolonial studies in general, and keep those in mind for our reflections on history, Black Consciousness, and the decolonial task of Black liberation theology:

> Can we produce a radical anti-systemic politics beyond identity politics? Is it possible to articulate a critical cosmopolitanism beyond nationalism and colonialism? Can we produce knowledges beyond Third World and Eurocentric fundamentalisms? Can we move beyond economic reductionism and culturalism? How can we overcome the Eurocentric modernity without throwing away the best of modernity as many Third World fundamentalists do?[103]

We can but try.

In his preface to the 2017 edition, Archbishop Emeritus Desmond Tutu hopes that readers of Biko's words might be so inspired by his life and commitment, and by Black Consciousness, that it changes lives and minds and ways of living. He hopes it would also help "to exorcise the horrible demons of self-hatred, and self-contempt that made blacks suck up to whites whilst treating fellow blacks as the scum they thought themselves to be."[104] But Desmond Tutu hopes for more: "Perhaps, it could just spark a black renaissance."[105] Perhaps it will, and we, the heirs of Black Consciousness and the legacy of Steve Biko, must make sure that it does.

---

103. See Grosfoguel, "Decolonizing Postcolonial Studies," 1.
104. Biko, *I Write What I Like*, xxv.
105. Biko, *I Write What I Like*, xxvi.

1

"Selfless Revolutionaries"
Black Consciousness, Black Theology, and the Validity of the Ethics of Global Solidarity and Resistance

Unremembering, Black Agency, and the Falling of the Idols

As I was working on this project, completely captivated by my rereading of Biko, four messages landed in my inbox. Two of them were from a youth movement and a group of students, invitations to virtual conversations, asking me to speak on current events and the "connection between the past and the present." Both groups expressed concern about how much of our history, including the history of the struggle against apartheid, "we don't know" because it is never properly discussed. Much is being forgotten, but much more is being suppressed, one email said. Two other invitations speak of plans for projects once circumstances allow, including an exhibition and series of discussions around the subject of "unremembering." The invitations are a surprise, an honor, and a delight. These younger colleagues reminded me of how, in a 2005 publication, I used the term in describing what I saw as the deliberate distortion of our recent history of struggle, how the role of the faith of the people, and in particular the prophetic church in that struggle, was being faded, ignored, or erased. I pointed out that throughout our history of struggle, religious faith, as a praxis of solidarity and resistance, was central to the oppressed themselves in that struggle, as, in fact, it had always been.[1] "During the 1980s, the time of our darkest oppression, faith, as the

---

1. Even secular historians who routinely minimize or ignore the role of faith in the struggles of South Africa's oppressed people have to admit that during the Defiance Campaigns of the 1950s, for example, "a mood of religious fervour infused the resistance" which was sustained throughout the period; the campaign was opened by "days of prayer" and volunteers "pledged themselves at prayer meetings to a code of love, discipline, and cleanliness." See Lodge, *Black Politics*, viii, 43–44. See also Boesak, *Tenderness of Conscience*, 106–17.

deepest source of inspiration for struggle and sacrifice, was the most salient feature of the struggle against apartheid and the resultant conflict between the church and the apartheid state had reached a level never experienced before."[2]

Yet, in our post-1994 history books and our political discourse, this, "apart from the blandest of acknowledgements," was never seriously recognized as the crucial aspect of struggle it really was. Inasmuch as the church or prophetic leaders from all faiths were mentioned, they were "almost always divorced from their faith and they are seen in, and used for, their political functionality rather than their prophetic faithfulness."[3] This was true for politics where our church gatherings and prayer services, so vital to our revolutionary resilience as well as our spiritual well-being, let alone the church's significant leadership in mass actions of civil disobedience in the streets, were blithely demoted to "excuses" under cover of which the "real" struggle was conducted. The role of faith, and the faithfulness of the prophetic church in service to the struggle in obedience to God, was relegated to service to the liberation movement, in obedience to the ANC. It is true for academia as well, where I detected "not only an anxiousness to ignore history as it happened... There is a conscious, and constant, effort to rewrite history by omission and commission."[4] I did not argue then, nor do I now, that the prophetic church and the people's faith were the only factors that mattered. I do argue that the role of the church was such that, without it, the struggle would have been significantly prolonged, and without it, the struggle would have taken on an entirely different character.[5] I called that process "unremembering," making a distinction between "unremembering" and "forgetting":

> A people might forget their history because the horrors of their past are such that they cannot bear further contemplation. Psychologists have taught us that the pain of suffering is often (and easily) blocked out in a collective act of forgetfulness. The violence inflicted upon persons can no longer be borne, and remembering is a way of carrying the memories with you. It is a victimization that never ends. This can be true of the perpetrators, too. They "forget" because they have an absolute need to forget, in a way which goes beyond mere denial. It is then not enough to say, "We did not know." Obliteration of the past is what is needed. As such, this is an act of suppression of memory, rather than simply of "forgetting."[6]

"Forgetting is common even among those people who are descended from slaves, like me," writes Gabeba Baderoon, speaking as a descendant of the slaves of the Cape

---

2. See Boesak, *Tenderness of Conscience*, 103.
3. Boesak, *Tenderness of Conscience*, 103. A full chapter in that work is devoted to this subject.
4. See Boesak, *Tenderness of Conscience*, 103.
5. As I will argue in ch. 4, by "church" here, I do not mean the institutional church. I am referring to the prophetic church, whose driving force is a theology of prophetic engagement and liberation.
6. Boesak, *Tenderness of Conscience*, 103–4. Today, Global South decolonial scholars would call this a form of "epistemicide." See the discussion in chs. 2 and 5 below.

colony and admitting just how hard it is to recall, remember, and deal with this part of our history even though it lasted for 176 years. She refers to the penetrating work of South African novelist and feminist literary scholar Zoë Wicomb, who writes of this same phenomenon, bringing, correctly, I think, the element of shame into the equation. This shame, Wicomb argues, "is the effect of the deep psychic costs of almost two centuries of extreme violence, and the further violence of being blamed for inviting that brutality." In turn, this has resulted in a phenomenon she called "a folk amnesia born of shame."[7]

This is how I defined unremembering then: Rather than forgetfulness, whether out of necessity brought on by powerlessness, or by design as a needful consequence of power,

> Unremembering is a deliberate political act for reasons of domestication and control. A people's history, or their memory, is falsified, rewritten or denied. This process is not a confluence of accidental political factors; neither is it the result of inevitable political [or historical] "shifts." It is an act of appropriation. Although it may serve psychological ends, as an act it is deliberately ideological and serves a political agenda.[8]

Key to understanding these processes is realizing the central role of power. Colonization disempowered colonized peoples by the violent erasure and appropriation of all that gave them meaning: the expectation of life, their lands and their sense of belonging, cultures, religions; and the possession of their bodies, personhood, and their consciousness of themselves. What we see now in the revolutionary waves in unprecedented solidarity across the globe are movements of empowerment. It is the realization that among much else, the history of imperialism and colonialism's rise is the history of the power of violence: dispossession and appropriation, unmaking and remaking, falsehood and unremembering. The matrix of power we discern in ongoing imperialism and renewed colonialism, which we now call coloniality, must be met with a new, energized matrix of power: The power to take a hold of that history, revealing its fraudulent face for what it truly is; unmasking its sacralized veneer as idolatrous depravity, exposing its pretentious "civilizing of the natives" as Frantz Fanon's "virtual Apocalypse."[9]

From this perspective, first priority is the reclaiming of the mind and the undoing of the systems and structures of oppression and injustice, in tandem with the

---

7. See Baderoon, "Remembering Slavery in South Africa." See for example Wicomb, "Shame and Identity," where she specifically discusses the effect of this phenomenon on the so-called "colored people" of South Africa, and even more specifically in the Western Cape, the place of origin for slavery in South Africa. Wicomb's "psychic costs over centuries" is the equivalent of Joy De Gruy's "post traumatic slave syndrome" as this pertains to African Americans. See De Gruy, *Post Traumatic Slave Syndrome*.

8. Boesak, *Tenderness of Conscience*, 104.

9. See Fanon, *Wretched of the Earth*, 251. See ch. 2 below.

building of systems of justice and equity. In that process, and in its own right, nothing is more important than the battle for the correction and reclaiming of history. In particular, this is happening in the onslaught on the statues of imperialism, colonialism, and racist white supremacy. This is important, not only because of the political and psychological value of symbolism, but also because it opens the way for genuine transformation at multiple levels. That is why the South African students of the Fallist movements set such a good example by following the removals of the symbols of colonialism with pressure on universities to decolonize their curricula, their teaching, and their approach to administration. So now, the debate is not just about symbols, but about the question: How can we turn this university, built on a Western model of education and with its Eurocentric educational perspectives, into a truly African university? And how can the university become a place that contributes to the building of a just, equal, and inclusive society? Bringing down the symbols of imperialism and colonialism is not by any means the totality of the revolution. But it is as close to its heart as it gets.

Very much like the youth driving this revolution today, another youth long before them, King Josiah, the boy who ascended the throne of Judah at eight years old, and a few years later launched a full-scale attack on the symbols of imperial religiosity in his land, the youth today are taking down all the idols of the imperial presence. Josiah did not start a violent revolt against the empire; by the time he was born, the political landscape had been shifting quite dramatically. But what he did was without question a textbook example of Martin Luther King Jr.'s "revolution of values." A few years into his reign, he began to see the lingering power of imperialism, what we today would call the "matrix of powers of coloniality."

We read of him in the book 2 Kings, chapters 22 and 23. What womanist theologian Katie Cannon said of prophetic black preachers could be said of Josiah. He lived "with one ear on the ground hearing the cries and longings of the people, and the other ear at the mouth of God."[10] Importantly, Josiah understood that history had presented him with unprecedented historical opportunities—a kairos moment, so to speak. With a keen sense of the political moment and an even keener sense of what God expected of him, Josiah sets his sights on fundamental, radical change, the only kind of change he knew would liberate his people. For a century, Judah was an oppressed, occupied, and exploited vassal of the Assyrian Empire. After the death of its god-king Ashurbanipal, whose name means, "The god Ashur is creator of an heir," the Assyrian Empire fell into chaos. Egypt was too weak to reassert its power, and Judah unexpectedly experienced a period free of foreign domination.[11] Reading and discerning the signs of the times, the young Josiah understood that a singular moment had arrived.

---

10. See Cannon, *Katie's Canon*, 115–16.
11. See Bright, *History of Ancient Israel*, 316–23.

Josiah, I suggest, realized four things. First, that the feared, ruthless leader of a feared, ruthless empire was only the "created heir" of a false god. He and his gods were what Jeremiah would derisively describe as "scarecrows in a cucumber patch" (Jer 10:5). That god-king, was after all, only flesh and blood, and was now dead. Still, his memory, and the awe and fear it aroused, was kept alive, not only in the hearts of the people, but by the omnipresence of the images he left behind. Second, that the moment has come; he could not wait, postpone, or procrastinate. Third, this was no time for the contemplation of incremental reforms; that because he was young, he could afford some tentative baby steps. He knew, with a wisdom beyond his years, that though *he* was young, the decimation and enslavement of his people was old. They had no time, and they could not wait. Fourth, Josiah understood that the planned reformation of his people could never be complete while the reminders of what had enslaved their bodies, hearts, and minds, and led them away from the God of their liberation, still stood around in all their glory. Images and statues are erected for a reason: to invoke both a sense of pride and identification, to be admired and worshiped, to solidify unquestionable authority. So Josiah understood: Those images, reminding the people both of their days of subjection and un-freedom, and of the glory of the empire that enslaved them, even though that empire had crumbled to dust, had to go. In his own way, Josiah understood what the youthful, selfless revolutionaries today understand so well: "Ashurbanipal Must Fall!" Incrementalism is the invention of the rich, the powerful, and the comfortable. If Josiah could stand next to South Africa's young revolutionaries in the 1980s, he, too, would have joined in that cry, *Sekunjalo!* "Now is the time!"

Can it be that this is the difference between the murders of Trayvon Martin in 2012 and Michael Brown in 2014 and the killing of George Floyd in 2020? Those first two murders, equally tragic, equally vile, equally cruel, equally seen as lynchings, did launch the Black Lives Matter movement, but somehow did not generate the energy necessary for a sustained movement of resistance at that time? That this time, Keeanga Yamahtta Taylor's "Obama illusion" is over, and the Trump reality has exposed the dark heart of the American Empire in all its rampant, violent destructiveness, no longer solely aimed at those of us in the rest of the world, but at Americans themselves, just as vulnerable as us? That what Jesus said of the Pharisees is fulfilled today: What Barack Obama has said in the dark will be heard in the light; and whatever Obama whispered behind closed doors, Donald Trump was now shouting from the rooftops (Luke 12:3)? Can it be that this time America can no longer continue to deny what the Global South, and black people, other minorities and poor people in the US itself have long known and had to endure?

I am recalling the words of journalist Bill Moyers about Donald Trump, but now equally undeniable of America as a decaying empire, too worn down by the truth to any longer prop up the lie: "Instead of a soul, Donald Trump has an open sore."[12]

12. See "Bill Moyers: Instead Of A 'Soul,' Donald Trump Has An 'Open Sore,'" YouTube video, posted by *MSNBC*, August 17, 2017, youtube.com/watch?v=zFL7tt-Pp1Y.

Moyers said this in 2017, not yet a year into the Trump presidency. It is a shattering judgment. Now, the "open sore" of American Empire is on full, frightening display, and so are its fatal fault lines. But the Black Lives Matter movement, like Hamid Dabashi's Arab Spring revolutions, turned out to be an "open work," a delayed, but not stoppable defiance. The embers never died, and they, fulfilling Martin Luther King Jr.'s prayers, have kindled a fire "that no water can put out." Thus, reading the death of George Floyd, though no different from the death of the hundreds of others lynched by the police as a sign of the times, have the Black Lives Matter revolutionaries, in their multi-racial, multi-generational, multi-gendered, multi-faith masses, like Josiah, selfless revolutionary of his day, realized that their kairos moment has come? That they, for this time, must embrace what King said was the innermost heart of the movement, "to save America's soul"? Or, more exact to the global inclusivity of their actions now, as Biko would put it, give the world the gift of "a human face"?

In great detail, the book named Second Kings tells us that Josiah began to remove all those symbols of false power, understanding that they were the symbols of a god created by Ashur, another false god that sought to replace the one God of Israel. He destroyed "all the vessels made for Baal, for Ashera, and for all the hosts of heaven; he burned them outside Jerusalem, in the fields of the Kidron" (2 Kgs 23:4). In a sentence highly critical of Judah's royal complicity with empire, the text reads that Josiah "deposed the idolatrous priests whom the kings of Judah had ordained"; he banned all the priests who "made offering to Baal, to the sun, the moon, the constellations, and all the hosts of heaven" (23:5). A false religion, handmaid of the empire, has no place in a liberation struggle. Then he went to the temple where Israel worshiped that thirty-five-foot statue of Ashera and "brought out the image of Ashera that was erected inside the temple, and burned it"; he demolished the houses of the male temple prostitutes that "were inside the house of the LORD," and he broke down "all the high places of the gates" (23:4–8). From verse 8 to verse 16, the chapter goes on and on, describing with an almost breathless intensity the destruction of everything—from the altars of sacrifice to the bones in the graves of those revered as iconic in the empire—that reminded of the empire, his people's enslavement, and their own faithless turning away from their God. The king disturbed the dead: they should not rest in peace and honor while their victims are still suffering the traumatic convulsions of the aftermath of their rule. Even their bones are turned to ashes. The long, detailed description is no superfluous rhetorical flourish. It is an attempt to make the reader *feel* the pain and the anger, to understand the radical depth of the transformation Josiah was after, step after step, act after act. It was, as South Africa's Pixley ka Isaka Seme, thousands of years later, would say of his own vision for an African renaissance, "a regeneration moral and eternal!"[13]

But then follows a remarkable exchange. As the king walked from place to place, personally overseeing these historic cleansing ceremonies, he saw another tomb.

---

13. Seme, "Regeneration of Africa," 439. See the discussion in ch. 2.

"What is this monument that I see?" he asked. The people of that city told him, "It is the tomb of the man of God who came from Judah and predicted these things that you have done against the altar at Bethel." Then the king said, "Let him rest; let no one move his bones" (23:17, 18). Amongst the hundreds of altars to the false gods and the hundreds of monuments honoring the iconized followers of the false gods, all those who exchanged the worship of Yahweh for the worship of the false god Ashurbanipal and the Mammons of empire, there was one exception. Amongst all the monuments erected to those who lived by the rules of empire, to those who profited from their complacency and benefited from their complicity, there was only one monument that stood for truth and righteousness and freedom. Besides the rediscovered Book, this one monument with its memories of hope and resistance, was Josiah's, and the people's, hopeful turning toward a new future. The one monument left standing was the monument of the prophet of God. The Bible does not tell us the prophet's name, but the people knew who he was, and they knew his work. They remembered him.

The invitation to participate in these projects initiated by the younger generation is an invitation to join the uprising against unremembering, which is now fast becoming one of the most meaningful and effective manifestations of the current, worldwide Black Lives Matter revolution. I am thinking of the sustained onslaught against colonial history and coloniality, not just in schools and the lecture rooms of universities, but on the streets and the parks and the city squares, in the toppling of imperialist and colonialist iconography.

In baffling succession, all over the world, the symbols of imperialist and colonialist history are falling. Notorious names associated with racism and white supremacy are being removed from buildings, and the iconography of power, domination, and subjugation, are coming down. And whether they are toppled or removed by governmental decree, this is done because of the pressure exerted by the people in the streets with protest and resistance. It is a most encouraging display of M. M. Thomas's vision of revolution as "power in the hands of the people as agents of change and symbols of dignity." They are "toppled." The people are claiming their agency; they are the creators of their own liberation. In America, a few toppled figures include Christopher Columbus, John Calhoun, Robert E. Lee, and Andrew Jackson. In Britain, it is the statues of that proud imperialist Winston Churchill, the hero who saved Britain from Hitler but could not overcome Ghandi, in his eyes the "malignant subversive fanatic, posing as a fakir of a type well known in the East, striding half-naked up the steps of the Viceregal palace."[14] And it is the slave trader Edward Colston.[15] They are all falling and drowning in this river of righteous, liberating iconoclasm.

In Hong Kong, in another revolution led by the young, the situation seems to be the other way around. The Chickeeduck children's clothing store has a white statue, erected inside the store. It shows a demonstrator wearing a helmet, gas mask, and

14. See Guha, "Churchill, the Greatest Briton, Hated Ghandi, the Greatest Indian."
15. See Landler, "With Edward Colston Statue Gone, Bristol Faces a Reckoning."

goggles. "Lady Liberty," they call her. She is life-sized, impossible to overlook. She is not there as a commercial attraction: she is there to serve the revolution. In one hand, she carries an umbrella—a symbol of mass protests in 2014—and in the other a flag that reads, "Free Hong Kong, revolution now."[16] The direct opposite of the images iconizing imperialist oppression, this one honors resistance against imperialist oppression. Standing high in a children's store, it displays something of an indestructible hope in the future. The children who look at the clothes on display in the windows and in the store must also look at her. Looking at her, they get it: On the streets, the masses are saying, *this must not be*. One day, she is saying, *this will be*. It is the Hong Kong version of *We Shall Overcome*, revolutionary music molded into plaster.

The authorities have ordered the owner to take it down. He refused. Here, the refusal to take down the statue displays the same revolutionary power as the determination to topple. It is the power of the powerless, and it is a power Beijing, whose overwhelming desire is to become the next world empire,[17] will seek to destroy, and will, despite its power, find out why that is so hard. My guess is that the presence of that one, single statue will create as much anger and humiliation for the mighty China as the presence of those millions in the streets who refuse to back down. So perhaps with the new security law, she will be taken down as the owner, like the hundreds of brave fighters for freedom, disappears into a Chinese prison.

One should be aware of the internal tensions within the Hong Kong revolution, however, and especially of the ever-present danger that the American Empire poses in its efforts to exploit these. As it did so often before, it will try to hijack this revolution and force its imperialist agenda down the throats of the people of Hong Kong knowing that in confronting as menacing a force as China, they are caught between a rock and a hard place. When the Hongkongers look at the US, they see imperialist opportunism and the fascist response to Black Lives Matter in Portland, Oregon. When they look at China, they see imperialist opportunism and the fascist response to Tiananmen Square. Still, the temptations turning on "the lesser evil" argument are great. Not just for the sake of the outcome of this revolution, but in the interest of geopolitical sanity and stability, Hong Kong must not become another Libya, or Egypt, especially since

---

16. See "Hong Kong Children's Shop Told to Remove Protest Statue." The statue is replicated in other places, and children are encouraged to make their own little "Lady Liberty" statues, from papier-mâché, wood, plaster, or anything that is handy. It is this kind of secondary, continuing revolutionary activity that the Powers That Be will find very hard to control or stop.

17. In many ways, Africa has become the testing ground for China's gentrified imperialist expansionism. The Chinese economic presence in Africa is growing rapidly, and is outstripping that of the United States and Europe. Chinese imperialism is far more subtle, far less aggressive and arrogant than that of the US. Hence, it is more effective, though in the long run not less extractive. While Barack Obama was heavily expanding US military presence in Africa through Africom, China was offering to help build infrastructure, expand mining operations, and offering loans on terms Africans would not get from the IMF, in all sorts of ways making Africa offers it found hard to refuse. While US imperialism is driven by typical capitalist instant gratification, China's eye is on long-term gain. See "Chinese Imperialism: A New Force in Africa."

Hong Kong's revolution is such a handy foil for actions against China. The chances that the revolutionary youth could still be wooed by China seem to be diminishing by the day. Conversely, that America has genuine interest in the fight for democratic freedoms the youth of Hong Kong are now waging, and therefore should be seen as an ally, is an illusion one should hope the youth of Hong Kong would be able to discern, and there are signs that this issue is very much on the agenda. Hongkongers should be on their guard, write JS and Promise Li, and the obvious pseudonyms speak for themselves:

> The two-faced support of Trump, [Sen. Tom] Cotton, and a whole cohort of right-wing politicians must be a wake-up call for Hongkongers. The US is not the bastion of freedom, liberty, or democracy that these right-wing politicians profess it to be.[18]

They warn about the hypocrisy and double standards of American politicians who cheer on the Hong Kong revolution but continue to employ harsh, repressive strategies and unbelievably vicious violence against protesters in the US:

> Just as these politicians don't care about Black lives, they don't care about the lives of Hongkongers either. Instead, their support for the Hong Kong movement has always been contingent on their broader geopolitical goals and is as fickle as the whims of US foreign policy.[19]

They make their plea: Hongkongers must be aware of those in their ranks who have ties with Trump and serve an imperialist agenda, and unequivocally "make their choice" for meaningful ties with the Black Lives Matter movement.[20] This call for unity and connections of global solidarity is urgent. The reactions of both China and the US to the events in Hong Kong are signs of just how high the stakes are.

South African students should take some pride in the fact that it is their own #RhodesMustFall revolution of 2015 and 2016 that initiated, and highlighted, the importance of such defiance for the empowerment and authenticity of the revolution.[21]

---

18. See JS and Promise Li, "Hong Kong Movement Must Stand with Black Lives Matter."

19. See JS and Promise Li, "Hong Kong Movement Must Stand with Black Lives Matter."

20. That America has interest in the fight for democratic freedoms the youth of Hong Kong are now waging and therefore should be seen as an ally is an illusion one should hope the youth of Hong Kong would be able to discern. For the moment, I weigh towards the possibility that the youth are not so naïve as to not understand the political factors at work. As much as they need international support and solidarity in the struggle against a ruthless world power like China, one hopes they would understand that America is not interested in their freedom. All this, in my view, does not diminish the goals of their revolution, their courage in standing for what they believe in, and their willingness to make sacrifices for those ideals. The one thing that would offer some kind of guarantee here, and keep the young revolutionists vigilant, would be their conscious relationship with the Black Lives Matter movement, and hence with other movements for freedom such as that in Palestine. See also Lyttleton, "The Black Lives Matter and Hong Kong protesters share methods and a cause, but fail to unite."

21. After months of protracted battle led by the students, Oxford University College finally decided to remove the statue of Cecil John Rhodes, showing that the current toppling of the statues stands firmly within the #RhodesMustFall tradition.

Still having to look at the images extolling the power and virtues of colonialism and apartheid in the streets and squares of Cape Town though, the challenges remain. From the images of Jan van Riebeeck and Maria de la Quelerie—who is, despite white history's claims, actually not the statue of Riebeeck's wife at all[22]—on their pedestals, to Boer General Louis Botha on his horse, proudly defying the aspirations of the people and the demands of the time, one knows: the job is far from finished. And one no longer wonders how it came to pass that the name the young generation so despise, Cecil John Rhodes, is so effortlessly, and without any apparent embarrassment, coupled with the name of that great icon of our liberation, Nelson Mandela in the towering Mandela-Rhodes building in St. George's Mall, Cape Town. To say nothing of the equally anomalously named Mandela-Rhodes Foundation.[23] It seems that this most painful of ironies is completely lost on the ones leading the "National Democratic Revolution." Perhaps the even more painful truth is that this is not ironic at all, and never was intended to be. In distinction to the people's revolution that was hijacked, this is a revolution that never was. But these are the kind of contradictions that are not sustainable. The people's revolution never really ended; its delayed defiance sparked anew in the streets of the cities of the world, and perhaps the empowering trend will be reversed this time, and in revolutionary reciprocity, South Africans will be inspired by the events overseas.[24]

Of course, the powers of imperialism are not taking this lying down. In London, Prime Minister Boris Johnson was not only furious, calling the actions of the protesters "absurd and shameful," he is ready, says journalist Stephen Castle, "to start a culture war" over these events. Experience teaches us, however, that when governments start, or incite, culture wars, they quickly, and inevitably, become real wars. Ask the victims of the "war on drugs," the "war against abortion," or the war against the LGBTQI community, to fight "the destruction of the family." Such unrighteous anger, defending such indefensible causes, once loosed and sanctioned, cannot long hide its violent heart. Defending such a brutal, violent past, how else can it present itself in the fight to hold on to it?

President Trump's reaction was also predictable. These privileged representatives and profiteers of imperialism talk as if the "absurd" and the "scandalous" is not the blood-soaked history and current reality of imperialism with its murderous greed, shameless looting, and incessant warmongering. No, "scandalous" is the fight against it, the rebellion against unremembering, the efforts to reclaim some truth of their own

22. "No image of Maria van Riebeeck exists. 'Her' statue in Cape Town in fact shows the wife of the chairman of the Dutch committee that helped to organise the 1952 Van Riebeeck festival in Cape Town." See Giliomee and Mbenga, *New History of South Africa*, 42.

23. Perhaps there is some awareness. The announcement on the website of the foundation reads, "We find, fund, and empower young Africans who aspire towards the kind of leadership Mandela embodied." Not a word about the kind of leadership Rhodes embodied. See www.mandela.rhodes.org.

24. As I write this, the statue of Cecil John Rhodes at Rhodes Memorial in Cape Town has been decapitated.

histories by the victims of imperialism. "Thuggery" is not the genocide of millions for the sake of profits and domination. No, in the twisted logic of empire, "thuggery" is the breaking of a window, always of more concern than a broken back, as in the case of Baltimore's Freddie Gray, or than the knee on someone's neck, choking them to death. "Scandalous" is not the police slaughtering David McAtee and leaving his body lying in the street for twelve hours, but taking to the streets demanding dignity and justice is. "Criminality" is breaking an unjust law. Kleptocracy is business as usual in the neoliberal "democracies." The first raises howls of indignation. The last raises nary an eyebrow.

This outrage continues at every level. As I write this, dozens of peaceful activists are facing years in prison after protesting on the front lawn of the Kentucky attorney general's house to demand he bring charges against the police officers who killed Breonna Taylor. On Tuesday afternoon, July 15 2020, writes journalists Jacey Fortin and Allyson Waller, a protest march through Louisville ended at the home of Daniel Cameron, the state's top law enforcement official. Louisville Metro Police Department officials arrested 87 people in total, charging them with felonies for "intimidating a participant in a legal process," as well as misdemeanors for trespassing and disorderly conduct.[25] They each face twenty-five years in prison, while the killers of Breonna Taylor have not even been arrested yet.

South African Black Consciousness thinker and poet Adam Small warned us against protest becoming "a form of begging."[26] What was seen in South Africa's streets in the 1980s and what is seen on the streets of the world right now is protest beyond begging. Calling such activism "vandalism," Trump decrees long prison sentences for them, forgetting the political, economic, and cultural vandalism imperialism visited upon the peoples and countries they invaded. Those on the streets of beyond-begging they call "scum," "lowlifes," and "looters." This while the visible evidence of their looting sits in shameless display in their museums, screaming their *j'accuse!* at those who drool over the ageless beauty of the art produced by the "savages" they robbed, frozen in imperialism's lie about where they truly belong. These representatives and defenders of empire do not have moral right on their side. What they have, *all* they have, is naked power, and what we see, and what they realize, is that on the streets of their capital cities and their small towns this power is being wrenched from their hands by the masses in revolt against empire. All over the world, the debates are fierce, but especially so in the instance regarding Africa: Belgium's King Leopold II and the Congo, and it is fitting that as an African I should turn to that now.

---

25. See Fortin and Waller, "87 Face Felony Charges." The fact these charges have now been dropped, does not change the outrageous nature of the action against these activists: that such charges were even a possibility in the first place.

26. See Small, "Blackness versus Nihilism," 14–15.

A Footnote, the Hidden Holocaust, and Black Agency

When American journalist/historian Adam Hochschild first published his meticulously researched and fascinating *King Leopold's Ghost* in 1998,[27] it did not get the attention it deserved from black circles, even though the reprisals from the Belgian establishment and the defenders of her colonial past were swift, public, and vicious. The book brought "howls of rage" from Belgium's older colonialist establishment, an article in *The Guardian* informs us. They called it "a scandalous book," and Barbara Emerson, Leopold's biographer, labeled the book "a shoddy piece of work" despite the author's meticulous research and the book's international acclaim.[28] It is not only the unvarnished history of Leopold's greed and unspeakable cruelty, and, as a result, Belgium's shameless profiteering from it all that angered them. It was especially the detailed discussion of the "hidden holocaust," in which no less than ten million Congolese were murdered, that raised their ire. Belgium's Prime Minister at the time, Jean-Luc Dehaene, asked by *The Guardian*'s reporter about the Congo legacy, chose the way of cool nonchalance: "It is not a strong emotional link anymore," he said. "It does not move the people. It's part of the past. It's history."[29] Sounding so much like white South Africans in their defense of apartheid for which there really is no defense, and the only thing left is to urge everybody to "move on." The past "is the past" and there is nothing one can do about it, except, of course, that the privileged children of empire, the "heirs of Ashur," continue to profit from it.

For a moment, it looked as if things seemed to have cooled down since then, or perhaps successfully suppressed and kept out of the Belgian public discourse. Here, too, the politics of manufactured consent seemed to have blended seamlessly with the politics of manufactured contentment. But the advent of the renewed Black Lives Matter revolution after the death of George Floyd changed all that. The Prime Minister did not reckon with the fact that Belgium's "people" were no longer the white, homogenous, complacent heirs of empire. Belgian's project of unremembering is under attack. The debates are raging again, and they are not so one-sided anymore. Belgium, that small but immensely rich country in Europe, and the center of the European Union's powerful bureaucracy as well as home to the headquarters of NATO, the symbolism of power from the past blending with the symbolism of power of the present, is all of a sudden swirling in a vortex of international revolution, caught completely off-guard. But it is confronting a new kind of power, its defenders facing not one author or a few journalists, but throngs of its own young people, white and black, but led by the

---

27. See Hochschild, *King Leopold's Ghost*.
28. See Bates, "Hidden Holocaust."
29. See Bates, "Hidden Holocaust." Belgium's current Prime Minister, Sophie Welmés, takes a view that offers more hope. She has called for "an in-depth" debate conducted "without taboo." "In 2020, we must be able to look at this shared past with lucidity and discernment," she said. "Any work of truth and memory begins with the recognition of suffering. Acknowledging the suffering of the other." See Petrequin, "Belgian king expresses regret for violence in colonial rule."

Belgian children of Africa. And they, in turn, are backed by millions across the world. The empire caught in the headlights.

Hochschild is not the first to try to raise some consciousness vis-à-vis King Leopold's, and Belgium's, scandalous, colonialist past. Hochschild tells us of two nineteenth-century black writers, George Washington Williams, the first foreigner of African descent to have discovered the suppressed history of African enslavement and exploitation and European greed and oppression, followed by William Sheppard, tried to shine a light on the workings of empire in the Congo. Their voices, like the cries of the oppressed in the Congo, were not heard, because the lives of the Congolese did not matter; and if those lives did not matter, why would the words of two Africans in the diaspora? Now, vindicated by the universal Black Lives Matter movement, those once-lonely black voices are being amplified, and these voices, through their sacrificial insistence to be heard, can never be unheard.

The young people of Belgium, like the young King Josiah, know that when you erect a statue of someone, it is meant to laud and honor the life and work of that person, to set up a model to be venerated, an example to be followed. It is meant to ask the world to join in the iconization of that person. In these cases, national pride requires, and equates with, national absolution. "This is who we are!" that statue proclaims, the empire whose sins are always forgotten on earth and always forgiven in heaven. This Josiah generation refuse to be part of this historic fraud. This is definitely not who they want to be. Hence their demand that every statue of Leopold, wherever it may have been erected across the land, has to go. The youth of Black Lives Matter are engaging, like the youth of 1976 in South Africa, in what we then called "the politics of refusal." In Al Jazeera English television's program *The Stream,* on June 22, 2020, spokesperson of the *Belgian Network for Black Lives,* Stephanie Collingwood Williams, explained: "It is not only about our lives today. It is also about all those lives throughout all those centuries *that never mattered.*" The movement is determined that they should matter now. That is the continuity that gives the movement such powerful authenticity. Like the realization that is beginning to dawn upon South Africa's younger generation, they too, against the grain of dominant narratives, insist that such iconoclastic events are not the *preclusion* of reconciliation; they are the indispensable *prerequisites* for reconciliation.

Here's the thing, though. In his book, Adam Hochschild explains that he himself, even though he had visited the Congo before, had not known about the "hidden holocaust." In the course of his research, Hochschild had come across a reference in a footnote to a remark in a report by Mark Twain, who mentioned that he was part of a worldwide movement against slave labor in the Congo in which ten million Congolese had been killed. *In a footnote!* As always, genocide and epistimecide are the inseparable spawns of imperialism. Hochschild was skeptical at first because statistics of mass murder are often hard to prove. But if this number turned out to be half as high, I thought the Congo would have been one of the major killing grounds of modern times. Why were these deaths not mentioned in the standard litany of our century's horrors? And why had I never before heard of them?[30]

It is a question colonized people have been asking for a very long time. The answer is manifold, I suppose, but the short answer is, *their lives did not matter*. At the heart of every answer, though, must be: the innate mendaciousness of empire, the desire of empire not only to withhold the truth, but to deliberately uphold the lie, since that lie is indispensable for the innocence of empire and empire's beneficiaries. But as we have learned from James Baldwin long ago, it is the innocence that constitutes the crime. By the time his research was done, Hochschild came to his inescapable conclusion: not only was it all true, it was a "death toll of Holocaust proportions."[31] So he took the footnote and placed it center-page, in the spotlight of historical truth telling.

There was, Hochschild assures us, no shortage of contemporary accounts of people who had been to Africa. There was, in fact, an abundance of "Africa travelers" and "adventurers," white "experts" on Africa, eager to recount their experiences in journals, diaries, and books. "The problem, of course," Hochschild admits, "is that nearly all in this vast river of words is by Europeans or Americans."[32] Except for the unheard and unheeded words of the two black journalists, Hochschild is right, and it remains a major problem as well as a major challenge today. Hence the necessity of decolonial studies and engagements with Eurocentrism for this generation. In that sense, Adam Hochschild is a kind of people's historian, much like Roxanne Dunbar-Ortiz and her *An Indigenous People's History of the United States*,[33] both following in the footsteps of the great Howard Zinn and his unsurpassed classic, *A People's History of the United States*.

And despite the howls of rage emanating from the circles of power and privilege, the people's movements continue to find allies in prophetic truth tellers. In her Foreword to Hochschild's book, Barbara Kingsolver writes about her own outrage. Scorched by the denials of those who support and benefit from the evils of empire, and by her own complicity, she writes about colonialism,

> We were enriched and bejewelled by it. Nearly every married woman I knew wore a diamond taken from African soil. The cobalt in our engines and aircraft, the rubber tires that underpinned our transportation and helped our wars, and going further back, the slave labor that built my nation's agrarian

---

30. See Hochschild, *King Leopold's Ghost*, 3.
31. Hochschild, *King Leopold's Ghost*, 4.
32. Hochschild, *King Leopold's Ghost*, 5.
33. See Dunbar-Ortiz, *Indigenous People's History*.

economy: all this prosperity came from a place unmentioned in our history books. This was not an innocent oversight.[34]

Indeed, it was not. Kingsolver writes against the dominant meganarratives of the privileged classes about King Leopold, praising him as a great Christian King, a "philanthropic monarch" whose troops did not enslave and kill, but instead fought and defeated slave traders who preyed on Congo's population, in this way brazenly overturning the truth of Leopold's and Belgium's true presence in the Congo. In this way, Adam Hochschild and Barbara Kingsolver join the voices of the millions crying out that black lives matter enough for them not to be silent. As I write, King Phillippe of Belgium has offered words of "sincere apology" to the people of the Congo. One should hope that the king will understand that words of apology do not begin to cover what is needed here. I sincerely hope that the revolutionary masses turning Belgium upside down today will look to South Africa and learn from our mistakes: a cheap reconciliation is no reconciliation. He should speak of repentance, which means reparation and restoration in ongoing deeds of justice toward Congo; a new historic project to undo the injustices done to the Congo. He should look, not only at his country's history, but to his country's wealth, acknowledge where that comes from and then do what is necessary. After a century of genocide, exploitation, looting, and dehumanization, words of apology are the low hanging fruit on a tree already poisoned by too many meaningless words of apology uttered by too many others. Hence, Barbara Kingsolver is not done:

> I hadn't fully considered the damage held over from previous generations, when the harm was not passive but harrowingly deliberate. Genocide leaves psychic scars on a surviving population. The Congolese men who voted for their first independent government in 1960, were the grandsons and great-grandsons of those who'd seen Leopold's forces arrive to usurp the whole of their land, terrorize them into subservience, and systematically extract every good thing from their lives. The tactics of labor coercion, the shackles and beatings, whole villages of wives and children held hostage until quotas were met, the hacked-off hands of those who still proved unwilling: these stories still live in the Congolese oral tradition, a century later.[35]

Those stories are now being recalled, without permission, against the will, and despite the very lethal, vengeful anger of the empire, and shouted out in millions of voices in countless languages across the globe, in the cry *Black Lives Matter!* This is the politics of refusal and defiance, girded by an ethic of solidarity and resistance, which, following Miguel De La Torre, we shall call "the ethics of *joder*."[36]

---

34. See Hochschild, *King Leopold's Ghost*, x.
35. Hochschild, *King Leopold's Ghost*, xi.
36. See De La Torre, "Doing Latina/o Ethics," 11.

Black Consciousness, Black Theology and the Ethics of *Joder*

That Black Consciousness and Black liberation theology seek to engender a global consciousness and an ethic of global solidarity and resistance is the argument of this book. But, as Biko insisted, we must start with the mind. "The most potent weapon in the hands of the oppressor," Biko tells us in as many ways as he can, "is the mind of the oppressed."[37] We will return to the concept "Eurocentrism" later in chapter 5, but here it is necessary to refer to it in order to introduce Miguel De La Torre's important insights. In this, I follow Marta Araújo and Silvia Rodriguez Maeso, who define "Eurocentrism" in this way:

> We consider Eurocentrism as a paradigm for interpreting a (past, present, and future) reality that uncritically establishes the idea of European and Western historical progress/achievement and its political and ethical superiority, based on scientific rationality and the construction of the rule of law. Accordingly, we propose that it is essential to debate Eurocentrism within the formation of Western knowledge and its claims for universal validity, since this provides a certain historical mapping of the world that unambiguously establishes which events and processes are scientifically relevant and how they are interpreted—simultaneously discovering and covering them.[38]

If, as we will argue throughout, Eurocentrism is a global phenomenon of power and dominance, a matrix of coloniality,[39] it should be countered by an ethic and praxis of transnational, intersectional, and transgenerational solidarity. As Black Consciousness also understood and insisted upon, this is necessary, writes Cuban American liberation theologian Miguel De La Torre in agreement, because

> Since childhood, those of us who resided in the underside of history have been taught to see and interpret reality through the eyes of the dominant culture, specifically white, heterosexual, upper-middle-class, patriarchal eyes.[40]

De La Torre writes in an effort to create an ethics "to liberate the colonized mind" from the Eurocentrism that holds it captive. We keep in mind that when De La Torre raises the matter of a "world view" historically conditioned to "normalize and legitimate" how they see and organize the world around them, he is speaking of a wider world than just the US. It produces a "racist and classist underpinning" that contributes to the metanarrative of how those within the dominant culture have developed their ethical perspectives.[41] Such a worldview and ethics create a situation where

---

37. E.g., Biko, *I Write What I Like*, 74.
38. See Maeso and Araújo, "Eurocentrism, Political Struggles and the Entrenched *Will-to-Ignorance*," 1.
39. See Grosfoguel, "Decolonizing."
40. See De La Torre, "Doing Latina/o Ethics," 5.
41. De La Torre, "Doing Latina/o Ethics," 8.

"complicity with US Empire is deemed normal."[42] Speaking of Latino/a people in the United States, but echoing Biko almost word for word, De La Torre states,

> Before we can speak about the liberation of our people from societal, political, and economical structures of oppression, we must first liberate ourselves from our own colonized minds, from equating the apex of ethical discourse with Eurocentric subjectivity. We begin the process of decolonizing our minds by not perpetuating the Eurocentric ethics that contribute to our own oppression.[43]

In other words, that ethic in itself constitutes a praxis of refusal and resistance.[44] Here, Silvia Rodríguez Maeso's and Marta Araújo's insights are to the point.

> As a paradigm for interpreting a (past, present, and future) reality that uncritically established the idea of European and Western historical *progress/achievement* and its political and ethical *superiority* based on scientific rationality and the construction of the rule of law, [claiming] universal validity.[45]

It is this ethical superiority that De La Torre, like Biko before him, puts into question. In trying to deepen our exploration of the meaning of Black Consciousness as an ethic of global solidarity and resistance, I suggest we turn to De La Torre's discussion of what he calls an ethic *para joder*.[46] De La Torre writes,

> *Joder* is a Spanish verb, a word one would never use in polite conversation. Although it is not the literal translation of a certain four letter word beginning with the letter "F," it is still considered somewhat vulgar because it basically means "to screw with."[47]

De La Torre also explains the "important difference in semantics."[48] It does not mean to "screw," but to "screw with." The word connotes an individual

> who purposely is a pain in the rear end, who purposely causes trouble, who shouts from the mountaintop, who constantly disrupts the established norm, who audaciously refuses to stay in his or her place.[49]

---

42. De La Torre, "Doing Latina/o Ethics," 8.

43. De La Torre, "Doing Latina/o Ethics," 5.

44. In 1979, in an address to the conference of the South African Council of Churches, I spoke of the need for the Black Church to adopt a "theology of refusal." See Boesak, *Black and Reformed*. Later, in 1983, at a Transvaal Indian Congress rally in Johannesburg, and calling for the formation of the United Democratic Front, I spoke of our resistance as an expression of "the politics of refusal." See Boesak, *Running with Horses*.

45. See Maeso and Araújo, "Eurocentrism," 1–22.

46. See De La Torre, "Doing Latina/o Ethics," 8ff.

47. De La Torre, "Doing Latina/o Ethics," 11.

48. De La Torre, "Doing Latina/o Ethics," 11.

49. De La Torre, "Doing Latina/o Ethics," 11.

African Americans know the phenomenon well. They call it "sass." The key words here are obviously those that describe the functionality of the term for oppressed communities: "purposely," "to cause trouble," to "audaciously refuse." De La Torre's "shouting from the mountaintop" has a prophetic sound the prophetic Black Church knows well. De La Torre remarks that some have been offended by his use of the term in public. However, "what is truly profane," he argues, "is not the word that is used but the oppressive death-dealing conditions under which Hispanics are forced to live."[50] Whether expressed in words, in attitude, or in actions, "an ethics *par joder* is an ethics that 'screws' with the prevailing power structures." It is no longer a choice, but an imperative. "Those who are among the disenfranchised, who stand before the vastness of neoliberalism that offers little hope for radical change in their lifetimes, have few ethical alternatives."[51] The ethics of *joder* is the ethics of the decolonized mind.

While the dominant culture, "including progressive ethicists," may be willing to offer charity and to stand in solidarity, "few are willing or able to take a role in dismantling the very global structures designed to privilege them at the expense of the world's majority."[52] Hence, that dismantling must come from the oppressed:

> When those who are disenfranchised start to *joder,* they literally create instability. An ethics that upsets the prevailing social order designed to maintain empire is an ethics that arise from the margins of society who are disillusioned and frustrated with normative Eurocentric values and virtues.[53]

The "order" of empire is disorder for the victims of empire. Marginalized communities, therefore, must call for and cause social disorder. To *joder* means one "refuses to play by the rules established by those who provide a space for orderly dissent that pacifies the need to vent for the marginalized but is designed not to change the power relationships within the existing social structures."[54] Meek acceptance of those rules, oppressive, exploitative, and dehumanizing as they are, is what the decolonized mind rejects, as it rejects definitions of "respectability" and "decency" as set by the hegemonic narratives of the dominant culture.

Joder challenges the "virtues" and "values" that subject the victims of empire to abuse, oppression, and dehumanization. Those values and virtues are designed to serve only the hegemony of the powerful, and it is only the colonized mind that submits to it without protest. In order to resist coloniality and the continued colonizing of the subaltern mind, De La Torre argues "that the best way for the powerless, the marginalized, the disenfranchised, and the dispossessed to radically counter the prevailing

---

50. De La Torre, "Doing Latina/o Ethics," 11. I will argue likewise in the discussion on "the politics of vulgarity" below.
51. De La Torre, "Doing Latina/o Ethics," 11, 12.
52. De La Torre, "Doing Latina/o Ethics," 12.
53. De La Torre, "Doing Latina/o Ethics," 12.
54. De La Torre, "Doing Latina/o Ethics," 12.

status quo is to *joder*."⁵⁵ Since ethics reflects praxis, De La Torre provides examples of *joder*: the young gang members from a Puerto Rican barrio in Chicago who evolved into a political social movement that fought for and demanded basic human rights and better social services. They demanded that Chicago Theological Seminary pay attention to the needs of the community where the seminary was situated. When there was no response, they, together with some seminary students, staged a sit-in at the seminary that lasted for days. Through targeted nonviolent actions that they employed elsewhere as well, they demanded that the seminary respond. The seminary caved and agreed to fund some of their projects, including low-income housing, a children's center, and a cultural center. The occupation ended only when the seminary agreed to the demands.⁵⁶ These were "gangsters" who in their "disrespect" for the rules, values, and virtues of "respectable society" offended hegemonic sensitivities but were ethically in the right, because their actions served the needs of the people.

I will argue here that Black Consciousness, too, employed the ethics of *joder*. The very idea of a liberated, self-conscious, determined mind set on breaking the centuries-old social, psychological, and political hold over the colonized, apartheid mind-set and standing up in resistance is the essence of *joder*. Like Jesus turning over the tables in the temple courtyard, simultaneously overturning the rules of expected behavior from the people of his class, *joder* is the deliberate overturning of the rules of expectation the dominant society lays upon the subjugated. The mass actions of civil disobedience, in the form of school boycotts, stay-aways from classes at colleges and universities, strikes and boycotts of white-owned shops, challenging the rules of polite society in their actions toward police in the streets of protest—these would come later, after the children of Soweto broke down the walls that held them back.

But even before that, in the way Steve Biko responded to situations in what, at best, could be described as constraining, if not intimidating, seeing what was at stake, the ethics of *joder* would be on full display as Biko testified at the BPC/SASO trial in 1976 and 1977. The editors of *I Write What I Like* made special mention of this when they, in the notes that introduce and frame the chapters containing Biko's testimony, recalled the moment when Biko was asked by the prosecution what he thought of Africans who work for the Security Police. "They are traitors!" Biko answered. The editors marvel, "And this in a courtroom ringed by armed Security Police, black and white!"⁵⁷ It is that *sass*, that bold expression of having overcome fear, of not giving anybody the satisfaction of entertaining the thought that Biko took their power seriously, that is *joder*.

The same ethic of *joder* is displayed as Biko engages presiding Judge Boshoff in that same BPC/SASO trial. In one instance, Boshoff tries to grill Biko on his use of the word "black." Boshoff wants to know why Biko refers "to you people" as blacks. "Why

55. De La Torre, "Doing Latina/o Ethics," 15.
56. De La Torre, "Doing Latina/o Ethics," 14, 15.
57. Biko, *I Write What I Like*, 135–36.

not brown people? I mean you people are more brown than black." Biko responds, "In the same way as I think white people are more pink than white."⁵⁸ This judge, clearly, does not deserve a more philosophical, reasoned response as to how black people prefer to refer to themselves, as Biko has repeatedly done in his discourses with black students, for example. Biko's respect for the court is a reserved decorum, for the formality of the court as court, not so much for the racist, politically biased judge.

Later on in the repartee, Boshoff, determined to get Biko to acknowledge that black people are not ready to govern, questions Biko on the situation in Kenya. He mispronounces the name of the Kenyan opposition leader. Boshoff calls him "Odinga Oginga," and wrongly thinks Odinga was assassinated. "No," Biko corrects him calmly and without missing a beat, "*Oginga Odinga* . . . is still alive." Again Boshoff, peeved at being corrected by a black man, presses: "Tom Mboya?" Biko schools him: "I think, My Lord, you are mistaking Tom Mboya with Kariuki. It was Kariuki who was murdered." Biko then continues his lesson in African history and politics. "Kariuki was the advocate on the one hand of the common man, the worker, the servant in Kenya, against this whole development in Kenya, of a bourgeoisie within the ruling party [driven by its leader Jomo Kenyatta]." Biko drives the nail into Boshoff's coffin when Boshoff tries to trump him, an attempt to trivialize Kariuki's political philosophy and influence, and to stop Biko's eloquent political exposition. Boshoff interrupts: "Yes, but Kariuki didn't survive all this?" To which Biko responds, and by now, the repeated "My Lord" has the ring of scarcely suppressed mirth, coupled with light, but devastating sarcasm: "Oh well, My Lord, several politicians don't survive. It seems like Verwoerd didn't survive."⁵⁹ Of course the court erupts in laughter. This, I suggest, is a perfect example of *joder*. This is how the decolonized mind deals with the colonial presence and colonial power. In these situations, it might still be power; but it is not allowed to be a *colonizing* power.

But how did this impact the Black Consciousness movement and its adherents? How did they, bereft of Biko's physical presence and inspired eloquence, respond to coloniality, white supremacy, and white power in the ongoing struggle? We find a clue elsewhere.

The editors of *Biko Lives!* tell of a moment, recalled by President Mandela while still a prisoner on Robben Island, as his "first encounter with the Black Consciousness movement," and one he would never forget.⁶⁰ After a conversation with the commanding officer of the prison, Nelson Mandela was walking back to the cellblock with him. Walking through a common room, they encountered a young prisoner sitting on one of the chairs. Mandela marveled at what followed. "These [Black Consciousness]

---

58. Biko, *I Write What I Like*, 115.

59. Biko, *I Write What I Like*, 141. Biko is referring to Hendrik Verwoerd, Prime Minister of South Africa, the ruthless and revered "architect of apartheid," who was assassinated in his seat in the House of Assembly (parliament) by a Greek immigrant, Dimitri Tsafendas, in 1966.

60. Mngxitama et al., *Biko Lives!*, 5.

fellows refused to conform to even basic prison regulations!" He tells of how the prisoner, perhaps eighteen years old, refused to stand up when the prison's commanding officer entered the room—a violation of prison regulations. He refused to take off his cap when commanded to do so—another violation. Then, in an even greater violation, he challenged the commanding officer to a verbal duel, demanding that the commander provide justification for those prison rules the young man clearly regarded with deep disdain, and had no intention of obeying. "What for?" When told that this was a regulation, he responded, "What is the purpose of it?" The commander, taken completely by surprise, and clearly embarrassed by this youthful disrespect in front of another prisoner, but not knowing how to handle this situation, "stomped out of the room" in frustrated humiliation.[61]

The question here is twofold: What does this behavior signify, and what is behind it? Is it simply youthful obstreperousness or naïve, and empty, bravado? Is it a youthful desire to seek some fame, even some kind of martyrdom, or is it perhaps something more? What it signifies, I suggest, is the praxis of an ethic of *joder*. In a situation of utter vulnerability, *in prison,* where his fate is not in his own hands, this young activist was demonstrating the power of the decolonized mind. This to the utter astonishment of a veteran of the struggle, participant in civil disobedience campaigns, a principal leader in the ANC's military wing, a man who planned sabotage and planted bombs. A man with the personality that would allow him to become one of his era's most iconized statespersons. What is behind it is a decolonized mind, a sense of power that does not come with the trappings of official office, a uniform, or the power of pain and suffering in one's hands. What it signifies is the willingness to risk whatever is necessary in order to deny white supremacy, white power, and white privilege a victory over the dignity of blackness. What is behind it is the refusal to bend to rules that denigrate and subject. That is the mind that refuses to be "the strongest ally of the oppressor." Even for a moment. His ethics of *joder* did not allow him to submit to the false power of white supremacy, not even for the sake of his own survival. What it signifies is the conviction that when in prison, when it matters, you do not follow prison rules. You take the rules that give you dignity and power with you into prison. In prison, there are times when even basic regulations become a test of fortitude. In prison, where the ethic of survival demands acute awareness of the conventional wisdom to "go along to get along,"

At all times, Black Consciousness demanded a dignity that would not tolerate intimidation or the erasure of black personhood. That young man knew what he stood for and what he was in prison for. He also knew what the prison commander stood for, and why *he* was on that island. Those two realities were not remotely comparable or equal. And between those two realities there was no middle ground. Betraying what he stood for, believed in, and what he was fighting for far outweighed the risk of

---

61. See Mngxitama et al., *Biko Lives!*, 5, 6.

whatever the commander could do to him. In the end, it was clear who in that situation wore the robes of authority, and it was not the white man in the uniform.

The ethic of *joder* would play out on a national scale with the United Democratic Front's defiance campaigns; in mass actions of civil disobedience and strikes; students refusing to go to school and university classes, bringing the country to a virtual standstill. It was the massive, popular expression of the ethics of *joder,* exposing and disturbing the disorder of the apartheid order; dismantling the structures of white power, exposing the "values" and "virtues" of what the dominant culture understood as "obedient," "decent," and "virtuous." Those young people were overturning the rules, embracing the necessity of revolutionary sacrifice, making the country ungovernable for the regime, shouting from the mountaintops that power belonged to the people.

There are other examples of the dismantling of hegemony's "decorum" and "civility." On May 5 2020, former US president George W. Bush released a video in which he sought to encourage Americans during the time of crisis caused by the novel coronavirus, calling on Americans to "unite" in this time of trial. It is not so much the political slickness of the video that surprises, as much as the reactions to it. Across the board Democrats, liberal establishment figures and "celebrity" Cable Network media figures fell over their feet to praise George Bush for this action. They "fawned" over him, said Krystal Ball and Saagar Enjeti, on their morning show on *The Hill*, "Rising." Bush, these liberals claim, is so much more "presidential" than Donald Trump. Even granting that Trump has set an exceptionally low bar, this is still surprising. Bush, they said, showed "real decorum" and "civility," striking just the right tone to "unite the country" in these difficult times. "Decorum" and "civility" are of course traits that Donald Trump does not possess. They "long for Bush to be president again." One should note that these are not the Trump sycophants from Fox News. These are the anchors of highly popular political shows on liberal networks such as MNSBC and CNN. Younger, more critical media voices, like Krystal Ball and Saagar Enjeti, saw it much differently.

But perhaps the one who read this best is Kyle Kulinski, on his show *Kyle Kulinski Show*. Kulinski exposes the shallowness of liberal political thinking, its distorted priorities, its rootedness in the privileged bubble of the political and economic elites in America. It also shows the arrogance of liberals and Democrats. "They," Kulinski says,

> look at Trump and they see somebody who is unhinged, who has no filter, who shoots from the hip, who's not at all polite, shows no decorum whatsoever, doesn't care about the rules of polite society, and that is Trump's biggest sin to them. So, in other words, Trump's biggest sin is not increasing drone strikes 432 percent. Trump's biggest sin is not continuing our seven or eight wars we are currently doing right now. It's not the 2017 tax cut law where 83 percent of the benefits went to the top 1 percent. It's not destroying the Consumer Financial Protection Bureau. It's not taking away your internet privacy rights. They do not focus on his policies.[62]

62. Kyle Kulinski, *Kyle Kulinski Show*, podcast audio, May 6, 2020, https://seculartalk.net/full-shows/.

Then Kulinski makes the point he really wants to make: Instead of looking for "civility" and "politeness," they should be looking "at the substantial harm Trump is causing."[63] Instead, they want George Bush back as president. They forget, he argues, that Bush is a war criminal who lied the US into a war with Iraq that has killed a minimum of 200,000 Iraqi civilians. They forget the Patriot Act, which, meant as an emergency measure after 9/11, has now become permanent, eagerly used by Bush's successors. They forget tax and deregulatory policies grossly favoring the rich, leading to the economic crash. They forget his torture programs. Bush, Kulinski insists, is "a war criminal and a torturer who should be in The Hague [in front of the International Criminal Court]."[64] In other words, what is truly profane and indecent is not so much Trump's impolite bahavior. Truly indecent is the bi-partisan support for the coddling of the billionaire class, the criminal exclusion of the poor and the vulnerable, the glorification of a blatantly racist culture of mass incarceration, the relentless militarization of American society and the mindless pursuit of endless wars. On the things they *should* attack Trump on, they can't, because they are complicit, and it is that complicity that is the truly indecent, objectionable thing. A mass expression of the ethics of *joder* is the only appropriate response to a situation like this.

Wendell Griffen is a judge and a black preacher in the prophetic tradition of Marin Luther King Jr. and Jeremiah Wright Jr. In 2019, at the anniversary of "one of the greatest massacres of black people in the state of Arkansas,"[65] it was decided to erect a memorial to commemorate the event and as a sign of reconciliation. Although an eminent figure in the city of Little Rock and Arkansas, and expected to be a prominent participant in the proceedings, Judge Griffen expressed outrage and launched a public campaign against the plans. Despite the participation of many of the black elites of Arkansas, and despite harsh criticism, Griffen remained "disrespectful" and "indecent." In prophetic rage at the politics of manufactured contentment, Wendell Griffen refused to be part of the event. This is the story as Griffen writes it, and in the interest of full context, and to let the power of prophetic truthfulness have its way, I will let him speak:

> The Red Summer concluded in my home state of Arkansas near the small, rural community of Elaine, where hundreds of black men, women and children were massacred by a white mob and federal troops over the course of several days beginning October 1, 1919.
>
> **No white person was arrested for or charged** with committing any of the murders or for planning the massacre or participating in it. Meanwhile, an all-white jury tried and convicted black men for the murder of two white men. The condemned men escaped death only through tireless and courageous

63. Kyle Kulinski, *Kyle Kulinski Show*.
64. Kulinski, *Kyle Kulinski Show*.
65. Griffen, "Monument to Black People."

efforts led by Scipio Africanus Jones, a black lawyer whose mother had been a slave.

Now, to promote tourism and line their pockets, descendants of the merchants, plantation owners, and political elite in Helena, Arkansas, who plotted, organized, carried out, profited from, and covered up the worst massacre of black people in Arkansas history, plan to "dedicate" what they call a "memorial" to the hundreds of black men, women, and children massacred a hundred years ago. The "dedication" ceremony is set for September 29 in Helena, twenty-five miles from Elaine.

Their "memorial" will stand on ground that includes a monument to several Confederate soldiers.

Their "memorial" is near the Phillips County Courthouse where black men tortured into making false confessions were unjustly tried and convicted of murder by a jury that included white men who were part of the posse that committed the massacre.

Their "memorial" in Helena is near the county jail where black men were beaten and electrocuted to obtain the false confessions.

Their "memorial" is where white plantation owners, merchants, bankers, and civic leaders—including religious leaders—whitewashed the massacre and have spent the past century denying it and intimidating people who inquired about it.

Elaine is where the massacre of hundreds of black men, women, and children happened and atrocities were committed in the name of white supremacy. Placing a "memorial" in Helena is as wrong as placing a "memorial" to victims of the recent massacre in El Paso in Allen, Texas—the home of the man who planned and committed that massacre.

Elaine is near the former community of Hoop Spur, where black men, women, and children attending a meeting at church the night of September 30, 1919, to plan their demand for fair pay for their work were attacked by white men who shot bullets into the church. White men later burned the church.

The Elaine Race Massacre happened after white men from Helena put out a lie that the black people meeting at that church were planning an insurrection to murder white people.

Wendell Griffen continues:

> **A century later, white people who claim to be "progressive"** intend to "dedicate" a "memorial" to the Elaine victims in the very place where the massacre was organized and the lie to cover it up was published.[66]

---

66. See Griffen, "'Monument' to Black People."

It was also argued that the memorial would serve reconciliation between blacks and whites in that still deeply racist and white supremacist state. Wendell Griffen and Lauri Umansky ask the questions an ethics of *joder* must raise in order to prophetically speak truth against the indecent power of decency, deceit and submission. To refuse to give credibility to such blatant erasure of the truth, such trivialization of violence and of the massacred, such unashamed fraud that parades as "forgiveness" and "reconciliation" is the only decent thing to do.

> The premature erection of a monument to reconciliation in nearby Helena seeks to mask, even entomb, living pain and turmoil. That must not happen. Open the casket. Let the people see. *Indeed, this leads to the crucial core of the matter.* After the casket is opened and the century-old corpse has been viewed, what then? Do we bury our shame, guilt, rage and sense of injury in polite ceremonies of "racial reconciliation" that leave unjust injuries unhealed, stolen land unreturned, age-old wrongs unconfessed and present vestiges of the segregation that defined Phillips County in 1919 costumed by a pricey slab of marble and granite?[67]

That sounds so much like post-1994 South Africa I think that Biko, had he lived, would have agreed wholeheartedly with his fellow revolutionaries in Arkansas. Reverend Griffen went on to work with the community of Elaine to have a commemoration that did not lie about history or serve as a cover-up for a fraudulent reconciliation. On the last Sunday of September 2019, Griffen, his white comrade in struggle Lauri Umansky, and a few others, joined the community of Elaine in worship. Inside, nearly two-hundred black people, many of them descendants of the 1919 Elaine Race Massacre, along with a few white allies, gathered to commemorate the centennial anniversary of that slaughter:

> We sang. We worshipped. We wept. We also raged against the injustices of white supremacy. We faced history. And we talked about what real reconciliation might look like for a community traumatized for generations by racism of every form imaginable, and then some.[68]

Griffen and Umansky conclude,

> Let us ask the ultimate question: Do we have the moral courage and tenacity to live and act as if we believe restitution and reparation are not merely possible, but necessary for racial justice to become reality? Faith in racial justice, like faith in other matters, is ultimately a choice, a moral decision. We must choose to believe that the power of love, justice and truth is stronger than the power

---

67. See Griffen and Umansky, "100-Year-Old Race Massacre."
68. Griffen and Umansky, "100-Year-Old Race Massacre."

of death, hate, oppression and evil. And we must fight like hell, collectively, to bring these beliefs into manifest reality.[69]

This is the ethics of *joder* at work within the American context today. It is not "polite" and certainly not acceptable to those in dominant positions of privilege and power, but it is prophetic, disruptive, life-giving, shouting-from-the-mountaintop truth speaking.

Then, as if all this was not already enough, came the unbelievable, unbearable eight minutes, forty-six seconds of police officer Derek Chauvin's knee on George Floyd's neck, which, in a very public execution—a lynching, James Cone would have said, and black leaders do—caused his death. That is being followed, as I write, by a wave of *joder*, the intensity of which was last seen after the death of Dr. Martin Luther King Jr. in 1968, and after the verdict in the Rodney King case in Los Angeles in 1992, though on a scale, in America and around the world, that not even those days of anger had seen. Inter-racial, intergenerational, inter-gender crowds of Americans are taking to the streets, marching for justice and dignity, confronting astonishing police and army violence, and in a non-racial cry that "Black Lives Matter!" sending the president into hiding in his White House bunker. Marching with them are other crowds in countries the world over, and soccer teams of the *Bundesliga* in Germany "take the knee" before playing their matches. In the British city of Bristol, in a vivid reminder of the #RhodesMustFall protests in South Africa, Black Lives Matter activists pulled down the bronze statue of seventeenth-century slave trader Edward Colston. Since then, it seems like a wave engulfing the world. All over, the images of the once-untouchable imperial heroes, the flags glorifying slavery and racism, the names of slave owners and the breakers of black bodies on the hallowed halls of learning of universities are now the targets of the revolt against unremembering. One truly stands in awe of such global revolutionary action against racism and police brutality protecting white supremacy and oligarchic rule, and for justice, dignity, and human rights. Since then more of the statues glorifying the colonial era and the reign of slavery and Jim Crow are being toppled all over the place. Steve Biko would have been as proud, for these are the actions of the "selfless revolutionaries" he pleaded for.

Selfless Revolutionaries

It is Fr. Aeldred Stubbs who alerts us to the great importance we must attach to a singularly meaningful phrase Biko uses in his correspondence with Fr. David Russell. These are Biko's thoughts on "the selfless revolutionary." I quote him in full so as to place the ensuing discussion in its proper context:

> Obedience in the sense that I have accepted it (i.e., in the belief that God has revealed in his laws inscribed in our conscience) is in fact at the heart of the

---

69. Griffen and Umansky, "100-Year-Old Race Massacre."

convictions of most selfless revolutionaries. It is a call to men of conscience to offer themselves and sometimes their lives for the eradication of an evil. To a revolutionary, State evil is a major evil for out of it flow other countless subsidiary evils that engulf the lives of both the oppressors and the oppressed. The revolutionary sees his task all too often of liberation not only of the oppressed but also of the oppressor. Happiness can never truly exist in a state of tension, even if the tension is only of conscience. Hence, in a stratified society like ours, those who have placed themselves on a pedestal spend too much time on the lookout for disturbances and hence can never have peace of mind. The South African society abounds with fear and is constantly in a state of frenzy. The revolutionary seeks to restore faith in life amongst all citizens of the country, to remove imaginary fears and to heighten concern for the plight of the people.[70]

To Stubbs, "the phrase 'selfless revolutionary' seems to be the clue to what Steve himself meant to die for."[71] Indeed, there is power in that phrase, the more so since it has a decidedly Jesus-like ring to it, and Aeldred Stubbs does draw those conclusions,[72] as does Njabulo Ndebele in his reflections on Biko's use of "the envisioned self."[73] Stubbs sees the selfless revolutionary most strikingly in Biko's insistence that the struggle is for the liberation of both the oppressed and the oppressor.[74] That inclusiveness and concern for the other, even as enemy, does express the meaning of a selfless revolutionary. I have dealt with what Paulo Freire called the "historic obligation of the oppressed" to free also the oppressor in a full chapter in a previous work.[75] In total agreement with Stubbs, I will here offer a somewhat different, or better perhaps, an additional perspective. Whether one wants to read this phrase in connection "with the mind of Christ" as Aeldred Stubbs does, or not, it stands out as a key to understanding Biko's philosophy of life, his commitment to the struggle, and his relationship with God. It is an intimate connection, and it shows that one cannot understand Biko, his commitment to the struggle for freedom and justice, and his death for that struggle if one does not understand his relationship with God.

This paragraph in Biko's memo to Fr. Russell is a passionate piece of writing. It seems to me that Biko is inviting us to make a vital distinction. There are revolutionaries, and then there are selfless revolutionaries. Biko speaks of selfless revolutionaries in the context of a discussion about his faith, God, and the struggle. He speaks of "obedience to God" that is "inscribed in our conscience" that compels those

---

70. See Biko, *I Write What I Like*, 241.
71. Biko, *I Write What I Like*, 241.
72. Biko, *I Write What I Like*, 241–42.
73. Biko, *I Write What I Like*, vii–viii; and see ch. 5, below.
74. Biko, *I Write What I Like*, 241–43.
75. See Boesak, *Pharaohs on Both Sides*, ch. 5.

"of conscience to offer themselves and sometimes their lives for the eradication of an evil."[76] To the revolutionary, here the great evil to be eradicated is the apartheid state and all it stands for. In that process, selfless revolutionaries see their task as the liberation of the oppressed as well as the oppressor. The selfless revolutionary knows that benefitting from oppression and exploitation causes constant tension, "even if the tension is only of conscience." Those who place themselves on "a pedestal" of white supremacy and superiority "can never have peace of mind." Such a state poisons the whole of society. For Biko, it is no wonder that "The South African society abounds with fear and is constantly in a state of frenzy." Biko knows well the results of that fear. Pernicious and persistent, it permeates South African society at every level. Earlier he makes the point that the "tripartite system of fear—that of whites fearing the blacks, blacks fearing the whites, and the government fearing blacks and wishing to allay the fears among whites—makes it difficult to establish rapport amongst the two sections of the community."[77] Because of this fear, "black people should not at any one stage be surprised at some of the atrocities committed by the government."[78] The manipulation of fear produces atrocities. We have seen that in South Africa and Nazi Germany, and we've seen that in the state of Israel, in the Balkan states, and Rwanda.

However, the selfless revolutionary knows that is a death-dealing condition. It is also unsustainable, and therefore she "seeks to restore faith in life amongst all citizens of this country" not only to remove the oppressor's "imaginary fears," but also "to heighten concern for the plight of the people."[79] To "restore faith in life"—i.e., meaningful life, life together in dignity, justice, and equality—is what selfless revolutionaries do. Selfless revolutionaries can see the hardened heart of the oppressor. Desperately afraid of Ubuntu and devoid of all feeling except for themselves, wrapped up in pre-emptive, ironclad victimhood, they dare not allow "concern for the plight of the people" to capture their heart, since that concern will bring on both their guilt and their judgment. Genuine compassion cannot hold hands with greed and domination. At the end of the road, what they have built for themselves is not only perdition, there is, as the well-known proverb says, also a mirror. Out of concern for their liberation and redemption, selfless revolutionaries seek to "heighten" concern and compassion in the hearts of the oppressor. That is a deed of redemption.

Oppression comes from a lust for power, an insatiable greed to devour. It gorges on a constant but lethal diet of acquisitiveness. It breeds self-centeredness, self-elevation, and self-aggrandizement. The selfless revolutionary knows this way of life is self-defeating and ultimately unsustainable because it is life-defeating. Hence the desire to "restore faith in life" in the oppressed as well as the oppressor. But Biko spoke thus because he understood something else. Apartheid, a system, ideology,

---

76. Biko, *I Write What I Like*, 241.
77. See Biko, *I Write What I Like*, 80–87.
78. Biko, *I Write What I Like*, 80.
79. Biko, *I Write What I Like*, 241.

and way of life was not only death dealing; it was death itself. People who put their faith in racism, supremacy, and a false and delusional sense of superiority, people who exploit and benefit from the exploitation, dehumanization, and annihilation of the other do not know life—they have, as the prophet Isaiah says, "entered into a covenant with death" (Isa 28:15). They cannot know peace, for violence is the way they sustain themselves. Those who make epistemicide a way of life will in the end have no stories of themselves to tell; at least, not without a sense of shame, after those stories have been revealed as stolen, and the braggadocio has been exposed as empty idol worship.

Already the prophet Habakkuk understood what kind of life this was:

> Look at the proud!
> Their spirit is not right in them,
> but the righteous shall live by their faith.
> Moreover, wealth is treacherous;
> the arrogant do not endure.
> They open their throats wide as Sheol;
> like Death they never have enough,
> They gather all nations for themselves,
> and collect all people as their own.
> Shall not everyone taunt such people and, with mocking riddles, say about them,
> "Alas for you who heap up what is not your own!" (Hab 2:4–6)

And Habakkuk also knew how it would end:

> What use is an idol
> once its maker has shaped it—
> a cast image, a teacher of lies? (2:18)

The selfless revolutionary understands this and seeks to "restore faith in life," so that all may have life, by finding ubuntufied, humanized ways of living.

However, none of this will be easy, and the selfless revolutionary will have to be ready "to offer themselves and sometimes their lives for the eradication of [this] evil."[80] Evil, Biko strains to make clear, cannot be alleviated. It has to eradicated. The selfless revolutionary does this in obedience to God, Biko knew: "If therefore, one speaks of obedience, one opens oneself up to tremendous challenges."[81] Then in an echo of Martin Luther King Jr., Biko continues, "Obedience to God implies deliberate maladjustments to so many evils in the Church and State."[82] King pleaded for "creative extremists" of love, freedom, and justice:

---

80. Biko, *I Write What I like*, 241.
81. Biko, *I Write What I Like*, 241.
82. Biko, *I Write What I Like*, 241.

> Was not Jesus an extremist for love: "Love your enemies, bless them that curse you, do good to them that hate you, and pray for them which despitefully use you, and persecute you." Was not Amos an extremist for justice: "Let justice roll down like waters and righteousness like an ever flowing stream." Was not Paul an extremist for the Christian gospel: "I bear in my body the marks of the Lord Jesus." Was not Martin Luther an extremist: "Here I stand; I cannot do otherwise, so help me God." And John Bunyan: "I will stay in jail to the end of my days before I make a butchery of my conscience." And Abraham Lincoln: "This nation cannot survive half slave and half free." And Thomas Jefferson: "We hold these truths to be self-evident, that all men are created equal . . . " So the question is not whether we will be extremists, but what kind of extremists we will be. Will we be extremists for hate or for love? Will we be extremists for the preservation of injustice or for the extension of justice? In that dramatic scene on Calvary's hill three men were crucified. We must never forget that all three were crucified for the same crime—the crime of extremism. Two were extremists for immorality, and thus fell below their environment. The other, Jesus Christ, was an extremist for love, truth and goodness, and thereby rose above his environment. Perhaps the South, the nation and the world are in dire need of creative extremists.[83]

And in even clearer language, Dr. King insisted that what the world of empire considered "maladjustment" were resistance and the signs of a truly well-adjusted life:

> There are some things in our nation and in our world to which I'm proud to be maladjusted . . . I never intend to adjust myself to segregation and discrimination. I never intend to become adjusted to religious bigotry. I never intend to adjust myself to economic conditions that will take necessities from the many to give luxuries to the few, and leave millions of people perishing on a lonely island of poverty in the midst of a vast ocean of prosperity. I never intend to adjust myself to the madness of militarism, and to the self-defeating effects of physical violence . . . And I call upon you to be maladjusted to these things until the good society is realized . . .[84]

Biko knew something of that "maladjusted" life. For King, it was clear, as clear as it would become in Biko's life and death, although he would not articulate it in these precise terms: "My ministry [is] obedience to the one who loved his enemies so fully that he died for them."[85] If Jesus's maladjusted life meant the cross for him, how could it be otherwise for those who love and follow him? For King, this obedience led him to Memphis, Tennessee, in embodied solidarity with the poor and the exploited, to the balcony of the Lorraine Motel, and to an assassin's bullet. For Malcolm X, in embodied solidarity with the poor and exploited, this obedience would take him from loyalty to

---

83. See King, *Radical King*, 127–46.
84. See King, "Remaining Awake," 268–78.
85. See King, "Beyond Vietnam."

Elijah Muhammad to the more perfect loyalty to Allah, and to the Audubon Ballroom where his murderers lay in wait. For Biko, in embodied solidarity with the poor and the oppressed, this obedience would lead him to a prison cell in Pretoria, to a torture chamber, and to the back of a police van, naked, covered only with a thin prison blanket, dying on his own. For those of us still alive to reflect on this, these are moments filled with awe. Shoeless, we stand on holy ground.

As King experienced, so did Biko: "Where do we draw the line? Do we allow ourselves to be obedient to God and at the same time obedient to a white-controlled, power-mongering institution like the Church of the Province?"[86] Biko speaks of the Church of the Province, since he himself was Anglican, and his correspondence was with an Anglican priest, both as priest, friend, and trusted comrade. Surely, the Church of the Province here stands for the church as a whole. There is not a single church or denomination in South Africa that can declare itself innocent in the face of this question.

Likewise, there is not a single activist who, at one time or another, did not have to ask this question with regard to her, or his own, denomination. It is another painful reality we are yet to fully overcome. Reverend Beyers Naudé, the white Dutch Reformed pastor who joined the black struggle because he could no longer live with white Christian nationalism, its false loyalties, its undeserved privileges, and its oppression of others, knew what this obedience meant, and what it called for. It cost him his position in his church, his acceptability among the Afrikaner community, and his guaranteed safety as a white person. For Naudé, too, it was the painful realization that Peter's bold declaration in Acts 5:29, "We must obey God, rather than human beings," was not just about obedience or disobedience to his government. It was a choice against his church. For him it was a question not merely of what he called "lesser loyalties," but of the salvation of his soul: "It is a choice between religious conviction and submission to ecclesiastical authority. By obeying the latter unconditionally I would save face, but lose my soul."[87] But even in this, he confesses to have learned from Steve Biko:

> Steve Biko challenges me to not keep quiet anymore but to voice my deepest convictions about what is right and true, to stand up for them and to suffer for them if necessary—even if this should mean that I have to endure condemnation and rejection by my own people.[88]

In his memo to Fr. Russell, Biko makes reference to "the conscience" even before he uses it in the context of selfless revolutionaries. In the first instance, he speaks about the "ultimate conscience of each living mortal."[89] Human beings, Biko says, "have enough power" to dull the sensitivity to our own conscience "and hence become cruel, hard, bad, evil"; however, "intrinsically somewhere" in us there is always something

---

86. Biko, *I Write What I Like*, 241.
87. See Naudé, *My Land van Hoop*, 159.
88. See Naudé, "Steve Biko, the Man and His Message," 79.
89. Biko, *I Write What I Like*, 241.

that tells us we are wrong.[90] Then, in his discussion on selfless revolutionaries, Biko speaks of the conscience at the heart of the selfless revolutionaries that compels them "to offer themselves, and sometimes their lives" in the struggle for freedom, justice, and dignity for the sake of others. It is clear that the conscience that "tells us we are doing something wrong" is not the conscience that compels us to "offer our lives."

When I wrote *The Tenderness of Conscience*, I did not speak of the human conscience in general, but of the *tender* conscience. I did not mean a conscience, as G. H. Ter Schegget so aptly put it, as "the alibi of the unscrupulous,"[91] but as the conscience we do not possess but that is awakened in us by the promises of God. The conscience that calls upon those promises for God's sake and for the sake of those who suffer. It is not just knowing about right and wrong. It is being touched and moved by things we are normally inured to—not just to the suffering of others, but to their hunger for justice, freedom, and dignity.[92] It is this tenderness of conscience, I wrote then,

> that leaves us open to the woundedness of others; that makes us take the risk of vulnerability ourselves. It is a spirituality that infuses politics with the sensitivity that knows we should not weep for wounds to be healed too quickly and for tears to dry too soon. It behoves us to weep with those who weep so we can more authentically rejoice when they rejoice . . . It is the unholy patience with the consequences of suffering caused by injustice.[93]

Perhaps Chelsea Manning, the young American soldier who could no longer stand the willful, senseless, and endless war in Afghanistan and Iraq is one of our world's best examples of a selfless revolutionary. Chelsea Manning is in prison in the United States because she had released "classified" documents of American soldiers engaged in the wanton killing of civilians in Iraq and passed them on to WikiLeaks. In 2010, she had first released those documents detailing abuses and war crimes against the people of Afghanistan and Iraq,

> unreported killings of civilians, the failure to adequately investigate accusations of torture; increased use of drones; and the use of special units to track down and kill individuals without trial, among other things.[94]

All this, of course, occurred under the reign of President Barack Obama.[95] Since then, she has repeatedly been hauled in front of Grand Juries, pressed to confess to

---

90. Biko, *I Write What I Like*, 237.
91. Ter Schegget, *Het Geheim van de Mens*, 131–144.
92. See Boesak, *Tenderness of Conscience*, 222.
93. Boesak, *Tenderness of Conscience*, 222.
94. See Maxwell and Chakravarti, "Chelsea Manning Against the Grand Jury."
95. More people have been prosecuted under the 1917 Espionage Act during the Obama-era than under all previous presidencies combined. Yet other high profile offenders like General Petraeus, Leon Panetta and others have gone entirely unpunished or have been treated lightly. Chelsea Manning remains, to date, the most egregious example of such unhinged justice. One will have to wait and

wrongdoing, put in prison, released again. Only to be arrested again and to repeat the process. At the end of his term, even though he could, and was asked to, the Nobel Prize winning president refused to pardon her. The revelations of his country's war crimes while he was Commander in Chief was just too much for him. Not many public figures have come to her defense, though others did. As I write, she is still in prison, and likely to remain there, a prophetic voice for truth, a selfless revolutionary who refused to be complicit in the murderous acts of her government.

Can a people develop this sense revolutionary selflessness and embrace an ethic of global solidarity and so set an example in global politics? The one phrase now hammered into us by the leadership of the World Health Organization, the general Secretary of the United Nations, by religious leaders, academics, and even politicians for whom the word did not even seem to exist prior to 2020, is "global solidarity." I remember the early 1970s, when "solidarity" became such a compelling word in ecumenical circles, an American church leader tried to convince me that solidarity was not "a biblical concept." The World Council of Churches tried to give expression to it in its Program to Combat Racism, and especially in its Special Fund to provide support for the educational and health programs of Southern African liberation movements. That was a solidarity that came with great costs. In the West, and in apartheid South Africa, the WCC was demonized as never before. Churches of the rich North punished the WCC severely by withholding their financial support for other WCC programs. Still, to its eternal credit and to our own everlasting gratitude, the WCC never gave in. I think that it altered the relationship forever. It is as if the rich churches of the North had decided never to let the WCC out of its control again. Sadly, today, the World Council is a mere shadow of the prophetic body it was during the turbulent years of the 60s, 70s, and 80s.

But to return to the question: Can a people develop this selflessness, this solidarity, on a global scale? And can this, too, be what Biko meant when he spoke of the greatest gift, to "give the *world* a human face"? Cuba seems to think so. Cuba's doctors were on the frontline in the fight against cholera in Haiti and against the Ebola virus in West Africa in the 2010s. Sending them now to one of the richest countries of the world to help fight the novel coronavirus, reports TeleSur, "is demonstrating the reach of its medical diplomacy."[96] Considering what is at stake here, however, I would suggest that what Cuba is demonstrating is of a different order than just "medical diplomacy." In truth, and especially in comparison to other countries who are shamelessly exploiting the presence of the virus to wage devastating war or to intensify already death-dealing sanctions, Cuba is demonstrating its revolutionary selflessness in its embodied solidarity. Dr. Leonardo Fernandez, sixty-eight, is the spokesperson of the group sent to Italy: "We are afraid, but we have a revolutionary duty to fulfill, so we

---

see what fate awaits WikiLeaks founder Julian Assange. See "Obama's War on Whistleblowers Leaves Administration Insiders Unscathed."

96. See "Cuba Comes to Italy's Aid."

take our fear and put it to one side."⁹⁷ As I write, a team of sixty medical personnel have just arrived in South Africa to help in the struggle against the virus. This is not fearlessness. What it is, as Leonardo Fernandez says, is selflessness.

Cuba has sent medical teams to other Global South countries, socialist allies such as Venezuela and Nicaragua, as well as to Jamaica, Suriname, and Grenada. That may be called "solidarity of the oppressed." But with Italy, a country in the European Union that is riding on the coattails, or better perhaps, hiding under the skirts of the American Empire, is going beyond that. When Biko used the term, he spoke within the same context as the commitment to the liberation of the oppressor, their "conversion" so to speak, convincing them to see that their own liberation is caught up in the liberation of the oppressed. That is an argument leaders like Luthuli, Mandela, and Martin Luther King Jr. used to make all the time. Here that motive is totally absent. There is no guarantee that Italy will break ranks with the rest of the European Union or the United States in its ongoing isolation of Cuba.

Not many countries are doing this or on this scale. And even in situations where there seemed to be a glimmer of this kind of solidarity, it is still difficult. Journalist Mike Davis speaks primarily of the United States, but his analysis is applicable to many more countries of the world.

> The leftward evolution of a new generation and the return of the word "socialism" to political discourse cheers us all, but there is a disturbing element of national solipsism in the progressive movement that is symmetrical with the new nationalism. We talk only about the American working class and America's radical history . . . In addressing the pandemic socialists should find every reason to remind others of the urgency of international solidarity.⁹⁸

Still, Fr. Stubbs is right. Biko is, and will remain, "a true martyr of Christ." Though, Stubbs hastens to add, "Not the Christ he could not consciously be often in communion with because of the disfiguring disguises with which the Church had distorted him. The Christ nonetheless of the poor and the oppressed, whose compassion he displayed, and whose passion for righteousness it was that drove him to his death."⁹⁹

It is the Jesus proclaimed by Black theology, who, despite everything, gave Biko hope. This Jesus is the ultimate selfless revolutionary. He is the Suffering Servant whose endless love for others was in his willingness to lose all, to give up all forms of majesty and all claims to privilege, to become acquainted with grief, taking on the form of a slave, to become "a man of sorrows" (Isa 53:3). It is no accident that Aeldred Stubbs and Njabula Ndebele found so much of him in Biko.

> He was despised and rejected by those who thought him a danger to their position of power and privilege within the status quo, *and* by those who found him

---

97. See "Cuba Comes to Italy's Aid."
98. Davis, "Coronavirus Crisis Is a Monster Fueled by Capitalism."
99. Biko, *I Write What I Like*, 243.

not pliable enough, as well as not hard enough, to fit into the predetermined mould of their revolutionary zeal. They knew, as we do, that the unimpressiveness of his incarnation was not the absence of his glory, but the heavenly solidarity with the poor and the lowly. Those who found him offensive would not look at him because looking at him means looking at the human face of the poor. They hid their faces from him because they could not bring themselves to look upon the misery their greed had visited upon the helpless. They held him of no account because the powerless do not feature in their reckoning except as sacrifices on the altar of political expedience. They held him cursed because he carried in his body the afflictions they have wrought upon the wounded by keeping them outside the gate, outside the circle of protection. They crucified him because he was the tender conscience that would not let go of their hardened hearts. But because God awakens in the hearts of the poor the longing for freedom, justice and contentment, they are doomed to hear his voice as long as the poor cry out. They shall have to face him as long as the poor have hope.[100]

And just as Womanist theologian Kelly Brown Douglas can speak of the murdered Trayvon Martin as "Jesus on a Florida sidewalk,"[101] so we can speak of Steve Biko as Jesus, naked in a police van from Port Elizabeth to Pretoria Central Prison. And just as we pray in the name of Jesus, the Crucified One, we pray in the name of Jesus, the Lynched One of Galilee.

---

100. Boesak, *Tenderness of Conscience*, 239.
101. See Douglas, *Stand Your Ground*, 179.

2

Rebels at the Lectern and in the Pulpit
Hegemony, Harmony, and the Critical Dimensions of Intellectual and Theological Integrity

A Rite of Passage

My *alma mater* in the Netherlands, the Theological University of the Reformed Churches in the Netherlands in Kampen, was a place that changed my life and thinking in ways I will never be able to adequately describe. It is now no longer in existence because of both economic austerity measures by the government and the dramatically changing ecclesial situation in Europe, impacting hugely on the formal training of prospective candidates for the ministry in mainline Dutch Protestant churches. Its impact would remain though: when I left, I was not the person who arrived there six years earlier. My supervisor, Gerard Rothuizen, spoke a deeper truth than either of us knew in his congratulatory speech after the public defense of my doctoral dissertation that day in June 1976, just before Soweto blew up. "You came here as a 'colored' minister of the gospel; you are leaving as a militant black theologian."

It was not a throwaway line, and it captured quite accurately my experiences through six years of study. Gerard Rothuizen knew what he was saying. At the start of the 1972/73 academic year, my professor and I had had fruitful discussions on a possible topic for my doctoral dissertation. A year later, however, we had a considerable difference of opinion over the new subject for that dissertation. Earlier, we had just about agreed on a study of what I would call "*Usus Eschatalogicus*: Toward an Eschatalogical Use of the Law."[1] Lutheran theology acknowledges two uses of the Law (i.e., the Torah); Reformed theology knows of three: the *usus civilis* (i.e., the civil or political

---

1. Inspired by a discussion in H. J. Heering's small but important and delightful study, *Ethiek der voorlopigheid*.

use of the Law), the *usus elenchticus* (i.e., the educational use of the law), and specific to the Reformed tradition, the *usus didacticus* (i.e., the rule of life for believers). I would explore the possibility of a fourth. For both of us it was an exciting prospect.[2] It was also a very proper European theological concept, fitting for such a prestigious theological institution. Now, however, I have changed my mind. I had undergone, I suppose one could say, a rite of passage.

I had just returned from a semester and most of the summer at Union Theological Seminary in New York City where I had met James Cone and his brilliant and provocative work, *Black Theology and Black Power*.[3] Later, I would also be introduced to the first collection of essays on Black theology from South Africa, published in London and banned in South Africa,[4] as I would be to Walter Rodney's still-gripping classic that today should be compulsory reading for those seeking to take part in the all-important project of decoloniality, Afro-plurality, and anti-imperialism.[5] The previous year, Gerard Rothuizen had introduced me to Dietrich Bonhoeffer, the brilliant young German scholar turned resistance fighter against the Nazis. In 1974, at the invitation of South African colleagues and friends, I returned to South Africa to attend a Black theology consultation in Hammanskraal. That close encounter convinced me that the direction my thinking was going was the right one. I had also begun to read Antonio Gramsci[6] and of course Frantz Fanon, whose foundational and brilliant work had begun to captivate a new generation.[7] Fanon, writes Jean Paul Sartre in his preface

---

2. My supervisor had himself written his dissertation on the civil use of the Law; see Rothuizen, *Primus Usus Legis*.

3. I am intentional in saying that I had met James Cone *and* his book. Sometimes meeting the person and reading their books are two separate events and separate experiences. With Cone, reading the book was meeting the man. The man was the living incarnation of the book: the fiery words, the righteous anger, the burning passion, the uncompromising, fighting spirit, the resolute commitment to the cause of black freedom. The book was the truthful, unflinching reflection of the man. It was the world's first encounter with what would become an abiding commitment for Cone, captured succinctly in the way he often described that commitment: "Writing is the way I fight." My stay in the United States also introduced me to most of that first generation of black theologians in the US, including Gayraud Wilmore, who would become my co-supervisor, many civil rights struggle veterans, superbly exemplified in the powerful preaching of Jeremiah A. Wright, and, to my utter delight, to the Black Church, its style of worship, black preaching, and its utterly unique music. It was, after my introduction to Kampen, a second wave of life-changing experiences, only this time more sweeping, more iconoclastic, and permanent. In a sure sign of the impact of Black theology and black theologians during that stay in the US, my pre-doctoral dissertation (in those days compulsory for admittance to the ThD program) was a comparative study of the ethics of Malcolm X and Martin Luther King Jr.; see Boesak, *Coming In Out of the Wilderness*. It was in the course of the writing of this small work that I learned to really appreciate Gerard Rothuizen, who, as a European theologian, showed a remarkable capacity to combine both learning, unlearning, critical reading, and supervision. There were many teachers at universities and seminaries in Europe at the time who did not deem Black theology a proper field of study. Rothuizen was not one of them.

4. Moore, *Black Theology*.

5. See Rodney, *How Europe Underdeveloped Africa*.

6. See Gramsci, *Selections*.

7. See Fanon, *Wretched of the Earth*.

to Fanon's most famous work, helped us understand what it meant that the world was divided into "men" and "natives." Between the two, he said, there were "hired kinglets, overlords, and a bourgeoisie, sham from beginning to end, which served as go-betweens."[8]

Fanon himself was scathing in his exposure of the Eurocentric view of the "natives":

> The native is declared insensible to ethics; he represents not only the absence of values, but also the negation of values. He is, let us dare to admit, the enemy of values, and in this sense he is the absolute evil. He is the corrosive element, destroying all that comes near him; he is the deforming element, disfiguring all that has to do with beauty or morality; he is the depository of maleficent powers, the unconscious and irretrievable instrument of blind forces.[9]

From the US, I had brought with me James Baldwin's *Fire Next Time*, in which was his "Down at the Cross: Letter From a Region of My Mind," a simply incredible piece of writing, reverberating with a power in today's contexts that is astonishing. Even at that early stage of my development, I could begin to discern that such unforgettable prose of elegant, eloquent rage could only come from the purifying fires of suffering, resistance, and liberation. Looking at this again, I am struck by the many times reviewers spoke about this work as "bitter" or "incendiary." But I now understand much better: They called him "bitter" and "incendiary" because this was writing that struck fear into their hearts, and *that* was because they could not deny the searing truth of it. This was the writing of a completely decolonized mind, a tormented and redeemed soul, for there is no redemption without torment. It was from within a shattered innocence and a shattering honesty, and it left his readers no reprieve, except if we were willing to go into the fires with him, and believe that we will together emerge purified and whole. Here again, I felt what I was to feel so many times, what Martin Luther King Jr. would call the "inescapable network of mutuality." The "Negro's past" Baldwin described so vividly was all our past:

> This past, the Negro's past, of rope, fire, torture, castration, infanticide, rape; death and humiliation; fear by day and night, fear as deep as the marrow of the bone; doubt that he was worthy of life, since everyone around him denied it; sorrow for his women, for his kinfolk, for his children, who needed his protection, and whom he could not protect; rage, hatred, and murder, hatred for white men so deep that it often turned against him and his own, and made all love, and trust, all joy impossible—this past, this endless struggle to achieve and reveal and confirm a human identity, human authority, yet contains, for all its horror, something very beautiful. I do not mean to be sentimental about suffering—enough is certainly as good as a feast—but people who cannot suffer can never grow up, can never discover who they are. That man who is

---

8. See "Preface" in Fanon, *Wretched of the Earth*.
9. Fanon, *Wretched of the Earth*, 40.

> forced each day to snatch his manhood, his identity, out of the fire of human cruelty that rages to destroy it knows, if he survives his effort, and even if he does not survive it, something about himself and human life that no school on earth—and, indeed, no church—can teach. He achieves his own authority, and that is unshakable.[10]

Such fierce writing had not penetrated my world before. To a certain extent, it helped me understand much better Cone's righteous anger, even as it helped to stoke my own. All these experiences together presented me with a truth that was both unassailable and inescapable: I would not simply be studying, but *doing* theology, and that for me, theology, as just about everything else, would never be the same again. There was, it seemed to me, a peculiar sense of innocence that I took with me to Europe and that initially attended my studies. An innocence about the uncritical acceptance of Eurocentric theological thinking as the proper, indeed, the *only* framework within which to study theology; about Western imperialism, racism, white supremacy, and white privilege; their relationship to academics in general and to religion and theology in particular. An innocence about the relationship between theology, church, race, and class; between apartheid, colonialist history, the Reformed tradition, and the Bible, and as a result, about white power and white wealth, black impoverishment and black powerlessness. Of course, it would take me some years to realize the connections between religion, ecclesial realities, and theology; and what we know today as heteronormative, patriarchal hegemony, and the frameworks, and limits, these set for our thinking. It would take even longer to understand Black Consciousness and Black theology's own toxic patriarchalism and the debilitating effects that would have on our thinking and praxis, and on the integrity of our revolution.[11]

There was the illusion that within and amidst all these manifestations, realities, and contradictions, theology somehow remained pristine and pure, detached from the fallen world of injustice, violence, and oppression, as long as my heart belonged to Jesus. That innocence first had to be unmasked as a pseudo-innocence, then understood as a fundamental enemy of faith and reason, dignity and theologizing, and then stripped away and completely discarded. Hence the title of my dissertation: *Farewell to Innocence*. Jesus remained, but the rest had to go.

From my mother, a woman with little formal schooling but with deep, abiding faith and wellsprings of wisdom, I learned those fundamental truths, "the first things" that opened my mind to understanding: that the central, inalienable, and enduring

---

10. Baldwin, *Fire Next Time*, 98–99.

11. Black theology in South Africa, as witnessed by one or two of the essays in the collection, were not totally unaware of our sexism. But I follow the distinction between sexism as an attitude, and patriarchy as a systemic issue. So it was possible for our writers to make mention of the fact that women should be treated as equals, but still had no problem with language and outlook that excluded women as a matter of course. I have endeavored to address these specific issues at different points in my work, but for the most recent, most detailed engagement of these, see Boesak, *Children of the Waters of Meribah*.

message of the Bible was liberation; that God was a God of justice and peace, the "protector of the widow and the orphan, and the defender of the defenseless" (Ps 68:5) as she would say in her prayers at the table. The words she did not use but certainly intimated, and that would become central to liberation theology, were God's preferential option for the poor and oppressed. That Jesus of Nazareth was the One sent by God to bring good news to the poor and liberation to the oppressed, to set the captives free, to heal the brokenhearted, and to announce the favorable year of the Lord.[12] Black theology confirmed, deepened, and enhanced these, enabled me to put them in words I could never find while under the tutelage of white apartheid teachers at my seminary, the seminary the white Dutch Reformed Church established for those "coloreds" from the "colored" branch of the Dutch Reformed Church "family" and who felt the call to ministry. Against that white-controlled, apartheid theology education, which if truth be told, would absolutely qualify as what America's Carter Woodson called "the mis-education of the Negro,"[13] Black liberation theology helped me articulate these truths in preaching, writing, and in actions in the streets of confrontation in the company of millions whose minds were bent on freedom.

Black theology and Black Consciousness also called for a thorough, intellectually endowed hermeneutical suspicion of all Eurocentric thinking. Through Gayraud Wilmore's irreplaceable and inspirational study I learned the truth about black religion and black radicalism, how these two forces came together and shaped the Black Church.[14] The challenge of this legacy for us in our times was clear. From Cone I learned that the theologian is "*before all else* an exegete, simultaneously of Scripture and of existence." Thus:

> To be an exegete of existence means that Scripture is not an abstract word, not merely a rational idea. It is God's Word to those who are oppressed and humiliated in this world. The task of the theologian is to probe the depths of Scripture exegetically for the purpose of relating that message to human existence.[15]

Cone insisted that

> Jesus Christ is not a proposition, not a theological concept which exists merely in our heads . . . He is an event of liberation, a happening in the lives of oppressed people struggling for political freedom. Therefore, to know him is to encounter him in the history of the weak and the helpless. The convergence of Jesus Christ and the black experience is the meaning of the Incarnation.[16]

---

12. See Boesak, *Children of the Waters of Meribah*, ch. 1, especially 14–21.
13. Woodson, *Mis-Education of the Negro*.
14. See Wilmore, *Black Religion and Black Radicalism*.
15. Cone, *God of the Oppressed*, 8.
16. Cone, *God of the Oppressed*, 32, 33.

Cone, like Gayraud Wilmore, was to become a teacher, a mentor, a partner in conversation, a friend and a brother, a comrade in our common struggles for freedom and justice. Their impact on my life and thinking is indelible. In the process, I understood better what Chief Albert Luthuli meant when he said, "I am in Congress *because of my Christianity*."[17] That does not only say something about the African National Congress, which from Luthuli's point of view today would be unbelievably unrecognizable. It also means that Luthuli's Christianity was fundamentally a Christianity unthinkable without it being a faith of the streets of struggle, in unbreakable solidarity with his people as they challenged the might of the apartheid regime *on the basis of their faith*. For him, faith had no meaning without this, and that is how it should be.

Steve Biko chastised us that while it was true that Christianity, in the hands of the white missionary, had been made the perfect instrument for the subjugation of our people, "*nowadays*," in other words, in the hands of Black preachers, in the pulpits of black churches, the Bible, as read, understood, interpreted and preached by us, still remained that perfect instrument of subjugation.[18] Now that black theologians occupy lecterns at universities, and blacks are the actual leadership of black churches or black majority churches, even global ecumenical organizations, Biko's challenge seems more urgent than ever before.

Like other colonized peoples, the indigenous peoples of the utmost southern part of Africa received the Bible and were first introduced to it as central to imperialist domination and colonizing manipulation. And Reformation or no, it would not matter whether in the colonization process the colonized were overrun by Catholics, Lutherans, Calvinists, Anglicans, or "Non-conformists" of whatever sort, they would all be representatives of the nations of the rich North, empires that had as their goal the theft of land and people, oppression, slavery, and genocide, all with the express intent of exploitation, deprivation, and enrichment. Invasion and colonization went hand-in-hand with domination and subjugation, and the Christianization of the people was unthinkable without the demonization of their culture and beliefs, that wide open door to the eradication of their history and their physical annihilation.

Inasmuch as it had to do with doctrine it was purely incidental.

I discovered how Dietrich Bonhoeffer, that extraordinary, brilliant young German theologian with a bright future in academia, turned into a partisan for the oppressed and the outcasts, a freedom fighter who joined the resistance and, ultimately, the plot to rid the world of Adolf Hitler and the Nazis. Bonhoeffer fascinated me from the beginning, but it was only recently, in truly groundbreaking works, that African American scholars Ralph Clingan[19] and Reggie Williams[20] helped us to properly understand this process in Bonhoeffer, and simultaneously for me, why I was so

---

17. See Luthuli, *Let my People Go!*, 147.
18. See Biko, *I Write What I Like*, 61.
19. See Clingan, *Against Cheap Grace*.
20. See Williams, *Bonhoeffer's Black Jesus*.

naturally attracted to this theologian from Germany. They show that for Bonhoeffer, everything changed fundamentally while in New York City in 1930. He attended church and taught Sunday school at Abyssinian Baptist Church in Harlem, listened to the fiery sermons of Rev. Adam Clayton Powell Sr., and learned the spirituals of the Black Church. He engaged with the black writers of the Harlem Renaissance, read Langston Hughes's "Christ in Alabama" and Countee Cullen's "The Black Christ" in which the historical Jesus is "the first in a succession of lynched black men in the South."[21] His heart was touched, his mind was gripped, and his life was changed when he was introduced to Langston Hughes's scorching words:[22]

> Most Holy Bastard
> Of the bleeding mouth,
> Nigger Christ,
> On the Cross
> Of the South

For Bonhoeffer, the learned German aristocrat with the protected life and the secured future, theology and life would be innocent no more. He now knew that the "White Christ" of complacent white American Christianity and of the white, nationalist Christianity of Germany was not the same as the "black Christ" of the ghetto, the Black Church and the black Harlem Renaissance writers in America.[23] He now also knew that in order to be truthful, one had to see life "from below, from the perspective of the outcasts, the suspects, the maltreated, the powerless, the oppressed, the reviled—in short, from the perspective of those who suffer . . ."[24] Instead of remaining in the safe environs of high academia, he became *a follower of Jesus*. In a word, as we will discuss below, Bonhoeffer, through his embrace of life and faith "from below" was able to take upon himself the "condition of blackness."[25]

Bonhoeffer no longer longed for a chair in one of Germany's great universities. He would find a home at the underground seminary of the Confessing Church at Finkenwalde, always marginalized, always under pressure, always threatened. He now understood better that the life of a servant of Christ must belong to the church. But Bonhoeffer did not mean a church disconnected from Christ in its disconnect from the world, a church turned into itself, trapped in the rituals of a meaningless religiosity or held in imperialist captivity without commitment to the transformation of the world. He meant a church "for others," one that understood and believed its confession that

21. See Williams, *Bonhoeffer's Black Jesus*, 54ff.
22. Quoted in Williams, *Bonhoeffer's Black Jesus*, 64.
23. Bonhoeffer refers to "a Black poet" who might have been Countee Cullen, whose work *The Black Christ and Other Poems* appeared in 1929, just prior to Bonhoeffer's arrival in 1930. See DeYoung, *Living Faith*, 28, 165n10. DeYoung follows Josiah Ulyses Young in this; see Young, *No Difference in the Fare*, 123.
24. Bonhoeffer, *Letters and Papers from Prison*, 17.
25. For the way I apply this phrase, see Boesak, *Black and Reformed*, 22–28.

Jesus Christ alone is Lord, and that it was to Christ, not to church or secular authorities, patriotic sentiments or a culture that provides political and economic privilege, to which the church owed ultimate loyalty and obedience. Bonhoeffer did not shun academic knowledge. Rather, he put it to use in the training of pastors for the Confessing Church—the church in resistance to Hitler and the Nazis.[26]

The commitment to Christ Bonhoeffer spoke of was a commitment to those the Nazis considered "less human," and therefore "less worthy" of life:

> You outcasts, you disadvantaged . . . you who are looked down upon . . . Blessed are you Lazaruses of all ages, you broken down and ruined, you lonely and abandoned . . . you who suffer injustice, you who suffer in body and soul; blessed are you for God's joy will come over you and be over [your] head forever. That is the gospel, the good news.[27]

It was a commitment he would not give up on. As a consequence, he would raise the critical question,

> Whether we Christians have enough strength to witness before the world that we are not dreamers with our heads in the clouds . . . that our faith really is not opium that keeps us content within an unjust world. Instead, and precisely because our minds are set on things above, we are that much more stubborn and purposeful in protesting here on earth . . .[28]

Bonhoeffer speaks of the "strength," the courage, to witness before the world. But first, the "world" he speaks of is a hostile world, a world in the grip of evil, quite specifically the world of Adolf Hitler, of the Nazis, of challenge and risk of persecution, of the ultimate limits of horror and death. He does not try to deny, minimize, or trivialize it. Second, he has, *by conscious decision*, left the safe and comfortable world of New York, Union Seminary, and Abyssinian Baptist Church behind. Third, the "witness" Bonhoeffer thinks of can no longer be words, how thoughtful and eloquent those might be. From now on witness could only be the act of taking a stand where Christ is to be found: in the places where the plagues fall, where death casts its shadow. The strength for this kind of witness comes not of earthly power, of connections with those in high places or of the guarantees of protective privilege. This is a strength that comes from personal faith in the empowering Spirit of God. And it is a strength that enabled him to commit his life to justice, freedom, and human dignity; in short, a new humanity.

It is clear to me just how immense a debt we owe to Ralph Clingan and Reggie Williams. Bonhoeffer would never have become so close to us in our struggles if we had not discovered that he was brought so close, not through Eurocentrism's prism, but through his life-changing encounter with the Black Church, black preaching,

---

26. For a more detailed treatment of the following passages concerning Bonhoeffer, see Boesak, *Kairos, Crisis, and Global Apartheid*, ch. 3, especially 69–74.

27. Bonhoeffer, *Ecumenical, Academic, and Pastoral Work*, 446, 447.

28. Bonhoeffer, *Ecumenical, Academic, and Pastoral Work*, 459.

black worship, and the fierce black writing of the Harlem Renaissance. This is what made him see both America and Germany, but the eyes were no longer only those of a concerned German. They were the eyes cleared by black suffering, black struggle, black resilience, and the joy of black resistance.

Reading Gramsci opened new possibilities from a field decidedly non-theological but essential for those wanting to understand the impact of academic work, in all its disciplines, on the lives of oppressed people.[29] But I also learned that although Gramsci could not be wholly and uncritically applied to the South African situation,[30] his thoughts about intellectuals and society remain invaluable.[31] First, and basic to his understanding, is the key observation that

> there is no human activity from which every form of intellectual participation can be excluded: *homo faber* cannot be separated from *homo sapiens*... [Every person] participates in a particular conception of the world, has a conscious line of moral conduct, and therefore contributes to sustain a conception of the world or to modify it, that is, to bring into being new modes of thought.[32]

That is without doubt the fundamental issue at work in this concept. No intellectual activity is "objective." If it is an activity "with a conscious code of moral conduct" that somehow "sustains a conception of the world"; it is not neutral, and it serves a political function.

Second, I learned about his concerns about hegemony; namely, the condition of one class, the ruling class, exercising dominance over the rest of society. He spoke of ideological hegemonic forces that manipulate individuals into consenting to their own exploitation. Third, how hegemony enlists the academy's and intellectuals' ideological power to do its bidding and to capture the minds of the masses into believing

---

29. See as a most recent example, and from an African feminist perspective, the excellent doctoral study of Ilze Keevy, where she analyzes Western philosophy, its embedded racism, and its impact on the lives of Africans: Keevy, "Western Philosophy," 62–117. See also Keevy, *African Philosophical Values and Constitutionalism*.

30. For example, Gramsci was heavily impacted by the realities of Italian and European politics between the two World Wars, by the raging battles between Fascism, Communism, and Democratic Socialism. Though all these elements were present, these dynamics did not apply to South Africa in the same manner. Neither do the tensions between Italy's "peasant South" and "urban worker North." The Roman Catholic Church of the beginning of the 20th century had an enormous impact on Italy's religious, political, social, and economic life. The Catholic Church, with the Vatican State as a political entity, carried considerable diplomatic presence across the world; the influence of the Pope as religious and political figure is still immensely powerful, but is seriously diminishing, as recent events in Chile (on priests and pedophilia) and Ireland (on the question of abortion), for instance, have shown. None of this was black South Africans' lived experience. In South Africa, the power of the white Dutch Reformed churches vis-à-vis the apartheid state was strong, but the situations were not comparable. Today, it is even less so. Besides, apartheid's uniqueness created for us a very particular situation. Nonetheless, Gramsci's thinking opened important avenues for the flourishing of our critical thinking.

31. These are returning themes for Gramsci, but see for our purposes Gramsci, *Selections*, loc. 131–61.

32. Gramsci, *Selections*, loc. 140–41.

that whatever those in power decide is for the best, is also for the good of society. Later, Edward Herman and Noam Chomsky would speak of "manufactured consent" by hegemonic forces—especially the media in their service to the dominant political structures, but also academia. Fourth, Gramsci taught us that those intellectuals who collaborated with the powerful classes are the "credentialed" intellectuals, those "sanctioned" by the powerful, placed in positions of authority in the academy so that their word carries the weight of the "respected" in a society that had bestowed upon them the badge of "respectability." That also gives them their authority and believability, which is their power. Fifth, he argued that it was a mistake to ignore, disregard, or trivialize the role of intellectuals. They are key in maintaining hegemonies. They generate and spread the ideas of the dominant group, serve their interests, and in that way work against the interests of the masses.

Over against what Gramsci called "traditional" intellectuals, he placed not "public" intellectuals, but "organic intellectuals."[33] These are not necessarily scholars, though they might be. They are not "sanctioned" or "credentialed" as "trustworthy social mouthpieces"; rather they are concerned with the practical matters of daily living as experienced by ordinary people. As theologians and preachers, in womanist theologian Katie Cannon's elegant phrasing, they had "one ear on the ground hearing the cries and longings of the people, and the other ear to the mouth of God."[34]

---

33. Gramsci holds that intellectuals are "organic" no matter their class affiliations and loyalties. That may be true. Here, however, I understand "organic" intellectuals, as opposed to "credentialed intellectuals," to be from among the oppressed masses, *working within the struggles for justice*, and they will find themselves in opposition to hegemonic powers and the intellectuals who serve those hegemonic interests. In the US for instance, I would describe Ta-Nehisi Coates as a public intellectual more prone to serving the interests of American hegemony, while for me, Cornel West is an organic theologian and intellectual. West himself describes the difference between the two of them and my experiences in the US compel me to side with West. "Coates and I," West writes, "come from a great tradition of the black freedom struggle . . . [however] the disagreement between me and Coates is clear: any analysis or vision of our world that omits the centrality of Wall Street power, US military policies, and the complex dynamics of class, gender, and sexuality . . . is too narrow and dangerously misleading." The issue is not condemnation of white supremacy, but Coates's failure to "connect this ugly legacy to the predatory capitalist practices, imperial policies (of war, occupation, detention, assassination), or the black elite's refusal to confront poverty, patriarchy or transphobia." See West, "Ta-Nehisi Coates is the neoliberal face of the black freedom struggle." What West calls "the neoliberal syndrome," is never more apparent than in the endorsements of black pubic officials and persons from the black elites for Joe Biden, the clear pro-establishment Democratic candidate in the 2020 US presidential race, and their rejection of Bernie Sanders whose democratic socialist policies would clearly be of more benefit to the poor and excluded masses in the US of which African American and Latinx communities form the vast majority. Unlike some poor whites who vote for Trump "against their own interests," these privileged and pro-establishment blacks vote for Biden precisely because he represents the interests of their class. In this matter, they act as if race is not an issue at all, whereas for the impoverished working classes, race still matters hugely.

34. Cannon, *Katie's Canon*, 115.

Harmony, Hegemony, Integrity

All these events and experiences together not only transformed my understanding; they redirected my studies and changed the course of my life. I understood my choices. If our people in South Africa were in a life and death struggle for freedom, justice, and dignity against impeccable imperialist forces; if the enemy had at their disposal a formidable array of weapons: political and economic power, science, religion, ideology, violence in all its manifestations, and had been using these for well-nigh three-hundred years, what did my six years of academic study in Europe mean? What should I make of these opportunities then opened only to a few of us? Was I to become a "sanctioned" intellectual, serving the interest of white hegemony? Was I to seek the safer position, offering a kind of harmony between what I knew to be right, but practically too filled with risk and clearly not the chosen path for "upward mobility"?

I was studying in Europe, enjoying six years of educational privilege I never knew and could never get at home. The fiery words Sartre learned from Fanon stubbornly held my feet to the fire. Those lured to Europe, and who succumbed to the temptations of the colonizer, he wrote, "were branded . . . as with a red-hot iron, with the principles of Western culture." They came home, if they ever did, "whitewashed." Sartre called them "walking lies who had nothing to say to their brothers, they only echoed."[35] Is that what I was destined to become, a whitewashed, walking lie?

I knew that apartheid was intent on offering black people the harmony option, who, in accepting, would be caught in the hopeless hypocrisy of "joining the system to fight the system," but I also knew that to be a fraudulent, undignified position, seeking the false comfort of political and intellectual neutrality. Black Consciousness has taught us, among so much else, that neutrality means taking the side of the oppressor without taking responsibility for it. Organic intellectuals, Gramsci argued, were those who emerged from "within a given social substratum and through the generation and proliferation of ideas, help the substratum to identify its own needs."[36] Black Christians recognized the truth of that idea. Was not Miriam in her prophetic leadership at the seashore and in the wilderness a prophet "from among the people"? So were the eighth-century prophets who stood up for justice for the poor and oppressed, against the power of the palace, the ruling elites, and the privileged classes. Was not Jesus of Nazareth the revolutionary prophet and teacher in his resistance against the Roman Empire and the ruling elites in Jerusalem from among the poor and oppressed in occupied Galilee?

Keeping in mind what we had learned from Fanon, on this point we had to go further than Gramsci, however. We should not *help* the oppressed to identify their needs. They *knew* their needs all too well. The Reformed tradition has understood this from the very beginning, as for example when Calvin stated that the oppressed

---

35. See the preface to Fanon, *Wretched of the Earth*.
36. Gramsci, *Selections*, loc. 141–42.

always, without anybody needing to explain this to them, "know that this confusion of law and order"—as Calvin calls states of oppression, domination, and exploitation—"is not to be endured." There is no condescension of the oppressed here at all. The longing for justice is "implanted in us [all] by the Lord."[37] I read Calvin's "not to be endured" not as a statement, but as an *injunction*, a call to radical obedience and action. When the oppressed rise up against injustice, it is not because some "agitator" or some better-equipped, self-appointed "vanguard of the revolution" tells them to. They are responding to a deeply human, divinely implanted impulse toward freedom and dignity. Besides, we were *from* the oppressed communities. We had no business standing on the bank trying to give theoretical directions to the masses in the roiling waters of struggle. We should, with our knowledge and commitment, *join* the oppressed in our common struggles for freedom.

And we had excellent examples. To name just a few, we had Lilian Ngoyi and Francis Baard, Sophie de Bruin and Helen Joseph. Their intellectual impact and political leadership in the Women's March, for instance, remain indelible. Were not Ella Baker, Rosa Parks, and Viola Liuzzo, the only white woman killed during the civil rights struggle in the United States, while working for voter registration, from among the people? And were not Dr. Abdurahman with his brilliant political foresight, Sol Plaatjie with his unsurpassed intellect and superb eloquence, and Albert Luthuli with his theological insights, political acumen, and fearless, nonviolent, militant leadership, and Trinidadian Henry Sylvester, who combined personal fortitude with undaunted political commitment to Pan-Africanism, or Martin Luther King Jr. from among the people? And so was Steve Biko, with his near-flawless understanding of black oppression, black internalized inferiority, white hegemonic superiority, and the need for and power of black resistance.

They not only had eloquence, but were, as Gramsci phrased it, "active participants in practical life," as "constructor, organiser, permanent persuader."[38] They were, to say it with John Calvin, persons "aroused by God" from among the people, who, in situations of oppression and injustice, "contemplated something altogether different" from what their oppressors envisaged and enacted.[39] That "something altogether different" was revolutionary, altogether set against the normalized, imperialist power structures of our societies. They were "organic" because, in the words of S'bu Zikode of the Shack-Dweller's Movement in South Africa, *Abahlali base Mjondolo*, they had the willingness, readiness, and ability "to be inside the struggles of the people and to be inside of the discussions inside the struggles of the people."[40]

Besides, we also had the example and legacy of W. E. B. Du Bois, one of the greatest intellectuals of the twentieth century, and not just in the United States of America.

37. Calvin, *Commentaries* 4:93–94.
38. Gramsci, *Selections*, loc. 141–42.
39. See Calvin, *Institutes* iv.xx.32.
40. Quoted in West, "People's Theology," 13, 14.

After the untimely death of his young son and the brutal lynching of Sam Hose in Georgia—tortured, strung up, burned, and dismembered by a gang of thugs encouraged by a mob of more than two-thousand whites—he made clear why he had left academia to throw himself into the real-life struggles of African Americans. "One could not be a calm, cool, and detached scientist while Negroes were lynched, murdered, and starved."[41] That is precisely what faced black intellectuals in apartheid South Africa.

Thus, my own choices were made. I would strive to be a liberation theologian, one who firmly embraces a radical Calvinism; rooted in faith, understanding as much as possible about my theological tradition and my theological choices; as much as possible about our political situation, the causes of and remedies for our oppression, and making my faith the basis for my participation in the struggle for freedom. If for Cone, as he so often put it, writing was "the way he fought," could I fight through my writing and preaching, and also in the streets of protest and struggle? I believed John Calvin was right: resistance to tyrannical powers was the duty, obligation, and privilege of a follower of Jesus Christ; and if the laws of government agitated against God's laws of justice, we should "pay them no regard whatsoever."[42] Such rulers have shown "contempt for God" and were seeking to "deprive God of God's rights"; namely, God's right and freedom to do justice to and demand justice and freedom for all of God's children.[43] Calvin understood that because he dedicated his life, not to entrench hegemonies, but to give voice to the suppressed voice of the oppressed, in which he heard, clearly and unequivocally, the voice of God. "It is then the same as if the Lord hears [Godself]," he wrote, "when [God] hears the cries and groanings of those who cannot bear injustice."[44]

As a theologian, a pastor, a preacher from the oppressed communities, and as an activist, this put me on an incontrovertible collision course with the apartheid regime, its structures and support systems, and its credentialed intellectuals. Our struggle would be against the white government with its awesome power, but also the white Dutch Reformed Churches, the progenitors, promoters, protectors and sanctifiers of apartheid; their theologians, pastors, and ecclesial leadership. The struggle would be for freedom, justice, and human dignity, and there could be no compromise. "We are not playing at politics," said Albert Luthuli, "we are bent on liberation."[45] And again, "Our struggle is a struggle and not a game."[46] Since power concedes nothing without a demand, it would mean confrontation at the risk of freedom and life. Luthuli left us with no illusions:

---

41. See Du Bois, *Dusk of Dawn*, 603.

42. See Calvin's sustained argument on obedience to civil government: Calvin, *Institutes* iv.xx.32.

43. Calvin, *Institutes* iv.xx.32. On my understanding of Calvin's position on illegitimate rulers "despoiling" God of God's rights, see Allan Boesak, *Kairos, Crisis, and Global Apartheid*, ch. 2, especially 56–60.

44. Calvin, *Commentaries* 1:2.

45. Luthuli, *Let My People Go!*, 147.

46. Luthuli, *Let My People Go!*, 124.

> We shall not win our freedom except at the cost of great suffering, and we must be prepared to accept it. Much African blood has already been spilt, and assuredly more will be . . . We do not desire to shed the blood of the white man; but we should have no illusion about the price he will exact in African blood before we are admitted to citizenship in our own land.[47]

It is this sober, truthful assessment of our situation, yet with the inescapability of participation that informed our understanding and our decisions. At issue between ourselves from the black Dutch Reformed churches and the white Dutch Reformed Church leadership, even, and sometimes especially, those who called themselves "enlightened" or "liberal," were the fundamental questions that would determine the ways we would go: Could the Reformed tradition be claimed to justify apartheid? Could apartheid be reformed or should it be irrevocably eradicated? Was apartheid a well-intentioned policy simply wrongly implemented, or was apartheid in fact politically irresponsible, sociologically irrational, morally reprehensible, and as such wholly untenable? Was apartheid merely a mistake, or was it fundamentally evil—a sin, a heresy, and a blasphemy? Was there time for gradualism and incremental steps toward never fundamental change while children were dying of hunger, illness, and designed neglect? Could the church be church if it were not in the struggle? Do we negotiate with Pharaoh, or do we do as God commanded: tell Pharaoh, "Let my people go!" Who determined the limits of struggle and who defined freedom?

In a word: Could we even contemplate seeking harmony with white hegemony? Many in my generation—in any case, enough to make a difference—could not, and like Albert Luthuli and the earlier generations, our own urge would be to "get into the thick of the struggle with other Christians," taking our Christianity with us, "praying that it may be used to influence for good the character of the resistance."[48] Theologically speaking, that meant that we were called to take our worship of God in the sanctuary and in the pulpit to our worship of God in the streets of protest and into the struggles for freedom and justice. These understandings delineated, for us, the critical dimensions of our intellectual, theological, and public integrity.

With the sterling examples of Christian participation, indeed, Christian leadership in the great moments of our struggle, black South Africans of my generation who understood the need for participation in the struggle for freedom did so on the basis of their faith, and taking their intellectuality and their Christian faith with them. The examples abound: the provocative brilliance of Steve Biko; the historic and courageous decisions on civil disobedience adopted by the South African Council of Churches in 1979 followed by my open letter to apartheid's Justice Minister Alwyn Schlebusch, offering a theological and biblical defense for those decisions;[49] the 1980 declaration of the

---

47. Luthuli, *Let My People Go!*, 124.
48. Luthuli, *Let My People Go!*, 148.
49. See Boesak, *Black and Reformed*, 32–41.

Alliance of Black Reformed Christians of Southern Africa, declaring apartheid a sin and its theological justification a heresy and a blasphemy, which became its proposal to the World Alliance of Reformed Churches, adopted at its General Council in 1982 at which meeting it also suspended the two white Dutch Reformed churches for their support of this evil policy;[50] the Theological Rationale for the Day of Prayer for the downfall of the apartheid regime in 1985;[51] the Belhar Confession of my own denomination written and approved in 1982 and formally adopted in 1986;[52] and one of the most influential ecumenical theological documents of the last century, the 1985 Kairos Document.[53]

The Kairos Document is especially important because it was written not by a committee of theologians, but circulated, draft by draft, by groups of Christians, which certainly included trained theologians like Frank Chikane and Albert Nolan, but finally was given its *imprimatur* by ordinary people of faith. Its groundbreaking distinction between state theology, church theology, and prophetic theology is today, globally, more relevant than ever. Its claim that it is a document that reflects a genuine people's theology is true in every respect. All this is the work of organic theologians and intellectuals whose commitment it was, and still is, to reject the claims of hegemony, to resist its control over the lives of the people, to put their intellectual endeavors at the disposal of the resistance.

And, not least, we had built relationships of strong solidarity, shared commitments to freedom and justice, common understandings of situations of oppression and exploitation across the globe. Through the Ecumenical Association of Third World Theologians we had engaged in rigorous and robust conversations, opening ourselves to the enrichment of trans-disciplinary scholarly engagement, critique and self-critique, and to the liberating and transformational processes of learning and unlearning. We learned from each other even as we learned the value of comradely mentorship, a situation in which James Cone had earned, and kept, a revered and unrivalled place.

Rethinking the African Renaissance

When in 1997 then-Deputy President Thabo Mbeki initiated his most ambitious project, the "African Renaissance," many of us welcomed it. I responded to Mbeki's vision with a monograph in which I argued for the full, critical, and wholehearted participation of those who truly understood the history of our struggle and its place in the history and the future of our continent.[54]

50. See De Gruchy and Villa-Vicencio, *Apartheid Is a Heresy*.
51. See Boesak and Villa-Vicencio, *When Prayer Makes News*.
52. See "Confession of Belhar."
53. For the text of the Kairos Document, see http://www.sahistory.org.za/archive/challenge-church-comment-political-crisis-south-africa-*kairos*-document-1985.
54. Boesak, *Tenderness of Conscience*. Mbeki would return to these themes in different ways again

Mbeki called upon intellectuals across Africa to join together with the people in the fight to "make foreign" all things that hold us back—from "backwardness" to the untenable position and role of women; to challenge the "disempowerment of the masses of our people." We must, he said, "dedicate ourselves to make sure to succeed in the struggle to make the masses of our people their own liberators." What we must also "make foreign" is the "abuse of political power to gain material wealth by those who exercise that power foreign to our continent and systems of governance."[55]

Mbeki invited us to "insert ourselves into the international debate on the issues of globalization and its impact on the lives of the people," and make our voice heard about what we and the rest of the world should do to achieve the development that is the "fundamental right" of the masses of our people. None of this will come about on its own, Mbeki warned, for the renaissance "will be victorious only as a result of a protracted struggle that we ourselves must wage."[56] It was an extraordinary call to vigorous and meaningful public intellectual engagement not often heard from heads of state.

Mbeki urged us to join that struggle, and from wherever we were situated "be ready to be rebels against tyranny, instability, corruption, and backwardness."[57] Hence the title of this chapter. As rebel in the academy, James Cone was without peer. His mantra, well known to all who ever talked with him, "Writing is the way I fight," was true in every sense. Had Mbeki's invitation extended to Africans in the Diaspora, Cone would have been one of the first to respond. It is a pity it didn't. The African renaissance as a project may have failed, but the realities of Africa still stand and cannot be denied, the challenges will not go away by themselves, and the invitation to us all, in the academy as well as in the church and in the general public is still an open one.

One important reason why I responded so positively was because in Mbeki's call I immediately recognized so much of what Black Consciousness had stood and called for. For me, as it might have been for others, Mbeki finally had to give recognition to the role of Black Consciousness in our struggle, and to its indispensability in what he called the "new struggle" for an African renaissance. We recognized in the terminology Mbeki used, in his reach for the great moments of achievement in Africa's past, and most of all in his acknowledgement that this would be a new kind of revolution. Mbeki seldom used Biko's name, just as he had not given credit to that brilliant black South African intellectual Pixley ka Isaka Seme, the one who in 1906 already had used that phrase, "the African Renaissance," when he called for "the regeneration of Africa," a "regeneration, moral and eternal."[58]

---

and again. E.g., Mbeki, *Africa*. An excellent example in which the call for a stronger and true engagement of Africa's intellectuals can be found in ch. 42, where Mbeki reiterates, "The call for Africa's renewal, for an African renaissance, is a call to rebellion." Mbeki, *Africa*, 300.

55. Boesak, *Tenderness of Conscience*, 1, 2.

56. Boesak, *Tenderness of Conscience*, 2.

57. Mbeki, *Africa*, 300.

58. Pixley ka Isaka Seme, "Regeneration of Africa," quoted in Karis and Carter, *From Protest to Challenge* 1:69–70. Like Mbeki would after him, Pixley ka Isaka Seme saw in the pyramids of Egypt

Selfless Revolutionaries

When Thabo Mbeki said, "As every revolution requires revolutionaries, so must the African renaissance have its militants and activists who will define the morrow that belongs to them in a way that will help our people restore our dignity," it was as a revolutionary, militant, nonviolent activist that I heard him, and *that* is what I responded to. It would take some years for most of us to realize just how much Mbeki's "revolution" differed from ours, or to what extent the ANC has succeeded in hijacking that revolution for its own political expediency.

But as Mbeki spoke, it was as if I had heard James Cone all over again as he, in 1984 already, reflecting on the Black Church—"where we have come from and where we were going"—spelt out his vision for a new social order.[59] That order, he wrote, must stress a universal black unity that should include an emphasis on the affirmation of the value of black history and culture. It must be decidedly and uncompromisingly non-sexist, because "a truly liberated social order cannot have men dominating women."[60] Then, in a bold step, certainly for America, albeit not for Martin Luther King Jr., Cone envisioned a new order that would be "democratic and socialist, including a Marxist critique of monopoly capitalism."[61] On this point, however, Mbeki's embrace of neoliberalism certainly caused too much of a gulf between him and the rest of us. Still, and which fits well with what Mbeki had in mind, "the new black perspective must be a global vision that includes the struggles of the poor in the Third World . . . There will be no freedom for anybody until all are set free."[62]

Here one can see how far Cone himself had come since 1969. He had learned from Martin Luther King Jr. and Malcolm X that the struggle for freedom is a global struggle. But Mamie Till Mobley, the mother of fourteen-year-old Emmett Till, brutally murdered by two white men in Mississippi in 1954, saw it even earlier. Defying

---

and Ethiopia the greatness of African civilizational achievement, "In such ruins Africa is like the golden sun, that, having sunk behind the Western horizon, still lays upon the world which he sustained and enlightened in his career."

59. See Cone, *For My People*, 202–7.

60. Cone, *For My People*, 203.

61. Cone, *For My People*, 204. This shows how far ahead of his time Cone was for Black America, (and most of the rest) but also how artificial, and superficial, our own debate on "white monopoly capital" has become as the essential truth and challenge of the reality and the argument were side-stepped, suppressed, or altogether ignored. It practically wilted under the severe pressure of the Gupta-guilt-by-association and public hatred in the self-serving political theatre that surrounded the Guptas, Zuma and what became known as "state capture." The catastrophic "state-capture" debacle during the Zuma reign was absolutely real and deserved the attention and vigorous opposition it got. That in the process, the equally disastrous reality of the power of white monopoly capital was not just underplayed but propagandized out of the equation, is a great pity. It is a short-term victory for what passes as justice in South Africa that has not brought us a single step closer to a resolution of the real problems such as our indefensible wealth-poverty gap, socio-economic strains, unrepentant racism, the severe challenges of social cohesion facing the country. Neither does it alleviate the tragic truth that South Africa's rulers remain beholden to the American Empire and its (white) surrogates here in South Africa. The election of billionaire Cyril Ramaphosa as president is not a solution for this deeper malady the country faces.

62. Cone, *For My People*, 20.

the pressure of the authorities, she kept her son's casket open. Not so that people would focus on her pain as a mother, but rather on the injustices done to her people, and that on a global scale: "The murder of my son has shown me that what happens to any of us *anywhere in the world* had better be the business of us all."[63] To complete the point: she left the coffin of her son open for the world to see, to be confronted, not so much as testimony of her suffering as a mother, but with the truth of white racism's apocalyptic violence as the deed was planned and done, white supremacy's evil and guilt as it was covered up, and white privilege's calculated complicity as the murderers were found "not guilty" by an all-white, all male jury in Mississippi.[64]

It should be to our eternal regret that what Mbeki called a "workable dream" has never come to fruition. It is probably true that the inherent contradictions—not least the tension between the idea of an African renaissance and the pre-negotiated preconditions set by the elite pacts between the ANC and South Africa's white rulers, and the ANC's embrace of neoliberal capitalism and its attending ideological demands—were simply unsustainable. These were contradictions created by an ANC too enthralled by the fractured benefits of an elite pact with white power in South Africa,[65] and in which Thabo Mbeki played a major role. What was simply unsustainable was the idea that an African renaissance could be birthed into, and sustained within, the life-threatening embrace of neoliberal capitalism. That fact alone may have made the plan implausible.

But something else was as important. In *Tenderness of Conscience*, I pointed out that ka Isaka Seme, in making his call so long ago, was clear that a renaissance of Africa could not simply be a political and economic project. It would not succeed if it was not at the same time a spiritual reawakening. It had to be "thoroughly spiritual and humanistic." Black Consciousness was such a movement, driven by a spirituality of politics with human dignity, equity, and social justice at its core. Pixley yearned for a renaissance that embraced not only the fact that African people are people who, though "not a strictly homogeneous race," see themselves as bound to "a common destiny," but even more "to a common duty to perform both towards God and to one another."[66] But as we saw in the Introduction, this was not language Mbeki was willing to embrace.

---

63. See, "Mamie Till." Emphasis mine. It is this global understanding of the struggle, which Mamie Till understood already then, and which Martin Luther King Jr., despite his sporadic connection with Albert Luthuli and his awareness of Africa's decolonization, came only to understand fully much later, around 1964, after his Nobel Peace Prize, that I am pleading for. It is also an understanding well grasped by the youth of the Black Lives Matter movement; see Boesak, *Pharaohs on Both Sides*, xvii, 52–53.

64. For further in-depth discussion of Mamie Till's stance within the broader context of women's agency and leadership in the struggles for freedom and justice and what I call "the Miriamic tradition," see Boesak, *Children of the Waters of Meribah*, ch. 3.

65. See Terreblanche, *Lost in Transformation*; Calland, *Anatomy of South Africa*; Bond, *Against Global Apartheid*; Bond, *Elite Transition*.

66. Pixley ka Isaka Seme, "Native Union," quoted in Karis and Carter, *From Protest to Challenge* 1:72.

However, it was not all Mbeki's fault. White intellectuals mostly already had what they wanted and got from the secret negotiated elite pact with the ANC (with Mbeki in the forefront), and consequently, in contrast to the white business community who looked toward expanding commerce, had little interest in the rest of the continent. While many black intellectuals responded well to the concept, most black intellectuals seemed doubtful.[67] It would not have been unreasonable for black South African intellectuals to wonder why we should get involved in an "African renaissance" seeing the very real racial fractiousness, unresolved social tensions, and unaddressed economic inequalities from the past drowning our present. Uncertain of the efficacy of the solutions proposed by an ANC drifting ever further away from the principles of the Freedom Charter, they were hesitant to wholeheartedly embrace this concept. Moreover, Mbeki's self-confessed "Thatcherism" surely cast a cloud of doubt over the plausibility of the whole exercise. An African Renaissance will surely not thrive if it is driven by such an exclusivist, exploitative, and destructive ideology as neoliberal capitalism.

But it is also true that it became a victim of internal political agendas, internecine ideological wars, petty jealousies, deadly envy, and a bent toward corruption and lethal political ambitions that were just beginning to show. Those, already present from the beginning of the new era, perhaps supremely exemplified by the notorious arms deal,[68] would come into full bloom in the Zuma era. Mbeki's vision was also a victim of an astonishing, if initially unacknowledged anti-intellectual syndrome, that had the gall to hide itself behind the legitimate desires and needs of our people and a pseudo intellectual defense of what it called a better understanding of the so-called national democratic revolution. This anti-intellectualism, like the distaste for the spirituality of politics, is ravaging South African politics.

There are, then, valid reasons for a critical assessment of Mbeki's tenure and it will surely come. Still, the African Renaissance project offered an excuse for something else entirely. This dream was trampled to dust by the dancing warrior-feet of those who, for reasons that had nothing to do with genuine revolution nor with the well-being of our people or the continent, wanted to make way for the great disaster that was to come, a calamity of their own making, and condoned by a people who, having lost their vision and with foolish bravado, seemed ready to perish. It is a catastrophe from which this country and our people will take years to recover.

But those of us from the prophetic church movement who heard and responded positively to Thabo Mbeki were not complete strangers to that call, as I have tried to show. Those documents I recalled were reflections on ongoing theological and political praxis. Some of us were scholars, but most of those involved in the struggle and in the formulation of those documents were not "sanctioned" by the academy, not

---

67. For a wide range of reactions from scholars, see Pillay and Pillay, "South African Intellectuals"; Mangu, "Democracy, African Intellectuals, and African Renaissance."

68. See Crawford-Browne, *Eye on the Money*.

"credentialed" as trusted social mouthpieces by the academy, the state, the media, or in many cases even by the hierarchical structures of our churches. In fact, the hostility of these sanctioned institutions was sometimes visceral. These intellectuals had authority because the people, in their struggle for liberation and justice, endowed them with it. Archbishop Tutu's wish, that the life and wisdom of Steve Biko would spark "a black renaissance" should be heard, heeded, and fulfilled. But if it does not heed Pixley's call for a moral, spiritual, and humanistic regeneration, it will die in its cradle. I stand by what I wrote in 2005:

> If our renaissance is made to be dependent on the sale of arms, which in turn depends on the creation and encouragement of fear, enmity, greed, distrust and death, and on the inhumane opportunism of global commerce which leaves no room for genuine concern centered on the people, but rejoices in get-rich-quick policies for the few, we are planting our tree by the side of a poisoned brook.[69]

I submit that it is the spiritual quality of our politics, more than anything else, that will help gift Africa and the world with that human face Biko dreamed of. South Africa gave so much hope to the world, I wrote then and believe still, not because we fought a successful violent revolution, but because we brought apartheid to its knees through our persistent struggle, our willingness to sacrifice, and the extraordinary moral courage of our people. What captivated the world during all those years was not our military successes, but our spiritual strength.[70]

Theology, Liberation, and the "Elusive Public"

Since the mid-1990s, Public Theology has become a fixture in the academy as well as an industry, much like our reconciliation and forgiveness projects. Worldwide, it seems, it is the push button for financial support for academic centers, seminars, conferences, and projects. According to the website of one fairly famous Centre for Theology and Public Issues, public theology is theology:

- One, that focuses on issues of public concern;
- Two, on issues that escape the public eye;
- Three, a theology that helps to shape debate and policy formation;
- Four, it is not about protecting the interests of the church but about drawing on the resources, insights, and compassionate values of the Christian faith to contribute to the welfare of society.

---

69. See Boesak, *Tenderness of Conscience*, 70.
70. See Boesak, *Tenderness of Conscience*, 70.

The "issues of concern" include "faith and justice," by which they mean "prison reform"; "faith and environment"; and "faith and good governance," understood as "the public good, equality, fairness, and social justice." They speak of "faith and society," which includes human dignity and the wellbeing of children.[71]

I do not consider myself a public theologian. I am not contesting public theology's right to exist, and these are all worthy goals. To me, however, it is clear: public theology is not liberation theology. Public theology is the child of the white, Eurocentric academy, offered as a substitute for liberation theology. Public theology may theorize about the people and their revolutions as a matter of public interest, but as far as I can see, it has no desire to be in the heart of those revolutions, organizing, supporting, persuading, as liberation theology is compelled to be, as I shall argue in chapter 7. As a liberation theologian, I do have some concerns. In an incisive piece, Tinyiko Maluleke has raised the same concerns as he speaks of "the elusive public of public theology."[72] At the core of his argument, framed much in the way I would do it myself, is his observation that the idea that public theology can address the anger in South African society without a theory of resistance as found in liberation theologies is not sustainable. Maluleke is right: the first question to ask is the question about public theology's public. Public theology speaks of "the public," but I have not seen serious discussion on the question: Which public? Whose public? Is it the public which consists of the dominant class? Is the public the public as perceived by the academy? Is there any serious debate about the public as those in our societies who have been robbed of their consent, their voice, and their agency? Is the public those who observe and theorize about the victims of empire, or is the public the victims of empire who speak for themselves as they struggle against empire?[73]

The question of who says what to which public is not new and remains pertinent. In the Bible, in 1 Kings 4:29, we read that God gave King Solomon "very great wisdom, discernment, and breadth of understanding as vast as the sand on the seashore," so much that Solomon's wisdom "surpassed the wisdom of all the people of the east, and all the wisdom of Egypt." But who wrote that? Solomon's priests and royal scribes, sons of Israel's newly established nobility, on the king's payroll, serving at his pleasure and seeking his favor. And other privileged and powerful men like them, claiming divine authority, included those words in what we know today as the Bible, the "Word of God." However, if we asked the thousands of Israelites, and the subjugated peoples Solomon pressed into forced labor to build his palaces and that magnificent temple to satisfy his lust for grandeur while their lands lay neglected and their families suffered

71. See "What Is Public Theology?"

72. Maluleke, "Reflections and Resources."

73. In a meticulous piece, South African theologian Dirkie Smit provides an excellent discussion of the issue in question in his analysis of Habermas's understanding of the matter. However, he does not reach beyond the philosophical framework set by Habermas, with no reference at all to the questions being raised here. See Smit, "What Does 'Public' Mean?," 11–46.

hunger, we would hear and see something entirely different. We would learn to see the bent backs, the calloused hands, the tired faces streaked with dust and sweat before we see the magnificence of those buildings. And we would ask: Who reaps the glory, and who pays the price? Or, if we asked the one thousand women whose lives he cut short and rendered meaningless because he made them wives and concubines, bartered for political expediency, and then left to languish in useless luxury, we should hear very different views on Solomon's famed wisdom.[74] From the dusty building sites and luxurious quarters of the harem both, we would hear the cries caught so poignantly by the psalmist (Ps 13:1), and the prophet Habakkuk (Hab 1:2). And we would remember Calvin's persuasive argument that in those cries it is as if God hears Godself cry.[75]

Leo X, according to historian Barbara Tuchman "undoubtedly the most profligate who ever sat on the Papal throne," was much admired for his largesse by his Renaissance constituents, who dubbed his reign "the Golden Age."[76] But, she writes, "it was golden for the coins that rained into their pockets from commissions, continuous festivities and entertainment, the rebuilding of St. Peter's and city improvement."[77] Those admirers and sycophants were Leo's public; the nobility, the upper clergy, the bishops and cardinals who called themselves "Excellency," and "Princes of the Church." But where did the money for these extravagancies come from? "From no magic source," Tuchman writes, "but from ever-more extortionate and unscrupulous levies by papal agents" wrung from the already-empty purses of ordinary people, the poor and the destitute whose need for succor and whose faith in the church had been so bitterly and ruthlessly betrayed. *That* public did not fawn and bow down in admiration. If they were bending down, they were bent down by the weight of the holy oppression and the sanctified exploitation the Pope and his public had pressed on them. So the questions remain urgent: Whose public? Which public?

Closer to home, the Western Cape's drought and water restrictions have seriously impacted the public. Even as we have had more rain this winter than in the three winters previously, water restrictions remain and the certain calamities of climate change

---

74. 1 Kgs 4:6 betrays a different and grim reality: "Ahishar was in charge of the palace; and Adoniram was in charge of the forced labor." "Indeed, 'forced labor' accurately describes the program of state slavery in Egypt from which Yahweh emancipated Israel in the Exodus. To find such an officer in Solomon's cabinet is a measure of how drastically Solomon has abandoned Israelite tradition [of egalitarianism]." See Brueggemann, 1 & 2 Kings, 58. Chapter 4 states that "the people of Judah and Israel ate and drank and were happy." The following verses overflow with praise for Solomonic opulence and extravagance. But, Brueggemann warns, this celebratory state of affairs concerned only *some* of the people. The upper classes were talking about themselves. The text expresses a "self-congratulatory innocence," however, for "the seeds of destruction that come with self-indulgence are already sown." Brueggemann, 1 & 2 Kings, 62. The anger of the other public, those at the bottom of Solomonic society, who "served Solomon all the days of his life," here completely ignored, will burst into revolt by ch. 12, bringing an ignominious end to the "united kingdom."

75. See Calvin, *Commentaries* 1:2.

76. See Tuchman, *March of Folly*, 126.

77. Tuchman, *March of Folly*, 9.

still hang over our heads. Unlike US President Donald Trump and his capitalist marauders, South Africans do not have the luxury of denying the dire consequences of human selfishness, greed, and carelessness on the environment, and the wrath of nature upon our feigned ignorance and willfulness will bear no excuses.

Recently, investigative journalist and indefatigable environmental-justice fighter Naomi Klein has argued for more honest specificity. It is not only human frailty and error in general that has caused our climate crisis, she writes, it is the unbridled capitalist greed of the few.[78] In Cape Town, people in the wealthy and middle-class suburbia are deeply concerned and sometimes angered because the lush gardens are now dusty and brown and ugly, and the worry is whether the next target might be the golf courses. But in the townships with rotted, neglected, and unattended leaking water pipes, many have been suffering under excessively high water rates for years. In squatter camps where there is perhaps one tap for every one hundred families, people argue that they have *always* had a water crisis. It was, however, ignored by the powers that be because the poor do not matter except at election time. So which issues escape which public's eye? Whose anger matters more?[79]

Is there in public theology serious acknowledgment of, and engagement with, the existence of oppression, exploitation, denigration, and exclusion of the vast majorities across the globe? Our societies do not exist in a void, but within the orbit of empire. Controlled in horrific measure by empire, they are subject to imperial punishment through a skewed and exploitative global economy, far-reaching political control, and arbitrary military interventions through endless wars, the goals of which are not combatting terror but political hegemony, regime change, cultural domination, control and exploitation of resources, and mind-blowing profits. Is there serious discussion of the imperialist nature of our global realities with the intention of resistance? In other words, is public theology also an anti-imperialist theology? I have not seen it.

According to Gramsci, the intellectual must know that at the heart of society's ills is the domination of a ruling elite and its embrace of capitalism. He is right, of course. Still, we have learned that the ravages of neoliberal capitalism come in many guises. We must take into account its workings on the particularities of race, gender, and sexual orientation, all of which are not incidental but the daily manifestations of a relentless war upon the poor and vulnerable. The poor and vulnerable are not collateral damage, they are the direct targets of exploitation and sometimes annihilation exercised with a ruthlessness that stuns the mind. They are the targets of a perpetual class war.

---

78. Klein argues, "Beyond capitalism humankind is fully capable of thriving within ecological limits." See Klein, "Capitalism Killed Our Climate Momentum."

79. Even if rains during the winter months are enough to break the drought, in reality the crisis for the poor remains. Conditions in the squatter camps and black townships remain the same, rain or no rain, and these still need to be addressed as a matter of political *and* moral urgency.

The basic assumption, the website says, is that "religion still matters." That is true, but the same question arises, and which we will address again: Which religion? Whose religion? What kind of religion? I do not have in mind the contrasting claims of say, Christianity and Islam, or Buddhism and Hinduism. Liberation theologians are bound to the still invaluable distinctions drawn by Frederick Douglass in 1846:

> I love the religion of our blessed Savior . . . which comes from above, in the wisdom of God which is first pure, then peaceable, gentle . . . without partiality and without hypocrisy . . . I love that religion . . . It is because I love this religion that I hate the slave-holding, the woman-whipping, the mind-darkening, the soul-destroying religion that exists in America . . . Loving the one I must hate the other; holding to one I must reject the other.[80]

I am speaking of the waves of Christian neo-fundamentalism imported from the US washing over Africa and much of the Global South with its toxic neo-colonialist package deal of scriptural selectivity, presented as "biblical inerrancy," violent homophobia, patriarchal power, and anti-justice agenda. Its justification of war and violence in the name of Jesus, its religious exclusivism and Christian chauvinism, coupled with unbridled political ambition in its so-called dominion theology, and its prosperity gospel grounded in the embrace of and enslavement to capitalist consumerist ideology. In its neo-colonialist alliances with capitalist power and the global media, it certainly is dragging Africa, its churches and its societies, to the edge of a disaster every bit as devastating as colonialism. This is the new heresy that, like the heresy of apartheid, has to be named and combatted.[81]

Pseudo-innocence is the death of intellectual integrity. "Good governance," "the common good," "democracy," "civil society," and "the public" are not innocent concepts. "Prison reform," for example, is meaningless without engaging the reality of the prison-industrial complex with racialized capitalism at its very heart.[82] While public theology is about bringing to bear the "virtues" of the Christian faith on public debate and policy making, liberation theology sees as its task the questioning of those "virtues" if they do not serve to rip the veil of complacency off the ugly face of imperialist, neoliberalist, capitalist reality. It is about joining the people in their struggles for freedom and justice, in embodied solidarity and critical engagement, knowing, with Bonhoeffer, that when Christ calls a person, he calls them to die; and with Martin Luther King Jr., that if we do not have something to die for, we are not fit to live. And yes, sometimes that much is at stake.

---

80. Douglass, *My Bondage and My Freedom*.
81. See McGee, *Brand® New Theology*.
82. See the searing analysis of the history and realities of incarceration in America as "a new racial caste system" in Alexander, *New Jim Crow*.

The Theologian as Permanent Persuader

The world of imperial domination in which we live and do our intellectual work today is a world, to say it with Helmut Gollwitzer, "shaken by deadly convulsions."[83] The combined wealth of the world's richest 1 percent has overtaken that of the other 99 percent in 2016. In 2016, more than half of the wealth in the world was in the hands of just 62 individuals, more than is owned by an entire 3.5 billion of the world's population. But that quickly became old news. By January 2017, Oxfam reported that the situation was much worse: just eight white men own as much wealth as half the world's population. One in nine people do not have enough to eat and more than one billion people live on less than $1.25 a day. As we will discuss in more detail in chapters 6 and 8, the Oxfam 2020 Report states that the inequalities in the world are now out of control.

In January 2017, the United States and the world witnessed a spectacle many were convinced they would never see, and all over the world misogynists, patriarchalists, and homophobes of every stripe, creed, and color; white supremacists and unashamed racists, from the New Nazis in Europe to the revived apartheid defenders in South Africa, and new apartheid creators in Israel arose emboldened.[84] The disastrous consequences of that election are now plain for all to see. Pointedly, and poignantly, for the first time perhaps Americans are experiencing in their own country what their country has been doing to other countries the world over. From Little Rock, Arkansas, Circuit Judge Wendell Griffen, who is also a Baptist pastor, writes after President Trump has announced that the US would withdraw its support from the World Health Organization. His words reflect the bitter realization many Americans do not care to avoid any longer.

> The unpleasant truth is that Donald Trump's presidency is both a curse on the United States and a curse from the United States on the wider world. Thanks to the election of 2016, the security of our nation, sanity of our world, strength of U.S. armed forces and our NATO allies, stability of our economy, tranquility of our society, and health and welfare of our population are threatened by one reality: the President of the United States is a vicious idiot. We are cursed. Welcome to the "new normal."[85]

Griffen is not the only one to use such harsh words. Almost one year before, journalist Charles Pierce, writing in *Esquire* magazine, saw it coming and likened Donald Trump to Mary Shelly's Frankenstein:

---

83. See Gollwitzer, *Way to Life*, xii.

84. I wrote this in Boesak, *Pharaohs on Both Sides*, ch. 7, within the context of the beginning of the Trump era. Today the situation is unquestionably worse, as we shall see in ch. 6.

85. See Griffen, "We Are Cursed."

> The president has a predator's gift for bringing out the native self-destruction in people for his own profit. What he has done in the last three years has been his masterwork in this regard. He doesn't plague himself with doubt about what he's creating around him. He is proud of his monster. He glories in its anger and its destruction and, while he cannot imagine its love, he believes with all his heart in its rage. He is Frankenstein without conscience.[86]

The organic intellectual, because of her deep connections with those who are the victims of these monstrous policies, will be sensitive to these realities and their impact on the lives of the most vulnerable in our society. The organic intellectual will not be distracted by the tweets with which Trump causes so much consternation and so much condescending—but misconceived—amusement while under that cover he does real damage to LGBTQI+ persons, women, mothers with babies, babies without mothers, and the earth. She would rather engage the evil system that produced him, and that system's capacity to produce yet more Trumps.

The organic intellectual will look at our institutions of higher learning and be aware of the perils of our untransformed institutions as "eugenic institutions," as Moroccan scholar Mohamed Ezroura describes them:

> Eugenic institutions producing particular individuals thinking according to particular [Eurocentric] mind-frames, and as a source of a particular form of knowledge that is highly shaped by Western (Anglo/American) textbooks and teaching methodologies.[87]

This mind-frame and these epistemologies, Ezroura argues, produce an "enslaved consciousness that carries fatal consequences."[88] The organic intellectual will not rest until that "enslaved consciousness" becomes a liberated, and liberating, consciousness.

In these times of manufactured consent, manufactured contentment, and revolutionary fervor, the organic intellectual will not only hear the words and observe the actions of the powerful and privileged, but will want to understand what lies *behind* those words and actions, as she will understand the difference between peacemaking, appeasement, and pacification. In a previous publication, I have raised the matter of the internal debates in South Africa around the issues of Africanness and African identity. Three years later, the debates, in the alarming solidifying of ethnic nationalisms, seem to have intensified. In those paragraphs, I called those ethnic contestations "quite scandalous."[89] South Africans, so far from freedom still, I wrote then, should not be deluded by these spurious debates. We should immediately discern Ezroura's "enslaved consciousness" and expose the false assumptions upon which it rests. While it is true that open, public discourse, with full acknowledgement of how these debates

---

86. Pierce, "This Was a Fascist Rally Down To its Bones."
87. See Ezroura, "Englishness."
88. Ezroura, "Englishness," 2.
89. See Boesak, *Pharaohs on Both Sides*, ch. 7.

reflect the skewed racialized politics of both colonial, apartheid, and post-apartheid South Africa are clearly necessary, one should not be unaware of the deeper political and historical issues concealed here. Apart from the fact that these debates are based on "race," not recognizing it as a political and social construct for the purposes of manipulation and control, these constructs also conceal something more sinister. So effectively used by the apartheid regime, they have been equally politically employed by the ANC's "Black and in particular African" policies after the ANC had sought to destroy the political legacy of the Black Consciousness movement by deliberately reinstating apartheid's racial categorization after their return from exile. Unsurprisingly, these are now the chickens come home to roost.

Neither should they be distracted by the question of how racist this is (even though it surely is), but should rather pay attention to the question: Why this debate *now*, and whose interests does it serve? Who, in this moment of national engagement of the all-important questions of decolonization, Africanization, and authentic Africanity, benefits from this useless distraction? But also, and importantly, what goes unnoticed? This, for instance: the pandemic that gender-based violence has become; the struggle for justice women have still not won and the fight for dignity and inclusion LGBTQI+ persons are far too much left on their own to fight. The struggle for the land as embedded injustice in our otherwise praiseworthy Constitution has just begun. The growing chasm between rich and poor, or the pervasive mediocrity and paucity of honor of our politics. All this, while we pay so much attention to the utter stupidity of whether people who are part descendants of the First Nations of South Africa and part-descendants of its slave populations brought from different parts of the world at the beginning of the colonization project are truly Africans? Why is the historical fact of the creole nature of all South Africans, beginning with our DNA, of no account? Why is the debate raging among the descendants of indigenous communities while the president, at the centenary celebrations of the *Afrikaner Broederbond*, an organization still deeply rooted in its toxic, white supremacist, apartheid soil, assures *them* that they have nothing to be concerned about—they *are* Africans? Why is the historic de-Africanization of South Africa's indigenous children, as Patric Tariq Mellet—one of South Africa's true, organic intellectuals—in his brilliant analysis calls it, including over the last twenty-five years, and the confrontation of real historical experiences of *all* Africans, especially slavery, not the proper political discussion? These detractions only serve the heirs of imperialism and colonialism in South Africa and their adopted black children.

In the current struggles for authentic Africanity, the decolonization of our minds, academic studies, and of the African church—intellectuals especially must be well-girded. Their role is crucial. It is a role that calls for the courage to be rebels—in the pulpit and at the lectern—against old and new tyrannies, from imperialist domination and post-colonial treachery to political backwardness such as heteronormativity and patriarchalism. And the goal still is to make our people the authors of their own liberation. And as I pleaded fifteen years ago,

> We must not make the imperfect our yardstick, nor the mediocre our consolation. We must not measure our progress by the comfort of the rich, but by the character of the justice we do to the poor and vulnerable. Judgement on our walk to our God-ordained destiny must not be taken from the privileged or the pampered circles of the powerful, but from the powerless, those whom Jesus calls "the least of these." The authority with which we rule in this country must not be derived from the approval of the mighty and the boastful, but must rest upon the hopes of the poor, the ones of unimpressive proportions, in whom the living God has invested the hope for life, and where our hope for life is to be found.[90]

And yes, in all of this our teaching, preaching, and actions will be a form of protest. But we will keep in mind that Adam Small, almost fifty years ago, warned us to be careful that protest does not become a form of begging.[91] He was right: protest, without the framework of fundamental analysis, fundamental understanding, fundamental transformation, and total commitment to the struggle for freedom will always be a form of begging. So we will not beg. But we will be rebels at the lectern and in the pulpit and if necessary in the streets until that different world becomes a reality. To bring it home completely, it is perhaps to Steve Biko we should give the last word here:

> In order to achieve real action you must yourself be a living part of Africa and of her thought; you must be an element of that popular energy which is entirely called forth for the freeing, the progress and the happiness of Africa. There is no place outside that fight for the artist or for the intellectual who is not himself concerned with, and completely at one with the people in that great battle of Africa and of suffering humanity.[92]

---

90. See Boesak, *Tenderness of Conscience*, 240–41.
91. Small, "Blackness versus Nihilism," 37.
92. Biko, *I Write What I Like*, 35.

3

"Who Will Rescue Me from This Body of Death?"

Black Theology, Black Consciousness, and the Quest for Meaningful, Humanized Consciousness

"A Systemic Negation and a Furious Determination"

"That imperialism which today is fighting against a true liberation of mankind," wrote Frantz Fanon, "leaves in its wake here and there tinctures of decay which we must search out and mercilessly expel from our land and our spirits."[1] We should note Fanon's phrasing here. John Calvin, we saw, insisted that the longings for freedom, justice, and dignity are "implanted" in us by God. That is, as the creation of this liberator God, freedom, justice, and dignity should be our "natural" state of being. Our being human all by itself should constitute it. Having to fight for it is, in that sense, an unnatural state of being. So Fanon's wording is correct. It is not us fighting against imperialism in the first place. It is imperialism fighting against the true liberation of humankind. Imperialism, in its boundless arrogance and overreaching hubris, is trying to turn on its head, alienate, and annihilate what the Creator had meant to be essential to human existence, and human beingness. Our struggles are so intense because the transgressions against the intentions of God—Calvin also speaks of the *rights* of God—are so enormous.[2]

Fanon was also one of the first to insist so fiercely on the totalitarian—by which I mean not only completely draconian, but also wholly comprehensive—nature of colonization and the colonizing presence. Speaking of Algeria, he wrote,

> In Algeria, there is not simply the domination but the decision to the letter not to occupy anything more [less?] than the sum total of the land. The Algerians,

1. Fanon, *Wretched of the Earth*, 249.
2. Calvin, *Commentaries* 1:87.

> the veiled women, the palm trees and the camels make up the landscape, the natural background to the human presence of the French.[3]

What Fanon saw in Algeria was, and remains, *ipso facto* true of any colonized situation. The process is all-pervasive, pernicious, deliberate, and relentless. It is true not only for the colonized population as a whole, its cultures, its religion(s), its ways of life. It preys on the particular, seeks to conquer the individual, to occupy the body, break the spirit, to own the soul. And if it cannot own it, to destroy it. In this situation, the colonized subject shall have to fight hard to create the necessary space for themselves to affirm and hold on to their humanity. In this respect, colonization is the true child of imperialism. It is possessed of and driven by a spirit of conquest and omnivorous acquisitiveness that leaves nothing to chance. Hence, we must, with Fanon, "search it out and mercilessly expel" not only from our lands, but also from "our spirits."[4]

In the eyes of the colonizer, nothing is sacred. Even in the music created by black people to rejoice in their humanity and their uniqueness, to rise above the onslaughts on that humanity, they will not find unthreatened refuge. In the United States, among the African slaves, their music, blues, jazz, and gospel, was such a place of refuge, survival, and resistance. Being a place of rejoicing in their uniqueness, the world of black music would also be the precious place of an alternative and empowered consciousness. The colonizer, intimating the threat, would encroach upon and seek to invade, or at least belittle, that is to say, disempower that space. "In their eyes," Fanon warns, "jazz should only be the despairing, broken-down nostalgia of an old Negro who is trapped between five glasses of whiskey, the curse of his race, and the racial hatred of the white men."[5] Imperialism's total onslaught was relentless, its aim was total destruction, and if that failed, total appropriation. They never conquered black music, however. It is then within the full context of this cultural, political, social, and psychological totalitarianism of coloniality that the need for an alternative, transformative consciousness arises, not simply as a form of protest, but as resistance.

Fanon raises these issues in a discussion under the rubric, "Colonial War and Mental Disorders."[6] He discusses a number of cases that he had treated and determined that the psychological damage was akin to severe trauma:

> It seems to us that in the cases here chosen the events giving rise to the disorder are chiefly the bloodthirsty and pitiless atmosphere, the generalization of

---

3. Fanon, *Wretched of the Earth*, 250.
4. Fanon, *Wretched of the Earth*, 249.
5. Fanon, *Wretched of the Earth*, 243.
6. Fanon, *Wretched of the Earth*, 250. On 250–92, Fanon documents case after case and shows how truly devastating this "Apocalypse" is. He writes, "The patient does not seem able to release his nervous tension. He is constantly tense, *waiting between life and death*." Fanon, *Wretched of the Earth*, 292. Emphasis mine.

inhuman practices, and the firm impression that people have of being caught up in a veritable Apocalypse.[7]

This situation does not only cause collective trauma, it becomes intensely personal, causing calamitous inner conflicts:

> Because it is a systemic negation of the other person and a furious determination to deny the other person all attributes of humanity, colonialism forces the people it dominates to ask themselves the question constantly, "In reality, who am I?"[8]

It stands to reason that if the colonizing experience was like "a veritable Apocalypse," it would take considerable and deliberate effort to fight the debilitating effects of it, and to overcome the consequences. The reality today is still one of deep, abiding, global coloniality, one of imperialist domination that permeates and seeks to control every sphere of life.

It is for all these reasons that in South Africa, where colonization has spawned apartheid, one of the most vicious historical instances of systematized, racialized hatred, exploitation, and oppression, the Black Consciousness philosophy was experienced as so powerful, so life-changing, so liberating, and was embraced so wholeheartedly by so many. And with regard to apartheid, Fanon was not wasting a single word: it was indeed a "systemic negation" of black personhood, dignity, and worthiness; a "furious determination" to establish and maintain white supremacy, white superiority, and white power. Those "tinctures of decay" have proved to be much more stubborn than even Fanon could have imagined.[9] The "cleansing power" of violence would prove to be a poor cure for these maladies. "Tinctures," as a "slight trace of something" may not even be the right word. Imperialism is no lingering odor, even of decay. And "here and there" must not lead us into temptation. It may be altogether too mild an expression here. As Fanon well knew, and said so in multiple ways, it is a toxic, pernicious, idolatrous presence, a matrix of power, whose lust for sacrifices from the poor and vulnerable has remained ceaseless and unquenchable.

Africans in America were not colonized as we were, but they knew the apocalypse was upon them from the first moment hostile hands were laid upon them to take them to some slave ship and hence to some foreign land. And they knew it through enslavement and Jim Crow and systemic, deliberately structured racist oppression in myriad and unspeakable ways until this very moment. James Baldwin was explicit:

> Negroes in this country—and Negroes do not, strictly or legally speaking, exist in any other—are taught really to despise themselves from the moment their eyes open on the world. This world is white and they are black. White people

---

7. Fanon, *Wretched of the Earth*, 250.
8. Fanon, *Wretched of the Earth*, 250.
9. Fanon, *Wretched of the Earth*, 249.

hold the power, which means that they are superior to blacks (intrinsically, that is: God decreed it so), and the world has innumerable ways of making this difference known and felt and feared. Long before the Negro child perceives this difference, and even longer before he understands it, he has begun to react to it, he has begun to be controlled by it. Every effort made by the child's elders to prepare him for a fate from which they cannot protect him causes him secretly, in terror, to begin to await, without knowing that he is doing so, his mysterious and inexorable punishment. He must be "good" not only in order to please his parents and not only to avoid being punished by them; behind their authority stands another, nameless and impersonal, infinitely harder to please, and bottomlessly cruel.[10]

In a passage that reminds us strongly of Biko's analysis of fear as "a determining factor in South Africa," Baldwin writes, but makes it intensely and almost frighteningly personal, chillingly echoing what African Americans call "the talk" black parents must have with their sons, and increasingly, with their daughters too:

The fear that I heard in my father's voice, for example, when he realized that I really *believed* I could do anything a white boy could do, and had every intention of proving it, was not at all like the fear I heard when one of us was ill or had fallen down the stairs or strayed too far from the house. It was another fear, a fear that the child, in challenging the white world's assumptions, was putting himself in the path of destruction.[11]

Perhaps nothing has expressed that furious determination more than the relentless violence visited upon black people, especially through lynching, an act in which black people, especially black men, were kidnapped, beaten, tortured, dismembered, and burned alive in full view of often large crowds of white people. The spate of murders of blacks, Latinos/as, Native Americans, particularly young men, but also many women, by police, security personnel, and civilians in the United States has risen alarmingly since the murder of Trayvon Martin in Sanford, Florida, on February 26, 2012. Black theologians have not only seen these murders as modern lynchings. They have, quite appropriately, likened them to the crucifixion of Jesus. James Cone has written movingly about this,[12] and so has, among others, Womanist theologian Kelly Brown Douglas.[13]

In a well-argued and persuasive piece on the historical reality of American fascism coming into full bloom under Donald Trump, American literature scholar Sarah Churchwell calls to mind the last "old-fashioned" lynching in America. In a passage

---

10. Baldwin, *Fire Next Time*, 26.
11. See Baldwin, *Fire Next Time*, 26–27.
12. See Cone, *Cross and the Lynching Tree*.
13. See Douglas, *Stand Your Ground*.

chillingly reminiscent of the Gospels' description of the arrest, trial, and crucifixion of Jesus, she writes,

> One of the last, and most horrific, public lynchings in America took place in October 1934, in the Florida Panhandle, where a crowd of as many as 5,000 gathered to watch what had been advertised hours earlier in the local press. Claude Neal was burned and castrated, had his genitals stuffed into his mouth, and was forced to tell his torturers that he enjoyed their taste. After he was finally dragged to his death behind a car, his mutilated corpse was urinated upon by the crowds, and then hung from the Marianna Courthouse.[14]

As I write this, my intrepid friends from the Samuel DeWitt Proctor Conference in the United States, who through their prophetic ministry keeps the world informed about these things, sent no less than three statements reacting to the then most recent lynchings. On February 23, 2020, in Brunswick, Georgia, Armaud Arbery, while jogging, was hunted down and shot to death by two white men, father and son. The incident remained obscure (which means the police were told, but did nothing about it) until video of the shooting was released more than two months later. I now have in front of me two more statements regarding the killings of a young woman, Breonna Taylor, in her home in Louisville, Kentucky, and of two young men in Indianapolis, Indiana, the place I called home while teaching in the US, all of them murdered by police, and all of them in a single week. The terrorizing of what Kelly Brown Douglas calls "the crucified class" seems to have no end.

Reflecting on the ongoing events after George Floyd's murder, Princeton University's Keeanga-Yamahtta Taylor writes of the long history of police brutality in the US. "African-Americans have been demonstrating against police abuse and violence since the Chicago riots of 1919. The first riot directly in response to police abuse occurred in 1935, in Harlem." She continues,

> In 1951, a contingent of African-American activists, armed with a petition titled "We Charge Genocide," tried to persuade the United Nations to decry the U.S. government's murder of black people. Their petition read: "Once the classic method of lynching was the rope. Now it is the policeman's bullet. To many an American the police are the government, certainly its most visible representative. We submit that the evidence suggests that the killing of Negroes has become police policy in the United States and that police policy is the most practical expression of government policy."[15]

---

14. See Churchwell, "American Fascism." For the full presentation of her argument, see Churchwell, *Behold, America*. The groundbreaking work of that intrepid nineteenth-century journalist and fighter for human rights Ida B. Wells remains required reading on this topic. See Wells-Barnett, *On Lynchings*; see also Bay, *To Tell the Truth Freely*.

15. See Taylor, "How Do We Change America?"

Keeping this in mind helps us to remember two things. First, that George Floyd's murder was only the spark amidst smoldering embers that never really died. Second, that police violence employed against black people is "the most practical," indeed, the most direct and revealing expression of government policy. For this reason, the call to defund and dismantle the police forces as they function today is so important and should be set as a litmus test for government's willingness to engage in meaningful transformation. The rope of the lynching mob is now indeed the police officer's bullet, or the bullet of any white civilian who will claim that merely seeing a black person in a space they regard as "theirs" makes them fear for their lives. And it does not always come from the barrel of a handgun. America's insane militarizing of its police forces and its equally insane gun laws have seen to that.

The reasons why lynching was so popular and deemed so necessary since the days of African enslavement in America never really stopped, and its return in gruesome public display in the first decades of this century with such a vengeance has all to do with the workings of white power, white supremacy, white privilege, white impunity, and white insecurity. Writes Brown Douglas:

> Lynching is about [white] power standing its ground against anyone it deems a threat. It is meant to be a deadly reminder to a suspect community of its "proper" place in society. It is about the protection of Anglo-Saxon white supremacy. It attempts to safeguard the "wages of whiteness."[16]

The so-called *Willie Lynch Letter*, purporting to be an address by a notorious slave-breaker to the slave-holding community in Virginia on Christmas Day, 1712, may be helpful here. It is a highly disturbing piece of writing: its words as brutal as the methods it prescribes. There is no evidence that this is a historical document. Most likely, it was written during the 1970s and, in fact, may have been intended as satire, meant to entertain a certain kind of audience with a certain kind of mindset, even as it betrays the mindset of its author. If it is indeed satire—and the fact that it is presented as a "Christmas message" might credit this—then its viciousness is all the more disturbing, though perhaps no less vicious or disturbing than the murder of the innocents described in the Advent story in Matthew's Gospel (Matt 2:16–18). It may have been misread by some individuals and published as "historical account," or it may have been published to bolster some political argument or sentiment. Perhaps it simply was the outpouring of the dark desires the author somehow wished could be (turned into) reality.

Satire or no, the brutality of slavery and the treatment of enslaved Africans, like the lynchings, are indisputable historical facts.[17] The *Lynch Letter* portrays colonialist

---

16. Douglas, *Stand Your Ground*, 173.

17. For South Africa see, e.g., De Kock, *Those in Bondage*, 146–97; and more recent, Mellet, *Lie of 1652*, 233–34. For the US see, Baptist, *Half Has Never Been Told*; Johnson, *Soul by Soul*. An article in the *Smithsonian Magazine* on Louisiana's Whitney Plantation Historic District probably illustrates this more vividly than anything else. See Keller, "Inside America's Auschwitz."

ways of working and thinking that Africans in America and blacks in South Africa find immediately recognizable. The breaking of the body and the capturing, and control, of the mind is exactly the experience of oppressed indigenous people in South Africa from the days of colonization and the introduction of slavery to the Apartheid era. So while the *Lynch Letter* is useless as a historical document, it is highly enlightening as a commentary on nineteenth- and twentieth-century race relations, as well as between racism and capitalism, by an unknown late-twentieth-century writer.[18] As such, it illustrates well the argument I am trying to make here.

In this letter, which I choose to read as satire, Willie Lynch traveled to Virginia to explain the logic of his philosophy and methods in a message to white Virginians. The "wages of whiteness," it turned out, would be enormous.[19] Lynch spoke of immediate actions for immediate benefit. He also outlined a long-range economic plan to make slavery as profitable as possible for which not only physical brutality, but also insight into psychology, was necessary. Lynch presented his three-step plan as a scientific process for breaking slaves, with an eye to secure their subjugation for generations. A more cold-blooded recipe for sheer terror to ensure white supremacy and power will be hard to find. We follow the steps as Lynch presented them.

As the public discussions around these twenty-first century lynchings grow, and liking it to the brutal murders of black people today becomes more and more common (even on the floor of the US Congress), we should remain vigilant. It is important not to let the familiarity that often-used language brings dull its real meaning. When establishment politics, their media propaganda models, and their echo-chamber punditry become comfortable with it, we should be on our guard. All too often, what becomes politicized becomes banal. The sacred becomes mere platitude, pearls thrown before swine. The context of its origination should not only always be uppermost in our mind; it should be the proper framework of every mention. While Willie Lynch did not actually exist, he should be in every discussion, for he represents what we are morally bound to keep in mind.

Step one, the male slave:

> Take the meanest and most restless nigger, strip him of his clothes in front of the remaining male niggers, the female, and the nigger infant, tar and feather him, tie each leg to a different horse faced in opposite directions, set him afire and beat both horses to pull him apart in front of the remaining niggers.[20]

Step two, the female slave:

> Take the female and run a series of tests on her to see if she will submit to your desires willingly. Test her in every way, because she is the most important factor for good economics. If she shows any sign of resistance in submitting

---

18. See Gonaver, *Peculiar Institution*.
19. See Goza, *America's Unholy Ghosts*, 100–2.
20. Lynch, *Letter*, 30.

completely to your will, do not hesitate to use the bullwhip on her to extract that last bit of resistance out of her.[21]

Goza comments,

> In case Lynch's audience didn't realize that this was a call for white men to rape black women, Lynch clarifies the need for "many drops of good, white blood, and putting them into as many nigger women as possible, varying the drops by the various tone that you want, and then letting them breed with each other until another cycle of color appears as you desire."[22]

This is sheer, unadulterated evil. Even just reading the words is already Fanon's "veritable Apocalypse," let alone having lived the experience as countless enslaved Africans certainly had to do. Note also how the repeated words "desire" and "want" and "submitting [to your will]," like vile drippings from his lips, express the lust for domination and acquisitiveness that is white patriarchal supremacy's very nature. Lynch cannot help himself. He is the high priest at racist capitalism's altar, calling on Moloch for the blessings of the highest capitalist gains.

Lynch's three-step recipe is well known and commented on. But for the purposes of our argument here, I want to draw special attention to the third step. Foundational to Lynch's whole plan is the capturing of the mind of the slave, to sow distrust, envy, and suspicion amongst the slaves themselves, set them against each other, always in competition for the approval of the slave owner. So before anything else, Lynch sets the frame, and here it is not the viciousness of the physical violence but the violence of the comprehensive annihilation of human bonding that strikes us:

> I shall assure you that distrust is stronger than trust and envy stronger than adulation, respect, or admiration. The Black slaves after receiving this indoctrination shall carry on and will become self-refueling and self-generating for hundreds of years, maybe thousands. Don't forget, you must pitch the old black male vs. the young black male, and the young black male against the old black male. You must use the dark skin slaves vs. the light skin slaves, and the light skin slaves vs. the dark skin slaves. You must use the female vs. the male, and the male vs. the female.[23]

The psychological value is huge. What Lynch prescribes is the preemptive destruction of any sense of togetherness, of discerning who the real enemy is, indispensable for common actions of resistance.[24] Of course, it is natural for Lynch to speak of the

---

21. Lynch, *Letter*, 31.

22. Goza, *America's Unholy Ghosts*, 100. See also Wood, *Lynching and Spectacle*; Waldrep, *Lynching in America*.

23. Lynch, *Letter*, 16. In the original printed form, selected words were both in bold and capitals so it would be clear what Lynch is presented to have considered important to emphasize.

24. It is the same basic principle taken over by apartheid in its racial and ethnic categorization of blacks, as "Bantu's," "Indians," and "Coloureds," each category allotted social, economic, and political

breaking of the horse and of the black person in the same breath, as part of the same process. Not only are they both considered chattel, they are both essential for the capitalist slave economy. However much the African person is considered an animal, though, Lynch knows that it is the human mind that he covets most. "Hence, both the horse and the nigger must be broken; that is breaking them from one form of mental life to another. *Keep the Body, take the mind!* In other words, break the will to resist."[25] For Lynch, it is necessary for that first black body to be totally destroyed, and as brutally as possible, otherwise the lesson of the psychological impact on the other slaves would be lost. So would, presumably, for the white slave owner, the pleasure of the power, so necessary to be established right at the start.

Step three: "Repeat," Lynch instructs. *Repeat*. In other words, the slave owner is encouraged to do this until the third end goal is achieved, for it is that end goal that is the heart of the matter, the way to secure permanent submission and the greatest profits. For the capitalist slave economy to prosper, for white power to be feared, for white supremacy to remain unquestioned, for white domination to endure, for white privilege to remain untouched, and for the rules of white society to remain unchallenged, do step one and two—repeatedly. *But keep the mind*. The terror must be internalized and the will to resist must be completely broken. Note how Lynch, over and over, uses the word "savage" for the black person in a vain attempt to mask, and deflect from, his own unspeakable and undisguised savagery. Note also that while the horse and the black person are coupled in this demonstration, the horse remains a horse. One cannot dehumanize an animal. The black person alone suffers the devastating degrees of denigration: person, slave, savage. It is, nonetheless, a savagery that will persist as the indelible hallmark of imperialism to this day.

Step three reads:

> Continually through the breaking of uncivilized, savage nigger, by throwing the nigger female savage into a frozen psychological state of independence, by killing of the protective male image, and by creating a submissive and

---

"privileges"—never rights—according to the level of its status on the ladder of apartheid's pigmentocracy and divide-and-rule designs. It is to the eternal credit of the Black Consciousness movement's philosophical and political acumen that this strategy was discerned so clearly, and so effectively combatted, overcome, and replaced by the practice of Black solidarity. "The importance of black solidarity to the various segments of the black community must not be understated," exhorted Biko. See Biko, *I Write What I Like,* 56. Biko then succinctly set it out in his famous four-point black solidarity argument. See ibid., 56–57. It is the culmination of the whole argument on the subject of black solidarity, perfectly understanding apartheid's Willie Lynch philosophy. See ibid., 52–57. On the same subject, Biko argues elsewhere, "Thus in an effort to maintain our solidarity and relevance to the situation we must resist all attempts at the fragmentation of our resistance. Black people must recognise the various institutions of apartheid for what they are—gags intended to get black people fighting separately [and therefore against each other] for certain 'freedoms' and 'gains' . . . " Ibid., 42. All these "gains" and "freedoms" were, of course, to be defined, granted, controlled, and managed by the white regime within the framework of "separate development," what Biko called "the deliberateness of the enemy's subjugation scheme." See ibid., 57.

25. Lynch, *Letter,* 27.

dependent mind of the nigger male slave, *we have created an orbiting cycle that turns on its own axis forever.*[26]

By "independence," Lynch means "abandonment," the woman being left entirely on her own, facing the torturer without any hope of resistance, protection, or rescue.

That is indeed the creation of a submissive and dependent black mind, that ultimate prize for imperialism and colonialism, that eternally orbiting cycle that turns only to serve white, capitalist, patriarchal power. It is this vicious cycle that Black Consciousness and black power set out, and still need, to break. That cycle turns, not as long as white power wants; it turns as long as black power allows it to. But in coloniality's power matrix, in too many ways, that cycle continues to turn; hence the absolute necessity for an invigorated Black Consciousness

A Pauline Dilemma

Because it is a systemic negation of the other person and a furious determination to deny the other person all attributes of humanity, we remind ourselves of Fanon's accurate observation that colonialism forces the people it dominates to ask themselves the question constantly: "In reality, who am I?" It is a question betraying utter despair.

For the psychiatrist Fanon, that was a question about the colonized person's psychological condition. For the person of faith, it is a compellingly spiritual question. It is a biblical question, and as such a profoundly theological question. So it is important to revisit the question Black Consciousness first posed over forty years ago and that has now resurfaced with such urgency: What can persons of faith learn from this philosophy that inter-relates consciousness, the issues of power, our Christian self-understanding, and our ethical praxis? What comes to mind and may be helpful as we ponder this, I think, is a classic text in the Christian Scriptures, the Apostle Paul's Epistle to the Romans 7:14–25. In this passage, Paul wrestles with an inner conflict, a very human dilemma, and the consequences this manifests in its grip on his life.

The passage is of course much more complex than I have space to enter into here, so perhaps it is a bit oversimplified, but this is how I read Paul's dilemma: his behavior, he confesses, is contrary to what his inner convictions dictate. He knows what he understands to be God's will for him, but his human desires and frailties, the personal sins and the pressures to submit to structural and systemic sins—what he calls "the flesh"—keep him captive, so that instead, "I do the very thing I hate" (v. 15). The conflict becomes acute: "I can will what is right, but I cannot do it. For I do not do the good I want, but the evil I do not want is what I do" (vv. 18, 19). I speak of "personal, structural and systemic sins," because Paul's struggle is not just a personal, inner one. It has as much to do with the societal structures, mores, and norms within which he

---

26. Quoted in Goza, *America's Unholy Ghosts*, 101.

is situated as a Jew living under Roman imperial rule, against which he witnesses and struggles, and their hold on his life.

Paul restates this universal human dilemma in different ways and utters the dramatic words, spoken, says James Baldwin, in his reference to this passage, "with a most unusual and stunning exactness"[27] and taken as our title for this chapter, "Wretched man that I am! Who will rescue me from this body of death?"(v. 24). The key to the understanding of this passage, I suggest, lies in Paul's words right at the beginning, and one can almost hear the sigh of utter perplexity: "I do not understand my own actions" (v. 15). Such is the power of internalized conflict, paradox, and the estrangement caused within a person. Black people certainly know all about it. It is as if I hear Steve Biko as he speaks of the black situation under apartheid. It is a confusion that encompasses all of life. The struggle to overcome this confusion and end the internal conflict is the struggle to open the way to meaningful life in every area of life. But without an adequate answer to the question, "In reality, who am I?" the confusion would, with insane jealousy, cling to its paralyzing embrace, and those caught in it would, to say it once more with Baldwin, "have no way whatever to remove this cloud that stood between them and the sun, between them and love and life and power."[28]

For the purposes of this discussion, this is, I suggest, an extraordinarily appropriate analogy. Within the context of the ongoing battles for the decolonization of the mind, the continuing tyranny of our unconquered racism, ethnicisms, and narrow nationalisms, this is a dilemma South Africans, black and white, in our continuing battles for meaningful social and political life together are well acquainted with, and we are still seriously struggling with it. We are not strangers to the conflicted alienation of the mind that comes from knowing what is right but doing what is wrong, because the doing of what is right inevitably brings with it the discomfort of risk, the pain of solidarity, and the dangers of commitment. It is a dilemma that manifests itself painfully in the shredded political, social, and economic life of the nation. And we are not the only ones: the dilemma is universal. So we hear Martin Luther King Jr.'s lament as he speaks to SCLC staff in 1967,

> The American people are infected with racism—that is the peril. Paradoxically, they are also infected with democratic ideals—that is the hope. While doing wrong, they have the potential to do right. But they do not have a millennium to make changes. Nor have they a choice of continuing in the old way. The future they are asked to inaugurate is not so unpalatable that it justifies the evils that beset the nation. To end poverty, to extirpate prejudice, to free a tormented conscience, to make a tomorrow of justice, fair play, and creativity—all these are worthy of the American ideal.[29]

---

27. Baldwin, *Fire Next Time*, 18.
28. Baldwin, *Fire Next Time*, 19.
29. See Mieder, *Making a Way Out of No Way*, 453.

Knowing what to do that is right, but lacking the courage to do it, produces, says King, "a tormented conscience." It is, however, a confusion we are prone to nurture and feed, rather than confront and dispel, because that confrontation means making choices and taking a stand, and these are choices that would reveal only too clearly how much we cling to the confusion itself as to a life raft for reasons of fear, privilege, and self-preservation. We then do "the very thing we hate," but the thing we hate is actually to our benefit, serves our interest, secures our position of power and privilege at the cost of the very humanity of others. The dilemma remains acute.

In parenthesis, but also for the sake of clarity: I read Paul, as one should the whole New Testament,[30] as literature from within the Roman imperial context, intended for the community of the followers of Jesus of Nazareth, victims of the empire. In these texts, it is as if the church is lurching between the desperate necessity to survive and the inescapable demand to *be* the church, the living *marturia* to the life, death, and resurrection of Jesus Christ, always in confrontation with the demands from the empire and the deified Caesar. In some of those texts, the followers of Jesus are being called, in subtle and sometimes not so subtle ways, to accommodation to the demands of empire. In other texts, notably the gospels and the authentic letters of Paul, they are being called to resistance against empire. They are called upon to form an anti-imperial, alternative society based on their faith, which in turn calls for loyalties higher than those to the Caesar, solidarity stronger than the lure of imperial privilege and patronage, and courage and resistance beyond the fear imposed by imperial terror.[31]

---

30. Scholarly consensus now holds that the only authentic Pauline letters are Romans, 1 and 2 Corinthians, Galatians, Philippians, 1 Thessalonians, and Philemon. Some portions of the so-called Pastoral Letters, such as 1 and 2 Timothy, as also the so-called house rules in 1 Peter, are understood as attempts to persuade the church to adapt to the expectations of and pacify the Roman Empire, especially regarding the questions of slavery, the position of women in society, and submission to imperial rule.

31. Steve Biko had virtually written off Paul as the main reason for the churches' "characteristic conservatism" that made him "shudder a lot." He thought that what he saw as Paul's conservatism was due to Paul's "Roman citizenship [which] tended to colour a lot of his interpretations. [Paul] saw Rome not as the enemy the people were hoping to be rid of by the advent of the Messiah, but as an institution to which God had given sanction and somewhat urged people to accept her authority." See Biko, *I Write What I Like*, 239. Biko is most probably basing this understanding on the famous passage in Romans 13:1–8, or perhaps, we should say, on the conventional reading and interpretation of that passage by the churches and conservative theology. I have offered a different reading of this passage in Boesak and Villa-Vicencio, *When Prayer Makes News*, 135–56. See also Boesak, *Kairos, Crisis, and Global Apartheid*, ch. 2. Moreover, there is a whole new school of thought in New Testament Studies, which, in my view correctly, reads Paul precisely within the context of his Christian resistance to the Roman Empire. See, e.g., Horsley, *Paul and Empire*; Horsley, *Paul and Politics*. For alternative readings of other portions of the NT, see Carter, *Matthew and Empire*; Herzog, *Parables as Subversive Speech*; Herzog, *Jesus, Justice, and the Reign of God*. Especially helpful, in my view, is Horsley, *Jesus and Empire*, and Horsley, *In the Shadow of Empire*. Most, though not all of these New Testament writings are intended to "equip the saints" in their daily life in opposition to the idolatrous demands of the Roman Empire and the pressures of the societies in which they lived, worked, and witnessed.

In accordance with growing consensus, it is my view that these and other texts from the New Testament do not simply reflect some esoteric, a-political view, concerned only with the transcendent dimension or our inner spiritual life. They all have deep political, social, and economic significance, not just for Paul's day, but for our reality as well.[32] Hence my understanding and contention that Paul's dilemma is applicable to our universal historical political and relational dilemma, the impact of the philosophy of Black Consciousness on that dilemma, and the lessons we may learn from it.

There are reasons why the philosophy of Black Consciousness has resurfaced as such a fascinating subject and the values it espouses are being revalued and once again held up as essential for our public life. Not only has Steve Biko's *I Write What I Like*[33] re-emerged as an eagerly read and studied text, but recent publications have also reclaimed Black Consciousness and the role it has played in our political history and in the life of a whole generation of activists.[34] This is a development to be wholeheartedly applauded.

In South Africa we are far more open today about the historic role of Black Consciousness than we were immediately post-1994, far more critical of the African National Congress' deliberate fading of this historic role in its own almost total claim on the history of South Africa's liberation struggle and its national life, and far more insistent upon the beneficial impact of the values of the Black Consciousness movement on South African society in its search for an open, non-racial, egalitarian democracy and creating for South Africa what Biko so earnestly sought and Nelson Mandela finally acknowledged, a "human face."[35] It is this "human face" which has the power to liberate us from the "body of death" and strengthen us in our struggle for meaningful life together. I understand "meaningful life" to mean a life wherein justice, equity, and humanity are given room to flourish, a society in which we embrace the rich diversity of our world with respect for the "dignity of difference,"[36] not as a tool for separation, estrangement, and enmity but as an instrument of genuine inclusivity and mutual affirmation. In this sense, it shall be clear, this is not an exclusively South

---

32. See, e.g., Boesak, "Theological Reflections," 59–72.

33. First published by Bowerdean Press, 1978, subsequently by Harper & Row, 1986, and since republished in South Africa, Johannesburg: Ravan, 1996, and Johannesburg: Picador Africa, 2006. The version I use here is the most recent one, published in 2017. The many reprints and editions of this work are ringing testimony to the continued relevance of Black Consciousness and Biko's thought. See also the thought-provoking volume *Biko Lives!*.

34. See, e.g., Boesak, *Tenderness of Conscience*; Ramphele, *Laying Ghosts to Rest*; and Mangcu, *To the Brink*. All underscore the continued relevance of Black Consciousness and Biko's thinking. See also Boesak, *Running with Horses*.

35. Biko, *I Write What I Like*, 47, referenced in Mandela's 2004 *Biko Lecture*; see Boesak, *Tenderness of Conscience*, 220. While Biko spoke of the "human face" as Africa's gift to South Africa as well as the world, Mandela here speaks specifically of South Africa.

36. See Sacks, *Dignity of Difference*.

African matter at all—it is universal. The need is not merely South African. It is a need for what scholars are increasingly calling *pluriversality*.[37] And it is global.

That there are valuable lessons to be learned from this renewed Black Consciousness quest is without doubt. In five points, I shall endeavor to explain what those lessons might be. I shall here reflect on Black Consciousness as first, a *critical, self-critical consciousness*, second as a *liberating consciousness*, third as an *empowering consciousness*, fourth as an *engaging consciousness*, and fifth as *humanizing consciousness*.

Black Consciousness as Critical, Self-Critical Consciousness

The first and perhaps most important reason why the impact of Black Consciousness was so powerful was because of its relentless honesty and unflinching insistence upon the truth about black people themselves. Of course, the Black Consciousness critique on white racist domination, what we called "the white power structure," was clear and unsparing. Biko knew exactly who and what the apartheid regime was. But he also understood clearly that "the white (Afrikaner) regime" could as easily be used as a scapegoat, a hiding place, an unholy sanctuary for all whites, especially the liberal (English speaking) white who claimed to criticize the apartheid regime but had no qualms soaking up the benefits the white racist structure provided.[38]

So early on, Biko understood Mahmood Mamdani's later but most valuable distinction, so crucial to a proper evaluation of our reconciliation process: that it should not so much have been about specific "perpetrators" of apartheid crimes and specific "victims" of those crimes—what Mamdani called "fractured minorities"—but rather about "beneficiaries" and "victims" of apartheid.[39] Instead of leading our efforts toward reconciliation to some regrettable and distorted outcomes, as it did, it would indeed have allowed us to confront society as a whole, its systems and structures and their workings, with the demands of justice.

Even then, Biko had argued that no matter how "sympathetic" (liberal) whites may be and how much they purportedly despised apartheid, as a group

> they are born into privilege and are nourished by and nurtured in the system of ruthless exploitation of black energy . . . and being white he possesses the natural passport to the exclusive pool of white privileges from which he does not hesitate to extract whatever suits him.[40]

---

37. See Maeso and Araújo, "Eurocentrism."

38. E.g., Biko, *I Write What I Like*, 66–79.

39. Mamdani, "Reconciliation without Justice": "If reconciliation is to be durable, would it not need to be aimed at society (beneficiaries and victims) and not simply at the fractured elite (perpetrators and victims)?"; see Boesak, *Tenderness of Conscience*, 189–90; Boesak, *Pharaohs on Both Sides*, ch. 4.

40. Biko, *I Write What I Like*, 71. It is probably not necessary to add that while Biko spoke mostly of the "English liberal," our experience with the "enlightened" Afrikaner liberal is exactly the same.

The essence of this argument is, within the context of our reconciliation debate today, as well as within the global context marked by imperial domination, powerfully relevant.

It is that same white (English-speaking) liberal class that proves Biko right as the TRC unveiled the depths of apartheid's racist depravity. Denial of responsibility for apartheid is a general white affliction. However, among English-speaking whites it goes particularly far. The cynical denial of any wrongdoing and any participation in apartheid, and hence any benefit from it, is a device English-speaking South Africans have especially used, and consistently. During the amnesty hearings, the Johannesburg newspaper, *The Star,* in an editorial, asked South Africans to avoid self-serving claims of innocence through ignorance. Then, in an amazing hypocritical twist, the editorial ends by urging whites to say, "Father forgive us, for we knew what they did." The "they" here clearly refers to the "perpetrators" of the "horrors" of apartheid. "They" are to be found solely amongst the Afrikaans-speaking white community "who alone shall bear that cross," I wrote in 2005.[41] The "we" are the English-speaking South Africans exonerating themselves from all blame for South Africa's imperialist colonialist (British) past, as well as for apartheid.

As if to emphasize the point and the white English-speaking liberal's innocence, the *Eastern Cape Herald,* another English language paper, objected strenuously to a call for white South Africans to take responsibility for reparations for the victims of apartheid. "The call," the paper argues, "is in effect to say that *all* whites benefitted from apartheid." The Afrikaners of course did, but not the English. "The fact that [white English-speaking South Africans] did well," the editorial stated, is not because they were part of an oppressive, exploitative system, but because "they realized that life must go on, even within an evil system."[42] Biko knew. And he told us so.

But that critical stance toward our white-controlled context did not begin to cover what Biko had in mind. The Black Consciousness he proposed was in the first instance a call on black people, had at its core an inescapable self-critical element, and that was Black Consciousness' main concern and point of departure. The "white power structure" could as easily be a hiding place for black people. The economic exploitation and material want of oppressed people were not to be denied, but Biko insisted that this was not the whole truth: "Material want is bad enough, but coupled with spiritual poverty it kills."[43] The spiritual poverty Biko refers to is not the spiritual emptiness the white Christian colonizers proclaimed to see in African religious life, devoid of any meaning and incapable of any meaningful relationship with God. It is the confession of our utter dependence on God's mercy and grace without which humane life is unthinkable. In contrast, Biko is speaking of the spiritual emptiness that ensues when one's humanity, one's personhood, one's worthiness as child of God

---

41. Boesak, *Tenderness of Conscience,* 189.
42. *Eastern Cape Herald,* March 25, 2003.
43. Biko, *I Write What I Like,* 30.

is denied and destroyed by racism, bigotry, and mindless hatred. It is Fanon's "systemic negation" we discussed earlier. Neither should what Biko says be confused with the spiritual poverty in Matthew's version of the Beatitudes. "Blessed are the poor in spirit," Jesus says in Matthew's version, "for theirs is the kingdom of heaven" (5:3).

In the mouth of Jesus, that beatitude is the subversive, counter-ideological language of challenge, defiance, and resistance, calling for "spiritual poverty," which here means an embrace of our dependency upon God, over against the arrogance and bloated self-sufficiency of the rich and powerful who considered themselves both socially and spiritually superior to the socially and materially deprived *am ha'aretz*—the common people, the peasants who lived off the land. We should not forget who the people are to whom Jesus is speaking here, the crowds of poor, oppressed peasants from occupied Galilee, many of them landless, laden with debt, perhaps enslaved until they would repay their debt—if they ever could. These were the people abandoned, exploited, and marginalized by their religious leaders in Jerusalem. Jesus spoke hope and life to them as none ever could before.

Jesus speaks to those outside the circles of privilege and power, those of unimpressive proportions, despised because of their "ignorance," fit only to be exploited, used, and then discarded. In this saying, Jesus resolutely levels the ground. The "poor in spirit" Jesus is addressing here, the poor, the destitute, the oppressed, those who hunger and thirst for justice, who mourn for lives destroyed by willful, random power, arrogance, greed, and hubris—these are the ones who shall see the reign of God overcome and overturn the reign of empire. They are the pure of heart who shall see God. These people, whose very lives seemed to them to be only a curse of endless demands and endless suffering, Jesus blessed. *Nine times* his "blessed are you!" resounds over them, not a guarantee of their invulnerability, but a refuge in the storms that await them as they follow him.

> Everyone who hears these words of mine, and acts on them will be like a wise
> man who builds his house on a rock.
> The rain fell, the floods came, and the winds blew,
> but it did not fall, because it had been built on a rock. (Matt 7:24, 25)

By blessing this demeanor before God and in life, Jesus criticizes the elites who think themselves better than others, holier before God and therefore with untrammeled access to God. The "poor in spirit" are blessed, and to them Jesus promises the kingdom of heaven with its justice and "all the other things" that shall be given to them (Matt 6:33). It is a promise of spiritual and material abundance, of flourishing and human fulfillment for this life and the next. It is a call for the radical inversion Luke's Beatitudes capture so well: "Blessed are you who are hungry now . . . Blessed are you who weep now. . . But woe to you who are rich, for you have received your consolation . . ." (Luke 6:20ff.).

Selfless Revolutionaries

In Luke's Gospel, of course, the Beatitudes are uttered in a much more direct, much more immediate way (6:20–26). It is as if Luke saw the need to remove all ambiguity, to stress the revolutionary nature of both the words and the One who uttered them. "Blessed are you, who are poor," Jesus says, "for yours is the kingdom of God." Here the blessings are juxtaposed by the "woes."

> Blessed are you who are hungry now,
> for you will be filled.
> Blessed are you who weep now,
> for you will laugh.
>
> Blessed are you when people hate you, and when they exclude you, revile you, and defame you on account of the Son of Man. Rejoice in that day and leap for joy, for surely your reward is great in heaven; for that is what their ancestors did to the prophets.
>
> But woe to you who are rich,
> for you have received your consolation.
> Woe to you who are full now,
> for you will be hungry.
> Woe to you who are laughing now,
> for you will mourn and weep.
>
> Woe to you when all speak well of you, for that is what their ancestors did to the false prophets.

Frantz Fanon may not have had much affinity for the Christian faith, but it is telling that when he searches for the most precise description of decolonization as a revolutionary project, he cannot but fall back on the words of Jesus of Nazareth. It is, perhaps, the only biblical text Frantz Fanon ever cited. "If we wish to describe it precisely we might find it in the well-known words, 'The last shall be first and the first last.' Decolonization is the putting into practice of this sentence."[44] This is the Jesus Fanon is reaching for in this sentence: the enemy of the Roman imperial occupier, the partisan of the poor, the oppressed, and the excluded, the revolutionary they had to crucify, the hope of the nations.

I suggest that Biko, in speaking of the "spiritual poverty" of the black, oppressed person is engaging in Black Consciousness as self-critical consciousness. If we understand it in that way, it points us to something deeper still. Jesus's story of the Pharisee and the tax collector at prayer illustrates this sublimely (Luke 18:9–14). The Pharisee represents the elite, wealthy, and spiritually superior class who participates with Rome in the oppression of the people. The tax collector, who collects taxes from the poor on Rome's behalf, represents the sellout, our *impimpi*. What Jesus wants to point out is that while they are both spiritually deeply impoverished, empty, and guilty before God, only one of them knew and acknowledged it. While the Pharisee's self-satisfaction and

---

44. See Fanon, *Wretched of the Earth*, 37.

self-sufficiency ring out in the temple, the tax collector beseeches God to replace his poverty of spirit with the richness of God's mercy and love. "Be merciful to me, a sinner!" Rather than illustrating the tax collector's "unworthiness" over against the Pharisee's spiritual superiority, thereby reinforcing his stereotyped "sinfulness," Jesus is speaking of *an entirely different relationship to God,* the kind, as with the tax collector Zacchaeus (Luke 19:1–10), that leads to remorse, repentance, conversion, and the doing of justice.

John Calvin captures the heart of it when he writes of our coming to the Table of the Lord:

> We come as poor people to a kind Almsgiver, as sick people to a Physician, as sinners to the Savior, and that this worthiness which God wants consists first and chiefly in faith, which ascribes and places everything in God and nothing in ourselves . . .[45]

On my reading, this is not a call to senseless self-denigration. Rather it makes of the Eucharist a call to a radical equalization and egalitarianism: we are *all* equally poor before God, equally undeserving of the mercy of God, and equally dependent on the grace of God, which grace makes us equally capable of doing what God requires: justice, mercy, and walking humbly with our God.

John Calvin himself sharpens this insight as if to avoid any misunderstanding. After Calvin's insistence that the Table of the Lord brings about the essential unity of the church, since it brings unity with Christ, he turns to the social effects of the sacrament which sharing Communion brings as an obligation:

> Now since he has only one body, of which he makes us all partakers, it is necessary that all of us also be made one body by such participation . . . We shall benefit very much from the sacrament if this thought is impressed and engraved upon our minds: that none of the brothers and sisters can be injured, despised, rejected, abused, or in any kind offended by us, without at the same time injuring, despising, and abusing Christ by the wrongs we do; that we cannot disagree with the brothers and sisters without at the same time disagreeing with Christ; that we cannot love Christ without loving him in the brothers and sisters; that we ought to take the same care of our brother's and sister's bodies as we take care of our own; for they are members of our body; and that, as no part of our body is touched by any feeling of pain which is not spread among all the rest, so we ought not to allow a brother or sister to be affected by any evil, without being touched with compassion for them.[46]

It also reminds us that the Eucharist is an act of radical faith and the expectation of the doing of justice. Without this, it becomes a meaningless ritual. Geoffrey Studdert Kennedy, the British World War I chaplain who returned as one of the most eloquent

---

45. Calvin, *Institutes* iv.xvii.42.
46. Calvin, *Institutes* iv.xvii.38.

voices for pacifism, had an astute understanding of what Calvin meant and had that radical expectation of the Eucharist:

> I have been to mass in churches where I thought it was sinful—sinful, because there was no passion for social righteousness behind it . . . Remember that medieval ritual was a natural expression of medieval life, which, at any rate, tried to consecrate all things to God . . . The way out is not to destroy ritual but to restore righteousness, and make our flaming colours the banners of a church militant here on earth.[47]

The kingdom that the spiritually and socially superior claim and take for granted as their right is in fact the inheritance of the poor: it is the poor who shall be "exalted." And expecting the fulfillment of that promise because it has not just been spoken but actually fulfilled in their hearing is living a life filled with revolutionary expectation and activity. That reign of God that embodies good news for the poor, liberation for the captives, justice for the oppressed, healing for the brokenhearted, freedom, restoration, and dignity for those possessed by the demons of fear, self-denigration, and hopelessness has come and is promised to *them*. "Those who are healthy have no need for a physician, but those who are sick. I came not to call the righteous, but sinners" (Mark 2:17). The context of this remark is the dinner at the house of a tax collector, Levi, in the eyes of the Pharisees with whom Jesus remonstrates here, a "sinner," unworthy of inclusion and redemption. Jesus's words are a rebuke, his reference to the "righteous" an ironic but stern reminder to those who consider themselves "righteous" that in Jesus's eyes, they are in fact the opposite. Your "righteousness" is in fact a sinful self-sufficiency. In your arrogance, you think you do not need God since you have already claimed God for yourselves and excluded from God's grace those you branded "sinners." But it is for them that I came, to save them from your oppression.

Biko's words echo those of Jesus in our political context. He speaks of that spiritual poverty which comes as a result of a life devoid of all meaning, drained of purpose by daily oppression, exploitation, and dehumanization; a mind robbed of all consciousness of the dignified, worthy self; full of the wretchedness that is emptied of self-belief and therefore completely subjugated to the will of the oppressor. It does not bring one closer to God: it stands in the way of one's true liberation and a meaningful relationship with God and with others. It is a totally paralyzing mindset. One could not join the struggle for the end of material poverty if one could not overcome the devastation of that spiritual poverty.

Economic want and political oppression were the external reality; spiritual poverty was the internal reality, the root of the problem. Biko's concern was to get to the issues that really mattered, what he called the "*first* truth, bitter as it may seem, that we have to acknowledge" and it is the fact that black people have lost their personhood:

---

47. See Kennedy, *After War*, 201–2.

> Reduced to an obliging shell, the black man looks with awe at the white power structure and accepts what he regards as the "inevitable position." Deep inside his anger mounts at the accumulating insult, but he vents it in the wrong direction—on his fellow man in the township, on the property of black people . . . His heart yearns for the comfort of white society and makes him blame himself for not being "educated" enough to warrant such luxury . . . [He has become] convinced of the futility of resistance and [has thrown away] any hopes that change may ever come. All in all the black man has become a shell, a shadow of a man, completely defeated, drowning in his own misery, a slave, an ox bearing the yoke of oppression with sheepish timidity.[48]

Then, in a perfect depiction of the Pauline dilemma we began with, and with the same stringent, self-critical honesty, Biko observes,

> In the privacy of the toilet his face twists in silent condemnation of white society but brightens up in sheepish obedience as he comes out hurrying in response to his master's impatient call. In the home-bound bus or train he joins the chorus that roundly condemns the white man but is first to praise the government in the presence of police or his employers.[49]

To hear this was painful; devastating actually, but it was nonetheless the truth, and those of us who understood and accepted it (and many couldn't) knew that we had to do more than just echo Paul's lament, "I do not understand my actions, wretched man that I am!" We had to see clearly what we had become, what has made us so, and especially how we were complicit in our own condition. This is what Black Consciousness helped us to understand. What Black theology did was to make us see how this situation alienated us not only from our true selves as God had intended, but also from others, and above all from God.

Black Christianity, too, did not escape. Biko accused the Black Church of "conniving" with an oppressive ideology and an interpretation of the Scriptures that had become a depressingly efficient instrument for the subjugation of the people. We did not just accept nor were we forced. We "connived" at an "appalling irrelevance of the Scriptures," a "colonialist-tainted version of Christianity" and had nothing liberating, comforting or humanizing to say in a country "teeming with injustice and fanatically committed to the practice of oppression, intolerance and blatant cruelty because of racial bigotry . . . where all black people are made to feel the unwanted step-children of a God whose presence they cannot feel . . ."[50]

---

48. Biko, *I Write What I Like*, 31. These sentences are so powerfully central to Biko's understanding of the workings of Black Consciousness that we shall have cause to return to them in this work, as we read them in the contexts of different arguments. Biko's gender-exclusivist language remains problematic, but I embrace fully the intention and truth of his argument here.

49. Biko, *I Write What I Like*, 30, 31.

50. Biko, *I Write What I Like*, 60–61.

The Black Church, in its colonized existence, was conniving with a form of Christianity that "*in its introduction* was corrupted by the inclusion of aspects which made it the ideal religion for *colonization* of the people"; and nowadays "in its *interpretation* (is) the ideal religion for the maintenance of the subjugation of the same people."[51] Biko accused the Black Church of no less than *active* participation in our own oppression.

Elsewhere I argued that Biko here misunderstood and underestimated the inherent radical nature and power of the Christian message.[52] I still think that is true. However, the central thrust of Biko's critique was nonetheless undeniable: for us the first step was the acknowledgment that indeed the most potent weapon of the oppressor was the *mind* of the oppressed. We had to begin with the decolonization of our minds, our grammar, and our actions; understand that it begins with pride and dignity and self-awareness. It does not begin with the demonization of white people—and ultimately there was no need for that—but rather with a new and right relationship with God and with the absolute insistence upon the worthiness of our own black personhood. It began with learning and embracing the maturity of self-criticism and putting an end to the "crime of our complicity" in allowing ourselves to be "misused and therefore letting evil reign supreme in the country of our birth."[53] Biko's language is strong, and brutally honest. Black people's "complicity" was "connivance" and a "crime," allowing evil to reign in South Africa.

This critical, self-critical awareness about ourselves, our faith, and our objective socio-political conditions was the bitter cup from which we had to drink in order to give life to that powerful force that changed a whole generation and the course of our country's history: Black Consciousness, Black theology, and black power. We understood that material and spiritual poverty created "mountains of obstacles in the normal course of the emancipation of black people,"[54] but we understood also the systemic nature of it, hence the emphasis on destroying "the white power structure" and the "systems of domination and exploitation."

We knew that we could no longer be "sacrificed to white self-centeredness and greed, or remain the victims of white alienation," as I argued in an essay in 1974,[55] or subjected to what black philosopher and writer Adam Small called "white nihilism."[56]

51. Biko, *I Write What I Like*, 61.
52. See Boesak, *Tenderness of Conscience*, 10.
53. Biko, *I Write What I Like*, 31.
54. Biko, *I Write What I Like*, 30.
55. Boesak, *Black and Reformed*, 4.
56. Small, "Blackness vs. White Nihilism," 14–15. See Boesak, *Black and Reformed*, 7, where Small states, "Although, therefore, protest shall play a role in our future actions, we must realize, nevertheless, that protest is itself a form of begging. We shall not, I repeat, beg. The primary form of expression shall be the manifestation of our blackness. We do not exist for the benefit of whites. We *exist!*" Protest, as important as it is, means that we are protesting against decisions that harmfully affect our lives. But it simultaneously means that we were not at the table where and when these decisions were taken, or at the table where the decisions for the changes we demand must be taken. This indeed makes protest a form of begging.

The key here, however, was the self-critical acknowledgment of our "sheepish timidity" and our complicity in our own oppression. This complicity was not just a political mistake. It was a sinful disposition, a betrayal of our being created in the image of God, people whose humanity was affirmed and celebrated by the incarnation of Jesus Christ. It was sinful self-denial. I do not mean self-denial as that readiness to give up all, even one's life for the sake of justice and the common good. I mean that self-denial that denies one's creaturely relatedness to God as being created in the image of God. One cannot put this too strongly.

It is John Calvin whose insights once again inform us here as he speaks of the inestimable value of human beings as beings created in the image of God: "God looks upon himself, as one might say, and beholds himself in men as in a mirror," Calvin says in a sermon on John 10:7.[57] And elsewhere he writes, "God's children are pleasing and lovable to him, since he sees in them the marks and features of his own countenance . . . Whenever God contemplates his own face, he both rightly loves it and holds it in honor . . ."[58]

So Biko is right when he concludes that black people had to take "serious cognizance of the deliberateness of God's plan in creating black people black," and this not with abject resignation and the grinding of teeth, but with pride and gratitude, and in celebration and a sense of moral agency.[59] So Black Consciousness was for us a critical, self-critical, and system-critical consciousness through which we sought to transform not only our minds but also the systems and structures that made meaningful life impossible. It was a redemptive self-critical consciousness with powerful implications for the self, for society, and for the transformation of the world.

Black Consciousness as Liberating Consciousness

The reality Black Consciousness was emerging into was the reality of white racist domination, of apartheid as the inevitable spawn of colonialism and slavery. It was a situation white people were intent on maintaining and strengthening through persistent political oppression, systemic economic exploitation, ruthless social engineering, psychological manipulation, and sustained levels of violence—personal, psychological, systemic, structural, and physical. All of this was held together by a vicious cycle of fear, punishment, and submission followed by reward.[60]

---

57. Quoted in Wolterstorff, *Hearing the Call*, 123.

58. Calvin, *Institutes* iii.xvii.5, cited in Wolterstorff, *Hearing the Call*. Wolstertorff concludes, "The thought is clear: God beholds what God has made. God observes that human beings are icons of Godself. God observes that they mirror God, that they are likenesses of God. In this God delights" (123).

59. Biko, *I Write What I Like*, 49.

60. Biko, *I Write What I Like*, 73–79. "White people, working through their vanguard—the South African Police—have come to realize the truth of that golden maxim—if you cannot make a man respect you, then make him fear you" (76).

Black Consciousness understood that fear not simply as a psychological phenomenon but as an inevitable result of the deliberate arrangement of the structures of power. It was a major determinant in our South African political reality. This fear had to be broken. That fear was a paralyzing cycle: it was born out of, and in turn bred powerlessness, and powerlessness, in its turn, "breeds a race of beggars," as the National Council of Black Churchmen in the USA observed in their 1966 statement.[61]

Black Consciousness, in its interconnectedness with Black theology and black power, infused black dignity with what Biko called a "singularity of purpose" toward the total liberation of black people at every level and in every sphere.[62] In this, one of its strongest weapons was its anti-tribalism, the antithesis of the tribalism so essential to apartheid domination and its non-racialism so essential to the creation of an alternative society and to the creation of a meaningful humanity. Black Consciousness rejected the artificially created and universally imposed racial and ethnic categories inherent to the apartheid state and the apartheid state of mind: "Bantu," "Colored," and "Indian." It was a concept that stood over against, indeed nullified, the concept of "multi-racialism" so precious to apartheid, especially toward the end, and so easily submitted to by even the liberation movement after its return from exile, so much so that it became a sensitive and contentious issue between the ANC and the younger activists who did not go into exile but came into political maturity through Black Consciousness and the struggle at home.[63]

The coining of the term "black" served several purposes. It was a political statement against the centuries-old colonialist divide-and-rule tactics, deeply embedded in the use of racial categories by the apartheid regime. It was an assertion of dignity and positive self-definition on the part of black people. It brought about a "solidarity of the oppressed" in the struggle against a common, and more precisely defined, enemy. It solidified the power of the oppressed masses, and it invalidated the false, but nonetheless sacralized, pigmentocratic structure of the South African political and social reality.[64] It required understanding, conversion, and embrace. What counted were no longer the pigmentation of our skin and the social connotations it signified, but our blackness and the dignity therein. It was our blackness that constituted our humanity, a complete and completely liberating reversal of the apartheid logic and the racialist mindset.

In this way, Black Consciousness became a liberating consciousness, moving us from a racializing paradigm to a humanizing paradigm. It destroyed the idolatry of white superiority mirrored in the myth of black inferiority; it saved us from the untruth that humanity could be conferred upon us through our submission to white superiority, because we now knew that could only be a stunted humanity. Finally, it

---

61. See the full statement from July 31, 1966, available on the archival webstie for the Episcopal Church: episcopalarchives.org/church-awakens/items/show/183.
62. Biko, *I Write What I Like*, 33.
63. See Boesak, *Tenderness of Conscience*, 12–15.
64. See also Ramphele, *Laying Ghosts to Rest*, 81.

liberated us from the heresy that we were merely God's "unwanted stepchildren," as Biko saw correctly, legitimized only through our acceptance of the step-fatherhood of whiteness.[65] This made for a radical understanding of human equality that white society was not ready to accede to, but that blacks insisted was non-negotiable.

This is why I say that personally I would never have been able to claim non-racialism as essential for our struggle and democratic well-being were it not for the non-racialism as understood and practiced by Black Consciousness. And since reconciliation without the recognition of essential human equality is not possible, this has immense consequences for the realization of reconciliation in our country today, not in the least regarding a crucial aspect Black Consciousness then had failed to attend to, namely the equality, dignity, and rights of women, as well as all persons so easily regarded as the alien "Other." A liberating consciousness today should be in the forefront in the struggle against patriarchalism, religious exclusivity, and heteronormative bigotry as these manifest themselves in South African and African societies as well as our global community.

Black Consciousness as Empowering Consciousness

The singularity of purpose I spoke of above was a purpose, Biko believed, "in the minds of black people to make possible total involvement of the masses in the struggle essentially theirs."[66] The enabling of their mind empowered black people to become the subjects of their own deliberation and the agents of their own liberation.

So here is the logic: it is a movement from personal empowerment to the empowerment of a community and a people. It is an empowerment of the mind in order to secure the understanding of the people of their own power to change their reality. It is an empowerment for the *total involvement* of the people—not just in terms of numbers but in terms of the liberation of their whole being. It is, furthermore, an empowerment for a *struggle*—there should be no misunderstanding about the fact that there is a struggle and there will be sacrifices and risks involved. It is, moreover, an empowerment to fight a struggle that is essentially theirs—in other words, no other person, no matter how well-meaning, can be their voice or replace their body in this struggle. It is *their* struggle, *their* freedom, *their* future at stake. There is no more powerful example of this than Soweto 1976 and what followed after into the 80s. It is, furthermore, about power, and it is about freedom—to shape their own destiny, to leave a legacy of dignity to their children, to rule their country with justice and equity, to rise to their full human potential, to make the world a better, more just, more humane place, to secure a safe space for the humanity of all. Using a term that we shall discuss

---

65. This is the underlying ideology in the racially inspired mission theology of the white Dutch Reformed Church (see Boesak, *Farewell*, 104–5), as well as in the theology of apartheid (ibid., 35).

66. Biko, *I Write What I Like*, 33.

in detail below, Fanon advised, "The new humanity cannot do otherwise than define a new humanity both for itself and for others."[67]

Once again, though, it must be clear that what Black Consciousness helped us to understand is as significant for the ongoing struggles of people everywhere and at every level. If we speak vaguely of having created "equal opportunities" for all, in education for example, but girl children are not empowered to make use of those opportunities because they are denied proper education by patriarchal power structures and attitudes, it is senseless. Under the South African Constitution, women are acknowledged as full citizens with all the rights and responsibilities men have always thought as naturally theirs. But unless women can, unhindered, claim the right to deliberately and purposefully empower themselves to possess those rights to the full, to remove whatever ceilings or walls may still exist, it remains an empty, paper promise.

To move from freedom and constitutionally guaranteed democratic rights to empowerment in order to realize those rights for every citizen, will of a certainty involve continued struggle. One shall be conscious, therefore, that one is called not just to the *undoing* of injustice that came with the systems our society has inherited from the old dispensation, one is called also to the *doing* of justice, that is, making sure that persons are not wronged, not treated unjustly, and that their rights are not being violated. But one shall also be conscious of the duty of constantly *seeking* justice; that is, bringing about justice in every situation of wrong one encounters.[68] It is, though, a struggle that is worthwhile, which cannot but succeed, for we depend not simply upon ourselves, but on what Biko, in an amazingly potent and meaningful phrase, called "the righteousness of our strength."[69]

Black Consciousness as Engaging Consciousness

It is almost axiomatic that if one embraces Black Consciousness as an empowering and enabling consciousness, it must lead to Black Consciousness as an engaging consciousness. It begins, as it must, with a personal engagement, a personal choice rooted in the discovery of the dignity and the demands of one's own personhood. It begins with the choice of knowing who I am, and not meekly accepting what the system of a racist construct wants, or more appropriately, *needs* me to be. That of course, has to do with identity, but it is an identity not defined by ethnicity, race, or class, but by the infinite worth of my humanbeingness.

---

67. Fanon, *Wretched of the Earth*, 246.

68. Wolterstorff makes a cogent and convincing argument regarding the way justice and injustice figure in the "scriptural story line of redemption"; see Wolterstorff, *Hearing the Call*, 175. Wolterstorff speaks of *doing* justice and *seeking* justice. I add a third: *undoing* injustice.

69. Biko, *I Write What I Like*, 135–55; see also Boesak, *Running with Horses,* 186, 187. Previously, I had devoted a full chapter to the discussion of this important concept; see Boesak, *Pharaohs on Both Sides,* ch. 5.

Once this discovery is made and the decision is taken, one cannot but become involved in the struggle for justice, which is the struggle for the redemption of the humanity of all. Ubuntu may have become a sometimes meaningless buzzword in different South African and global contexts today, but for Black Consciousness it was always crucial as well as central.[70] Hence Steve Biko's statement,

> We regard our living together not as an unfortunate mishap warranting endless competition among us but as a deliberate act of God to make us a community of brothers and sisters jointly involved in the quest for a composite answer to the varied problems of life.[71]

Here Biko links the "deliberateness" of God's act "to create us black," a statement I shall have cause to discuss more fully below, to the deliberateness of God's act to make us a human community. The celebration of blackness was not a solitary, isolationist, exclusionary act, but an act affirming human connectivity and community. Contrary to the apartheid mindset, God's "deliberateness" (both in creating blackness and in creating community) is not a curse, but a blessing. So our contribution to the world community, to that essential dignity that true, reconciled, inclusive humanity demands, is not on the terms of artificial racial or ethnic constructs, nor on the false premises of superiority and inferiority, but rather on the basis of our undisputed human worthiness.

The engagement called for is an engagement not for its own sake, but for the sake of others, in the quest for systemic, political, economic, and social transformation, and a truly reconciled community. It places the need for individual fulfillment within the context of the need for justice and human dignity for all. It calls for an understanding of not just what oppressed people might *need*, important though that is, but more deeply, of what they *deserve*. Because what *they* deserve is what humanity and all relation deserve: justice, dignity, equality, meaningful life.

It is an engagement fully aware of its risks and consequences—for oneself, first of all, and those might be severe, as we have seen in the life and death of Biko himself as well as thousands of others. But *not* making those choices and not being engaged bring even more severe and tragic consequences for the people, and for the human community, as a whole.

It is this persistent strain, together with its intimate connectivity with Black theology, that made Black Consciousness such a profoundly spiritual movement, as Mamphela Ramphele has correctly observed. She says,

---

70. See Biko, *I Write What I Like*, 44–51; see also Boesak, *Farewell*, 152, where I refer to the principle of Ubuntu as sacred concept in Black theology, "as real as Africa itself . . . one is only human because of others, for others. This is Black Theology. It is authentic, it is worthwhile. It is, in the most profound sense of the word, gospel truth." See also "Liberation and the Churches of Africa" in Boesak, *Black and Reformed*, 70–78. The belief that justice for black people will secure justice for all humanity is not exclusive to us. James Cone speaks of black people as "God's Suffering Servant who are called to suffer with and for God in the liberation of humanity." Cone, *God of the Oppressed*, 178. It is a thought with a long history in black struggles for justice. See Boesak, *Pharaohs on Both Sides*, ch. 6.

71. Biko, *I Write What I Like*, 42.

> The Black Consciousness movement was a profoundly spiritual movement that understood the importance of the psychological dimension of freedom. The "human face" that Africa would bestow on the world, as Biko said, could only emerge from a deeply spiritual ethos that went beyond conceiving human rights in legalistic terms. Value-based freedom, as defined in the BCM formulation, transcended the trappings of materialism.[72]

I suggest that there is a great need for this kind of freedom in the world today, the value-based freedom that transcends the trappings of materialism and the trap of exclusivism, and roots itself in a "deeply spiritual ethos." In South Africa, as elsewhere, Black Consciousness would find that transcendence in the theological expression of that consciousness, namely black liberation theology, with its rootedness in liberation and compassionate justice, seeking to respond to what Biko called "the appalling irrelevance of the interpretation given to the Scriptures," and Christianity's "inward-directed definition of the concept of sin . . ."[73]

So we worked towards a prophetic and activist Black Church, joined in a black solidarity that transcends all barriers of denomination and ethnicity, sharing the black experience and a critical understanding of Western, Eurocentric Christianity and theology. We sought a black understanding of the gospel firmly rooted in the belief that the gospel of Jesus Christ proclaims the total liberation of all people and that the God of Jesus Christ is the God of the oppressed. Our call was for a theology of refusal, engagement, and resistance rather than a theology of acceptance and acquiescence; away from a theology that subjugates the people to a theology that seeks to liberate the people and tries to point humanity to a better way.[74]

That better way includes dealing with the realities of racism, the denial of it and the necessity of the deconstruction of whiteness that still plays such a crucial role in our so-called "post-apartheid" and "post-racial" societies, and in the way of operation of our global realities today. The meaningful humanity we are striving for will not be realized unless these realities are faced and dealt with.

Innocence and Victimhood

"Farewell to Innocence" is the title of the dissertation I wrote in 1976, which ended with a description of Ubuntu as a crucial concept in Black theology.[75] The title reflected the intention to help both black and white people in South Africa to understand what it meant to live in a world forged by our "pseudo-innocence," a childishness that

---

72. Ramphele, *Laying Ghosts to Rest*, 81.

73. Biko, *I Write What I Like*, 56.

74. E.g., Moore, *Challenge of Black Theology*; Boesak, *Farewell to Innocence*; Mofokeng, *Crucified among the Cross-Bearers*; Cloete, *Hemelse Solidariteit*; Tutu, *Voice in the Wilderness*.

75. I have since found this paradigm useful in other contexts as well; see Boesak, "Theological Reflections on Empire," 59–72.

completely distorts reality. It closes our eyes to matters we believe too horrendous to contemplate, or simply refuse to see, causing us to make a virtue out of powerlessness, weakness and helplessness, the myths behind which we hide from ourselves and the Other. It is an innocence that leads to a rootless utopianism—either an idealization of the present situation, an apathetic political non-consciousness, as opposed to an active consciousness, or to a futile escapism into a better world than the present.

As this pseudo-innocence cannot come to terms with the destructiveness in oneself, in others or in societal structures, it actually becomes self-destructive. It is this innocence which uses the "ideal" to blind people so that they do not see the distortions and atrocities of the present. It blinds, paralyzes, and cunningly uses all means at its disposal to cover up and rationalize guilt and wrongdoing. It is an innocence which, for its own justification, trivializes, ignores, or deliberately excludes the reality of evil. This false innocence itself, therefore, becomes demonic. It effectively blocks off all awareness and all sense of responsibility. The enduring gift of Black Consciousness is that it rescued us from this pseudo innocence.

This is a paradigm very apt for the situation we find ourselves in today and crucial for the deconstruction of whiteness in our still racialized societies and for a world under imperial rule. Both the reality and the deepest causes of our deepest concerns—the frightening and growing gap between rich and poor, the blatant rise of racism and ethnic mobilization, our declining levels of trust in our politics and the structures of law, our waxing social and political anger with its devastating personal consequences, especially for women, all speak to this. Our unraveling social cohesion, our stumbling reconciliation processes worldwide, and our hesitant reach toward an inclusive, nonracial global community—what Martin Luther King Jr. had called the "Beloved Community"—are often all denied or ignored or downplayed with a bland but pernicious pseudo-innocence that can only lead to disaster.

Historically white consciousness never manifested itself simply in the attitudinal expressions of a mindset in personal, individual relationships. Rather, it always came in the guise of legality, the pretense of civilizational propriety, and the harshness of societal, economic, and political power structures. It solidified itself into a system in which pigmentation was *the* determinant of one's social, political, economic reality and more importantly one's human designation, of human status, acceptability, and potential. It determined privilege as birthright.[76]

As such, white consciousness was not a benign state of affairs willed by God, and as it is defended even today, always with good intentions;[77] nor the result of uncontrollable historical, evolutionary developments. It was, in fact, a deliberate, systemic, sustained assault upon the dignity of black personhood and hence upon the worthiness of God. It was the deliberate creation of systems of power and privilege that

---

76. See Wise, "Whites Swim in Racial Preference." See also Battalora, "Whiteness." On critical race theory, see Matsuda et al., *Words That Wound*.

77. E.g., De Klerk, *Last Trek*; Gaum and Gaum, *Praat verby Grense*, 44–45.

became so pervasive and insidious that, seen through white eyes, it is hardly noticed as a manifestation of racist exclusivism. We called this consciousness "false" because it is deeply alien to and destructive of true humanity, even while it was so much a part of the privileged consciousness that whites seemed almost oblivious to it and hence "innocent" to its disastrous consequences for others. And here lies the root of apartheid as a "crime against humanity."

The response of Black Consciousness to this reality was not the denigration or denial of humanity in whites—even though it did claim moral superiority in the struggle. It was, rather, the insistence that in denying black people their humanity, whites were losing their own, and that it could only be reclaimed to the measure that whites knew that their humanity could only be found in the recognition and embrace of the humanity of blacks. It is in this context that the expression "blackness as condition," which whites could adopt if they joined blacks in the struggle for liberation—ours, and theirs—should be understood.[78]

Today such expressions of white consciousness are still rampant in the dominant structures of the global society, above all economic and patriarchal and capitalist. But equally disturbing, in post-1994 South Africa at least, it presents itself in other crucial ways; in our stuttering reconciliation project from which justice, dignity, restitution, and restoration have been fatally de-linked, and that right from the start. In the persistence of racism and ethnic isolation for private, white gain: from the white Afrikaans churches to white tax payers and other white civic organizations, with a scarcely disguised racist agenda of Afrikaner cultural and political mobilization.

A different factor, but with the same ramifications, is the appalling indifference by English-speaking South Africans who still clothe themselves in the false innocence that they were never beneficiaries of apartheid. I have referred to the English language newspapers above. Here, however, are the political practicalities of it. Charles Villa-Vicencio, who served on South Africa's Truth and Reconciliation Commission (TRC), offers a powerful example in the form of the Democratic Alliance, South Africa's official parliamentary opposition, and its prominent representative, Douglas Gibson. Before the TRC, Villa-Vicencio states, the DA "distanced themselves and the English-speaking community from what they saw as an Afrikaner-imposed ideology," and, echoing what we discussed about the phenomenon of "victimhood" earlier, in fact presenting themselves as more or less innocent victims of that Afrikaner-inspired ideology.[79] Indeed, Douglas Gibson would some years later severely criticize a civil society initiative calling on whites simply to acknowledge that they benefited from apartheid, insisting that as a white person, he had attained "no benefits" from the apartheid system. Villa-Vicencio comments, "The DA made no attempt to persuade or enable whites to acknowledge culpability for accepting the benefits of apartheid

---

78. See Boesak, *Black and Reformed*, 22.
79. See Villa-Vicencio, *Walk with Us and Listen*, 102.

or to take responsibility for any form of reparation."[80] This, as James Baldwin rightly stated, is the innocence that constitutes the crime. Journalist Elna Boesak saw this as well, and points out that more often now this denial takes on a more subtle and thus more dangerous form: the "emergence of a new 'identity of victimhood.'" What is more blatant now, however, is the arrogance.[81]

In white circles, it is a condition experienced from loss of political power, guaranteed socio-economic advantage, and privileged insulation. From my point of view, this new victimhood is a classic manifestation of pseudo-innocence. It is disastrous in its perceived necessity and fatal in its effectiveness. It seeks to close down the past without dealing with it or recognizing its unfinished business. It acts as if the past has no bearing whatsoever on the present, and thus the continuing suffering of the real victims of the past's unfinished business is first blurred, then trivialized, then rendered invalid because the past that caused their privileged situation, and the present that perpetuates that situation, are set aside by the new victimhood. Victimhood focuses completely on itself to the exclusion of all others. Self-obsessed, it is the exact opposite of Black Consciousness—it is not engaging, nor empowering, nor humanizing. It disempowers the real victims by denying the injustice still being done because it blames the victims' continued misery and poverty on themselves. Because it does not know true solidarity, it cannot share the pain of others, knows no repentance, does not invite forgiveness and healing. Because it refuses human equality, it cannot respond to the call for reconciliation.

It nurtures a false consciousness because it is rooted not in actual injustice, but in the loss of political power and the exclusive right to opportunity and privilege, which is portrayed as injustice. It is false because it equates this diminishment of power with the loss of freedom and dignity. It is false and dangerous because in this equation "equity," "freedom," and "dignity" cannot exist in a democratic society because this democracy is not defined by, controlled by, and resonant with the demands of white consciousness and white privilege.

But this understanding of white consciousness finds its counterpart in what South African political commentator Xolela Mangcu calls (black) "racial nativism" which he describes as "exclusionary" and "intolerant"; black people who, in turning racist themselves, forgot that Biko argued that being black is not a matter of pigmentation, but a "reflection of a mental attitude."[82] Mangcu reminds us not just of Biko, but also of Cornel West, for whom Black Consciousness is a "political and ethical construct that embraces values of service, love and care, discipline and excellence"; and of Aime Cesaire, who observed that blackness is historical, "there is nothing biological about it."[83] The racial nativists work with hierarchies of blackness and suffering and

---

80. Villa-Vicencio, *Walk with Us and Listen*, 102.

81. See E. Boesak, "Alienation, Reconciliation and the Rubicon Between," 4: "Today the blatant arrogance with which it is positioned central to any and all debate on reconciliation is quite startling."

82. Mangcu, *To the Brink*, 2, 3.

83. Mangcu, *To the Brink*, 78.

new expressions of ethnic differentiation to safeguard political and economic elitism. So their claim on Biko and Black Consciousness is false and completely invalid.

Equally it is true of the privileged minority in the black communities already so far removed from the realities of the South Africa they have left behind on their rush to an exclusive, elitist Promised Land: the poverty, the misery, the disillusionment, the loss of trust and hope, the anger; but also the longing for equality, justice, and dignity. Economist Sampie Terreblanche makes the point that in our recent history South Africa has moved from (English) segregation to (Afrikaner) apartheid to what he calls "non-racial elitism."[84] This is true, but just as with Jakes Gerwel's assertion that South Africa is enjoying significant "deracialization of capital,"[85] meaning the rapid creation of a small, super-rich, elite black class, the word "non-racial" tends to lose all meaning here. In this instance, a continued sense of victimhood is coupled with unbridled entitlement, once again denying justice to the real victims of continued economic and social injustice. Larger than the wealth-poverty gap we can clearly see is the consciousness gap that we "innocently" deny.

Black Consciousness as Humanizing Consciousness

The lessons we can draw from Black Consciousness are crucial for our ongoing search for a meaningful life together in our burgeoning democracy; in our continued struggle for justice, equity, and human dignity, and in the creation of a global Beloved Community. We must seek to embrace the values and the legacy that Black Consciousness offers: a consciousness that is critical and self-critical, liberating, engaging, empowering, and finally humanizing.

For black people, this means not exhibiting their blackness as a means of entitlement, privilege, power, and exclusion, but reasserting the search for human dignity as Black Consciousness has taught us, reclaiming the concept of Ubuntu not as a trendy catchphrase or a substitute for justice, but as a liberating, humanizing, inclusive walk of life. For white people, it means that they are not regretting or rejecting their whiteness, which only leads to either a completely meaningless paralysis of guilt, a bottomless pit of self-pity, or, in the absence of genuine remorse, to a disastrous hardening of the heart.

Whites, and for that matter all South Africans, and, it seems to me, increasingly our world community, should simply be convinced that in embracing the humanity of others they are embracing their own, and in *that* greater scheme of being, pigmentation and what is called "race" are entirely irrelevant. Together we discover that this is also true of a certain view of masculinity and sexual orientation and the yearning for the power that comes with patriarchal and hetero-normative domination, as it is true of cultural imperialism and the desire for cultural domination.

---

84. See *Die Burger*, October 13, 2009.
85. Gerwel, "National Reconciliation," 284.

On this point, however, we can readily see how the boundaries of race are already being transcended, and how a self-critical, system-critical, liberating, engaging, empowering, and humanizing consciousness impacts upon the process of transformation in persons black and white and on society as a whole. What this is leading to, we should hope, is not new forms of racialized consciousness, but the creation and nurturing of a new, open, and de-dichotomized human consciousness. This is not "post-racialism," but my understanding rather of non-racialism, as genuine, inclusive humanism.

Black Consciousness's scathing critique of the white liberal who "possessed the natural passport to the exclusive pool of white privileges" and soaked up the benefits of apartheid while purporting to despise it, is equally true of black, newly-privileged South Africans and the collaborators of imperial domination in societies of the Global South. They now possess access to power and use that power to oppress, subjugate, and marginalize others. Black Consciousness uttered that critique as a particular critique of those whites who never identified with the struggle as articulated and led by blacks, who wanted meaningless multiracial integration which left the structures of power, injustice, and inequality intact; even those whose hearts may have been in the struggle, but whose bodies never were. In contrast, Black Consciousness strove for meaningful life together, justice, equality, and the human dignity of all.

Within that context, as I have argued, Black Consciousness advocates spoke of blackness as a "condition," and the invitation to whites to take upon themselves that condition, consciously rejecting privileged, dominant white consciousness, by sharing the vision and joining the struggle so that black *and* white should be free.

In my view, South African history, and as likely the history of the American civil rights struggle, offers many and deeply inspirational examples of this hope-giving reality, and we have seen this with our own eyes. Today, after the murder of George Floyd, this reality is on joyful, unrestrained display on the streets of American cities and towns, as it is in so many cities across the world. This is true also of the global struggles for justice against patriarchy and heterosexism, ageism and sexism; all forms of discrimination and domination and for the life of the earth. The lines of ethnicity, race, sexual orientation, and gender are fading rapidly, and solidarity amongst humanity for the life of humanity and creation is openly and defiantly celebrated. That is a precious thing to behold, and it is right that so much attention is paid to it. The mere presence of such boundless and borderless energy and solidarity is in itself a most powerful rebuke of the racist, supremacist, exclusivist forces that so furiously seek to capture and swallow us whole.

But what always lies behind the public, nonracial, inclusive participation in the freedom and justice movements are personal struggles, choices, and decisions; *kairos* moments of discernment, conversion, and commitment. And for every personal decision there are personal consequences, sometimes intensely so, that we do not know about. Perhaps, in our celebration of the collective outpouring of solidarity, and in the collective suffering of official punishment, we do not pay enough attention to the personal decisions that make this happen. If we do, the collective becomes much more meaningful and inspirational. Revolutionary fervor without revolutionary love cannot hold.

These same realities remain true. In the new and ongoing struggles for freedom, dignity, and inclusion in the world, we are still called to the making of fundamental choices, to accept the vulnerability of risk, isolation within, and expulsion from communities of privilege. In joining the struggle for liberation in South Africa then, whites walked away from their crippled consciousness, protested their alienation from humanity, turned their backs on white exclusivism, and in embracing the condition of blackness embraced meaningful life. They found the courage to say "no" to white society's privileged existence in ways that were fundamental to life and death. Choosing for blackness as condition and engagement in the struggle freed them from the compulsions of whiteness in a racialized society and they embraced a different consciousness, not alienated from their truest humanity. They were welcomed and participated in a struggle whose nature and quality were a fundamental inversion of the apartheid, racialist logic:

> The nature and the quality of our struggle for liberation cannot be determined by the colour of one's skin, but rather by the quality of one's commitment to justice, peace and human liberation. And in the final analysis, judgement will be given, not in terms of whiteness or blackness, whatever the ideological content of those words may be today, but in terms of the persistent faithfulness we are called to in this struggle.[86]

And again,

> We are doing what we are doing not because we are white or black; we are doing what we are doing *because it is right*. And we shall continue to do so until justice and peace embrace and South Africa becomes the nation it is meant to be.[87]

It is time, however, to give full meaning to these words, to deepen our understanding of Ubuntu and the meaning of a liberated, liberating consciousness, to broaden this inclusiveness and affirmation beyond race and the poor, so that it be inclusive of the dignity of women and non-heterosexual persons. That will be the singular contribution to the ubuntufication of our world today.

So the question remains, looking with un-starred eyes at our country and our people today as white and black elites, in a mockery of true non-racialism, join hands in privilege and power in the renewed exploitation of the impoverished black masses: Can these values be as inspirational, transforming, life-giving today as they were in the past? Can they help us in the new struggle, not so much for racial equality and

---

86. Boesak, *Running with Horses*, 151.
87. Boesak, *Running with Horses*, 151.

the end of apartheid but for global economic and social justice, dignity, and inclusion for all? Is it possible to change, to stop the alienation, estrangement, and confusion, overcome the life-stifling contradictions and self-created dilemmas, to replace this crippled consciousness and through repentance, forgiveness, healing, and the restoration of compassion find a different, whole, and wholly human consciousness, to clothe ourselves with the condition not so much of blackness but of humanness?

Can we again do what we should do *together*, not because we are white or black, but because it is *right*? I suggest that it is possible. But there are no shortcuts, no place for amnesia-induced histories, no euphemisms for justice, dignity, and equality. And there can be no subtitles: our own voices have to be heard. There can be no substitutes: our own bodies have to be there, next to one another, facing together what is before us, so that we can see together the humanized future that awaits us.

Where to begin? Perhaps we should simply start with the recognition by Nelson Mandela, when, in his 2004 Biko Lecture, he finally acknowledged the absolute indispensability of the true meaning and need of Black Consciousness for South Africa today. As a nation we have made great strides, Mandela says, but it is at the level of what we once referred to as "the reconstruction of the soul" that we might have crucially fallen behind:

> The values of human solidarity that once drove our quest for a humane society, seem to have been replaced, or are being threatened, by a crass materialism and pursuit of social goals of instant gratification. One of the challenges of our time... is to re-instill in the consciousness of our people that sense of human solidarity, of being in the world for one another and because of and through others. It is, as Biko did at that particular moment in history, to excite the consciousness of people with the humane possibilities of change... To bestow on South Africa the greatest possible gift—a more human face.[88]

I submit that that human face is not a disembodied set of values, nor the legalistic fulfillment of constitutional requirements in order to respond to the rules of civility or political correctness. It is the cultivation, nurturing and living of a truly human and humanized consciousness, a way of life in response to each other's humanbeingness, the embrace of each other in a common search for reconciled humanity, cherished diversity, and meaningful life.

---

88. Cf. Boesak, *Tenderness of Conscience*, 220.

4

"A Restless Presence"

Black Theology, the Prophetic Church, and "Post-apartheid," "Post-racial" Challenges

"A Church That Makes Me Shudder"

Steve Biko had almost completely written off the church. Not God, or Jesus, but the church. It was not only the church's "colonialist character," its "institutionalization," its "bureaucratization," or its denominationalism that bothered him. "Where does the truth lie?" he asked. "With the Methodists or Anglicans, with the Catholics or Jews, with Jehovah's Witnesses or the Seventh-Day Adventists?"[1] He is equally dismissive of the "strongly conservative" Dutch Reformed churches and their "Calvinism," which, he thought, "fetched" their theology from "the philosophy of [the Apostle] Paul."[2] He would rather find "the truth" in what the church evidently could not offer him.[3] Not in the churches' fragmented and contradictory "truths" of religious dogma and competing claims of rightness, but rather

> in my ability to incorporate my vertical relationship with God into the horizontal relationships with my fellow men; in my ability to pursue my ultimate purpose on earth which is to do good.[4]

---

1. See Biko, *I Write What I Like*, 238.

2. Biko was not wrong about the conservatism of the white Dutch Reformed churches, but he could have been unaware of the fact that their "Calvinism" was a perverted, racist Calvinism and would be exposed and condemned as such first by South African black theologians who had learned so much from him, and later by the worldwide family of Reformed churches. Similarly, he did not live long enough to be aware of the sharp departure from the conventional readings of the writings of Paul and the discovery of just how much Paul did see the Roman Empire as an enemy of the people. E.g., Horsley, *Paul and Empire*; Horsley, *Paul and Politics*.

3. Biko, *I Write What I Like*, 239.

4. Biko, *I Write What I Like*, 238.

This is an indictment with the sound of divine judgement. If the church cannot make loving and creative space for people, enabling them in their "ability to pursue [their] ultimate purpose on earth," we may rightfully ask, what in heaven's name is then the purpose of the church on earth? The church *must* do what our political systems can only *try and hope to do*, and that is give us soul and purpose. It may not be entirely an exaggeration to ask that if Biko found the church to be an obstacle in the way of black people's revolution, and therefore their emancipation, did he, by that very fact, also find the church a stumbling block to their true humanization? Through our politics—if it is the politics of humanity, decency, integrity, and honesty—we must give, we will hear Biko say elsewhere, South Africa and the world "a human face." But should, because of Jesus, that "human face" not be a given with the church, so that in our hesitations, stumbles, and failures in our struggles for the human face of our politics, we might be able to turn to the human face of the church for comfort, guidance, inspiration and empowerment?

The church's "characteristic conservatism" made Biko "shudder a lot."[5] More seriously, it stood in the way of his understanding Christ. "My God—if I have to view Christ as such—is so conservatively interpreted at times that I find him foreign to me," he wrote to Fr. David Russell in 1974. On the other hand, he says, "if I accept him and ascribe to him the characteristics that flow logically from my contemplation about him and his work, then I must reject the Church almost completely . . ."[6] Can such a church even vaguely claim to be "activist"? That is, be deeply, transformatively involved in the struggles of the people? Not simply, and perhaps paternalistically, be "the voice of the voiceless," but understanding the art, and necessity, not only of standing by their side, but standing *aside*, when the moment comes, so the oppressed can speak for themselves?

James Baldwin had the same searing critique of the church. At a young age, he began preaching. The boy preacher charmed the congregation, even though for him, the pulpit was like "being in the theatre."[7] His own deceit in this regard did not bother him, for he knew the character of those in leadership, just as he knew "where the money 'for the Lord's work' went."[8] At first, there was an overwhelming "excitement," which Baldwin describes in stunningly beautiful and moving terms:

> There is no music like that music, no drama like the drama of the saints rejoicing, the sinners moaning, the tambourines racing, and all those voices coming together and crying holy unto the Lord. There is still, for me, no pathos quite like the pathos of those multicolored, worn, somehow triumphant and

---

5. Biko, *I Write What I Like*, 238.
6. Biko, *I Write What I Like*, 239.
7. Baldwin, *Fire Next Time*, 37.
8. Baldwin, *Fire Next Time*, 38.

transfigured faces, speaking from the depths of a visible, tangible, continuing despair of the goodness of the Lord.[9]

Still, he discovered he was searching for something more. The church did not offer him solace, even though he desperately needed it. But just as desperately, he wanted the church to be something other than it was:

> I was even lonelier and more vulnerable than I had been before. And the blood of the Lamb had not cleansed me in any way whatever. I was just as black as I had been the day that I was born. Therefore, when I faced a congregation, it began to take all the strength I had not to stammer, not to curse, not to tell them to throw away their Bibles and get off their knees and go home and organize, for example, a rent strike.[10]

That does indeed sound like something Biko could have said.

In his personal memoir in *I Write What I Like*, Fr. Aelred Stubbs devotes much attention to Biko's remarks on the church. He understands Biko's strong feelings about the church, but notes that first, "It was not Christ that [Biko] rejected, only the 'unbelievable' Church dogmas about him. Second, that 'Black Theology' seemed to give him hope."[11] Words like these, together with Biko's blistering critique of the Black Church,[12] make me wish Biko had lived long enough to experience the impact of his philosophy, work, and life on the Black Church in South Africa, its awakening and leadership in the struggle in the late 1970s and throughout the 80s, and on Black liberation theology to this day. The "activist church" I am about to discuss, like the "dogmatized Christ," was indeed completely "foreign" to him. It is not that the prophetic church in the discussion that follows has been faultless or anything near perfect. But it is true that in its determined efforts to follow the revolutionary Jesus of Nazareth, helping South Africans find their purpose in life for the times in which we lived, joining God in God's struggle for justice, dignity, and freedom for God's children, it came as close to being the church Biko longed for, though no doubt still far from the church Jesus longed for. It is the restoration of this vision of the church for which I will be arguing for in this chapter.

At this point in our history, however, the concept "church activism" at best seems almost an anachronism. At worst, it is only a memory of what was a scant forty years ago, the main characteristic of what was known as the "prophetic church" in South Africa. Granted, the post-1980s era was marked by some of the most extraordinary events in our history. In a 2005 publication, I discussed this matter in some detail and proposed some reasons for the virtual disappearance of the prophetic church in South

---

9. Baldwin, *Fire Next Time*, 33.

10. Baldwin, *Fire Next Time*, 39.

11. Biko, *I Write What I Like*, 240. See also Stubbs, "Martyr of Hope," in Biko, *I Write What I Like*, 175–244.

12. See Biko, *I Write What I Like*, 58–65.

Africa.¹³ Now, in the new context of our democratic era, with enormously challenging issues confronting the country and its people, the prophetic voice that gave such direction in the 70s and 80s is still not heard, and its presence is hardly felt.

In this chapter, I propose to discuss my understanding of "church activism," (re)visit some historical contexts of such activism, then discuss church activism in "post-apartheid" times.¹⁴ Throughout I shall argue that the church we are speaking of is not the institutional church but what Martin Luther King Jr. called "the church within the church, a true ecclesia and the hope of the world,"¹⁵ driven by a radical gospel of justice, hope and liberation. That is the church not captured by what the South African 1985 *Kairos Document* calls "state theology," and neither by "church theology," but rather engaging in "prophetic theology."

Colonial conquest of South Africa in the middle of the seventeenth century brought with it racism, dispossession of the land, exploitation, dehumanization, oppression, slavery, and genocide. With it came Western Christianity, central to the colonialist project and the global outreach of Western imperialism. But simultaneously it saw the birth of the first signs of church activism, by which we mean the prophetic engagement of Christians in public witness and action on the basis of their faith, and on behalf of dispossessed, enslaved, and oppressed communities, imagining an alternative future.¹⁶

Immediately we must make three observations: One, the recognized church was the established church, deeply rooted in Europe, its ecclesial, cultural, and political

---

13. See Boesak, *Tenderness of Conscience*, ch. 5, in which I discuss the role of the church in "post-apartheid" society. See especially 154–68.

14. I place "post-apartheid" in quotation marks since I believe, and will argue throughout this book, that even though apartheid has formally been removed from South Africa's legislative books, its realities are visible everywhere.

15. In King, "Letter from a Birmingham Jail," 127–46; also King, *Testament of Hope*, 300.

16. Here I do not speak of "prophet" in, for example, the way German sociologist Max Weber does. Much of what we see in so-called "prophetic" movements, and the use of the term "prophetic" in most fundamentalist, Charismatic churches that have become such a powerful phenomenon today, is in accordance with Weber's definition. Weber understood a "prophet" to be the charismatic leader of a cult, a collective of individuals made to feel especially vulnerable and alienated by society at large. The prophet's purpose is to organize life in a way that optimizes the accomplishment of salvation. The ultimate goal, however, is preserving itself. See Weber, *Economy and Society*, 59ff. It goes without saying that power over others plays an extraordinarily large role here. In my understanding, prophetic witness and ministry is a way of following the example of the biblical prophets, especially the eighth-century prophets, for whom justice for the poor, protection of the orphans, and defending the widows and strangers was central to their message. In this sense, "prophetic" means not only standing up for the oppressed, but also standing up to the powerful that ruled their lives and oppressed them. The doing of justice was at the heart of a true and faithful relationship with Yahweh, as well as at the heart of true worship of Yahweh. To know the Lord was to know and do justice (Jer 22:16). This was also the heart of the life and ministry of Jesus of Nazareth, whom the poor and oppressed in occupied Galilee recognized as "a prophet powerful in speech and action before God and the whole people" (Luke 24:19). With the biblical prophets and Jesus, the goal is not self-preservation, but rather the preservation of society through the undoing of injustice and the doing of justice, the defense of the weak and powerless, and the liberation of the oppressed.

traditions, the church of the white settler and slave-owner. The other was the church as represented by the oppressed and colonized and those seeking identification with the colonized; those who saw in the gospel a call to recognize the situation of oppression, to heed the voice of the oppressed, and to seek justice for the oppressed. Two, from the beginning there were two manifestations of the church, two readings and understandings of the gospel, and two applications of the gospel to public life. Thus, two fundamental hermeneutical constructs became clear: a hermeneutic of hegemony, oppression, and possession, and a hermeneutic of protest, resistance, and liberation. Three, there were two understandings of the role of the church and of Christians in public affairs. These understandings were underpinned on the one hand by a theology of conquest, appropriation, and justification, and on the other by a theology of prophetic challenge and resistance.

This is a distinction that has persisted throughout South Africa's colonial history, and it has found expression in every era, sometimes in movements and sometimes in courageous, faithful individuals who carried the torch for prophetic Christian witness in South Africa.[17] There was the church that lived in the center, benefitting from conquest and enslavement, and there was the church in the margins, and of the marginalized, seeking to resist both the enslavement of people and the appropriation of the gospel for that enslavement. In both, the church was actively involved: on one side for the establishment, maintenance, and justification of imperial and colonial designs, and on the other for the sake of justice and rights of the colonized.

The one church saw itself as "church" because it was recognized as such by the state, clothing itself with ecclesial power, more often than not allied with political power and with the power of tradition and the dominant culture. The other, representing the powerless and destitute, did not claim any alliance with, or protection of, earthly power. In fact, it almost always found itself in resistance to political powers and often in conflict with ecclesial power structures. It found its strength precisely in its powerlessness, recognizing in that powerlessness more of the church who first

---

17. Apart from well-known and acknowledged examples such as the committed Christian leadership of the African National Congress from its beginnings to the 1960s, one thinks of Christians such as Anglican priests Trevor Huddleston in the 1950s and Bernie Wrankmore in the early seventies; Rev. Beyers Naudé and the Christian Institute in the 60s and 70s; Revs. George Plaatjies and Izak Theron of the Dutch Reformed Mission Church in the 60s; the black student and youth Christian movements, the brave black clergy (and a smattering of whites) who aligned themselves with, and had such a great impact on the resistance movements of the 70s and 80s. As a matter of interest, but in its context today surely as important as the role of Beyers Naudé in the white Dutch Reformed Church in his time, is the persistent prophetic faithfulness of the five theologians in the Netherdutch Reformed Church of Africa the second white South African church suspended from the membership of the World Alliance of Reformed Churches in 1982 for its theological and moral justification of apartheid. Andries van Aarde, Johan Buitendag, Yolanda Dreyer, Ernest van Eck, and James Loader all paid a price for their witness to the Netherdutch Reformed Church of Africa in their efforts to move the church towards an unequivocal, and remorseful, condemnation of apartheid as sin and heresy and a commitment to justice. In his "Autobiographical Reflective Notes" van Aarde writes movingly about this part of his life, see van Aarde, *Jesus, Paul, and Matthew* 2:316–37.

presented itself to the world as the followers of Jesus of Nazareth over against the realities and murderous pressures of the Roman Empire. *That* is the ecclesial tradition it seeks to emulate, rather than the tradition of throne and altar that became the hallmark of Christianity since the Constantinian era. That church understood that to truly glorify the holiness of God, one has to do that in the sanctuary as well as in the streets of protest, discerning the signs of the times through the eyes of the suffering children of God.

Charles Villa-Vicencio spoke of these last-mentioned Christians within the church as "a restless presence that has disturbed the church."[18] The "restless presence" we are speaking of here is not the church as a whole, certainly not Biko's colonized, institutionalized, bureaucratized church. I speak of the prophetic church, an alternative to the Christianity of the established church, a church in tension with and in resistance to both society with its systematic injustices, and the dominant church with its embedded, privileged complacency. It represents the difference between those who always seek ways to negotiate co-existence with the hegemonic powers that rule society, and those drawn to, and gathered around, Jesus of Nazareth, the defender of the poor and powerless, the revolutionary teacher who exposed and resisted the established powers of the palace and the temple, and who was rejected and crucified by those powers on the cross of an occupying power. Like him, they too live in resistance, in the margins of the institutional church and of society, representing a radical rather than an accommodationist Christianity.[19]

There is still much debate, and rightly so, on the role of the missionaries of the early colonial years and some are extremely critical of that role. They are convinced that in the final analysis missionaries were no more than sometimes tacit, sometimes conscious, agents of the imperial powers. They were justifiers of the colonialist project who, despite their good intentions, identified Christianity too much with Western civilization, and whose designs with the "Natives" were in line with their own "basic allegiance."[20] For by far the majority of missionaries that is unquestionably true. Others stress the difference between this kind of missionary (of the Dutch Reformed or Lutheran churches, for example), and the missionaries of the London Missionary Society (LMS) who, they argue, championed the cause of the indigenous people against the racial exclusivism and oppression of the settlers.[21]

I do not hold the view that all LMS missionaries had pure motives or even that all of them made the choice to stand with the indigenous peoples in their struggle for justice and rights. But I do believe that *some* of them did. Even a critical observer

18. Villa-Vicencio, *Trapped in Apartheid*, 5.

19. This church is sometimes referred to as the "prophetic minority," but by the mid-80s this church, which Frank Chikane has called "the church of the streets," had decidedly become, albeit not for long, the "prophetic majority."

20. Cf. Villa-Vicencio, *Trapped in Apartheid*, 43–48.

21. See De Gruchy, *Church Struggle in South Africa*, 12–14.

such as Charles Villa-Vicencio must admit that Johannes van der Kemp, for example, saw the needs of the indigenous people differently than some other missionaries, who saw only the need to be Christianized, i.e., Westernized. "The need van der Kemp witnessed was socio-economic, not evangelical, and he committed himself to strive for the political and economic rights of the oppressed."[22]

As a descendant of the Khoi and the San, the First Peoples of this land and the first to bear the brunt of imperial conquest, dispossession, slavery, and annihilation in South Africa, I cannot simply write off the efforts by missionaries such as van der Kemp as if they do not matter. They did matter to the indigenous people then in their uneven struggles with the conquerors, and they matter to this generation now. Van der Kemp and the few who made the choice for justice became the bane of the settler society and their churches. The hostility from colonial settlers and settler government was visceral. Because they married indigenous women, they were called "immoral"; because they took up the cause of the oppressed and exploited native peoples, they were accused of "meddling in politics." Because they enlisted public opinion overseas and sought to influence government decision-making processes, they were called "traitors." Because they were passionate about justice and unflinching in the exposure of injustice, they were called "one-sided."[23] Van der Kemp's public witness to the Dutch governor of the Cape, Janssens, was not open to misunderstanding: "I could not forbear to warn him of the displeasure of God who most certainly would hear the cries of the oppressed."[24] When all is said and done, "the church's struggle against racism and injustice in South Africa really begins in earnest with their witness in the nineteenth century," says John De Gruchy, and he is right.[25] No wonder Janssens would report,

> If the harm that missionaries have done in the Colony . . . is weighted against the good they have done, it will be found that the harm is very serious and the good amounts to nil. Most of these missionaries (rogues!) should be sent away with the greatest possible haste . . .[26]

---

22. Villa-Vicencio, *Trapped in Apartheid*, 58. See also Enklaar, *Life and Work of Dr. J. T. van der Kemp*.

23. See Boesak, *Tenderness of Conscience*, 135. See also Sales, *Planting of the Churches*, 51.

24. Villa-Vicencio, *Trapped in Apartheid*, 58.

25. De Gruchy, *Church Struggle in South Africa*, 13. Johannes van der Kemp arrived in South Africa in 1799, and almost immediately tensions between him and the colonialist government, as well as the colonists, surfaced. The tensions rose as the situation of the colonized worsened, and van der Kemp remained a fighter for justice until his death in 1811.

26. Sales, *Planting of the Churches*, 51. Villa-Vicencio writes that these missionaries regularly found themselves in conflict not only with the colonial authorities but also with other missionaries who were differently inclined, as well as with the authorities of the established church. John Phillip argued that it was the task of the missionary to "defend the weak against the strong," to which Weslyan missionaries objected strongly. See Villa-Vicencio, *Trapped in Apartheid*, 58. Concerning the tensions between Bishop John Colenso and the authorities in Natal and Governor Theophilus Shepstone, see 62; and with Colenso's own Archbishop in Cape Town, see 16, 61.

Still, Villa-Vicencio's point is well taken. Indigenes remained caught in historical processes fraught with ambiguity, suffering from the "unintentional collusion" between the humanitarian desire of the missionaries and the selfish, exploitative motives of others.[27] So it makes sense that indigenous people who had turned to Christianity would continue to search for the meaning of the gospel for themselves. The more indigenous people would come to understand and interpret the gospel for themselves, and the more they sought their own indigenous, contextual understanding of the gospel as it pertained to their own lives, the more they understood the shortcomings in the interpretation of missionaries, however well meant.

The more also they understood the need for an interpretation of the gospel for the world of political, economic, and human subjugation and alienation in which they had to live. That indigenous interpretation would, in time, take on a decidedly different form from the Eurocentric Christianity whites brought, shaped by what Gayraud Wilmore would call a "radicalized Black Christianity."[28]

Some of the first signs of this would be seen in the "Ethiopian movement," those first black independent churches who broke away from established "mission" churches and aligned themselves with the African Methodist Episcopal Church, powerfully drawn to it by the radical theology and teachings of Bishop Henry McNeal Turner, who visited South Africa in 1896.[29] Their grounds for breaking away were not so much doctrinal, but rather cultural, and even more, political, and they at first raised deep fears among the white population, including the missionary circles. Perceptions of "Ethiopianism" later changed, and they were regarded as less of a political threat. Nonetheless, historian Richard Elphick maintains, much modern scholarship has tended to conclude correctly that the movement was deeply political. Their breakaway was resistance to white supremacist, colonialist rule and politics in society that was so precisely reflected in the church. Zimbabwean historian J. Mutero Chirenje, writing in the 1980s, provocatively concluded that "if the activities of the Ethiopian movement and allied organizations . . . are viewed in the context of their time, they will be seen to be no less acts of self-determination than are armed struggles for national liberation now taking place throughout southern Africa."[30]

It was that radicalized black Christianity that would infuse a spirit of resistance, give birth to the anti-colonial Christian millenarianism of Khoi leader Jan Paerl after

---

27. Villa-Vicencio, *Trapped in Apartheid*, 48, quoting historian C. W. de Klewiet, *Imperial Factor in South Africa*, 159.

28. See Wilmore, *Black Religion and Black Radicalism*.

29. See Elphick, "Evangelical Missions," 119. The first important independent church in South Africa, the Thembu Church, was founded by Nehemiah Tile, a Weslyan preacher, who broke with the mission in 1883 as a result of his political views and activities. Over the next generation African churches seceded from a great variety of missions, with noted leadership such as Mangena Mokone and James Dwane; see Elphick, "Evangelical Missions," 118–19.

30. Cited in Elphick, "Evangelical Missions," 121.

the failed Khoi uprising of 1788,[31] and the rise of early black theological critique in the work of Khoi evangelists Cupido Kakkerlak, Hendrik Boezak, and Klaas Stuurman. Its spirit would move in the poignant, poetic protest in John Ntsikana's "gospel as fabulous ghost" from 1884.[32] From this historic stream would also come the prophetic Christian leadership in African nationalist politics in the nineteenth and twentieth centuries with leaders such as Dr. John Dube, Rev. James Calata, Pixley ka Isaka Seme, Sol Plaatjie, and teacher and lay preacher of the Congregational Church Albert John Mvumbe Luthuli.

In this regard, Gayraud Wilmore's observation is correct:

> What we may call "White Christianity" in Europe and North America has made a deep impression upon blacks everywhere, including Africa. But blacks have used Christianity not so much as it was delivered to them in racist white churches, but as its truth was authenticated to them in their experience of suffering and struggle, to reinforce an enculturated religious orientation and to produce an indigenous faith that emphasized dignity, freedom and human welfare.[33]

That, in South Africa, would be the first stirrings of Black liberation theology, in many ways the heart of a radical black agency in the beginning.

Decades of Tumult and Decision

The 1950s were a decade of tumult with political activism reaching its height in the historic Defiance Campaign—a nation-wide campaign of sustained, non-violent resistance with massive civil disobedience, strikes, and demonstrations as a response to the victory of the National Party at the polls in 1948 and the establishment of apartheid as official policy of the land. It was a watershed in the history of black resistance against oppression in South Africa.

Characteristic of the Defiance Campaign was the strong Christian tone set by leaders and followers alike. "A mood of religious fervour infused the resistance," writes South African historian Tom Lodge.[34] There were days of prayer where volunteers pledged themselves to "a code of love, discipline and cleanliness," and to prayer and fasting. Even though there were also speeches "in the strident tone of Africanism," Lodge tells us, "more typically the verbal imagery involved ideas of sacrifice, martyrdom, the triumph of justice and truth."[35] Lodge calls them "ideas," but they were

---

31. See Viljoen, *Jan Paerl*.
32. Cf. Mphahlele, *ES'KIA*, 298. See also Boesak, *Tenderness of Conscience*, 136–37.
33. Wilmore, *Black Religion*, 25.
34. Lodge, *Black Politics*, 43.
35. Lodge, *Black Politics*, 44. See my discussion on the permeation of a Christian ethic of resistance in the Defiance Campaign in Boesak, *Tenderness of Conscience*, ch. 4, but especially 106–17.

in fact the lived experience and firm convictions of people who took their faith into the struggle for justice and freedom. They understood and experienced the truth of Luthuli's testimony, "The road to freedom is via the Cross."[36]

These black Christians were members of churches where blacks were in the majority but with white leadership, a point that drew Biko's consistent critique.[37] As a result, they could not avoid the dilemmas of the English-speaking churches who in turn shared those dilemmas and sense of apartheid-entrapment with the black, so-called mission churches of the DRC with their white "missionary" leadership: an acute ambivalence towards the struggle for political and human rights of the oppressed majority. They suffered under the weight of white paternalism, imposed white guardianship, and a Euro-centric, pietistic theology that separated the spiritual from the secular and created a devastating "inwardness" that left them helpless to deal with the "this-worldly" situations of oppression, exploitation, and humiliation. But above all was the fact that the political and economic interests of the white leadership ultimately coincided with the interests of white South Africa and its white minority government. These churches, even though numerically overwhelmingly black, could not wholeheartedly stand up for justice because, sharing Villa-Vicencio's judgment of the English-speaking churches, it had "rationalized the demands of the gospel, heeding the demand of the rich and powerful rather than the cries of the poor and oppressed."[38] In this era, it was not the institutional church but the prophetic witness of Christians like Chief Albert Luthuli and Father Trevor Huddleston who kept the flame alive.

Ultimately, though, it was left to black Christians themselves to join the struggle—they could not wait for their hesitant churches to show the way. Rather, they followed Albert Luthuli, his theological convictions, and his radical, charismatic Christian leadership:

> It became clear to me that the Christian faith was not a private affair without relevance to society. It was, rather, a belief which equipped us in a unique way to meet the challenges of our society. It was a belief which had to be applied to the conditions of our lives; and our many works—they ranged from Sunday school teaching to road building—became meaningful as outflow of Christian belief.[39]

Neither would working together with those who were not Christian deter them. Again Luthuli, affirming the foundations of inclusive, inter-religious, and human solidarity that were to characterize the anti-apartheid struggle in the years to come:

> For myself, I am in Congress precisely because I am Christian. My Christian belief about human society must find expression here and now, and Congress

36. Luthuli, *Let My People Go!*, 232–36.
37. Biko, *I Write What I Like*, 58–65.
38. Villa-Vicencio, *Trapped in Apartheid*, 6. See also De Gruchy, *Church Struggle in South Africa*, 37ff. See also Boesak, *Tenderness of Conscience*, 137–40.
39. Luthuli, *Let My People Go!*, 147–48.

is the spearhead of the real struggle. Some would have the Communists excluded, other would have all non-Communists withdraw from Congress. My own urge, because *I am a Christian*, is to enter into the thick of the struggle, with other Christians, taking my Christianity with me and praying that it may be used to influence for good the character of the resistance.[40]

Luthuli and the growing number of Christians who joined the struggle on the basis of their faith—these were the prophetic church, the restless presence disturbing both church and society, giving witness through prophetic speech and action, shaping an alternative imagination and enacting it.

If the 50s were a decade of hopeful, activist tumult, the 60s brought a tumult of another, albeit particularly dangerous and sinister kind. On March 21, 1960, the Pan-African Congress staged a peaceful demonstration against the so-called Pass Laws, marching toward Sharpeville police station near Johannesburg, and the struggle took yet another historic, fateful turn. Police opened fire with live ammunition, killing sixty-nine persons and wounding over one hundred and eighty-six others, most of them shot in the back.[41] Sharpeville would, more than the Defiance Campaign, become the iconic turning point of the struggle in South Africa. Government reaction was immediate, much harsher, much more oppressive, and much more brutal. Liberation movements and activists were banned, political leaders and hundreds of activists arrested and imprisoned, exiled and driven underground. It was the decade of the end of the Treason and beginning of the Rivonia trials and the emergence of Nelson Mandela. Draconian "security legislation" multiplied and political activity was severely suppressed—a harbinger of even worse to come. Albert Luthuli was awarded the Nobel Peace Prize in 1960, and the world began to take serious notice of the struggle for freedom in South Africa. In another fateful turn, 1960 was also the year the African National Congress decided to form its military wing, *Umkhonto we Sizwe*, and make violence part of the strategy of struggle.

In his statement at his trial, Nelson Mandela explains why:

> We of the ANC had always stood for a non-racial democracy, and we shrank from any action which might drive the races further apart. But the hard facts were that 50 years of nonviolence had brought the African people nothing but more and more repressive legislation, and fewer and fewer rights . . . I came

---

40. Luthuli, *Let My People Go*, 146–47. Emphasis mine. Scott Couper, in his excellent historical study, makes the point that in this, as in so many other things, Luthuli's leadership was decades ahead of the church. "Prior to the formation of the United Democratic Front in 1983, the wider church would not work with and alongside communists, Muslims and black nationalists in a broad-based movement and formed by the congresses as Luthuli did, and did well. During the 1950s and 1960s, whites and insularity dominated the Christian churches . . ." Couper, *Albert Luthuli*, 64–65.

41. In Evaton, also close to Johannesburg, the protest was broken up by low-flying fighter jets, and in Langa, near Cape Town, three people were killed and twenty-seven injured in a baton-charge by police. See Couper, *Albert Luthuli*, 86.

to the conclusion that as violence in this country was inevitable, it would be unrealistic to continue preaching peace and nonviolence.[42]

For the churches, too, Sharpeville was a turning point. At the urging of the World Council of Churches, the Cottesloe conference was called where the situation was discussed by the WCC and its South African member churches, and the Cottesloe Declaration was issued. The Rev. C. F. Beyers Naudé of the Dutch Reformed Church, deeply disturbed by the massacre at Sharpeville, challenged his church on the issue of its moral and theological justification of apartheid. Tensions continued to rise, and he was finally forced to break with his church to become the head of the Christian Institute of South Africa and its mouthpiece, *Pro Veritate*. The South African Council of Churches and the Christian Institute published the "Message to the People of South Africa" in 1968. Father Cosmas Desmond would be the courageous witness from within the Catholic Church who worked in the then-apartheid "homeland," Ciskei, and would later stir the conscience of the church and the world with his book about the "discarded people" of South Africa's homeland system.[43] The World Council of Churches held its Assembly in 1968, instituted its Programme to Combat Racism a year later, and in 1970 inaugurated the so-called Special Fund—the most controversial action in its whole history and a huge, probably permanent affront to the churches of the rich North—to provide financial support (for humanitarian purposes) to Southern African liberation movements.

Albert Luthuli died in 1967. In the leadership of the ANC-in-exile, the strong, prophetic Christian influence would, but for the voice of Oliver Tambo, all but disappear. But in South Africa, after a hiatus of almost ten years, through Black Consciousness, black liberation politics would arise again in defiance of both an increasingly militarized and despotic state and its minions in the black communities, and at its center would be a revived, radicalized black Christianity.

The Boundaries of White Leadership

Charismatic, black Christian leadership in the struggle was always aware of the limitations of the churches under white leadership, a point Biko was at pains to make.[44] Already, Albert Luthuli had uttered a sharp critique of the lack of prophetic witness from the church in the midst of the growing crisis of the times. He acknowledged, apart from the oppressive security apparatus, the hold government had on churches in terms of things such as building sites, yearly leases, permits, etc., but grew far more concerned about the churches' response to such pressures. He decried "white,

---

42. Mandela, "Ideal For Which I Am Prepared to Die," in Clarke, *Great Speeches*, 232–33.
43. See Desmond, *Discarded People*.
44. Biko, *I Write What I Like*, 63.

paternalist Christianity,"[45] but his critique was not just aimed at the white leadership of the church; he accused the black pastors of a lack of prophetic courage, as well. "I am extreme on this point," he warns, echoing Martin Luther King Jr.'s "extremism for justice,"[46] and goes on to explain why:

> The threat is that, if a sermon, or a congregation, or a bishop displeases the Department, the site will cease to be available. Parsons must not talk politics—yet much orthodox Christian teaching can be called "politics" . . . This threat has many Christian ministers and organizations virtually cowering, as of course the government intends. What is becoming of Christian witness? . . . Let us lose church sites and keep Christian integrity. I disagree with those who want to "save something from the wreck" because what I see happening is the wreck of Christian witness . . .[47]

What agitated Luthuli was that some leaders in the church sought to "save something" from the wreck of church/state relations as if that were the most important thing. Luthuli, however, was concerned about the wreck the church was making of its prophetic faithfulness. The ordained leadership and trained theologians think pragmatically, the lay preacher/activist and people's theologian thinks theologically and prophetically. Both strains of thought are political of course, but the difference between the pragmatic, accommodationist politics of the institutional church and the radical, prophetic politics of the people's theologian is profound. And it is his prophetic insight that shames, challenges, and saves the church. He is the faithful one, the restless presence, consistent with his commitment from the beginning, calling for a "spirit of defiance":

> Laws and conditions that tend to debase human personality—a God-given force—be they brought by the State or other individuals, must be relentlessly opposed in the spirit of defiance shown by St. Peter when he said to the rulers of his day, "Shall we obey God or man?"[48]

Scott Couper gallantly defends the institutional church against Luthuli's claim that the church "did almost nothing" in the matter of the closure of Luthuli's beloved educational institution, Adams College.[49] I think, however, that for Luthuli there is more at stake. Luthuli's concern was not simply the church's reaction to the closure of Adams College, but the church's overall lack of courage and prophetic clarity vis-à-vis the liberation struggle *as a whole*. What Luthuli saw, and the church did not, was that its virtual silence, the "wreck of Christian witness" regarding the liberation for all South Africa's oppressed people, rendered it almost helpless, and irrelevant, even when it came to defending its own institution. One cannot fight with integrity for one's own

   45. Luthuli, *Let My People Go*, 125.
   46. See King, "Letter from a Birmingham Jail."
   47. Luthuli, *Let My People Go!*, 131–32.
   48. See Karis and Carter, *From Protest to Challenge* 2:486.
   49. Couper, *Albert Luthuli*, 64.

issues when one is not wholeheartedly in the fight for *all* matters. Adams College's enforced closure was not an isolated incident, but the logical outcome of an evil policy and a corrupt system that Luthuli had been praying for the church to wholeheartedly struggle against, and it could not, or would not. When a struggle for freedom is going on, there is no merit or integrity in fighting for isolated church or denominational matters, as if the church is isolated from the all the struggles of the people. The struggle for the freedoms of the church must be embedded in the struggles for the freedom of the people. It may be this failure, on top of the deep disappointment over the fact that he did not have the unqualified support of the African leadership of his church in the struggle against injustice in South Africa that prompted Luthuli's "strange" silence on the closure of the college in his autobiography.[50] The church could not see what Luthuli saw: that justice, and freedom, as the church's witness, are indivisible.

For the new generation, too, the boundaries of white, liberal church politics became increasingly clear.[51] Without discarding the value of those who truly became part of the struggle, one must realize the limitations of the extent to which by far the vast majority of white Christians wanted to commit themselves. It is true that they did offer protest, but it was constrained by their caution, their desire to compromise, and the pressures of white solidarity. The Trevor Huddlestons, Beyers Naudés, and Cosmas Desmonds were few and far between, and they were not church leadership. Analysis of the two major church statements after Sharpeville will bear this out.

The Cottesloe Declaration[52] was a statement written in the wake of Sharpeville, with the blood still visible on the ground. In my view, the statement seeks to be a "responsible," "balanced" appraisal of the South African situation, hoping that its careful language would not agitate whites in general, and the white government in particular, too much. Crucially, the statement recognizes that "all racial groups who permanently inhabit our country are a part of the total population, and we regard them as indigenous." These "racial groups" have an "equal right to make their contributions . . . and share in the ensuing responsibilities, reward and privileges." But what does this mean if there is no clear condemnation of apartheid, the Bantustan policy, nor of the 1913 and 1936 Land Acts that sought to give legitimization for the laws that gave 73 percent of the land to whites? Since there is no clear vision of a non-racial, democratic

---

50. Couper, *Albert Luthuli*, 63: "Many African Congregationalists proved even more wary of Luthuli's increasing involvement in politics than their former white American ecclesial paternalists who harboured concerns with the ANC's, and hence Luthuli's links with communists."

51. Biko would rail insistently against white liberals, those who did more harm than good because they regarded themselves as "not responsible" for apartheid. See the chapter, "Black Souls in White Skins" in Biko, *I Write What I Like*, 20–28. A liberal white colleague in the then-Dutch Reformed Mission Church, a fixture in the church's leadership for years, constantly described himself as "a white man with a black heart," proving Biko's point, and never understanding how much the younger black generation considered him a "Trojan Horse" of white liberalism. See also ibid., 66–79.

52. For the text of the Cottesloe Declaration, see Naudé, *Neither Calendar Nor Clock*, 226–29. For the text of the "Message," see Naudé, *Neither Calendar Nor Clock*, 233–36. In this subsection, I rely on an earlier discussion of this; see Boesak, *Kairos, Crisis, and Global Apartheid*, ch. 3.

society and a radical shift of power relations in politics and society, one is entitled to ask: What kind of society and government are black people expected to make their contributions to? Who decides on the "rewards," and what those might be, if power remains in white hands? Will those be the rewards blacks will share with whites *after* reparations and restoration of land, and after the enactment of policies that will fundamentally address the deep, shameful, and unsustainable socioeconomic inequalities that makes South Africa the most unequal society on earth?

And what does "groups who permanently inhabit out country" mean when the Declaration states that it has "no objection in principle to the direct representation of *coloured people* in parliament"?[53] This is a plea for the inclusion of "coloured" people in the "white" parliament, under white control, with white power intact and undisturbed, with the exclusion of the vast majority of South Africa's people. Does this mean tacit approval of Bantustans? What about the black majority, apartheid's "Bantus," who, according to the apartheid dispensation, did not permanently reside in "white South Africa," were not citizens of the country, and therefore have no right to be represented "in parliament"? Cottesloe's persistent thinking in racial categories will prove to not be helpful in South Africa's search for a nonracial, open, egalitarian society.

It is exactly this kind of enlightened apartheid logic that made Black Consciousness rail against the ambiguities of white, liberal politics in South Africa. And it is this mindset that would eventually lead to P. W. Botha's 1983 Constitution with its Tri-Cameral Parliament which was so roundly rejected by so-called colored and Indian people in the formation of the United Democratic Front and the boycott of those apartheid elections on both political and moral grounds.[54] It shows also just how out of touch with black aspirations white church leadership were, despite their good intentions.

There is another, even more serious matter, and one that will come back to haunt us in the reconciliation process that was meant to deal with South Africa's past and steer us into the direction of what would be called "a shared future" with "common goals." Cottesloe declares that "the present tension [after Sharpeville] is the result of a long historical development and all groups bear responsibility for it." It is a key sentence in the Declaration since it calls up historical contexts for the massacre, and it

---

53. I emphasize this because of the long history of the debate whether the whites would allow "coloreds," who had a qualified vote until removed from the voter's roll in 1951, as distinct from "Bantus" who had no right to vote at all, to participate more fully in the apartheid state government. The Bill was challenged by many in the "colored" community and was declared invalid and unconstitutional by the Supreme Court. After enlarging the Senate, the National Party pushed through the Bill and it became law. Although mainly driven by liberal whites, it was a debate some "colored people" vigorously participated in, mostly for, but many against. The community was divided between the benefits of the vote through which "coloreds" could then fight for the vote for all, and the argument that any participation in the system guaranteed the legitimization of the system, and that participation in apartheid means taking responsibility for apartheid. The generation of the seventies and eighties completely rejected the idea of such privileging at the cost of the majority.

54. See Boesak, *Running with Horses*, 77ff.

raises some fundamental questions. On whose behalf, one wonders, does the Declaration really speak? What does that historical context become, seen through the eyes of the powerful and privileged? How is such a-historical analysis possible? Exactly how is this "historical development" understood? Even a superficial glance at history reveals the long, and amazingly patient, engagement by black people in their struggle to make white South Africa understand "the things that make for peace," and the contempt with which this was treated by successive white minority regimes over decades. "How long?" cried out Albert Luthuli, echoing the agonized cry of the prophet Habakkuk, "How long before the Union's African people are seeking a new embodiment of new wishes? How long before, out of the depths they cry, 'If the man of peace does not prevail, give us the men of blood'?"[55]

This is not a call "from blood to blood." It is not a call of vengeful desperation caused by the loss of faith in nonviolent militancy. Neither is it a rallying call for the justification of violence as some have made it out to be. It is a cry of mourning for the hardness of heart in white South Africa, and the temptation for the people, in response to that hardness, to risk their soul in embracing what is closest to their oppressors' hearts. After Sharpeville, in December of 1960, the ANC made its decision to establish *Mkhonto we Sizwe*, the military army that would henceforth engage the apartheid regime with violence. With this, and the history that led to this decision in mind, Luthuli goes on to raise the question the men who wrote the Declaration did not ask. It was a decidedly *political* question, but as a political question, Luthuli made it a profoundly *moral* question, namely: Who *created* the dilemma? Who is really to blame for the decision to turn to violence? Certainly not the leaders of the ANC, whose patience, after more than fifty years of nonviolent struggle, of knocking on the door of reason, whites, from the colonialists in South Africa to the imperialists on the throne and in the corridors of power in England, had kept firmly closed, had finally worn out?[56] And Luthuli knows where the blame lies. With the white government who refuses to abandon a policy of racist oppression, and with their white supporters for whom the benefits of oppression and the treasures of exploitation were more precious than the blood of their black compatriots, especially in the light of the decades of extraordinary patience and endurance. "How easy it would have been," Luthuli makes plain in his Nobel Lecture, "for the natural feelings of resentment at white domination to have been turned into feelings of hatred and a desire for revenge against the white community."[57] That did not happen, however, and the reason why it did not happen was not accidental. It was because, "deliberately and advisedly, African leadership for the past fifty years... had set itself steadfastly against racial vaingloriousness."[58] Albert

---

55. See Couper, *Albert Luthuli*, 182.

56. This does not include the more than a hundred and seventy years of armed resistance against the colonialist settlers by the Khoi and San peoples.

57. See Couper, *Albert Luthuli*, 230.

58. Couper, *Albert Luthuli*, 182.

Luthuli, in sharp and supremely elevated contrast to the apartheid regime, did not believe that the use of violence was a show of strength, or racial superiority, or that it brings on respect or honor. It was mere "vainglory."

So the language of the Declaration, so carefully designed to couch deliberate processes of oppression and dehumanization in acceptable terms, is in truth a euphemism for the annihilation of the culture(s) and religion(s) of the indigenes in consciously designed acts of erasure—what we have come to recognize as "epistemicide." The words "historical developments" are here offered as a euphemism for a genocidal history of imperialism and colonialism, of Christian invasion, dispossession, and deliberate extermination of the indigenous peoples of the land. Why put the blame for the violent response of the apartheid regime to the nonviolent protests of March 21 on the black protesters instead of on the government, their police, and their army? Why seek justification for the *causes* by shifting blame to the *response* to those causes? Why shift the blame from white South Africans who were benefiting from colonialism and apartheid for centuries to "all groups"? Surely they knew that those "Whites Only" signs were not just meant for separate entrances or separate schools, for social amenities or for benches in parks, cars in trains, and the most beautiful beaches? Why such a deliberate lack of understanding for the root causes of the conflict? Such acquired innocence may be necessary for the oppressor, but it is deadly for the oppressed. And as I have argued before, it is this pseudo-innocence that constitutes the crime.[59] The Sharpeville massacre, and its immediate aftermath, is not something black people should even remotely take responsibility for. Albert Luthuli was abundantly clear on that point.[60]

Why could the white representatives of the churches, at least as direct beneficiaries of apartheid if not its direct perpetrators, not take responsibility for the intransigence of the white government, backed by the white voters, its resolute resistance to calls for peaceful change and for the utter failure of the church to unequivocally stand up for justice? Beyers Naudé did so, privately at first, and publicly, a few years later, setting an example that few, even in that much later stage, would be willing to follow.[61] Why force the victims to share responsibility for their oppression, the denial of their rights, and their death, with the authors, perpetrators, and beneficiaries of their oppression? Why must the protesters be made to feel guilt at their protest, at the audacity of their hope, at the display of their courage to demand rights, justice, and equality in

---

59. See "Introduction" in Boesak, *Farewell to Innocence*.

60. "And now, as never before the government is responsible for the civil violence that takes place." Luthuli, *Let My People Go!*, 228.

61. Speaking of forced removals as a "slow process of death," Naudé says, "And you know, I must feel the agony of this because I know that the people who are in control and in power doing this, these are my people. I cannot deny that I am an Afrikaner. I am nothing else but an Afrikaner . . . yet in that sense I don't see myself to be there—then the *agony of that separation . . .*" Emphasis mine. Then Naudé poses the issue that "separates" him from the Afrikaner: "What are the basic roots, what are the deepest roots of such an injustice, of such inhumanity? How do we continue to justify it, and that in the face of the fact that the whole world outside is turning like South Africa? This is wrong, this is inhuman, and this is evil . . ." See Naudé and Sölle, *Hope for Faith*, 9–10.

the land of their birth? But owning the critique of the system, as Beyers Naudé was willing to do, means resisting the system, and resisting the system means separation from that system and all its privileges and benefits. Not many whites were willing to do that. If not, though, the critique is nothing more than guilt-ridden, self-serving political theater, something oppressed people have no use for at all.

Likewise, the "Message to the People of South Africa" is a strong theological statement, emphasizing the unity of humankind, the sinfulness of separation and apartheid. It introduces the terms "false faith" and "a novel gospel" with regard to apartheid and its (implied) moral and theological justification, and calls for reconciliation. But it is, alas, a theological statement devoid of contextual understanding, and therefore of prophetic power and endurance. Nowhere is there any mention of social and political justice, no articulation of black aspirations, no sign of recognition that there was a struggle going on—despite the campaigns, trials, and deaths—and that God was calling the church to take sides in that struggle. It speaks of reconciliation, but there is no specific challenge to the white community on what reconciliation in our socio-political context might mean: remorse, repentance, justice, restitution, restoration, and the kind of forgiveness that signifies a profound shift in power relations.

However, one must be careful not to judge these events and actions with the flawless wisdom of hindsight. It is better to measure such statements within their own contexts; that is, by the known demands *of the oppressed* at the time, in whose name these church leaders, the majority of whom were white, took it upon themselves to speak. To begin with, we place these statements against the light of the views of a white Anglican priest, Trevor Huddleston, who, unlike most whites, did learn from blacks. His *Naught for Your Comfort* is a scathing attack on white oppression and white complacency coming from a priest who took the people's demands seriously.[62] Read against the light of Albert Luthuli's autobiography, it is as clear a Christian witness for justice as this country has ever seen, and, from a purely political point of view, Mandela's statement at his trial, his almost scientific analysis of the reasons for the ANC's choice for violence "after fifty years" of nonviolent resistance. More to the point, the church leaders also had Luthuli within their reach, as fellow Christian, who believed that on these matters, it is black voices that should be heard.[63]

> *Africans Should Categorically Reject the Bantustans Because*: they purport to meet our demand for direct participation in the government of the country by some pseudo plan of self-government which is falsely acclaimed by the government as conforming to the traditional form of government in African society . . . *The progress of Bantustans will not be judged on the affluence of a few: chiefs, traders, civil servants and professional people who are hardly* 12

62. Huddleston, *Naught for Your Comfort*.
63. See Luthuli, *Let My People Go!*, 176–77: "I see no clever strategy in leaving [whites] to attribute fictitious attitudes to us when in fact we have *real* attitudes of our own." His aim was "to ensure that if the whites are ignorant of the realities, the fault does not lie with us."

percent of the people. What will matter more is the raising of the general standard of living of the masses of the people to progressively approach a civilized standard of living.[64]

There could have been no doubt whatsoever about the aspirations of black South Africans at the time, the demands they were making, the sacrifices they were called to, or the grim determination of the government to uphold and defend white supremacy. Equally clear were the noble aspirations they articulated on behalf of all South Africans, as the Freedom Charter of 1955 testifies.[65] White leadership simply found it too hard to speak prophetically, or failing that, to stand aside and let black leadership speak for the people. Even the best of white leadership failed to grasp this. Dr. Frits Gaum, one-time leader of the DRC and, in his context also one of the most liberal thinking persons, unwittingly still finds himself defending the motivations for, and the intentions of, apartheid even though he himself has long since abandoned defending the policy itself.[66]

As part explanation of this instinctive defense, Gaum quotes Roman Catholic Archbishop Denis Hurley of Natal, a highly respected white liberal, at the time also Chair of the Institute for Race Relations. "My personal view," Gaum reports Hurley as having stated in a meeting in 1966,

> is that separate development as Christian solution for the race question could be acceptable if it meets four conditions. One, the policy must be implementable. Two, it must have the consent of all concerned. Three, there must be a proportional sharing of sacrifices, and four, the rights of all people must be safeguarded in the period of transition. *In principle, there can be no objection to an honest and just sharing of South Africa amongst all its racial groups.* But nobody can convince me that what is happening at the moment is either just or "sharing."[67]

It is not clear to me what the statement "the rights of all people should be guarded in the period of transition" means. Gaum provides no further clarification. Uppermost, already though, are the questions: What rights are meant here? Who defines those rights, and who is to "guard" them? "Rights" in prosperous, developed, "white" South Africa, cannot possibly be the same as "rights" in a Bantustan, under some tinpot dictator appointed by the apartheid regime. The most logical understanding, I suggest, must be the desire for white privileges and rights to be guaranteed in a possible process of transition between white minority regime and democracy, which became

---

64. In Couper, *Albert Luthuli*, 80.

65. "We the People of South Africa, black and white together . . . declare . . . South Africa belongs to all who live in it . . . We the People . . . equals, countrymen and brothers . . ." See Luthuli, *Let My People Go!*, 237.

66 See Gaum and Gaum, *Praat Verby Grense*, 46.

67. Gaum and Gaum, *Praat Verby Grense*, 46. Emphasis mine.

reality thirty years later, and which is exactly what whites bargained for, and got, in the secret talks and in the negotiations. With regard to what amounted to blanket amnesty for the apartheid human rights abusers, it was called "transitional justice," or more boldly, "restorative justice." With regard to real economic power remaining in the hands of whites, South Africa chose for neoliberal capitalism. The new black elite got what they called "deracialization of capital." The masses got undeserved, increasing impoverishment. And we ensconced the right to keep most of the land in white hands in the clause on private property in article 25 of the Constitution, all of it sanctified by the Constitution's sacred foundation: Ubuntu and reconciliation.

However, the question remains: Transition from what to what? Furthermore, why on earth did the bishop think that apartheid, in whatever form, would ever have "the consent" of all concerned? And how could there be any realistic expectation that whites (if they are included in Bishop Hurley's calculations) who support apartheid precisely because blacks shared all the sacrifices and whites all the benefits would be willing to share *any* of the sacrifices necessary to make apartheid work, if these sacrifices could even be calculated? American civil rights leader Jesse Jackson always spoke of "sharing the pain." With more than 350 years of colonization, dehumanization, slavery, land theft, genocide, and apartheid, can whites really share the pain, or make up for it, even if they wanted to? If, as we have learned over the past twenty-five years, whites' greatest desire is to "move on," is that even possible?

But finally, the point is not what could convince the Archbishop. Who should be convinced are the black oppressed masses of South Africa, and they were always clear on what they wanted. One glance at the Freedom Charter should make that abundantly clear. This is exactly the kind of attitude and presumptuousness that made Biko so critical of the white liberal. Why is it so difficult for white people to let go of their craving to decide what is good and acceptable for black people? The point is that the struggle leadership never spoke of accepting Bantustans under certain "conditions." They always spoke of *unconditional* freedom in the land of their birth.

Radical Black Christianity

The decade of the 70s brought Steve Biko and Black Consciousness and Black liberation theology, renewed black political activity, the concept of black power, the unequivocal rejection of white paternalism, Soweto and the children's revolution. All this came with a challenge to black people never experienced before. Steve Biko confronted black people with what he called "the first truth, bitter as it may seem, that we have to acknowledge," and it is the fact that the black person has lost their personhood; that we were "reduced to an obliging shell," that all in all, the black person has become "a shadow of a man completely defeated, drowning in his own misery, a slave, an ox bearing the yolk of oppression with sheepish timidity."[68]

Steve Biko accused the Black Church of not just complacency, but of "conniving" with an oppressive ideology and an interpretation of the Scriptures that has become a depressingly efficient instrument for the subjugation of the people. We did not just accept, we "connived at an appalling irrelevance of the scriptures . . . a colonist-trained version of Christianity" that has nothing liberating, comforting, or humanizing to say in a country "teeming with injustice and fanatically committed to the practice of oppression, intolerance and blatant cruelty because of racial bigotry . . . where all black people are made to feel the unwanted step-children of a God whose presence they cannot feel . . ."[69]

Those words, and the actions of the children of Soweto and across the country, reinventing and redefining the struggle for liberation in myriad ways, were the challenges the Black Church had to meet. It was a challenge to the church's preaching, teaching, and understanding of its role in public affairs.[70] But it could not be the church that perpetuated a colonized theology, conniving with the oppressor and standing sheepishly by the wayside while the children were being slaughtered. As a result, the 70s saw a fundamental renewal of the Black Church, the prophetic church, the restless, disturbing presence for the church and society. It was a church defined not by doctrinal affiliation nor ecclesiastical sanction or denominational understanding; but rather by obedience to Christ, by faithfulness to the prophetic call of the gospel, by receptiveness to the spirit of the ancestors such as Jan Paerl, Sol Plaatjie, and Albert Luthuli. The fighting spirit of the women of the 1956 march, and the compelling, sacrificial presence of the children.

In 1979, at an SACC conference, I tried to spell out what such a Black Church should be:

- This is a church that embraces a black understanding of the gospel as a gospel of hope, liberation, and justice. It is a gospel that speaks directly to our situations of oppression and subjugation. It is the result of a painful, soul-searching struggle of black Christians with God and with the meaning of God's Word for their lives today.

- This church has wrestled with black history—a history of suffering and degradation and humiliation caused by white racism. They refuse to believe that the gospel could corroborate the narrow, racist ideology white churches were preaching and white theologians were giving respectability through their teaching.

- This church knows that the God of the exodus and the covenant, the God of Jesus of Nazareth, was different from the God white Christianity was proclaiming.

---

68. Biko, *I Write What I Like*, 30–31.
69. Biko, *I Write What I Like*, 60, 61.
70. E.g., Boesak, *Finger of God*, 1–17.

- This church believed that the gospel of Jesus Christ does not deny the struggle for black humanity, and it is with this light from God's Word that they went into the struggle, both within the church and outside of it.

- Out of this struggle emerged the Black Church, a broad movement of black Christians, joined in a black solidarity that transcends all barriers of denomination and ethnicity. It shares the black experience, the same understanding of suffering and oppression, and the same struggle for liberation from all forms of oppression, firmly rooted in the belief that the gospel of Jesus Christ proclaims the total liberation of all people and that the God of Jesus Christ is the God of the oppressed.

- We made one other point: We must remember that in a situation such as ours blackness (a state of oppression) is not only a color; it is a *condition*. "And it is within this perspective that the role of white Christians should be understood . . . I do not speak of those who happen to be leaders in the black churches. Nor do I refer to those who happen to be in control of churches where black are the majority. I speak of those white Christians who have understood their own guilt in the oppression of blacks in terms of corporate responsibility, who have genuinely repented and genuinely converted; those who have committed themselves to the struggle for liberation and who, through their commitment, have taken upon themselves the condition of blackness in South Africa. In a real sense, they bear the 'marks of Christ.' They are part of the black church not as lords and masters, but as servants, not as 'liberals' but as brothers and sisters, for they have learned not so much how to do for blacks, but to identify with what blacks are doing to secure their liberation . . . this is the black church . . ."[71]

The Black Church rejected the anemic, inadequate theology of accommodation and acquiescence, of individualistic, other-worldly spirituality foisted upon us by Western Christianity; that taught us to accept the existing unjust order as God-ordained. We embraced, rather, what I called a "theology of refusal"(in tandem with the "politics of refusal")—a theology that refused to accept God as a God of oppression, but rather as a God of liberation who calls people to actively participate in the struggle for justice and liberation.[72]

Lewis V. Baldwin makes very much the same point with regard to the Black Church in the United States,

> There was a consensus of beliefs, attitudes, values, and expectations that bound them together despite the incidentals that distinguished them from one another. Thus they were able to establish to a broad, interdenominational tradition of shared involvement in the struggle for a just and inclusive society . . .[73]

---

71. See Boesak, *Black and Reformed*, 21–22. See also Boesak, *Running with Horses*, 48–62.
72. Boesak, *Black and Reformed*, 26.
73. Baldwin, "Revisiting the 'All-Comprehending Institution,'" in Smith, *New Day Begun*, 18.

It is perhaps not unimportant to note two things at this point. One, this Black Church included those whites who made the choice for justice and liberation, thereby, within the context of the times, taking upon themselves the "condition of blackness."[74] Two, the apartheid establishment against which we set ourselves was the white minority government and its collaborators in the black communities, its apartheid institutions in the so-called colored and Indian communities and in the Bantustans, none of which would have existed without the willing cooperation of black people making *their* choice for apartheid and its rewards. This was a huge step away from the racial separatism of pure apartheid, the disengaging paternalism of white liberalism and the multi-racialism of modified apartheid, toward the non-racialism South Africa cannot do without.

Four theological documents from the 1980s best demonstrate this phase of the struggle and the character of this prophetic, activist church as described above. First is the Charter of Alliance of Black Reformed Christians of Southern Africa.[75] In this charter, black Reformed Christians, till then hopelessly divided by a history of missionary domination in Southern Africa, deliberately attempt to rescue the Reformed tradition from the perversion of the ideologically driven theology of apartheid. This step gave Reformed theology a new identity in Africa, a new vitality in the ecumenical movement, and played a decisive role in the ultimate decision of the World Alliance of Reformed Churches to declare apartheid a sin and its theological justification a heresy.

Second is *The Belhar Confession*, written and proposed in 1982 and finally adopted by the Dutch Reformed Mission Church in 1986. The Confession is the church's stand against the heresy of the theology of apartheid and the church's theological understanding of and guidance in its prophetic participation in the continuing struggles for justice ever since. It consists of four articles centered on unity, compassionate justice, and reconciliation. Uniquely describing the church as "the possession of God," it calls upon the church to "stand where God stands," namely, with the poor, oppressed, the wronged, and the destitute. It confesses God as the God of indivisible justice, and calls for the church to fight against *any* form of injustice *wherever* it may be found.[76]

Third is the well-known *Kairos Document*, produced by the so-called Kairos theologians, and published by the South African Council of Churches and the Institute of Contextual Theology. It was the first of a series of "Kairos Documents" that saw the light in many countries across the world and in my view, one of the most important ecumenical documents of the twentieth century. It was a powerful exposure of "State

---

74. If this sounds like a paradox, it is what I would call a "redemptive paradox." The point here, again, is to underscore that for Black Consciousness, this was the gateway to non-racial inclusivity. In the end, it was not "race" that was the main determinant of a person's being and existence, but a person's humanitarian consciousness, their commitment to the liberation of all humanity.

75. De Gruchy and Villa-Vicencio, *Apartheid Is a Heresy*, 161–68. The Charter was adopted by the Alliance at its conference in Hammanskraal, South Africa, on October 26–30, 1981.

76. The text of the Confession can be found in an appendix in Boesak, "To Stand Where God Stands."

theology" and "Church theology" versus "prophetic theology," always recognizing the urgency of the times and the moment of truth (*kairos*): knowing that the stakes are immeasurably high; it is a matter of life and death. In these situations, neutrality is no longer possible, the church must make choices, since God is a God that takes sides. It exposed injustice and oppression, violence and exploitation, exclusion and class struggles, offering severe critical analysis of the role of the church in these struggles. There is also deep self-critical awareness of our own complicity and hence a call for conversion, prophetic action, and participation in struggles for justice.[77]

Fourth, there is the call for the day of prayer for the "Fall of Unjust Rule," in 1986. The language of the "Theological Rationale" accompanying this call speaks for itself:

> Now, on 16th June, and twenty-five years after the dawning of this phase of resistance, it is right to remember those whose blood has been shed in resistance and protest against an unjust system. It is also right that we as Christians reassess out response to a system that all right-thinking people identify as unjust. We have prayed for our rulers, as is demanded of us in the scriptures. We have entered into consultation with them, as required by our faith. We have taken the reluctant and drastic step of declaring apartheid to be contrary to the declared will of God, and some churches have declared its theological justification to be a heresy. We now pray that God will replace the present structures of oppression with ones that are just, and remove from power those who persist in defying his laws, installing in their place leaders who will govern with justice and mercy.[78]

These documents demonstrating the difference between hesitant, paternalistic, white leadership and radicalized black leadership caused severe oppressive responses from government and the white establishment and deep division within the churches, even "anti-apartheid" churches. But it established simultaneously a radical theological departure and a new grammar for the churches, and it defined the role of the churches in public affairs and in struggles for justice in new ways. It brought together a new kind of church across boundaries of denomination and race and doctrine, committed to the justice the gospel calls for and the liberation of the oppressed people of South Africa.

We realized that the banning of liberation movements also meant that "the church has become more important than ever before as a vehicle for expressing the legitimate aspirations of black people."[79] Rejecting false notions of love, reconciliation, and peace without justice and restoration, shunning the "cheap grace" of political accommodation to apartheid, we called for full and meaningful participation in the struggle. We called for the church to "initiate and support meaningful pressure to

---

77. E.g., Smit, *Essays in Public Theology*, 251–54.
78. Boesak and Villa-Vicencio, *When Prayer Makes News*, 26.
79. Boesak, *Black and Reformed*, 27.

the entrenched system as a nonviolent way of bringing about change . . . to initiate and support programs of civil disobedience on a massive scale and challenge white Christians especially on this issue . . ."[80] and worked for divestment and sanctions on the apartheid regime. We called support for the World Council of Churches' Program to Combat Racism including its Special Fund with its humanistic support for liberation movements.

We challenged the white church and establishment on its hypocrisy regarding the issue of violence—why the violence of the oppressed in response to tyranny and in service of their freedom was condemned, but the violence of the state in defense of an evil system was not challenged. We called the church from white guardianship to black leadership, from sympathy to engagement, from a theology of protest to a theology of resistance and struggle. The role of this church in the struggle during the 1980s and in the non-racial United Democratic Front is now a matter of record, and the dawn of democracy in South Africa is not conceivable without the role of the prophetic church, a conscientized black leadership and the infusion of radical, black Christianity. For it was in response to the challenge of Biko and the children of Soweto that the prophetic church arose, claimed its historic responsibility, and honored the ancestor-prophets on whose shoulders we stood.

Activism in "Post-apartheid" South Africa

After 1994, it was as if the voice of the prophetic church in South Africa had died. As I pointed out above, reasons for this have been advanced and most of them are probably valid,[81] but it depends on where one stands when these arguments are made. The issue for prophetic faithfulness is never who is in power, but whether those in power are using it in the service of compassionate justice and dignity and especially for those most vulnerable. For the small elite who have hugely benefited from change in South Africa in the last twenty-five years or so, the quality of our liberation is decidedly different than for the vast majority of our people who remain crushed under the heavy burden of chronic poverty, deepening hopelessness, and angry disillusionment. The true measurement of good government, John Calvin stressed, is whether it does justice and defends and maintains the rights of the poor. Calvin is not speaking of charity, goodwill, or trickle-down capitalism, but of justice and *rights*.[82]

South Africa is a country of vast and unsustainable inequalities.[83] Unemployment is unacceptably high, especially among the youth; service delivery to the poor

---

80. Boesak, *Black and Reformed*, 30.

81. E.g., Boesak, *Tenderness of Conscience*, 156–157.

82. Calvin, *Opera 45*, 82.

83. The new, multi-racial elite (20 percent of the population receives 74 percent of the GDP, while the poorest of the poor (53 percent) received 6–8 percent. Even ten years ago, Archbishop Njonkongkulu Ndugane described poverty as a "time bomb"; see *African Monitor Poverty Report*.

is such that we have had five years of unending, increasingly violent protests on the streets of our townships. The anger is deep and abiding. We have seen the reckless militarization of our police force, and almost as a matter of course, instances of police brutality have become alarmingly high. Police have orders to "shoot to kill" and so they do: from toddlers in cars parked in driveways to teenagers at a party to protesters against government corruption to a young woman who accidentally backed her car into a stationary police vehicle.

Our children will be presented with the legacy of the utter foolishness of our having bought arms worth more than R 60 billion in a deal fraught with suspicion of corruption, when there is no discernible threat to the country and while we know the greatest threat to our security to be poverty, inequality, and our lack of social cohesion. These are the issues crying out to the activist church in "post-apartheid" South Africa. Colonialism, slavery, and apartheid were not disparate and separated historical phases—the one was the logical consequence of the other, built upon the foundation of the other. Nor were they just a matter of attitudes; they were solidified in political, social, economic, religious, and judicial structures of oppression and exploitation. Racism was at the heart of it for over 350 years. Racism is still a controlling category of South African society and perhaps we should remember at least three things here: First, the way, as a system of oppression, racism creates both victims and beneficiaries; second, its enormity and its all-encompassing reality; and third, the fact that its effects, for both victims and beneficiaries, are trans-generational.

We have removed all the racist, apartheid legislation from our books, but we are still a deeply racialized society. When one thinks of it, and this is perhaps a fourth factor, one is struck by the permanentization of separation in the spatial, physical, psychological, economic, and social legacy of apartheid, and one wonders how we shall ever overcome it. Racist incidents still abound, racist talk comes from both sides of the color line, our political discourse is replete with it, and the ANC has, to the distress of millions, brought back apartheid's official racial categorization. In South Africa, what Emerson and Yancey call "the three dimensions of whiteness"[84] is a present reality. White South Africans call every effort to rectify the wrongs of the past "racism-in-reverse," and by the same token resist the process of genuine transformation. Every decision to put a black person in a position of responsibility, whether in sports, business, or the academy has to be justified; a white appointment guarantees automatic meritorious virtue.[85] We are beset still with racial inequality, racial alienation, and

---

84. Emerson and Yancey, *Transcending Racial Barriers*, 12, 13. They identify white structural advantage, white normativity, and white transparency.

85. As a very recent practical example as a phenomenon that repeats itself regularly, see the heated public debate on the selection for the Springbok rugby team for the 2012 Rugby World Cup, *The Cape Argus*, June 2, 2011. For a more systematic, theoretical argumentation, see Cromhout, "Die Vermyding van Etniese Spanning." Cromhout refers to the pervasiveness of "racism" by which he means what is called "racism in reverse"—in, for example, the (Afrikaans) "language debate," the changing of street names and names of towns, and the South African government's "ideology of transformation."

racial division. The activist church will have to manifest the genuine non-racial community South Africans and the world desperately need and which South Africa has made a pillar of our struggles for such a long time.

Genuine non-racialism is fundamentally different from the shallow "color-blindness" that comes from a denial of racism and its pernicious effects of white supremacy and its systemic pervasiveness. The insistence on South Africa as having become a "color-blind" society blinds us to the permanency of separation, as well as to ongoing racial micro-aggression, which is the "brief commonplace daily verbal, behavioral or environmental indignation, whether intentional or unintentional, that communicate hostile, derogatory or negative racial slights and insults toward people of color."[86] For the vast majority of our people, we are not a post-apartheid, post-racial society. I would suggest that the measure for whether this is so lies not with those few who have become collaborators and beneficiaries of the global neoliberal capitalist empire, but as Albert Luthuli suggested even then, with the masses of those whose hunger and thirst for justice have not been satisfied, the most vulnerable and woundable in our society, those forced to stare at life from the bottom of the well. For them, as the fiery Henry Highland Garnet differently, but much more truthfully, put it so long ago, "There are Pharaohs on both sides of the blood-red waters."[87] The activist church is called to discern this fundamental truth and act upon it.

The activist church will have to learn to see these realities, like the Accra Confession says, "through the eyes of those who suffer." Then we too will "discern the signs of the times," see a "scandalous world that denies God's call to life for all." We, too, will hear that "creation continues to groan in bondage" as the "plundering of the earth" continues. We too will see the "dramatic convergence of political and military might," and that economic systems are "a matter of life and death."[88] Then we too shall experience the righteous anger that comes from suffering injustice and indignity. We need much more than our current heretical embrace of free-market, neoliberal, capitalist prosperity. We need Robert Franklin's prophetic radicalism with social justice as the goal,[89] just as we need King's early insight that "the roots [of economic injustice] are in the system rather than in men or faulty operations," that "something is wrong . . . with capitalism . . . [that] there must be a better distribution of wealth and maybe America needs to move toward democratic socialism."[90] We have to hear and heed Steve Biko, who warned us that a few black faces in office will not bring fundamental change. Without a completely new economic policy, that is, away from neoliberal capitalism,

---

86. See et al., "Racial Micro-aggressions."
87. See Wilmore, *Black Religion*, 120. See also Boesak, *Pharaohs on Both Sides*.
88. See "Accra Confession."
89. See Daniels, "Doing All the Good We Can," 178.
90. See Dyson, *I May Not Get There with You*, 87, 88. See also Boesak, *Coming In Out of the Wilderness*, 38–41.

"our society will be run almost as of yesterday."[91] The challenges are at once local and global: poverty and wealth, socio-economic justice, and the domination and salvific claims of neoliberal capitalism; the challenge to end gratuitous violence, state and private terror, and global war; gender justice and patriarchal domination; justice and the dignity of human sexuality; environmental justice and the security of the earth and its resources for all.

Finally, the activist church shall have to be inclusive in the broadest sense, not just on the matter of race, gender, and sexual orientation, all matters that begs our attention,[92] but open to responding to the urgent call of interreligious solidarity in the ongoing struggles against oppression.[93] This is not just because the anti-apartheid and civil rights struggles have already shown the way. The threat to world peace in all its manifestations is often carried by multi-religious fundamentalism. The struggle for world peace and justice must be carried by interreligious solidarity. Besides, the thrust of peaceful revolution towards justice, democracy, and a new, meaningful, humane way of life in the world today at the moment comes from North Africa and the Middle East. It is there, in the midst of those momentous events, where vital decisions are being made, determinative not just for them, but for the future of our world. In the twentieth century, it was the civil rights struggle in the US and the anti-apartheid struggle in South Africa that presented the international community with the moral choice for justice or injustice, dehumanization or humaneness, right or wrong. Right now, that decision is presented by the renewed revolutionary stirrings across the Global South, but most urgently still by the Palestinian struggle for freedom and the right of return. It is by its sensitivity for these situations that the prophetic church today will regain its authenticity. This is what King called "the right side of the world revolution."[94]

In this way, and only this way, radical, activist Christianity can continue to make its valuable contribution to a worldwide activism for the sake of the people of the world and the earth, remaining a restless presence in the church and in the world. Perhaps then the young Steve Bikos of today will find the church a place where they may be encouraged and supported in their pursuit of their ultimate purpose on earth, "which is to do good."[95]

---

91. Biko, *I Write What I Like*, 169. See the detailed discussion on this issue in ch. 7.
92. See chs. 5, 6, and 7.
93. See Esack, *Qur'an, Liberation and Pluralism*.
94. King, "Beyond Vietnam," 240.
95. Biko, *I Write What I Like*, 238.

5

Testing the Inescapable Network of Mutuality

Luthuli, King, and Biko—Global Challenge, Global Solidarity, Global Resistance

A Tent and a Voice at Midnight

The year was 1968, the year of my ordination as a twenty-two-year-old in Immanuel Dutch Reformed Mission Church congregation in Paarl, South Africa, a town at the foot of the mountains nestled in the breathtakingly beautiful Winelands country of the Western Cape. My congregation was in turmoil, in the throes of forced removals as a result of apartheid laws: as it would everywhere, the Group Areas Act, the refinement of the 1913 and 1936 Land Acts, had come to Paarl. It struck with its familiar, relentless cruelty. Most of the town had been declared a "white" area. All those classified "non-white" were forcibly removed to east of the river, had their homes confiscated or bulldozed, their sacred buildings desecrated: sold insultingly cheap—communities under this sword of Damocles had no power, nor the strength to negotiate with the inevitable—to be used for something more useful to white people, or razed to the ground. Families who had lived there for generations would hold out as long as they could. Finally, however, they would be moved, their communities and memories, their history and their dreams violently uprooted, sometimes eventually obliterated. Epistemicide indeed does take on many forms. All of a sudden, the beauty of this place—a "pearl" glittering in the Boland sunrise—would be forever scarred by the ugliness of apartheid from which there would be no escape anywhere. It was a time of great upheaval, turmoil, and anger; a time in great need of the word of prophetic truth. I, however, was completely unprepared for the challenges of justice to my ministry.[1]

---

1. There is yet another side to this story, a powerful encounter with an older woman in the church, her exposure of my theological and political inadequacies, and her challenge to and encouragement in my ministry; see Boesak, *Running with Horses*, 33–34.

It was the year of the discovery of the total inadequacy of my theological training at my seminary where I was tutored by teachers from the white Dutch Reformed Church who believed in the theology of apartheid, white supremacy, and the divine right of the Afrikaner as God's chosen people to lay claim to the land of my ancestors, the determination of my future, the content of my dignity, and the definition of my identity and my freedom. It was the year of the first phase of my farewell to that bland but toxic mixture of Reformed theology, European pietism, and Afrikaner *Volksromantik,* that utterly distorted version of the radical Calvinist tradition, what Martin Luther King Jr. called "a completely other-worldly religion which makes a strange, un-biblical distinction between body and soul, between the sacred and the secular."[2] At least, in the version they presented to their "daughter churches." For themselves, they had no trouble using Calvinism for their own Christian-National, political ambitions and political rule. This would be the year of the discovery that my discontent with the world and the church, as they were, was total. King's powerful, rhythmic litany of "divine dissatisfaction" with American apartheid would become mine with South African apartheid.[3]

It is not as if I had not seen and experienced the devastating workings of the Group Areas Act before. The destruction of Cape Town's famed District Six and Johannesburg's Sophiatown and their communities was already becoming the stuff of dreadful legend. Somerset West, my hometown a scant hour away, was hit by those same laws, and my family was one of thousands who had lost our homes. So the anger, the sense of injustice, and the frustration of not being able to do anything meaningful about it were not new. But I was not asked to stand in the pulpit, preach about this particular evil in Somerset West; I was not expected to offer succor, comfort, and the promise of justice from the Word of God to my people as I was in Paarl. In Somerset West, I was a teenager, angry at what was happening to my family, not yet fully seeing the wider implications of these events and not yet reading the signs of the times the way I would later. In Paarl, I was a pastor who was called upon to speak to the angry and fear-filled hearts of my church, on behalf of all our people struck by this injustice, and in the name of the God of justice. This is just one of the many reasons why I have such complete understanding for the preachers of the gospel and Imams and pastors in occupied Palestine as they seek to serve their people engaged in the life and death struggles against the Israeli occupation, the brutalities of land-theft and war.

---

2. See King, *Radical King*, 142. In truth, this process had already begun in earnest with my introduction to Rev. Beyers Naudé in 1965, and his careful explanation of the pivotal importance of the need for moral, biblical, and theological justification of apartheid in the ideology and practice of that system in the Afrikaner mind in general. But it was especially true for those in the Afrikaner community for whom it was so absolutely crucial to have "God on their side." However, the difference in understanding this intellectually and employing that knowledge in one's ministry, preaching, and activism was considerable.

3. King, *Radical King*, 178–79.

It was also the year of the publication of the South African Council of Churches' *Message to the People of South Africa,* the attempt by mainly white theologians to articulate the sinfulness of apartheid, following on the 1960 *Cottesloe Declaration.*[4] But it was simultaneously the dawning of my understanding that in a situation of struggle, pain, and suffering, commitment means, to quote Rev. Beyers Naudé, that "the time for pious words is over."[5] My pious words from the pulpit would not be enough, would not assuage the hunger and thirst for justice in those sitting in the pews, and would not suffice in the struggle against a system declared a crime against humanity, a sin, a heresy, and a blasphemy.

In April of that year, Martin Luther King Jr. was murdered, and while the stunned grief that reverberated around the world echoed in Black South Africa, in the pages of an Afrikaans Sunday paper they reported it with undisguised glee. I did not know him of course, but I knew *of* him. Clearly though, the apartheid regime *did* know him, or enough about him, and greatly feared him and his influence, especially on young, black South Africans in danger of discovering the power of faith in the revolutionary gospel of Jesus of Nazareth. Nothing could be read of or about King. His books, recordings of his sermons and speeches, everything he had said, were banned by the government: forbidden. Possessing, reading, and disseminating banned material was an offense against one or other of the vast array of draconian laws enacted by the apartheid regime. In this time, Rev. Dale White of the well-known Wilgespruit Conference Centre in Johannesburg, a preacher, activist, and mentor to many from the Johannesburg townships, went on trial because, amongst other deeds considered seditious by the apartheid regime, he had disseminated a recording of a Martin Luther King speech.

In September of that year, I was leading the Bible study at the week-long spring camp for the Association of Christian Students. Some three hundred young people from high schools across the country, the few teacher colleges we had, and the one university college persons classified "colored" were forced to attend. At some point during that week, someone whispered in my ear and asked whether I wanted to listen to "a secret tape." It was a tape recording of Martin Luther King's sermon at the

---

4. See the discussion in ch. 3 above. See also Boesak, *Kairos, Crisis, and Global Apartheid,* 76–82. These documents, however well meant, lacked completely the urgency of involvement in the struggle, of having taken sides in the struggle, even of an awareness that a struggle was going on. Of black Christians' wrestling to connect their faith to that struggle, or that the choice for "obedience to God" actually meant *commitment* to and *participation* in that struggle as the critical dimensions of one's faith such as Albert Luthuli showed by example throughout his life, there is practically no sign.

5. These words are from a key sentence in a crucially important article in which Naudé defends his decision to openly support the World Council of Churches' Program to Combat Racism and its Special Fund that provided financial support to Southern African liberation movements. The article, significantly titled, "The Parting of the Ways" (*Pro Veritate,* October, 1970), signals the intensification of the tensions between Naudé and the white population of South Africa, Afrikaans and English speaking alike as Naudé's solidarity with the freedom struggle signified more and more personal commitment and involvement. See Boesak, *Kairos, Crisis, and Global Apartheid,* ch. 3, especially 75–82.

National Cathedral in Washington DC, earlier that year, "Remaining Awake through a Great Revolution,"[6] which included King's masterful retelling and application of the Rip van Winkle story. Perhaps it was a copy of the same recording Rev. White was on trial for.

In that sermon, Martin Luther King utters one immortal word after the other, and over the years, reading and rereading would reveal other words of power in this sermon. But what, at that time, really caught and held my attention were the words that have become the title of this chapter. Their relevance seem to have only deepened since Dr. King voiced them all these years ago:

> All life is interrelated, and we are all bound up in an inescapable network of mutuality, tied in a single garment of destiny. Whatever affects one directly, affects all indirectly. For some strange reason I can never be what I ought to be, until you are what you ought to be. And you can never be what you ought to be until I am what I ought to be. This is the interrelated structure of reality.[7]

This chapter discusses the impact of that concept on the generation that was to lead the struggle in its final phase against apartheid. It seeks to explore the meaning of those words for Martin Luther King Jr., his work, and his life, and their impact on his growing understanding of its truth concerning worldwide struggles for freedom and justice. It seeks, secondly, to understand their meaning in the interconnectedness with Albert Luthuli, his Christian leadership in the struggle against apartheid in South Africa. Third, it will ask to what extent, within the context of the strong reemergence of Black theology and Black Consciousness, this concept has lessons to offer South Africans as we struggle to find the right ways towards genuine democracy in post-1994 South Africa, and in our connectedness with worldwide struggles for justice, as we search for a global ethic of solidarity and resistance.

The Inescapable Network of Mutuality

Listening to that smuggled-in tape that night, I was struck with awe, not just by that voice, by the gripping, soaring rhetoric, or by what I would come to know as the rhythmic, mesmerizing cadences of Black preaching from America. I was moved by the prophetic unfolding of the story for us at that time; by the sheer power of the truth he spoke so plainly and fearlessly. I did not know him, did not understand American politics or the struggle for racial justice there—certainly not in the way I was beginning to understand more and more the dynamics of our own struggle—did not even

---

6. This was a recording of the sermon King preached at the National Cathedral in Washington DC, which was to be his last full Sunday sermon before his death four days later; see https://kinginstitute.stanford.edu/king. For the text of the sermon, see King, *Testament of Hope*, 268–78. King makes reference to this story in several speeches and sermons before this final delivery; see, e.g., King, *Where Do We Go from Here*, 170.

7. See King, "Remaining Awake," 268–78.

know where precisely Washington DC, was. Why then was I so moved, so stirred with anger, so compelled by the power of his words? Why was I so convinced that we, black South Africans and the Black Church in South Africa, were the ones sleeping through the great revolutions of our time, including our own? Why did I feel that I understood intuitively what black Americans were enduring, hoping and fighting for; that our struggles were intertwined, that the justice King was talking about as the longing of his people and the desire of God, was also the justice our people called for, in my church and right through South Africa? Why did I immediately understand that our thinking was too small, unworthy both of our situation, our calling, and our God; that we were so intent on the "windows of opportunity" opened ever so slightly at the whim of the powerful and privileged that we did not even see the doors opened wide by the God of history?

It was not because of the rudimentary connections between the anti-apartheid struggle and the civil rights struggle that certainly did exist at the time but that we were mostly unaware of. I did not then know that in 1962 Martin Luther King Jr. and Albert Luthuli were the two most significant signatories to the appeal to Western governments to isolate the apartheid regime through sanctions and divestment. And in this relationship there was a radicalization in King that paralleled his radicalization vis-à-vis the American situation. Whereas, for example, in 1958 King referred to the apartheid regime as a "government who sponsors a more rigid program of segregation,"[8] that euphemistic language was gone by 1965.[9] Nor did I know of King's real admiration for our own Defiance Campaign of the 1950s and Luthuli's fearless leadership, inspired by his Christian faith. Lewis V. Baldwin, that great King scholar, has written more extensively than anyone on the relationship between King and the oppressed in South Africa from the time King assumed the pastorate of the Dexter Avenue Baptist Church in Montgomery, Alabama, in the mid-1950s.[10] Baldwin also discloses the growing relationship of comradeship between Albert Luthuli and King, even though the two men never met. Their convictions, commitments, and leadership acted as mutual inspiration.[11]

King understood the interconnectivity, and wanted South Africans to know that he thought that South Africans were involved "in the far more deadly struggle for

8. See Baldwin, "Coalition of Conscience," 53–82.

9. King's awareness of the interconnectivity and interdependence of our struggles would grow as his commitment to both would deepen. See King, "Let My People Go," a speech given on December 10, 1965, in support of the anti-apartheid struggle, in King, *Radical King*, 107–12. His powerful opening sentences set the tone for the judgement on apartheid, its leaders and beneficiaries, and the call for nonviolent, militant resistance on an international scale. Note the telling overturning of the word "savage," one of colonialism's favorite descriptions of the colonized. "Africa does have spectacular savages and brutes today, but they are not black. They are the sophisticated white rulers of South Africa who profess to be cultured, religious and civilised, but whose conduct and philosophy stamp them unmistakably as modern-day barbarians." King, *Radical King*, 107,

10. Baldwin, "Coalition of Conscience," 54; see also Baldwin, *Toward the Beloved Community*, 5.

11. Baldwin, "Coalition of Conscience," 58.

freedom."[12] As a South African, I appreciate the show of solidarity. However, even taking into account that in Sharpeville's 1960, we were still four years away from the bombing at 16th Street Baptist Church in Birmingham, Alabama, which killed four young black girls, one has to wonder whether in his desire to show that solidarity, King forgot about the extraordinary violence faced by black Americans. I am thinking not only of the over four-thousand lynchings over the years that were going on even as King spoke, but also of the massacres that dwarfed the Sharpeville massacre: the so-called Red Summer massacre in Elaine, Arkansas, in October 1919, when over a hundred African Americans were slaughtered by gangs of white men.[13] I am thinking also of the Tulsa, Oklahoma, massacre of 1921, when mobs of white men destroyed a thirty-two-block neighborhood nicknamed "the Black Wall Street." Black businesses and homes were destroyed, at least 176 black residents (the numbers are still unclear) were killed, some of them buried in mass graves.

Still, King's words resonated with us. It was because what King said rang undeniably true: "We are caught in an inescapable network of mutuality, tied in a single garment of destiny. Whatever affects one directly, affects all directly." And then, in words that years later I would recognize as echoes of Ubuntu, making the universal intensely personal and the personal intensely political: "For some strange reason I can never be what I ought to be until you are what you ought to be. And you can never be what you ought to be until I am what I ought to be."[14] It was the first time I had heard that expression even though King had been using it much earlier.[15] Suddenly my world was wider than apartheid-confined South Africa, the struggle became broader, deeper, more inclusive, more demanding, encompassing much, much more than the struggle against apartheid. It became international and multi-faceted. Many years later, we would speak of "global apartheid."[16]

With time, I would understand why there was such a strong spiritual kinship between Martin Luther King Jr. and Albert John Mvumbi Luthuli, that most remarkable Christian leader of the African National Congress in the 1950s,[17] as I would, through my own intense involvement in the 1980s, come to understand the spiritual kinship between the civil rights struggle and the anti-apartheid struggle. I would also come to understand why, in his acceptance speech for the Nobel Peace Prize in 1964, Luthuli would be the only person King would quote by name. Their radical, combatant love for their people was grounded in their complete love for Jesus Christ. He

12. Baldwin, "Coalition of Conscience," 66; Baldwin, *Toward the Beloved Community*, 45–46.

13. See Brown, "Remembering 'Red Summer.'" See also the Introduction, above.

14. King, "Remaining Awake," 269.

15. As he did in his commencement address at Lincoln University on June 6, 1961; see King, *Testament of Hope*, 208–16.

16. According to South African economics scholar Patrick Bond, this very appropriate term was first introduced by former president Thabo Mbeki at the World Summit for Sustainable Development, Johannesburg, 2002; see Bond, "Is the Reform Really Working?," 817–39.

17. See King, *Testament of Hope*, 224–26.

was preaching in Washington DC, but he was talking about, and to, all of us. On that day, I—and as I would discover later, a large section of my generation—embraced Martin Luther King Jr., and even in this we were not the first, as we have already seen. From the moment Walter Sisulu appealed to King for solidarity[18] and King's growing involvement with South Africa through the American Committee on Africa, this embrace was a reality.[19]

But for my generation it was an *initial* embrace. King, we ourselves, and that embrace would become much more complex, even as for me it became more compelling.[20] That embrace would deepen to more critical dimensions, and as Martin Luther King became more radicalized, our embrace would become the embrace of the *radical* King.[21] This process of radicalization would illustrate, in ever deepening fashion, how serious King was when he reminded his audience at the National Cathedral of the poet John Donne's famous words, "Any man's death diminishes me because I am involved in mankind. Therefore never send to know for whom the bell tolls, it tolls for thee." Then he went to say, "We must see this, believe this, and live by it . . . if we are to remain awake through a great revolution."[22] King said one other thing that stirred me deeply, and which would become a guiding light for my activism in years to come: "Somewhere we must come to see that human progress never rolls in on the wheels of inevitability. It comes through the tireless efforts and the persistent work of dedicated individuals who are willing to be co-workers with God."[23]

No one has argued more eloquently for, and allowed us to understand and appreciate the global reach of Martin Luther King Jr.'s thought and work more than Lewis V. Baldwin, King scholar of great stature. In his valuable and meticulous selection of King's speeches and addresses that reflect King's international spirit and his genuine love for humankind as a whole and his commentary on them, Baldwin makes us see the "interconnectedness of these concerns in King's consciousness, and also his perspective on and contributions to world liberation movements."[24] King's ringing and blistering attacks on "the new order" of war and destruction, and his infinitely hopeful reflections on "The World House" that come together in King's dream of a global "Beloved Community," are as shattering as they are moving. As Baldwin takes us on a journey with King, from his learning from Gandhi to his admiration for India's Jawaharlal Nehru, to South Africa's anti-apartheid struggle, to that of Namibia, "the UN's stepchild," we learn of King's increasingly radicalized views on global poverty,

18. Baldwin, "Coalition of Conscience," 55.
19. For King's role within the US Anti-Apartheid Coalition, see Baldwin, "Coalition of Conscience," 54–69.
20. Baldwin, "Coalition of Conscience," 70–78.
21. See King, *Radical King*.
22. King, "Remaining Awake," 270.
23. King, "Remaining Awake," 270.
24. See King, *In a Single Garment of Destiny*, loc. 202.

global war, and the worldwide struggles against both. Baldwin is utterly persuasive as he opens our eyes to King's broad "Global Vision of Human Liberation" and the particularities of King's participation in "Breaking the Bonds of Colonialism."

But for us as South Africans it was the bond with our own Albert Luthuli, forged in the 1950s when Luthuli was the leader of the Defiance Campaign, and King of the budding civil rights struggle in the US, both movements of militant nonviolence, both men living presentations of a radical black Christianity that spoke to us most forcefully. Baldwin lets us see King's leading role in international solidarity with our struggle beginning with the "Declaration of Conscience" in the late 1950s. This apart from the later appeal signed by both, to world governments to pass sanction legislation on the apartheid regime:

> The Declaration of Conscience, signed by 123 heads of state, religious leaders, and scholars, actually symbolized, perhaps more than anything else, King's efforts to establish links between the struggle in the American South and the black South African anti-apartheid cause.[25]

As we find ourselves in the process of rethinking and re-appreciating Black Consciousness and Black liberation theology and the role Steve Biko played in both those movements, we inquire to what extent some of the fundamental truths Martin Luther King Jr. has tried to teach coming generations are still relevant, and what we can learn from those in our current, continuing struggles, and as Black Consciousness and Black liberation theology reassert themselves in South Africa's public life. Although never as explicitly as it could have been, we have discovered signs that Biko was very aware indeed of this "network of mutuality." Not only as he constantly falls back on the work of other Africans such as Aimé Cesairé and Frantz Fanon,[26] but also as he draws on the lives and works of African American heroes. He leans on words by Frederick Douglass, in turn claimed by both Martin Luther King and Albert Luthuli, as we shall see below, to strengthen his argument for the South African context,[27] as he takes over that powerful phrase from the memorable 1966 statement from the National Committee of Negro Churchmen, "Powerlessness breeds a race of beggars."[28] As he writes about African cultural values he identifies easily with Black spirituals and jazz as music "from their African heritage." If he had been able to read James Cone on this subject, he would have agreed that those "slave songs" were not only "sorrow songs"; they were also resistance songs, and as such, freedom songs.[29] It would have gladdened his heart even more to know that these songs, far from portraying the kind

---

25. See King, *In a Single Garment of Destiny*, loc. 260.

26. E.g., Biko, *I Write What I Like*, 72, 78.

27. Biko, *I Write What I Like*, 100: "Power is never handed over on a plate," and "The system concedes nothing without a demand."

28. Biko, *I Write What I Like*, 86.

29. Biko, *I Write What I Like*, 47. See Cone, *Spirituals and the Blues*.

of "colonized theology" Biko despised so much, were actually expressions of radical Christianity, of political and cultural rebellion, claiming and affirming black people's essential humanity in the face of brutal oppression.

A Witness to Be Borne

For South Africans, as we have pointed out above, the 1960s was a decade of great tumult and deep disorientation. In Langa township in Cape Town, but especially at Sharpeville, the people's aspirations were sledge-hammered into the ground by apartheid's brutal power. The government banned the liberation movements, their leaders and their activists. Black political activity, such as survived, was driven into exile or underground. Leaders were imprisoned. Robben Island, long a symbol of banishment and resistance, became iconic. The vibrancy of Christian activism that had become a hallmark of the Defiance Campaign had been virtually abandoned. The prophetic church had lost its voice. Our world was shaken. What was left was Luthuli's yearning for its return:

> It is my hope that what began, in the way of Christian involvement and thinking out, at the time of the Defiance Campaign, will not simply drain away, leaving Christians in despondency and impotence, adapting themselves fearfully to each new outrage, threat, and assault upon the people in our care. There is a witness to be borne, and God will not fail those who bear it fearlessly.[30]

Towards the end of the decade and the beginning of the 70s, the young generation embraced Black Consciousness and Black theology. They rediscovered their power in the challenges of Black Power. The young activists who in 1976 and from 1983 onwards took their faith, anger, and hope into the streets of protest and the manifold ways of militant, nonviolent resistance had heard Luthuli. And they did so with a depth of courage that will continue to amaze and shape history, because like Luthuli, they knew, and experienced, that "God will not fail those who bear [that witness] fearlessly."

In 1948, apartheid became the official policy of South Africa. Unvarnished white supremacy, always present, was turned into the law of the land in ways the country had not known before. Though not called by that infamous name, apartheid itself, as a political, social, and economic state of reality in colonial South Africa was not new. There were, however, three remarkable things about apartheid in the hands of Afrikaner Calvinists that uniquely shaped our struggle:

One, apartheid, even though a drastic intensification of the segregation policies brought by colonialism and a consequential historical development of slavery, was a direct result of the continued intervention and unceasing hard work of the white Dutch Reformed Church. In fact, as Rev. D. P. Botha argued persuasively some time

---

30. See Luthuli, *Let My People Go!*, 132.

ago, apartheid was a political policy in many ways derived from and based on the mission policy of that church, in place since 1857.[31] Botha makes extremely valid and valuable points regarding the Dutch Reformed Church and its pivotal role in the coming "social revolution" in the ascendance to power of the National Party.[32] Hence it was with complete justification that the official organ of the DRC, *Die Kerkbode*, wrote in jubilation that the victory of the National Party at the polls that year was not just God's divine will, but asserted proudly that apartheid was "a church policy."[33] Two, and this too was quite unique, also put in place was an elaborate, systematic theological construct called the theology of apartheid. Not simply satisfying itself with random proof-texts from the Bible, the theology of apartheid was a systemic, well-thought out biblical and moral justification of the policy. Intertwined with a uniquely Afrikanerized dogmatism—a South African twist of neo-Calvinism—it was absolutely essential to the upholding of the policy and to the construction of the myth of white chosen-ness, white innocence, and white divine right.[34]

Three, after 1948 the resistance from the majority of the population moved from what Nelson Mandela would later call "constitutional protest" to open defiance. That gave rise to the nonviolent campaigns of the 1950s known as the Defiance Campaign, and sporadically into the first months of 1960, challenging the unjust apartheid laws and practices with mass actions of civil disobedience until the brutal crackdowns of the regime forced an end to it all, at least for that time period. After the Defiance Campaign, other acts of nonviolence resistance such as the "Potato Boycott" of 1959,[35] as well as the subsequent campaigns against the municipal beerhall system, the dipping tanks, and especially the hated "Pass Laws,"[36] had no institutional church support.[37] However, Christians participated in their thousands, considering themselves part of a people's movement led by strong Christian leadership like Albert Luthuli and

31. Botha, "Church and Kingdom in South Africa," 68–69.

32. The success of the National Party as it stormed toward a majority in the 1948 elections D. P. Botha described as "the Dutch Reformed Church on the verge of victory." The DRC was responsible for no less than "a revolution, a total disrupting of the very fabric of the social life in South Africa up till that stage." Botha mentions how the DRC proclaimed with some pride that it "never preached politics," but it had no need since it had government policy, henceforth called apartheid, "which is her own brainchild . . . Her missionary policy has grown out to become a full-fledged secular gospel for the salvation of South Africa." Botha, "Church and Kingdom in South Africa," 68–69.

33. See "Apartheid as Kerklike Beleid, I."

34. Kinghorn, *Die N.G. Kerk en Apartheid*; Lombard, *Die Nederduitse Gereformeerde Kerke en Rassepolitiek*.

35. Luthuli, *Let My People Go!*, 215–17.

36. Luthuli, *Let My People Go!*, 215–17.

37. Albert Luthuli, lamenting the hesitation of the churches regarding the Defiance Campaign and the escalating repression from the apartheid regime, writes, "What did the churches do about this? Except for the lone stand made by Bishop Reeves, who refused to hire church buildings out for the Verwoerd secular education for serfdom, almost nothing." Luthuli, *Let My People Go!*, 131. His critique is scathing. He speaks of "the wreck of [prophetic] Christian witness," and what he fears was a "slow drift into a Nationalist state religion" (132).

Robert Sobukwe. What we saw was the emergence of the prophetic church, what Martin Luther King called the "inner, spiritual church, the church within the church, the true *ekklesia* and hope of the world,"[38] and what South African pastor/activist Frank Chikane would refer to as "the church of the streets."[39]

As a result, and authenticating the truth preached more than a century ago already by Frederick Douglass,[40] followed by Albert Luthuli[41] and Martin Luther King Jr.,[42] that the oppressor never surrenders power without a struggle, the 1960s also brought us the Sharpeville massacre, the consequent suppression of all black political activity, the banning and exile of black political leadership, the banning of the liberation movements, the Rivonia trial, following the Treason Trial of the 1950s, and the imprisonment of hundreds of activists and leaders, among them Nelson Mandela. In the aftermath of Sharpeville, in December 1961, the African National Congress took the decision to embark on military struggle, a decision that would cause deep divisions within the movement as well as between its most prominent leaders, Albert Luthuli and Nelson Mandela.[43] That decade also saw Mandela's capture, the Rivonia Trial, and his imprisonment with many others. We would not see him for the next

---

38. King, *Radical King*, 142.

39. In contrast, because the Black Church in the United States was an institution owned and run by African Americans, and had such a strong history of prophetic leadership in the struggle against slavery and racial oppression in the US, the civil rights movement had considerable support among laypersons as well as clergy, even though it has to be said that even here, it was not the Black Church as a whole that supported the struggle. The degree of resistance to King's leadership, the Southern Christian Leadership Conference, and the struggle in general from many Black Church leaders, their churches or representative bodies was astonishing, and shameful. Dr. Joseph H. Jackson from Chicago, then president of the powerful National Baptist Convention, a body that never gave formal support to King's work and that of the SCLC, is probably the most notorious example. There are reasons why some Baptist ministers, like Dr. J. Alfred Smith of Allen Temple Baptist Church in Oakland, CA, and others, broke away and formed the Progressive National Baptist Convention that stood in clear solidarity with Dr. Martin Luther King, Jr. and the civil rights struggle. Nonetheless, it is fair to say that without the prophetic Black Church in the US there would have been no Martin Luther King Jr. and no civil rights struggle. See Baldwin, "Coalition of Conscience," 59; also Wilmore, *Black Religion and Black Radicalism*. Just as in South Africa, it is wise to remember the distinction between the institutional church and the prophetic church.

40. "Power concedes nothing without a demand. It never did, and it never will." See Douglass, "If There Is No Struggle."

41. "Our struggle is a struggle and not a game—we cannot allow ourselves to be daunted by a harshness which will grow before it subsides. We shall not win our freedom except at the cost of great suffering, and we must be prepared to accept it. Much African blood has already been spilt, and assuredly more will be . . . We do not desire to shed the blood of the white man, but we should have no illusion about the price he will exact in African blood before we are admitted to citizenship in our own land." See Luthuli, *Let My People Go!*, 124.

42. "Lamentably, it is an historical fact that privileged groups never give up their privileges voluntarily . . . We know through painful experience that freedom is never voluntarily given by the oppressor. It must be demanded by the oppressed." King, *Radical King*, 13.

43. See Couper, *Albert Luthuli*; also Boesak, *Kairos, Crisis, and Global Apartheid*, 182–92.

twenty-seven years. Albert Luthuli died in 1967.[44] Sharpeville was a defining moment for the apartheid regime, as it was a defining moment for the struggle.[45] It also became a defining moment for the churches.

While the white Dutch Reformed churches were in full support of apartheid, the white, moderate leadership of the multi-racial English-speaking churches responded with resolutions and statements, all the while seeking to calm the waters, calling for caution, and warning against "extremism" and violence "from both sides." In this, too, we understood Martin Luther King Jr.: we too saw a church

> more devoted to "order" than to justice; who prefers a negative peace which is the absence of tension to a positive peace which is the presence of justice . . . [white church leaders who] paternalistically believe they can set the agenda for another man's freedom . . .[46]

What King says about "moderate" white church leaders here is *ipso facto* true for liberal white South Africans, clerical and secular both, who found it hard to resist the temptation to set the agenda for black freedom.[47]

Chief Albert Luthuli's response to mining magnate Harry Oppenheimer, unsurprisingly similar to his response to white liberal church leaders, is a case in point. "After a preliminary declaration of his understanding of the African point of view," Luthuli recalls, Oppenheimer "took us to task over what he sees as the excessive nature of our demands and methods, such things as the demands for votes and the methods of public demonstration and boycott." The "extremism" of the oppressed masses "made it difficult for him and others like him to persuade 'liberal-minded people'" of his own group of the justice of those demands.[48] Luthuli relates what he told the white contingent. What was important for Oppenheimer to understand, was that

> however "unpleasant" our demands might seem, they are real demands, and that it was far better that white South Africa should here and now know their nature than be constantly taken by surprise by being admitted to our thoughts installment by installment.[49]

---

44. To this day the unease surrounding his death, whether he really "got lost," wandered toward the railway lines and was killed accidentally by a train, refuses to come to rest.

45. In the same way, I argued elsewhere, the Marikana massacre of 2014 has become a redefining moment for the ANC, it will continue to have far-reaching consequences for the ANC as a political movement and its political and moral leadership in politics in South Africa. See Boesak, *Dare We Speak of Hope?*, 6–10.

46. King, *Radical King*, 135.

47. The language and argumentation in the section on "Church Theology," and the subsections "reconciliation," and "violence" in the South African *Kairos Document* would reflect these viewpoints quite powerfully.

48. Luthuli, *Let My People Go!*, 166.

49. Luthuli, *Let My People Go!*, 166–67.

Towards the end of the decade, Black Consciousness would embrace this same political suspicion and revolutionary impatience with "the white liberal" who simply could not conceive of black people's agency in shaping the agenda and pace of their own struggle for freedom, who were always afraid of black "excessiveness" in our demands, and disapproving of black people's desire to define their own freedom. White liberals are so engrossed in their prejudices, writes Biko, that they cannot believe that blacks can formulate their own thoughts without white curatorship.[50] Biko raises the matter of white liberals twice, as subjects of separate discussions underscoring the importance of those debates at the time.[51]

What we desperately needed in fact was not the cautionary cowardice of white paternalism, nor the endless patience, resignation, and pseudo-innocent complicity of black conformism, but the "maladjustment" (King's term) of the eighth-century prophets of the Hebrew Bible in their unremitting challenge to the powers of oppression and injustice and their prophetic faithfulness, and the extremism of Jesus in his outrage at injustice in his love for justice. So the question always is, King argued, not *whether* we should be extremists, but rather *what kind of* extremists we should be.[52] What we needed was a church who understood the radical demands of the gospel, the interrelatedness of life, and the indivisibility of justice. A church that understood that there was a revolution going on in the world—in Africa, Asia, Latin America, the United States, and in South Africa. But the decade of the 1960s also saw the silencing of the prophetic church in South Africa. And, like Luthuli, we should be "quite extreme on this point," and like Luthuli, not be afraid to say it.[53]

When Martin King called for the United States and for all people of good will to "get on the right side of that revolution" because "the great masses of people are determined to end the exploitation of their races and their lands . . . They are awake and moving toward their goal like a tidal wave,"[54] he was talking *about* us as well as *to* us. Those "shirtless and bare-footed masses" of the world were *us*. Referring to this "tidal wave" of revolutionary change as the "continuing story" for freedom from the time of the exodus, he said, "Something within has reminded the Negro of his birthright of freedom, and something without has reminded him that it can be gained."[55]

But if African Americans should see God at work in history and be reminded of their birthright by the struggles for freedom and justice in Africa, Asia, and Latin America, should we, conversely, also not see God at work in the civil rights struggle

---

50. See Biko, *I Write What I Like*, 20–28; 66–79.

51. "These are the people who argue they are not to blame for white racism and the country's inhumanity to the black man, these are the people who claim that they too feel the oppression just as acutely as the blacks . . ." Biko, *I Write What I Like*, 69.

52. King, *Radical King*, 138.

53. Luthuli, *Let My People Go!*, 132.

54. King, *Where Do We Go from Here*, 170.

55. King, *Where Do We Go from Here*, 170.

in the United States, and should not *we* be reminded of *our* birthright because of *their* struggle? Is "the network of mutuality" not also networks of unbreakable solidarity and revolutionary reciprocity? And is the "single garment of destiny" not our common destiny of peace, freedom, and human dignity? And is the human dignity we seek not also for the whole human community, including our oppressors, not just for ourselves alone?[56] The answer, it seems to me, is a clear "yes." The interconnectedness, the network of mutuality, is also more than politics. It is fundamental to our common humanity, to our obligation to restore to the world a human face.

But here is something remarkable. While the prophetic church in South Africa was driven underground, silenced by suppression and fear, the banning, imprisonment, and the killing of its prophets—a time in which the "Word of God was scarce" (1 Sam 3:1), a time of crisis and testing for prophetic faithfulness—God allowed a new generation to hear the Word from another part of the world. The prophetic church in the United States was not silenced, but had in fact begun to gain a new strength and a new urgency, driven by new insights into the crises of their own society and our world. At a time when Martin Luther King Jr. was maturing into greater, deeper, more radical wisdom, seeing with clearer eyes the indivisibility of God's justice, the oneness of God's world, the inescapable network of mutuality, and the single garment of destiny—this is the time this message, a secretly smuggled tape recording, comes to awaken the prophetic church in South Africa, reminding us of the way in which the prophetic church in South Africa had inspired the Black struggle for freedom in America. This is no coincidence, but the way the Spirit of God works to keep God's work of liberation and hope alive in the world.

Understanding the Solidarity of Struggle

The most remarkable thing about Rip van Winkle, King pointed out, was not that he slept for twenty years, but that *he slept through a revolution.* That was certainly true of the church of my generation, and of us, the children of that generation. And it took King's words to help wake us up. We embraced Martin Luther King because he awakened us to the fact that we, too, have been in a struggle, but like Rip van Winkle, my generation have mostly been asleep while momentous events were occurring in Africa and around the world. We were asleep in another aspect, as well. In our many urgent discussions, debates, and engagements with each other about the unfolding struggle and our role in it, we discovered that those of us calling ourselves Christian activists have mostly been dealing with effects, rather than with causes. We were dealing mostly with the *effects* of racism, the *effects* of poverty, the *effects* of disenfranchisement. It was time to wake up, understand, and engage the *causes.*

---

56. See Boesak, *Pharaohs on Both Sides,* 147–68.

So towards the end of the 1960s and into the 1970s, with the coming of the Black Consciousness movement and the courageous and impeccable leadership of Stephen Bantu Biko, we began to think about the deepest roots of white supremacy and racism; the *causes* of powerlessness and the meaning, use and abuse of power; the *systems* of economic exploitation and the systems of domination rampant in the world. We began to think how these systems work nationally and globally, our subjection to them, our compliance with them, and our complicity in them. We began to understand better how white racism, as a particular South African phenomenon, was entrenched in white supremacy and white privilege globally and how these functioned as manifestations of white power, hand in hand with social engineering, economic exploitation, and political oppression.

In 1963, in the "Letter from a Birmingham Jail," Martin Luther King Jr. uses the phrase "the white power structure" only once, almost as a casual afterthought, and confined to the city of Birmingham. Later, towards the end, he would use that phrase much more thoughtfully, much more systemically, much more globally. We came to understand that phrase, its reality, and its consequences for South Africa, and for the world we live in. It also indicated a radicalization in King's thinking that would grow in maturity and effectiveness in his ongoing engagement with power structures in the United States, and as the United States exerted its power across the world, though he would not come to recognize it explicitly as the power exerted by *empire*.

We took King seriously, too, when he spoke of his distinction between constitutional rights and what he called "God-given" rights. We understood him to mean that *he* understood that while the United States had a Constitution, that same Constitution saw black people as three-fifths of a human being, therefore not guaranteeing the human rights, the God-given rights, of black people. In that constitution, equality was mentioned, but selectively applied; freedom was a word but not a reality; dignity was not even mentioned. So it was necessary to appeal to something that came from "beyond the dim mist of eternity," that no document from human hands could deny, redefine, change, or diminish. Yet, time after time, Martin King would appeal to that Constitution, in an effort to find common ground with what white America would consider the proud foundation of their democracy, for them the "greatest in the world."[57]

In South Africa, in contrast, we had no constitutional democracy. The Constitution was a racist, apartheid construct. There could not even be the pretense of appealing to the Constitution, but following Martin, we appealed to our God-given rights. Not just the right to freedom, but the right to freedom that guaranteed and protected dignity; not just the right to vote but the right to have a voice; not the right to pursue

---

57. It was an inherently contradictory appeal however, and not sustainable, but King clung to it because like Frederick Douglass before him, he believed that the Constitution guaranteed the freedom of all Americans, not just white people. The Constitution did not sanctify racism, they believed, but rather revealed the utter hypocrisy of white Americans. Calling them out on it was the moral responsibility of Blacks. Malcolm X, of course, like Henry Highland Garnet before him, held the opposite view. See "Introduction" in Cone, *Martin & Malcolm & America*.

individual happiness but the right to secure the common good in the name of our shared humanity. We fought for the right not to go hungry; not to be exploited, not to be exiled at will; the right to shelter, the right to have choices, the right to hope and work for a better, more humane, more just world. It is this understanding, fashioned in the vortex of struggle, burnished in the flames of hope, and moulded on the anvil of sacrifice that informed the values of South Africa's struggle and its current Constitution, one of the most progressive documents in the world with the exception of our flawed private property clause.[58]

In the deepening dimensions of our struggle, we also came to deepened understanding. We came to realize that for Martin "the network of mutuality" could not have been just a geographical inescapability, but an embraced, qualitative, humanistic inclusivity. Hence it was quite natural for us, in the writing of the *Belhar Confession*, to insist upon understanding God as first and foremost the God of compassionate justice, "the One who wants to bring about justice and true peace on earth." For that reason, *Belhar* urges the church "to stand where God stands," to "witness and strive against *any* form of injustice," so that for *everyone* who is despised, rejected, wronged, destitute, excluded or discriminated against "justice may roll down like waters, and righteousness like a mighty stream." Hence also the firmness of the rejection, as it is in the affirmation: "Therefore, we reject *any* ideology which legitimates *any* form of injustice."

The "inescapable network of mutuality," King believed, included black as well as white, African Americans as well as oppressed people across the globe. As it included poor whites, poor blacks, and poor Latinx from all parts of America he was recruiting for the "Poor People's March," its call for radical justice would have had to include women and LGBTQI+ persons, who were also an inextricable part of the "single garment of destiny." Following Martin Luther King Jr's (radicalizing) logic, such a conclusion, I argue, is entirely plausible.[59] Because without them, the women, LGBTQI+ persons, and the differently abled, our humanity would never be complete. While over half of humanity would remain excluded, we could never be whole. Full humanity, in every sense of the word, requires full, egalitarian inclusion. We would, as King himself understood full well, never be what we ought to be, unless they are what they ought to be. It was, for me, an extraordinarily liberatory understanding.[60]

---

58. As I write, the debates in South Africa on the amendment to the Constitution to change clause 25 to allow the restitution of land without economic compensation are raging across the country. It may have been unnecessarily postponed for twenty-five years, but it is not too late and absolutely imperative in order to make our reconciliation process credible, durable, and sustainable.

59. See the convincing case made by West, "Gay Rights and the Misuse of Martin," 141–56.

60. See Boesak, *Kairos, Crisis, and Global Apartheid*, 112–17.

The Road to Freedom

We listened and agreed because we knew it to be true, when King told us that "freedom is never voluntarily given by the oppressor; it must be demanded by the oppressed."[61] From our own history, we understood that freedom is always the fruit of struggle and pain and sacrifice. We recognized it because King echoed the words of our own Albert Luthuli, who taught us that "the road to freedom" is not only long and hard, but for Christians it is "via the CROSS."[62] Nelson Mandela, like Luthuli before him, testified that the ideals of the struggle are ideals we should live for, and, if necessary, be ready to die for.[63] It is well worth repeating the well-known, but never superfluous words of Frederick Douglass, more than 160 years ago:

> If there is no struggle, there is no progress. Those who profess to favor freedom and yet deprecate agitation are men who want crops without plowing up the ground; they want rain without thunder and lightning. They want the ocean without the awful roar of its many waters. The struggle may be a moral one, or it may be a physical one, and it may be both moral and physical, but it must be a struggle. Power concedes nothing without a demand. It never did and it never will . . . The limits of tyrants are prescribed by the endurance of those whom they oppress.[64]

So when the time to join the struggle came and we recognized God's *kairos* for our generation, we asked God to forgive our complicity and our cowardice and we embraced the radical demands of the gospel, for ourselves and for our struggle. But because King convinced us that struggle without love is freedom held captive, we tried, under the most difficult circumstances, to remember as Biko, following what Paulo Freire taught us, that liberating the oppressor is our historic obligation, and that the ubuntufication of the world is integral to the call for justice.[65]

It is for that reason that in the final analysis, black South Africans, in our choice for reconciliation, chose political justice rather than victim's justice; distributive justice

---

61. King, "Letter from a Birmingham Jail," 131.

62. Luthuli, *Let My People Go!*, 232–36. There is a reason why Luthuli spelled those words out in capitals. He did not just mean the "cross" that one bears as one enters a struggle for freedom and justice. He means the cross on which Jesus was crucified, because he dared to challenge the powers and principalities of his time. The Romans crucified him as a rebel and a revolutionary, one who threatened their power and hegemony. He means that Christians who joined the struggle will have to keep that cross in mind so they can correctly understand the cross they have to bear for the struggle. For us, more than the Cause, that Cross defines the struggle.

63. See Mandela, "I Am Prepared to Die."

64. See Douglass, "If There Is No Struggle."

65. Perhaps Cornel West put it best in his description of "the radical King": "The radical King was first and foremost a revolutionary Christian . . . whose intellectual genius and rhetorical power was deployed in the name of the Gospel of Jesus Christ. King understood this good news to be primarily radical love in freedom and radical freedom in love, a fallible enactment of the Beloved Community or finite embodiment of the Kingdom of God." West, *Radical King*, xv.

rather than retributive justice; justice for the living rather than revenge for the dead; a reconciled future rather than an unforgiven past; a shared hopefulness rather than a negotiated despair. That is what the ongoing struggles are all about.[66] The challenge, therefore, is how to step away from the politics of manufactured contentment while holding on to the politics of radical reconciliation.

When King spoke of the power of nonviolence, he reminded us of our own struggle and how we, under pressure of the violence and intransigence of the oppressor, chose the road to violence, in the process often becoming more like the oppressor than we had wanted to be or could foresee that we would. Nothing would make that destructive becoming clearer than our South African version of white Americans' lynching—the necklace. We remembered then that Luthuli told us that we should not succumb to the oppressor's invitation to join the oppressor's desperation; that he prayed that through all the temptations our soul would remain intact; that he pleaded with us not to give up the militant, nonviolent struggle. Even when under severe pressure from his own movement, and from no less a charismatic, courageous and brave leader of the younger generation, Nelson Mandela, Luthuli nonetheless thought that the oppressor's incessant violence was "vainglorious," and that our imitating the oppressor would be equally vainglorious. That should not be the way for us. And so, leaning upon the wisdom of Albert Luthuli, it was possible for a new generation, after the decade of quiet despair, even while respectfully understanding the choices Nelson Mandela and his generation thought they had to make in their time, to return to those methods in the 1970s and 1980s, and build a movement of militant, nonviolent resistance that would ultimately break apartheid's back.[67]

Never losing sight of the agonizing circumstances that forced our elders to make that decision, and never losing our respect for them and their reasons for making those decisions, we never passed judgment. Like Luthuli, we understood that the stakes were high and the pressures almost unbearable. Nonetheless, we would define and defend our own choice for what Albert Luthuli called nonviolent militancy.

As I have done before, I readily concede that this view is and has always been a point of serious contestation among those engaged in struggles for freedom. In these weeks of writing, African Americans, in a veritable homicidal frenzy, are being slaughtered by police as if a new, brazen, and terrorizing display of their power and impunity has suddenly become necessary. And so it has, as it always is for any empire crumbling under the weight of its own violence, hubris, and God's judgment. Ahmaud Arbery in Brunswick, Georgia, followed by Breonna Taylor in Louisville, Kentucky, Dreasjon Reed and McHale Rose in Indianapolis, Indiana, all within a matter of weeks. Then

---

66. That South Africans have in fact not experienced justice for the living in our reconciliation process to make that "shared future" possible, durable and sustainable, remains the challenge for this generation; see Boesak and DeYoung, *Radical Reconciliation*. See also Boesak, *Pharaohs on Both Sides*, especially chs. 4, 5, 6.

67. See Boesak, *Running with Horses*.

came the murder of George Floyd in Minneapolis, killed by a policeman kneeling on his neck, choking him to death.[68] This last murder caused an eruption of protests across the United States, and like the apartheid regime with us, the US regime's response has been vicious and will become exponentially so. Who knows what awaits us as the revolutionary fervor in the hearts of Americans of all races continues to burn? As the fear in the hearts of the powers and principalities grows, so will the retribution. The anger of the people is both righteous and unstoppable. In my mind, I am back in the South African struggle, in the years of the States of Emergency in the 1980s. Not surprisingly, as with us then, in America the debate on how black people should respond, on violence and nonviolence, is back. And rightly so.

As an almost inevitable consequence of all this, a young, black Baptist pastor, Rev. Paul Robeson Ford, has written on "the right of black people to defend themselves, same as white people." He writes about the armed African American groups who demonstrated publicly with their guns, in accord with their state's "right to carry" laws, and exercising their Second Amendment rights. So, Ford says,

> While these scenes have been unsettling to many, I am proud of each and every one of these young black men and women who have shown up in this way. I am proud of them because of the courage and conviction they have demonstrated, and how they have walked in the footsteps of Williams and others. But I am also proud to see them highlight one of the central issues in the two most recent high-profile killings of black people by police or vigilantes: black people have the right to defend themselves by the same means that their white counterparts do.[69]

My aim here is not to enter that seemingly endless, and senseless, debate on American gun laws, or on what Americans call their "Second Amendment" rights. Others have more than adequately done so, and dealt with it decisively.[70] Here I propose to simply share from our own South African experience. We, too, have known those moments of utter darkness and rage-filled misery. We have known the deadly provocations of the police, the heartless political opportunism of the sell-outs, and the depraved indifference of the oppressor.[71] This depraved indifference is ostentatiously manifest in just about every tweet from the (former) president of the United States about these matters, as clearly as it was in then-Minister of Police Jimmy Kruger's "It leaves me cold," when confronted with the murder of Steve Biko by his security police forces.[72] It is

---

68. New, shameless acts of police brutality seem to occur every day, and one literally cannot keep up.

69. See Ford, "Black People Have the Right to Defend Themselves."

70. See the brilliant work, Dunbar-Ortiz, *Loaded*.

71. "To constitute depraved indifference [the person's] conduct must be so wanton, so deficient in a moral sense of concern, so lacking in regard for the life or the lives of others, and so blameworthy as to warrant the same criminal liability as that which the law imposes upon a person who intentionally causes a crime." See the USLegal website: definitions.uslegal.com/d/depraved-indifference/.

72. See "Biko's imprisonment, death and the aftermath," *South African History Online*, https://www.sahistory.org.za/article/bikos-imprisonment-death-and-aftermath.

the same depraved indifference on such blatant and shameless display in the criminal behavior of America's police forces with regard to African Americans and other minorities. For decades now, the police in America have taken over the role the Ku Klux Klan used to play. That is true not just for the police officers who are actively committing the crime; it is true also of those who look on without lifting a finger, those who stand as if on guard, making sure no one from the surrounding public interferes, making sure compassion and decency do not get in the way of power and death. It is true of the cowardly black officials and "leaders" who benefit too much from the system to turn against that system,[73] who take it upon themselves to call for calm, "reasonableness," and "responsibility," arguing for the validity of incremental change even as police leave dead bodies lying in the street for twelve hours.[74] Those who try to cover their hypocrisy by calling on the name and legacy of Dr. Martin Luther King Jr. as if the mere evocation of that name places them on higher moral ground and proves them right. Those who, while making their pious speeches over the dead bodies, surreptitiously slip in the propaganda of the very political establishment that caused, maintained, and feeds off the conditions of racist oppression and exploitation in order to keep the people captive to that establishment and their corrupt systems as if there were no truth to see or speak. Those who, while profiting from the system, castigate those who not only criticize but reject the system that excoriates them, as if they have no self-respect, and as if they have no right to call and work for something altogether different.

It is true of the white law officials, prosecutors, and the politicians who over the years have learned to take for granted that blindness to their perfidy is their birthright. Those whose first instinct is to excuse and justify the criminals, rarely charge them with murder, and of the court systems that always seem to find reasons to exonerate them. It is true of the white and black *agents provocateur,* paid by the system to join the marches, not to fight oppression, but to incite to violence so as to give police brutality legitimacy, and to distract from both the provocations to violence from police and the righteous cause of the revolution. Hiding behind their more-radical-than-thou facade, these people do not ever join the struggle; they join only the marches where they serve the vile purposes of their masters. It is true of the white and black moderates who in the face of these travesties try to drown the cry, "Black Lives Matter!" in the trivializing equalizer, "All Lives Matter!" that is supposed to be the morally superior ground: not as blatant as "Blue Lives Matter!" Meanwhile, the oppressive, violent system shrugs and marches on. We have seen it all. So yes, the anger is both right and righteous.

---

73. I watched with little surprise as former Obama National Security Advisor Susan Rice confidently described the protests over the death of George Floyd as the result of foreign interference, "right out of the Russian playbook." See Evans, "Susan Rice."

74. See Chávez, "Louisville Police Leave Body in the Street"

In 1985, after the massacre of more than forty demonstrators by the South African police in Langa township near Uitenhage in the Eastern Cape, commemorating the Sharpeville massacre on March 21, I stood up to preach the second eulogy, with twenty-seven coffins, including those of young children, lined up in front of us. The police released only those twenty-seven bodies, but the community insisted there were more than forty dead or missing. Archbishop Desmond Tutu was the other preacher. The very first words out of my mouth, as years later I was reminded by someone, only fourteen years old then, and who was there on that day, were, "I am so angry!" It is true: I was. So were the people. For many of us, certainly for me, the aim never was to find ways to suppress or preach away the anger. The deeper, more strategic question always was, how do we find creative, nonviolent ways to channel that anger? And, having found those ways, how do we keep the anger *righteous*?

And so it would be right through those dark, dismal years, with over forty-thousand activists in prison, 40 percent of them children under eighteen, in detention without trial, and with hundreds tortured and killed by police and army. Funerals—one every week, it seemed—became moments of confrontation, of conscientization and mobilization. "Don't Mourn, Mobilize!" were the words emblazoned on T-Shirts worn by activists at the funerals. So it was when I accompanied a mother from Gugulethu to the morgue in Salt River near Cape Town where the bodies of those shot dead in a protest march were kept. I was there when the policeman told her to find her son's body, then told her to lick his whole face, as a "test" to "prove" that he really was her son. As she did this, because she was a mother, the policemen stood there, snickering. I felt the anger, and it was right and righteous. I was there in Elsie's River township, in 1981, when Bernard Fortuin, fifteen years old, was shot down in the street. I was there when his mother, while he lay dying, tried to break through the crowd and the police cordon, crying, "He's my son!" I was there when the policeman—not white, this time—hit her with the butt of his rifle and screamed at her, "Let the bastard die!" I felt the anger, and it was right and righteous.

The years between 1976 and 1990 were the years of protest, in the pulpit, on the stage at rallies, and on the streets. And yes, I saw the police descend on peaceful marchers with shamboks, dogs, and guns. Sometimes helicopters. They would wade into the masses, always beginning to hit the girls first, always aiming for their breasts, knowing how that would infuriate the boys. Then we have to read in the press that our peaceful march "quickly deteriorated into violence," and what a pity that was. And always, I would have to respond to the question whether I "approved" of the violence, as if the violence were started by us and not provoked by the police; as if the violence of the state was proof of the failure of nonviolence. It was a question meant to annoy and distract, not to inquire and learn, as if the apartheid system as a whole was not an affliction of deadly violence upon the lives and bodies of black people in every conceivable way; and as if police brutality were not only the very tip of the iceberg. Of course, there were some who reminded us of the powerful and always relevant words of Martin Luther King Jr., that the riots "were the voice of the unheard," and rightly so. That will always be true. In these times, however, we should also remind the world of another King, the radicalized King whom we so easily forget, but who Keeanga-Yamahtta Taylor has called our attention to in her brilliant book, and now again in a very recent article, and it captures our times perfectly:

> I am not sad that black Americans are rebelling; this was not only inevitable but eminently desirable. Without this magnificent ferment among Negroes, the old evasions and procrastinations would have continued indefinitely. Black men have slammed the door shut on a past of deadening passivity. Except for the Reconstruction years, they have never in their long history on American soil struggled with such creativity and courage for their freedom. These are our bright years of emergence; though they are painful ones, they cannot be avoided.[75]

The righteous anger of Paul Robeson Ford is a shared anger. I will not judge his choice for violence. "Brave and just" South Africans, as Luthuli called them, did so, Nelson Mandela among them. Paul Robeson Ford writes,

> When, at every level, the government of the United States of America finally learns how to defend *all* of its citizens in the same way that it has historically defended *some* of its citizens, then the rest of us will not have to defend ourselves by any means necessary. When police everywhere finally learn to protect *all lives* and not just some, then we can begin to look at them as the servants that they are supposed to be. Until then, look for more black activists to show up armed for battle in states with open carry laws. And don't be surprised if black preachers like me offer them a blessing as they step out to protect the unprotected and brandish the sword that may finally usher in peace-with-justice.[76]

Reverend Ford distances himself from Martin Luther King Jr., but professor Taylor holds up another King who is "not sad" at the riots, because in a particular historic moment, they light up the "bright years of our emergence." Martin Luther King Jr. writes these words, says Taylor, "in the weeks before his assassination, while the 'eminently desirable' Black rebellion rose in the streets of the United States, exposing the triumphalist rhetoric of the American dream as meaningless."[77] As I have argued throughout this chapter, *this* is the King who was also the *becoming* King, the clear-eyed, radical, revolutionary King who does not cling to dogmas, what Biko would call "absolutes,"[78] but staying in the heart of the struggle, understanding even better what it means to be a militant, nonviolent, revolutionary. This is the King we embraced, whom

---

75. See Taylor, *From #Black Lives Matter to Black Liberation*, 1, 2.
76. Ford, "Black People Have the Right to Defend Themselves."
77. See Taylor, *From #Black Lives Matter*, 2.
78. See ch. 6 below.

we recognized in our dark years, reminding us that such years should be embraced as our "bright years of emergence." They are painful, but they are unavoidable, because they are *made* unavoidable. Perhaps through our faithfulness and commitment, we can turn them into the bright years of contagious courage and stubborn hopefulness.

Unquestionably, it is Ford's right to make that choice, if he believes that the circumstances demand it, and he accepts responsibility for those black people, even armed to the teeth, taking on the ultra-militarized, racist, American police and armed forces, incited by, and justified by, a raw jihadist in the White House. Ford departs, he writes, from Martin Luther King Jr., in that King wanted to make nonviolence a life-style as well as a strategy:

> As a strategy, it has taken us through many valleys and up to great heights. As a strategy, it has emphasized the sacrificial mindset that is required to usher in lasting social change. It has imitated the Way of the Cross and the moves that our Savior Jesus Christ made as he healed the sick and raised the dead and willingly went to Calvary, chastising Peter for his impulsive violent aggression along the way.[79]

But as "a way of life" he infers, it should be rejected. To prove his point, Ford then adds, "and yet, our Savior also declared, 'I have not come to bring peace, but a sword'" (Matt 10:34).

I would suggest, however, that Ford would be better off citing Mandela, as he also does, rather than Jesus for support. I have preached on this very text in 1977, while the fires set after "Soweto" on June 16, 1976, were raging across South Africa, and the students, my congregation at the University of the Western Cape, were right in the middle of it. We wrestled with the questions of violence and nonviolence on a daily basis, at times when the chapel was an oasis of rest and spiritual renewal between deadly confrontations with the forces of apartheid. There is no sign, here or anywhere else in the gospels, that Jesus was calling for violence as a "strategy." The difference between Jesus's peace and that of Albert Luthuli and Martin Luther King was not that Jesus was willing to use the sword, and that therefore, Jesus's peace was "real," because it was "peace with justice." In fact, there was no difference at all. Does that mean that justice can only be brought through violence? Somewhat like Mao Tse Tung's belief that true freedom can only come through the barrel of a gun? That is a rather superficial reading, one that supposes a juxtaposition not found in the text. With Jesus, from his first sermon in Nazareth, quoting the prophet Isaiah, to the very end, there never was such a thing as "peace" without "justice," and it was never the willingness to use violence that made "justice" embrace "peace." Not in Psalm 85, not with Isaiah, and not with Jesus.

Within the context of Matthew 10, especially verses 34–42, the issue is not violence or nonviolence, but the radical, sacrificial obedience that causes us to follow Jesus in

79. Ford, "Black People Have The Right."

his resistance against the Powers That Be in Jerusalem as well as Rome. That resistance consists of making choices that are radical in their departure from the choices that the powers of evil make: for violence, oppression, exploitation, and dominion. Those are choices that make us radically different, and so will make the world a radically different place. That is an obedience that will call for radical choices, and those choices will bring painful but unavoidable divisions, touching on the most intimate family relationships. Those choices will also bring painful consequences, including losing one's life. Those choices will invite violence, but will discern that it is not violence that brings peace or justice. Those are the choices we are still called to make. Jesus spoke at such length about this obedience and those choices, because he understood the temptations and pressures living under Roman oppression and occupation brought. Jesus does mention "rewards," but the retribution of the powers is much more immediate, and much more real, than the rewards Jesus offers. That is why, in that same chapter, Jesus spoke so earnestly about fear. "Do not fear them," he says repeatedly. "Do not fear those who kill the body but cannot kill the soul, rather fear [God] who can destroy both body and soul in hell" (Matt 10:28)—the text I preached the Sunday after Biko's death in September 1977, with informants and security police present in the chapel, and many of the students on our campus in prison.[80]

In all these situations, we have found one must respectfully weigh at least four questions: of morality, inevitability, positivity, and responsibility. Violence from the side of the oppressed is always counter-violence. As we have learned from Albert Luthuli, the moral question is not: Why the violence from the oppressed? It is, rather: Who is responsible for the causes of the violence, and who is it that made nonviolent change impossible? "It was only when all else failed," Mandela reminded the court at his trial, "when all channels of peaceful protest were barred to us, that the decision was taken to embark on violent forms of political struggle . . . We did so not because we desired such a course, but solely because the government had left us with no other choice."[81] Albert Luthuli, in remaining steadfast in his own choice for militant, nonviolent resistance, nonetheless spoke of Mandela and the others as embodying "the highest morality and ethics." The apartheid regime and its beneficiaries "have put the highest morality and ethics in the liberation struggle in a prison where it might not survive."[82] Luthuli was not referring to the decision by Mandela and the ANC to ultimately turn to violence, I think. He was referring to those high and impeccable moral standards, embodied by Mandela and the others, in fact by the oppressed people of South Africa as a whole for so long. That morality that, against all odds and in the

---

80. "Don't try to lie to us," said Colonel Nel, the leader of the interrogation team, and elder in the white Dutch Reformed Church, when I was in solitary confinement in 1985 in Pretoria Central prison. "We've got a room full of suitcases filled with tapes of every sermon and speech you ever gave, and videos of all your marches." It was true. They did have all those suitcases.

81. See Mandela, "Second Court Statement, 1964," cited in De Gruchy, "Dilemma of Violent Resistance," 48.

82. See Couper, *Albert Luthuli*, 172ff.

face of the severest provocations has kept the struggle nonviolent for so long, that has honored the noblest goals of the struggle for decades in the face of the immorality of unspeakable oppression. It was those high moral standards, clung to so tenaciously, which were now punished with imprisonment, where they "might not survive." And if they did not survive, where would South Africa go then? Most importantly, moreover, this is a question that can only be asked by the oppressed themselves. Those who drive, maintain, and benefit from oppression dare not ask this question. It simultaneously answers the "inevitability" question. Over and over, Martin Luther King Jr. reminded Americans of the words of John F. Kennedy, "Those who make peaceful revolution impossible, make violent revolution inevitable."[83]

But further: Is it possible that such violence can sometimes have a positive effect, so that the revolution benefits from it? The answer, I suggest, is yes. Two instances come to mind. First, when Cuba joined the revolutionary forces of Angola's liberation movement to defeat the South African army at the now-famous battle of Cuito Cuanavale, in March 1988. Whatever one's view on this event—stalemate, tactical withdrawal, or defeat—consensus is that it was "one of the turning points in South African history. The fighting led to the withdrawal of South African, ANC, and Cuban presence in Angola, and to the independence of Namibia."[84] The "turning point" consisted of more, of course. Not only did that battle contribute to the defeat of Jonas Savimbi's UNITA forces, the black surrogates of the United States with its imperialist agenda in Southern Africa. It also dealt a heavy blow to the myth of the invincibility of the South African Defense Forces, the mightiest army on the continent, and to the equally enduring myth of the unconquerable power of white supremacy, and gave a much-needed boost to the African National Congress's image and to the struggle in South Africa in general.

But that was war. What if we looked at a more personal example, a more personal decision, one with far more personal consequences? My mind goes to the decision of Dietrich Bonhoeffer to not only join the resistance to the Nazis, but also the plot to assassinate Hitler. Bonhoeffer himself makes it abundantly clear that that decision was not taken lightly. Neither was Nelson Mandela's in South Africa some thirty years later. But Mandela grappled with his decision as part of a collective, as a freedom fighter and political strategist, weighing the historical, political, and practical realities, possibilities, and consequences. God or Jesus or the Bible, did not come into play. Bonhoeffer wrestled with his decision as a follower of the Jesus of the Sermon on the Mount, as a freedom fighter whose highest loyalty was not to an organization or even a cause, but to Christ. But his freedom as a freedom fighter is also a freedom before God, and the freedom fighter, no matter how noble the intentions, remains a fallible human being. The Christian freedom fighter's actions are never simply in obedience to the pressures of the Cause, but always in obedience to God. For the Christian in the

---

83. Kennedy, "Remarks," 13.
84. See "Battle of Cuito Cuanavale 1988."

struggle, the issue of obedience to God always problematizes the question of obedience to the Cause. Here again we hear the echo of Paul's agony, "Oh wretched man that I am!" Hence, Bonhoeffer struggles with the freedom of having to make a decision, with the responsibility that that freedom entails, and with the guilt it inevitably brings.

In a thoughtful essay, John De Gruchy writes about the dilemmas faced by both Bonhoeffer and Mandela. The situations in Germany and South Africa (as the assassination of Prime Minister Hendrik Verwoerd proved) were vastly different, of course. Killing one white leader, even the Prime Minister, would not have the same impact at all as killing a dictator, revered and iconized as Hitler indeed was, without whose presence everything would indeed fall apart, making it the turning point of history. Of Bonhoeffer, De Gruchy says,

> His decision was both an ethical and a strategic one. Morally, *not* to act in such a way was worse than committing such a violent deed. Strategically there seemed to be no alternative to ending the war and Nazi terror than through killing Hitler.[85]

In a dictatorship, the killing of the revered leader could save millions of lives. That was the reasoning behind the plot, and strategically, that was correct.

But even more important was Bonhoeffer's struggle within the context of Christian responsibility. The paragraphs in his *Ethics* on these matters are sobering and humbling. Human beings are given freedom by God to act. Yet, they are responsible to God for their actions, he writes. There are morally ambiguous situations in which they have to exercise their freedom. Not to act would be irresponsible, but there is no guarantee that the act of free responsibility is untainted by sin. One cannot turn to the support of others or seek justification in the decisions and actions of others as if one has no personal responsibility and no personal relationship with God. "They themselves have to observe, judge, weigh, decide, and act on their own."[86] So even if the act is a collective one, the responsibility remains intensely and irrevocably personal. That responsibility understands that an act of violence against the other incurs a guilt we cannot deny or trivialize, as it entails vicarious suffering for the good of others. It is a responsibility that brings us before God, before whom we confess our guilt, and to whose judgment we submit ourselves. Such responsibility understands that "there is no possible scenario that would allow the Christian to remain without guilt . . . [but] this guilt is surrendered to Christ who is a merciful judge."[87]

So in making our choices in this regard, we allowed the experiences of these Christian freedom fighters to haunt our minds. That struggle generation made no judgment, but we looked at Jesus, Bonhoeffer, Luthuli, and Biko, more than at

---

85. See De Gruchy, "Dilemma of Violent Resistance," 48.
86. See Bonhoeffer, *Ethics*, 284.
87. Bonhoeffer's words to a young comrade; see Zimmermann, "Bonhoeffer and Nonviolence," 200, 201.

Mandela, Che Guevara, and *Mkhonto we Sizwe*. This would remain a seriously contested issue, and not everyone would be persuaded. Nonetheless, we thought we had good reason. Violence, I argued, and will continue to argue, has an awesome irreversibility. It destroys the chances of genuine peace and reconciliation in the irremediable destruction of the other. It casts the other in the mould of an unchangeable, incontrovertible enemy. It systematizes as well as depersonalizes the other as the eternal enemy. After the violent blow is struck, there are no more options left and the last word is already drowned in blood. Violence takes on a life of its own, feeds on human emotions far stronger than we realize, releases a relentless, deadly dynamic we are first not prone, then not able, to stop. It sweeps reason and better judgement aside as in ritualistic helplessness not acknowledgeable to ourselves we respond to the call of blood to blood. Lifting the sword destroys the soul. Nonviolence appeals to our better selves, to the truth we know about ourselves as well as the other, but too often deny: that in our creaturely, relational existence and our common humanity we are created to affirm, choose, and celebrate life rather than death. Nonviolence affirms the humble acknowledgment of the possibility that we might be wrong, that the other may be redeemable. Nonviolent militancy does not deny the existence of evil, and neither does it try to trivialize it. It purposefully seeks to open possibilities for our creativity in resisting, confronting, and overcoming evil. It opens the way for the choosing of another path, to the ubuntufication of the other, because it longs for the affirmation of our humanity in the redeemed humanity of the other. Violence, in its irreversibility, is a reach too far for mortals such as us. Nonviolence acknowledges the existence of holy ground: such as taking the life of another. We dare not tread upon it.[88]

In making those choices, we did not only follow Albert Luthuli, Martin Luther King Jr., and Steve Biko. We also heeded James Baldwin, who, in the midst of some of his most fierce and fiery writing, asked us all, in America and the rest of the world, to consider this:

> I am very much concerned that American Negroes achieve their freedom here in the United States. But I am also concerned for their dignity, for the health of their souls, and must oppose any attempt that Negroes may make to do to others what has been done to them. I think I know—we see it around us every day—the spiritual wasteland to which that road leads. It is so simple a fact and one that is so hard, apparently, to grasp: *Whoever debases others is debasing himself.* That is not a mystical statement but a most realistic one,

---

88. Not everyone accepted this view, of course, and the debate raged throughout the 1980s, but there is no gainsaying that it was embraced by the vast majority during those final phases of the struggle and held its ground as the bedrock of their belief and their participation in the struggle. Honest appraisals of the situation in the 80s will confirm that the violence in the streets was almost always violence provoked by infiltrators, *agents provocateur*, or the police, and all within the broader framework of counter-violence to the inherent violence of apartheid. But this view on violence and nonviolence remains my own firm conviction, even more so in a world drenched in blood through perpetual, needless, global war.

which is proved by the eyes of any Alabama sheriff—and I would not like to see Negroes ever arrive at so wretched a condition.[89]

But there is still another thing that I have learned, and it is crucial. When one calls for nonviolence, and one asks young people to face the systematized indifference of a whole criminal state—police and army brutality, shamboks, tear gas and dogs, imprisonment and torture, guns and possible death woefully long before one's time—one cannot do so from a pulpit or a stage, and then step away. One cannot do so in a book or article. One has to do so from the front of the lines of anger and protest, there with the people, facing the danger, same as they do. Just as we had learned that true worship was worship not just in the pulpit and the sanctuary, but in the streets of protest for justice. That is called revolutionary authenticity. And even though the then-Minister of Police Louis le Grange called my clerical robes my "battle dress," the only weapon I had in my hand was my Bible. So the call one makes is a choice one makes, but never just for others. If we make the choice, we have to be there, with mind, body and soul, to face whatever comes, and then be ready to face the division the consequences of that obedience brings—between me and my church, between me and the powerful in my community who do not want their lives, and their relationships with the even more powerful, disturbed; between me and the Powers That Be, whose hegemony depends on my submission and my complicity. But Jesus does not even mention those. Jesus talks about the divisions between me and my parents, my siblings, between me and my wife—one's foes are not only the oppressor, his quislings, and his guns, but one's "family and one's household." There is a reason why, in these verses, Jesus keeps it so intensely personal and does not even mention "authorities" of any kind. *That* is the sword Jesus speaks of here. The consequences when we stand up against the powers is something Jesus does not avoid, as we have seen. And those consequences will surely come.

Radicalization and Domestication

Across the world, whenever the name Martin Luther King Jr. is mentioned, it is inevitably in conjunction with his famous Washington DC march "I Have a Dream" speech.[90] But let me confess: the Martin Luther King Jr. whom the generation of young struggle activists embraced is the King of '66, '67, and '68 rather than the King of '63: the global citizen who recognized the global challenges of racism, poverty, and war, rather than the King who remained enchanted by the American dream. *That*

---

89. Baldwin, *Fire Next Time*, 83.

90. Martin King is in full flight on the cover of a book titled *Speeches That Changed the World*, reprinted twice, among forty-nine great historical figures, beginning with Jesus of Nazareth (the Sermon on the Mount). Abraham Lincoln has only one; King has two—the "I Have a Dream" speech and his last address, given on the eve of his assassination in Memphis on April 3, 1968: "I Have Seen the Promised Land."

Selfless Revolutionaries

King had become America's favored son, stripped of his radicality, domesticated in dozens of presidential speeches—from Ronald Reagan to George W. Bush to Barack Obama—about his life on his birthday, his dream so hopelessly American that it is being claimed by the far right without a blush.[91] Our embrace was of the King who, by 1966, had discovered that it was not at all about a seat at a lunch counter, but all about systemic justice; not so much about integration as about dignity and equality, and even then with the question attached: What *kind* of equality in what *kind of society*? Hence his emphasis not so much on integration anymore but on the creation of a beloved community whose yardstick was justice to the poor and most vulnerable.

As a result, the King we embraced saw the triple evils of racism, militarism, and capitalist exploitation. *That* King embraced the political and economic potential of democratic socialism. That was the King who saw perpetual impoverishment as a critique of capitalism rather than as a mere by-product of racism; the King who mused that America should find a different economic system. "There must be a better distribution of wealth and maybe America must move toward a democratic socialism."[92]

We were captivated by the King who observed and understood the revolutions that engulfed the world in his times, not because the people involved were simply prone to violence, but because they were, he said, "revolting against old systems of exploitation and oppression," the King who could now see and identify with the "shirtless and barefoot people of the land [who] are rising up as never before."[93] This is a radicalized Martin Luther King Jr., whose choice of words echo both Franz Fanon's "wretched of the earth" and the Hebrew Bible's *am ha'aretz*, the people of the land, the poor and powerless peasants of Judea and Galilee who had so often revolted against their Roman imperial overlords.

That King who, in reference to the war in Vietnam, saw even then what would be and would remain, even more so today, "the deepest malady within the American

---

91. Probably the worst examples of the domestication and abuse of Martin Luther King can be seen in the way Americans from the far right have been shamelessly using him to defend their racist stances (e.g., right-wing Fox News TV personality Glenn Beck), their resistance against affirmative action, a dignified minimum wage, and gender-justice issues. Even worse is the abuse of King in defense of America's war policies. Baldwin and Burrow use the publications of Clarence B. Jones, a one-time King advisor turned rabid conservative Republican who argues that King would have supported George W. Bush in his invasion of Iraq and Afghanistan and his war policies in the Middle East. See Jones and Engel, *What Would Martin Say?*; Baldwin and Burrow, *Domestication of Martin Luther King Jr.*, 29–54; also Jones, *Behind the Dream*. "Indeed," writes Michael Eric Dyson, "conservatives must be applauded for their perverse ingenuity in co-opting King's legacy and the rhetoric of the civil rights movement." Dyson, *I May Not Get There with You*, 12.

92. Dyson, *I May Not Get There with You*, 88. Dyson explains how King was much more explicit on the subject of his leanings toward democratic socialism in private than in public, and he found this statement "remarkable." However, in an early comparative study on the ethics of Martin Luther King Jr. and Malcolm X (1974), I have probed the development of King's thinking on this matter and already then came to the conclusion that King was a "latent socialist." See Boesak, *Coming In Out of the Wilderness*, 39, 41.

93. See King, *Where Do We Go from Here*, 33.

spirit": that war is poisonous to the soul of a nation, and that "[America] can never be saved as long as it destroys the deepest hopes of men [and women and children] the world over."[94]

But I am afraid that means that the King that we embraced is the Martin Luther King America has so devoutly and effectively domesticated and so determinedly watered-down, the King America wants so feverishly to forget.[95] For far too many in the rest of the world, as well, it is the King least remembered, least celebrated, least honored. It is disturbing to see how much effort is going into creating a Martin Luther King more manageable, a prophet more palatable, a leader more pliable, a preacher more controllable.[96]

But one, crucially important reason why, despite its undeniable beauty and soaring rhetorical heights, black South Africans of my generation were (and are) less drawn to the "I Have a Dream" speech is not just because it has been so abominably abused over the last fifty years, made devoid of meaning, but it is also because, for us, people of the Global South, the American dream is such a threatening, frightening thing. Malcolm X had persistently referred to the American Dream as the "American Nightmare" for African Americans,[97] and by 1967, King would concur. Referring to his speech at the Lincoln Memorial in 1963, he confessed, "I talked to the nation about a dream that I had had, and I must confess to you today that not long after talking about that dream I started seeing that dream turn into a nightmare."[98] Malcolm X was clear on this matter from the very beginning, but for perhaps too long King held on to the myth that freedom for Blacks is ultimately secured because of America's *inherent* commitment to freedom. In consequence, in light of the disappointment Barack Obama turned out to be, and the shameless racist bigotry, the fascist tendencies of Donald Trump, and the feckless elasticity of Joe Biden, it is not unfair to ask a question of African American brothers and sisters. Is at the core of the dilemma you face

---

94. See King, *Radical King*, 204. See also Glenn Greenwald's reflections on the relevance of King's Riverside Church speech on Vietnam, and the lessons he draws for the US and the world today. Greenwald, "MLK's Vehement Condemnations of US Militarism."

95. See Baldwin and Burrow, *Domestication of Martin Luther King Jr.*; Dyson, *I May Not Get There with You*; and Cornel West's Introduction in King, *Radical King*.

96. The same process of domestication can be seen in the way Mandela has been "re-invented" and thoroughly domesticated by conservative and liberal forces alike, both in South Africa and abroad, to suit their own political agenda; see Boesak, *Pharaohs on Both Sides*, 169–93.

97. See Malcolm X, *Speaks*, 12. In one of his last speeches given at Cory Methodist Church in Cleveland, Ohio, April 3, 1964, Malcolm remained uncompromising on this matter: "No, I am not an American. I am one of the 22 million black people who are the victims of Americanism. One of the 22 million black people who are the victims of democracy, nothing but a disguised hypocrisy. So I am not standing here speaking to you as an American, a patriot, or a flag-saluter, or a flag-waver—no, not I. I'm speaking as a victim of this American system. And I see America through the eyes of the victim. I don't see any American dream, I see an American nightmare" (12). But even if Malcolm could not completely foresee the consequences of American exceptionalism for people of the Global South today, he would not have been surprised at all.

98. King, *Trumpet of Conscience*, 75–76.

not perhaps the idea you have embraced from before King's days up to now, that your freedom is, as King put it, "the goal of America," and that your destiny is "tied up in the destiny of America"?[99] And: "We will win our freedom because the sacred heritage of our nation and the eternal will of God are embodied in our echoing demands."[100] It was apparently very hard for King to distance himself from the belief in the core decency of America and especially in American exceptionalism.[101] Surveying American politics and the role of African Americans in it since the victories of the civil rights struggle, it would have been better if in this respect King had been more like Malcolm.

What if, we might ask, with humility and some trepidation, but nonetheless with love and as honestly as we can, "the destiny of America" is indistinguishable from America's "manifest destiny," which is not freedom, justice, and equity, but rather based upon invasion, exclusion, expansionism, exploitation, genocide, and imperial domination the world over?

What if the American dream can be upheld and realized only by perpetual war not in service of freedom or democracy, but in service of greed and the pursuit of profits whatever the costs? And that nothing would matter because those costs would be borne by the darker-skinned people of the world, the poor and vulnerable in America itself, people of color, women, immigrants and their children—all of them as disposable as the throw-away consumerist system demands.

What if the pursuit of the American dream has become the unbearable nightmare of those of us in the rest of the world, where the name "America" does not conjure up "sweet dreams of liberty"—no matter how stirringly King's voice captures them—but night sweats drenched in terror, displacement, and pain? Filled with images of such things as "extraordinary rendition" and torture, perpetual war, and endless occupation, cluster bombs, drones, computerized death, and the very real threat of nuclear destruction?

What if we admit that Barack Obama's famous chant, "Yes, we can!" has migrated from an inspiring, hope-giving slogan to a fearsome expression of brute power, even as he celebrated his successful run for the presidency, taken to the White House as the supposed fulfilment of King's dream? President Obama, shaking our dreams of renewed hopeful politics to the core, had so consistently, and devastatingly, shown throughout his term in office that he was as far from King's real dream as one could be. So for the

---

99. King, *Radical King*, 142.

100. King, *Radical King*, 143; King, *Testament of Hope*, 277.

101. King wrote this in his "Letter from a Birmingham Jail" in 1963, but he has consistently clung to this language till the end; see, for example, in the sermon from 1968 under discussion, King, "Remaining Awake," 277. It is a curious mixture of Christian nationalism, patriotism, and American exceptionalism, perhaps an unsolved contradiction of which King was not unaware that needs a more in-depth discussion than can be done in this chapter. Following King's path toward radicalization, I would like to believe that King, like with his growing understanding of "the American dream," would have changed his mind on this issue. In my view, however, seeing how dismayingly strong black support is for Joe Biden in the 2020 Democratic primary race, the epitome of this ideological enslavement, it would have served American politics, and Black politics in particular, better if King had seen this earlier.

seven countries in which he waged war, and for the peoples of Venezuela and Iran and North Korea crippled by his sanctions, and through them for the rest of us, "Yes we can!" became, "We exploit, attack, wage war, maim and kill, *because we can!*?"[102]

What if the American dream is no longer—and, if one should ask Native Americans, never has been—the dream of a hopeful, compassionate people driven by the love for justice but the agenda of a heartless empire held captive by an outrageous, dehumanizing, God-defying ambition for world domination? What if we understood that the American dream is not really a glittering vision "from sea to shining sea," but the dark reality of a Christian invasion, of genocide, and land theft? The systemic executions from coast to coast of people of color by militarized police, who, from Sanford, Florida, to Ferguson, Missouri; from Standing Rock, North Dakota, to South Minneapolis, Minnesota, are, for this South African, a disorienting and frightening mirror image of the South African apartheid security forces at their worst. What if the shining "city on a hill" has become the fig leaf for desolate reservations, where the right to operate a casino is intended to make up for a hundred Trails of Tears? Of neglected and disinvested inner cities, calculatedly being prepared for gentrification, America's own gentrified version of South Africa's forced removals? Of dire but officially ignored poverty, oppression, and dispossession; of black neighborhoods under siege, and white suburbs imprisoned by ignorance and indifference? What if the words of the American dream are no longer "America the beautiful"—no matter how hauntingly beautiful Ray Charles renders that song—but the lyrics of a nightmare: "Bury my heart at Wounded Knee"; "Don't shoot, I don't have a gun"; or "Please, don't let me die"; or "I can't breathe"?

If Martin Luther King Jr. were alive today, standing not in Selma, Alabama, but in Ferguson, Missouri; not in Birmingham, Alabama, but in New York City and Staten Island; not in Montgomery Alabama, but in Standing Rock, North Dakota; not in Cicero, Chicago, but in poverty-stricken Thembisa and Khayelitsha? Not in Jackson, Mississippi, but in gang-infested Bishop Lavis, Cape Town, or in that occupied, open-air prison camp called Gaza? Not in South Los Angeles but in the sprawling miasma of misery that we call "squatter camps" or more euphemistically, "informal settlements"? What if today, he were called to stand, not with sanitation workers in Memphis, Tennessee, but with mothers and grandmothers in that "Wall of Moms" in Portland, Oregon, facing SS troops made in America? What would those compassionate eyes see; what would that heart filled with revolutionary love for Christ and the world yearn for; what would that mind set on freedom think; what would that prophetic tongue say; what would those feet, restless for justice, do? Next to these questions, Clarence Jones's question, "What would Martin say?,"[103] asked in an effort to put Martin Luther King Jr. on the side of George Bush's senseless and brutal Iraq war is not only completely nonsensical, it is utterly banal and indescribably treacherous to the man and his legacy.

102. See Boesak, *Dare We Speak of Hope?*, 90–122; also Ali, *Obama Syndrome*.
103. See Jones and Engel, *What Would Martin Say?*

Selfless Revolutionaries

The lessons from the life, commitment, courage, and power of Martin Luther King Jr. are far from fully learned. Much remains. The King we learned to love and embraced is the King who taught us to stand up for justice, because injustice anywhere is injustice everywhere, and make those vital choices, his voice soaring in the National Cathedral: "On some positions, cowardice asks the question, is it expedient? And then expedience comes along and asks the question, is it politic? Vanity comes along and asks the question, is it popular? Conscience asks the question, is it right?" King concludes, "There comes a time when one must take the position that is neither safe, nor politic, nor popular; but [we] must do it because conscience tells [us] that it is right."[104]

These are the penetrating questions South Africans and, I dare say, Americans, in our restless and as-yet unfulfilled search for an open, nonracial, nonsexist, people-centered, egalitarian, inclusive, humane democracy cannot avoid. As, in this time of resurging racism, tribalism, and ethnocentrism, of all-consuming self-interest and self-destructive entitlement, we cannot avoid the question of loyalties. "Our loyalties must transcend our race," King said, because he understood the necessity of genuine nonracialism. "We deem ourselves bound by allegiances and loyalties which are broader and deeper than nationalism," because he understood the essential oneness of our world and the call toward a common humanity. As a consequence, even if it meant speaking out *against* the leaders and politics of his own nation, he *had* to speak out "for the weak, for the voiceless, for the victims of our nation, and for those it calls enemy, for no document from human hands can make these humans any less our brothers [and sisters]."[105] It is as if King had read and understood clearly John Calvin, who long ago spoke words that would echo in King's "inescapable network of mutuality" and "single garment of destiny":

> The name "neighbour" extends *indiscriminately* to every person, because the whole human race is united by a sacred bond of fellowship . . . *To make any person my neighbor it is enough that they be human.*[106]

South Africa's Beyers Naudé understood King, as he understood the crucial nature of the distinction between what he called "loyalties and lesser loyalties," the courage it would take to make that decision, and the courage it would take to sustain it:

> In the Afrikaner society there is such a deep sense of loyalty . . . Loyalty to your people, loyalty to your country, loyalty and patriotism have in a certain sense become deeply religious values . . . So that anybody who is seen to be disloyal to his nation, to his people, is not only deemed to be a traitor, but in the deeper sense of the word, he is seen as betraying God.[107]

---

104. King, "Remaining Awake," 277.
105. King, *Radical King*, 206.
106. Calvin, *Opera 45*, 613. Emphasis mine.
107. Naudé and Sölle, *Hope for Faith*, 11.

I have written extensively about the choices Beyers Naudé had decided to make, but it is worthwhile repeating the gist of it here.[108] It is because he understood the totalitarian nature of that loyalty and its demands that he understood so well its consequences, and the choices it presented. A choice for those loyalties would be in direct opposition to the choices for Christ he had made. For that very reason he was always so clear on the demand for Christian obedience and loyalty to Christ above all, and the extent to which loyalty to Christ alone would make one understand the place of "lesser loyalties," and how these lesser loyalties not just competed with one's loyalty to Christ, but in fact displaced it. It was especially dangerous since the "lesser loyalties" claimed to be of God, and resisting them was presented as tantamount to resisting God. Then "lesser loyalties" actually become "false loyalties." It is this combination of courage and conscience, of insight and foresight, that enabled Beyers Naudé to see earlier and more clearly than others the deep and complex roots of the heresy of apartheid. It was not just the formal theological and biblical justification. It was, as well, and dangerously so, the informal, insidious, and all-pervasive cultural embodiment of a false, deceitful, carefully inculcated consciousness that presented itself as loyalty and as Christian.

South Africans are once more faced with the vexing question of loyalty—to race or ethnic grouping, to tribe and class, to historical truth or self-serving myths; to gender justice and equality or patriarchal privilege and power. To an exclusivist, homophobic, transphobic, body armor of othering, or to the embrace of inclusive humanism. To the interests of the country and all its people or to the interests of the Party, the rightful demands of the people or the benefits of patronage and self-serving entitlement. Beyers Naudé had learned from both Dietrich Bonhoeffer and Martin Luther King, as he had learned from Steve Biko.[109] It is once again time to make those choices. We are indeed caught up in this "inescapable network of mutuality" in this "single garment of destiny."

The King we embrace is the King who taught us the power of love as the most potent force in human relationships as well as in politics:

> Darkness cannot drive out darkness, only light can do that. Hate cannot drive out hate; only love can do that. Hate multiplies hate, violence multiplies violence, and toughness multiplies toughness in a descending spiral of destruction. The chain of evil . . . must be broken, or we shall be plunged into the dark abyss of annihilation.[110]

---

108. See Boesak, *Kairos, Crisis, and Global Apartheid*, 85–90.

109. "Steve Biko's death has helped me to wake up to my life, my true liberation . . ." And again, "Steve Biko challenges me to not keep quiet anymore but to voice my deepest convictions about what is right and true, to stand up for them and to suffer for them if necessary—even if this should mean that I have to endure condemnation and rejection by my own people . . ." Hansen, *Legacy of Beyers Naudé*, 79.

110. King, *Strength to Love*, 53.

Selfless Revolutionaries

The King we love and embraced is the King who taught the world that hope is indispensable:

> God grant that we will be participants in the newness [that God is creating] ... If we will but do it, we will bring about a new day of brotherhood [and sisterhood] and peace. And that day the morning stars will sing together and the children of God will shout for joy.[111]

We embraced Martin Luther King Jr. because he embraced our own Albert Luthuli, one of the most inspiring examples of Christian commitment to the struggles for freedom and justice the world over, and who today, above the desperate denials at the sickbed of our rainbow-nation dreams, still speaks to his people, urging us to discard the destructive politics of illusion and instead invest ourselves in the uplifting politics of hope and commitment:

> The task is not yet finished. South Africa is not yet a home for all her sons and daughters. Such a home we wish to ensure. From the beginning our history has been one of ascending unities, the breaking of tribal, racial, and creedal barriers. The past cannot hope to have a life sustained by itself, wrenched from the whole. There remains before us the building of a new land, a home for [people] who are black, white, brown, from the ruins of the old narrow groups, a synthesis of the rich cultural strains which we have inherited ... Somewhere ahead there beckons a civilisation, a culture, which will take its place in the parade of God's history beside other great human syntheses, Chinese, Egyptian, Jewish, European. It will not be necessarily all black, but it will be African.[112]

Such is the power of the networks of mutuality. These are the witnesses to prophetic truth, prophetic faithfulness, and prophetic courage recognizable in all movements across the world dedicated to the subversion of systems of injustice, domination, and subjugation; to freedom and the militant, nonviolent transformation of societies; to the protection of life upon the earth. Such lessons we have scarcely begun to understand, it seems to me, but they are nonetheless indispensable for a life of dignity, peaceability, and human flourishing, and for a democracy that is inclusive, humane, durable, and sustainable.

---

111. King, "Remaining Awake," 278.
112. Luthuli, *Let My People Go!*, 230.

6

In Search of Our Human Face
Black Consciousness, Indivisible Justice, Inclusive Humanity, and the Politics of Vulgarity

The Quest for True Humanity

"We have set out on a quest for true humanity," said Steve Biko in an early 1970 essay, his contribution to South Africa's very first anthology on Black liberation theology,

> and somewhere on the distant horizon we can see the glittering prize. Let us march forth with courage and determination, drawing from our common plight . . . and our brotherhood [and sisterhood]. In time we shall be in a position to bestow upon South Africa the greatest gift possible—a more human face.[1]

Arguably, this is one of the most crucial insights from Biko's considerable wisdom, and one vital for our developing and maturing understanding of both Biko's thought and our situation today. To begin with, the bracketed words in the quote above, "and sisterhood," indicate wholehearted concurrence with feminist critique of Biko's thinking, and perhaps of all male thinking in Black Consciousness circles, on the question of gender, the equality of, justice for, and respect for the dignity of women. Sociologist Zimitri Erasmus writes of Biko, "He addresses black men and white people of liberal persuasion, but he excludes black women. Thus he leaves untouched the humiliations and injustices of gendered hierarchies."[2] That critique is completely justified, and thinkers like Fanon and Cesairé are not excluded. Being "a child of one's times" is a universal affliction, and it sometimes takes time to discover new ways of understanding. It is a shortcoming we have to admit and a *mea culpa* we have to express and work

---

1. See Biko, *I Write What I Like*, 108.
2. See Erasmus, "'Race' and Its Articulation of the Human," 58, 59. See also P. D. Gqola's fresh and insightful critique on this issue in "Contradictory Locations."

much harder to eliminate. I have recently pointed out this issue several times, making the argument that as black males, we might have been converted from our sexism, but we have yet to overcome our patriarchalism.[3] Today Biko would have written "our common humanity," but at the beginning of our movement our understanding of gender justice, gender equity, and inclusiveness lacked the sensitivity.

In reflecting on Biko's search for our human face, I need to underscore three further points here. First, Erasmus has full appreciation for what she calls Biko's "humanism." She mentions some examples: Biko's assertion that blacks are not "an extension of a broom or an additional leverage to a machine." His insight that "beyond material well-being the fact of being human should be the centre of our social and political concern." His belief that it is through these "material and spiritual projects" that blacks will be able to "give the world a more human face." Nonetheless, she worries about "moments" when he "locates his humanism in a romanticised construction of African culture as 'pure,' 'close to nature,' characterised by beliefs in the 'inherent goodness of man.'"[4] Except that the belief in the "inherent goodness" of human beings is not solely an African phenomenon, Erasmus is essentially correct. In his discussion on "Some African Cultural Concepts," Biko once again raises the specter of romanticizing African culture when he quotes Zambia's former president Kenneth Kaunda with approval as Kaunda writes about Westerners' cultural tendency to "cut out the dimension of the spiritual." Unlike the Westerner, Biko adds,

> [Africans'] close proximity to Nature enables the emotional component in us to be so much richer in that it makes it possible for us, without any apparent difficulty to feel for other people and to easily identify with them in any emotional situation arising out of suffering.[5]

Kaunda's—and Biko's—observation about Africans' closeness to nature is doubtless true. However, reading the rest of the sentence one cannot help but wonder what Biko's reaction would have been if he had lived to see the brutality of what was called "necklacing." First during those desperate years of struggle, when only black persons suffered this fate (not a single white, the real cause of the problem and the real reason for our oppression, was necklaced), then of African foreign nationals in the streets of our townships in the xenophobic rage that gripped the country in 2008, in 2012, and again in 2019. Would he still have blamed it on "the advent of Westerners" who have "changed our outlook almost drastically,"[6] or would he have insisted on a deeper, more self-critical analysis, as he has done in other instances? Would he have pondered

---

3. See, e.g., Introduction in Boesak, *Children of the Waters of Meribah*. The argument of that work is that Black liberation theology needs to shift its lens completely on this issue: from our reading of the Exodus story, to the place of women in the ministry of Jesus, to their place in society and in the church. See also my 2005 work, Boesak, *Die Vlug van Gods Verbeelding*.

4. Erasmus, "'Race' and Its Articulation," 59.

5. Biko, *I Write What I Like*, 51.

6. Biko, *I Write What I Like*, 51.

with Uganda's Mahmood Mamdani over the bewilderments, the paradoxes, and the painful contradictions in those times when victims become killers, as in the Rwandan holocaust?[7] Would he have agreed with South African novelist Sindiwe Magona as she anguishes about necklacing as an instance during our struggle when "Ubuntu took flight"?[8] I think so, because with Mamdani, he would have recognized the vile shadow of colonialism stalking these events,[9] and with Magona, he would have acknowledged the frightening power of human frailty[10] haunting even the best intentions in our struggles for freedom.

7. See Mamdani, *When Victims Become Killers*.

8. See Magona, *Mother to Mother*.

9. This realization is evident throughout Biko's thinking of course, but see especially his discussion on "some African cultural concepts." Biko, *I Write What I Like*, 44–51.

10. Even though Biko is clear about the harmful legacy of colonialism on the indigenes, their culture, psyche, and ways of life, he never argues that Africans are infallible, or, theologically put, "without sin." He speaks of the "ultimate conscience of each living mortal" given by God and believes "that man has enough power to dull his sensitivity to his own conscience and hence become hard, cruel, evil, bad, etc." Unwilling to turn his back on the possibility of some goodness in humankind, however, Biko hopes that "intrinsically somewhere in him there is always something that tells him he is wrong." Biko, *I Write What I Like*, 236, 237. He had this disposition even towards the whites who ran the apartheid regime. As late as May 1976, during his testimony at the BPC trial, Biko stated that in his view, "this government is not necessarily set on a Hitlerised course" (153). The editors of *I Write What I Like* noted that June 1976 and the years following proved Biko wrong (135), and in a way they are right. There is no question about the sympathies of generations of Afrikaners for the Nazi cause and the chilling similarities between many apartheid laws and the Nazis' Nuremberg laws were not imaginary. The accusation that the apartheid regime, not least in the violence it unleashed upon the oppressed, was as evil as the Nazis' was not wrong, either, and the title of Heribert Adam's article, "The Nazis of Africa: Apartheid as Holocaust," reflects a serious discussion. The references in the black resistance literature of the 1950s and '60s to the regime and its supporters as "the *Herrenvolk*" were not out of place either. Yet one cannot say that the regime had plans to annihilate black people by the millions, as King Leopold II did in the Congo, or Hitler did with the Jews. Perhaps that is what Biko had in mind. The point we are making, however, is a different one. Ultimately, theologically speaking, Biko, perhaps inadvertently, may have pointed to an enduring dilemma for the regime and its followers. The Afrikaners' desire for their racist and violent policies, and themselves, to be seen as "Christian," presented them with that excruciating dilemma. Andries Treurnicht, Dutch Reformed Church theologian, rabid Afrikaner nationalist and right-wing political leader whom we quoted above, proves the point. I repeat that quote here: "I know of no policy as moral, as responsible to Scripture, as the policy of separate development . . . If the . . . Christian Afrikaner can be convinced that there are no principles or biblical foundations for this policy of separate development, it is but a step to the conviction that it is un-Christian or immoral. And if we believe it is un-Christian or immoral it is our obligation to fight it." A. P. Treurnicht, *Credo van 'n Afrikaner*, cited in Villa-Vicencio, "All-Pervading Heresy," 59–60. This was a theological conviction with deep resonance in the Afrikaner mind and heart and with far-reaching political consequences, forming one of the indispensable pillars of apartheid. This was what made the 1982 declaration by the World Alliance of Reformed Churches that apartheid was a sin and its theological justification a "heresy" theologically so devastating for the Dutch Reformed churches, psychologically so shattering for the Afrikaner in general, and politically so effective for South Africa's apartheid politics. We exposed that policy as deeply unwise, morally bankrupt, unchristian, and idolatrous. Afrikaners could no longer credibly deny that, but most of them could not fight it even then. But they were forced to sit and watch as the heresies that made them powerful, and rich and superior branded them and their churches forever. That call upon the name of the Lord, however false, wore them down, I wrote elsewhere. "Those who call upon that Name cannot but be overpowered by that Name. So the apartheid

Second, this is important, for in the current, heated debates on decolonization, decoloniality, Africanization, and Africanity, there is such a marked re-appreciation of these concepts in Black Consciousness and Biko's thought that the warning seems appropriate. I will argue that Biko's "human face" was never intended to be confined to "blackness" as "racial" category, and that his political understanding of blackness was always an inclusive Africanness. This is already illustrated in his understanding of the concept of "black solidarity."[11] Within this context Biko encouraged all of us—those categorized, dehumanized, and racially designated by apartheid's racialized obsessions—to understand liberation as of "paramount importance in the concept of Black Consciousness, for we cannot be conscious of ourselves and yet remain in bondage. We want to attain the envisioned self, which is a free self."[12]

That freedom, I suggest, was the freedom to express ourselves as "complete in ourselves," by which I mean completely and fully human, a concept we will further explore below. From a Christian point of view, first, that "envisioned self" was grounded in our being created in the image of God, "in our likeness," says God (Gen 1:26), not an "aberration from the 'normal' which is white."[13] Furthermore, it is grounded in the incarnation of God in Christ who became human and identified completely with us. In fact, argues womanist theologian Kelly Brown Douglas, "Jesus' ministry showed his intimate bond with the demonized outcasts of his day."[14] Nowhere, Douglas argues, is this more evident than in the story of Jesus and the Samaritan woman (John 4:1–42):

> By transgressing into Samaritan territory and by interacting with a Samaritan woman, Jesus (again as God's incarnation) is affirming the sacred worth of

---

establishment denied the gospel while preaching the gospel, betrayed the Name while calling upon the Name; but all the while, inexorably, unavoidably, eroded their ability to resist the power of that Name." See Boesak, *Tenderness of Conscience*, 167. Was this, perhaps, what kept them from becoming completely "Hitlerized"?

11. See Biko, *I Write What I Like*, 56. "Being black is not a matter of pigmentation—being black is a reflection of a mental attitude." Ibid., 52. The apartheid-created and apartheid-serving determinations ("Bantus," "coloureds," "Indians" etc.), as well as the apartheid-induced associations of apart-ness, racial and ethnic validity in relation to "whiteness," and rivalry, (as related to apartheid's pigmentocratic scale of status, acceptability, and privileges); should be resisted and discarded. It is apartheid's intention that we "hold each other in contempt." Ibid., 56. We must guard against racial and ethnic fragmentation and remember that "we are oppressed because we are black . . . [therefore] we must cling to each other with a tenacity that will shock the perpetrators of evil." Ibid., 108. What we "should at all times look at" is that "we are all oppressed by the same system," "by varying degrees" (ibid., 56) to create and increase division and tensions within the oppressed communities. It is a "deliberate ploy to stratify" us and should be exposed as "the deliberateness of the enemy's subjugation scheme." This in contrast to *God's* "deliberateness to create black people black." Ibid., 53. That is to say, God's deliberate intention to declare blackness God's complete, created humanness, captured in the divine satisfaction: "and indeed, it was very good" (Gen 1:31).

12. Biko, *I Write What I Like*, 53.

13. Biko, *I Write What I Like*, 53. We return to the phrase "envisioned self" later on in this chapter.

14. See Brown, *Stand Your Ground*, 181.

this woman. In other words, any human narratives and constructs that suggest otherwise do not vitiate her status as a "good creation."[15]

That is exactly the point we are trying to make here. No racist, white supremacist narrative or construct can negate the "good creation" of God's deliberate intent to create black people black. Jesus's identification with the despised, the poor, and the oppressed has been central to Black liberation theology. James Cone describes the lynchings, the humiliation and pain and suffering, the unholy glee of the lynch mob as they stood around and cheered, took pictures and cut off body parts as souvenirs. Cone then writes,

> The cross was God's critique of power—white power—with powerless love, snatching victory out of defeat . . . The lynching tree joined the cross as the most emotionally charged symbols in the African American community—symbols that represented both death and the promise of redemption, judgment and the offer of mercy, suffering and the power of hope.[16]

For Cone, as for Kelly Douglas Brown, following the writers of the Harlem Renaissance early in the twentieth century, the crucifixion was a first-century lynching. In a supremely eloquent argument, she writes about the murder of seventeen-year-old Trayvon Martin in Florida. Contrasting the cross with the state of Florida's "Stand Your Ground" law, she too sees the cross as a first-century lynching, exhibiting "white power and Anglo-Saxon supremacy."[17] The crucifixion is meant to intimidate, terrorize, as well as destroy. It is an instrument of forced submission to evil. Yet, "the cross is at the heart of black faith," she writes. It is the irrevocable symbol of unearned, undeserved, senseless suffering. Douglas speaks of seeing Jesus "in the face of Trayvon."

> That Jesus was crucified affirms his absolute identification with the Trayvons, the Jordans, the Renishas, the Jonathans, and all the other victims of the stand-your-ground-culture war. Jesus' identification with the lynched/crucified is not accidental. It is intentional.[18]

Jesus, as the incarnation of God, has been this from the beginning, but the cross is his ultimate identification with the "crucified class" of his day, that is, the poor, oppressed, exploited, and marginalized class of occupied Palestine. "The crucified class in the first-century Roman world was the same as the lynched class today."[19] The Matthean question today, Douglas goes on to say, might be,

---

15. Brown, *Stand Your Ground*, 175–76.
16. Cone, *Cross and the Lynching Tree*, 3. See my treatment of the Rizpah story from 2 Sam 21 in Boesak and DeYoung, *Radical Reconciliation*, ch. 2.
17. See Douglas, *Stand Your Ground*, 172–203.
18. Douglas, *Stand Your Ground*, 174.
19. Douglas, *Stand Your Ground*, 174.

"But Lord, where did we see you dying and on the cross?" And Jesus would answer, "On a Florida sidewalk, at a Florida gas station, on a Michigan porch, on a street in North Carolina. As you did it to one of these young black bodies, you did it to me." The tragedy of the cross is the tragedy of stand-your-ground war. It is in the face of Trayvon dying on a sidewalk that we see Jesus dying on the cross. *To know the extent of God's love, one must recognize the face of Jesus in the face of Trayvon.*[20]

South Africa's Siya Khumalo expresses it this way:

> The masters of the world's kingdoms thought Jesus was their trophy, but he was actually the underdogs' trophy. For the rulers of this world unmasked their capacity for evil and discredited themselves in their violence against Jesus. Christ crucified was the vindication of those hitherto called "sinners" and "criminals"; those who crucified him washed this band of misfits completely in his blood. Jesus was the heartthrob to the maginalised, lover of the rejected. Some of our churchwomen address him as "Soka labafelokazi": *Casanova of the widowed.*[21]

So the claim is stunning in its righteousness, completely comforting and empowering in its rightness, "Jesus on a Florida sidewalk," and Jesus as "the Casanova of the widowed." Put another way, if Jesus is indeed re-crucified in the crucifixion of black persons today, the inscription over him on the cross would not read "King of the Jews," but "Black Lives Matter."

Within the context of the Roman imperial world, the incarnation of God as human being is not a mere metaphysical concept. It represents a "concrete, political alternative," writes Dutch theologian Bert Ter Schegget.[22] For God reveals that it is in this Jesus, the One who has "emptied himself," taking the form of a slave, and in so doing identifying with the pain and suffering of the most humiliated and despised—in this love to the very end—that God has entered into the human story, demonstrating true majesty. For "precisely as slave is he very God. If God is the God of *this* Jesus, the hidden victory shall come to light."[23] It may be hidden now, but it will come, as sure as the dawn breaks the dark of night.

That immensely empowering truth is the message of the persecuted church to the mighty Roman Empire: the servant, the emptied One, the one you crucified in the most horrific death the empire could imagine, is Lord. The slave reigns! As for the Christians in the Roman Empire, likewise for us, it represents that "concrete, political alternative," and it is an alternative that must be *enacted*. That foundational biblical truth is the grounds for true equality because it is the obliteration of all inferiority and

---

20. Douglas, *Stand Your Ground*, 180. Emphasis mine.
21. See Khumalo, *You Have to Be Gay*, 255.
22. See Ter Schegget, *De Andere Mogelijkheid*, 44–45.
23. Ter Schegget, *De Andere Mogelijkheid*, 48, 49.

false pretences of superiority. As far as Black liberation theology's participation in our current debates is concerned, it remains an important insight. For black Christians, this consciousness is an unmissable basis of non-racialism; it is an indispensable foundation upon which the true egalitarian society, as Biko would have it,[24] must be built. It was on this philosophical basis that the United Democratic Front was founded as a truly non-racial, inclusive movement, and as such it sought to mobilize South Africa's masses.[25]

"Full Humanity Requires Freedom"

I should make a third point. As a Reformed theologian, I read Biko's idea of the "human face" as echoes of John Calvin's concept of "full humanity." In his commentary on Matthew 2:9, Calvin writes, "Full humanity *requires* liberty."[26] Calvin understood that full humanity, that is, meaningful life as free children of God endowed with inalienable rights to worthiness, justice, equity, having choices, and living with dignity, cannot be realized while people remain in the chains of social hesitation, economic deprivation, and political ambiguity. It requires freedom. *Full humanity,* not as in the "three-fifths of a person" clause in the Constitution of the United States that gave such validity to the concept of the enslaved African as property, to be bought, owned, and sold by whites. The clause was finally scrapped, writes Paul Finkelman, but "the taint remains."[27] Subsequently, black Americans in general would be regarded as not fully human, with "no rights which the white man is bound to respect," as the scandalous 1857 Dred Scott US Supreme Court decision declared. The consequences of that mind

---

24. Biko, *I Write What I Like*, 169.
25. See "Introduction" in Boesak, *Running with Horses*.
26. Calvin, *Commentaries* 2:9, 87.
27. See Finkelman, "Three-Fifths Clause." Finkelman explains, "The three-fifths clause provided the extra proslavery representatives in the House to secure the passage of the Missouri Compromise of 1820 (bringing Missouri in as a slave state); the annexation in 1845 of Texas, which was described at the time as an "empire for slavery"; the passage of the Fugitive Slave Act of 1850; the law allowing slavery in Utah and New Mexico; and the passage of the Kansas-Nebraska Act in 1854 (which opened the Great Plains and Rocky Mountain territories to slavery). None of these laws could have been passed without the representatives created by counting slaves under the three-fifths clause." In the course of this writing, President Trump issued a memorandum that proves why Finkelman's judgment is so sound. "Donald Trump's new memorandum to exclude undocumented immigrants from the next round of congressional apportionment is morally repulsive, illegal, and impossible. It is repulsive because it borrows the logic of the notorious Three-Fifths Clause to declare that undocumented immigrants are not full "persons" under the Constitution. It is illegal because it seeks to exclude these immigrants from a state's population when counting how many seats each state gets in the House of Representatives, which violates the Constitution," writes Mark Joseph Stern. Yet Trump and his supporters will try to have this memorandum enacted. See Stern, "Trump Wants to Strip House Seats from States under Three-Fifths Clause."

set, writes historian Walter Johnson, are palpable in the mindless havoc racism and white supremacist nationalism are causing in that country even today.[28]

Calvin insists on *full humanity*, not "once born," "broken," "split," or "burnt" outcaste as the Dalits of India are designated.[29] Not "creatures," English for the decidedly derogatory *"skepsels"* as white South Africans used to call us and describe us in their Afrikaans dictionaries to make sure that on the farms and on the streets, in school and in church, in formal speeches and casual conversations this is drilled into us: creatures, "non-whites" who are considered less worthy, less trustworthy, less deserving, less human. So, Biko is saying, South Africa will have acquired that human face only when all its people have acquired full humanity.

Full humanity, not a situation where "race" determines one's acceptability to the human community, or where the poor are *tolerated* yet exploited, because they will "always be among us" (and remain a source of cheap labour). Or where women are *tolerated* yet abused, because they are "the weaker sex" (but necessary for procreation and service to men); or where LGBTQI+ persons are *tolerated* despite their sexual orientation, yet despised, discriminated, and physically hurt, because we "hate the sin, but love the sinner" (and that strokes our sense of moral superiority). *Full humanity*, treated, accepted, and honored with indivisible justice, inclusive dignity, and unqualified equality. *Full humanity*—a life not ruled, poisoned, and destroyed by fear, which Biko called a soul-destroying force.[30]

However, full humanity, according to John Calvin's firm conviction, "requires freedom." *Requires,* that is, *demands,* not *desires,* not merely longed for or requested, and certainly not begged for. If this is the case, this means struggle, for full humanity does not flourish in situations of oppression, injustice, discrimination, dehumanization, and indignity. Furthermore, this is the result of a freedom defined by the oppressed and the powerless themselves, not the scraps that are thrown from the table of the privileged who think that their power justifies their sacralized hegemony.

The quest for true humanity is inextricable from the struggle for justice, dignity, equity, and freedom. That is why, on numerous occasions, Calvin speaks of tyranny, that is, political oppression, economic exploitation, and dehumanization through unjust laws and practices, as totally unacceptable, as rebellion against God, a denial of the rights of the powerless and a denigration of the rights of God. Consequently,

---

28. The consequences of that infamous "Dred Scott decision," argues legal scholar Walter Johnson, are impacting African Americans to this day. See Johnson, "No Rights Which the White Man Is Bound to Respect." See below, ch. 7.

29. See Human Rights Watch, *Broken People*, 1–2. It is not surprising either that Dalits themselves are referring to their situation as one of "apartheid," another way of expressing "the condition of blackness." See, e.g., Sathianathan Clarke's reference to apartheid and the Dalit situation, "Dalit Theology: An Introductory and Interpretive Theological Exposition," in Clarke et al., *Dalit Theology*, 17.

30. Biko, *I Write What I Like*, 73–79.

Calvin insists that to not rise up in resistance against that oppression is "cowardice"; rising up against it is a sacred duty.[31]

Biko is not naïve, however. He knows that it is a struggle and that we are in it for the duration. Biko foresaw what post-1994 South Africans are now having to come to terms with: the end of official apartheid and a black face in high office would not mean the end of that struggle.[32] He spoke of the "distant horizon," not in an effort to discourage and certainly not in a spirit of defeat in the face of apartheid's formidable might. Biko spoke with clarity of mind from a deep, experiential understanding of the nature, durability, and adaptability of evil, a truth we learned from Henry Highland Garnet, Albert John Mvumbi Luthuli, and Martin Luther King Jr., namely that power is never surrendered voluntarily. It has to be wrested from the hands of the oppressor.

Long ago, the nineteenth-century African American abolitionist, literary giant, and freedom fighter Frederick Douglass made it clear in his incomparable way:

> If there is no struggle, there is no progress. Those who profess to favor freedom and yet deprecate agitation are men who want crops without plowing up the ground; they want rain without thunder and lightning. They want the ocean without the awful roar of its many waters. The struggle may be a moral one, or it may be a physical one, and it may be both moral and physical, but it must be a struggle. Power concedes nothing without a demand. It never did and it never will . . . The limits of tyrants are prescribed by the endurance of those whom they oppress.[33]

Biko, who had in fact quoted Douglass verbatim on this issue,[34] broke the literary flourish down, telling South Africans in plain language what this practically meant for our own struggle:

> In a true bid for change we have to take off our coats, be prepared to lose our comfort and security, our jobs, and positions of prestige, and our families, for just as it is true that "leadership and security are basically incompatible," a struggle without casualties is not struggle.[35]

We have always known this, but the period of the late 70s and especially the 80s, which no less than twice declared a State of Emergency, would prove how true this observation was. At this point in our history, the realization of Biko's dream still remains South Africa's greatest challenge. This dream, which Biko saw "far, on the

---

31. Calvin, *Commentaries* 1:10.

32. Biko, *I Write What I Like*, 170.

33. See Douglass, "If There Is No Struggle."

34. See Biko, *I Write What I Like*, 98, 99. The words, "We must expect that the limits of tyrants are prescribed by the endurance of those whom they oppress" (100), are directly from Douglass as the above citation shows, even though Biko does not credit him. Biko does not make use of footnotes in this publication.

35. Biko, *I Write What I Like*, 97.

distant horizon," is still as distant. All our challenges—the grim, continuous impoverishment of the vast majority of our people, the unconscionable gap between rich and poor, our unconquered racism, our stuttering social cohesion, the tragic failures of our reconciliation process, our battles with crime and corruption, our utterly shameful gender-based violence, bigotry, misogyny, and homophobia; and the bewildering brutality of South Africans against each other—are captured in the longing for our country to have "a more human face."

Biko said this in the midst of a struggle against one of the most inhumane systems the world has ever known, labelled a "crime against humanity" by the international community. Apartheid was a vicious, violent, totalitarian system, not just in the unsurpassed draconian nature of its laws and their application, but in the destructive totality of its claims upon every area in the lives of the oppressed. Now we have to recall Biko's words, for twenty-five years into our democratic experiment, this struggle for indivisible justice, human dignity, and inclusive humanity is still not over, and the poor, women, and the LGBTQI+ communities are bearing the brunt of it.

Africanity, Indigeneity, and Afro-plurality

I raise these matters so that in the heat of the new debates on Africanity and Eurocentrism, indigeneity and Afro-plurality, anti-blackness and humanism, they are not forgotten. They deserve our full attention.

At the core of Unisa's Simphiwe Sesanti's discussion on these matters is the argument that tapping into (subjugated) African knowledges is essential to dismantling neo-colonialism in education and other spheres. In this process, he argues, Afrocentrism is the absolute key. Sesanti speaks of an almost universal, historically unbroken African culture as "central" to an Afrocentric education. Afrocentricty is

> a philosophical perspective associated with the discovery, location, and actualizing of African agency within the context of history and culture . . . a quality of thought and practice rooted in the cultural and human interests of African people . . . Afrocentricy is interested in what Africans traditionally regarded best in education before colonial invasion.[36]

Sesanti pleads for a return to "African concepts" such as Ubuntu and "traditional African precepts" such as *feta kgomo o tshwaremotho*, which "informed Africans' approach to economics, the giving of compassion," and the work towards the "elimination of poverty, criminality, and greed."[37]

The issue here is not that these values actually existed (and hopefully still do) in various African communities, or not that these values can indeed make the kind of spiritual and material contribution towards giving the world the "human face" Biko

---

36. Sesanti, "Afrocentric Education," 34–40, 35.
37. Sesanti, "Afrocentric Education," 36.

hoped for. I have argued in this same vein in my first writings some forty years ago, yet also cautioning (though with hindsight that caution was far too muted) that we should not uncritically accept everything that purports to be "African culture,"[38] and later argued for a serious problematizing of concepts such as Ubuntu.[39] Cautioning against "a romanticised construction of African culture," as Erasmus does, is entirely appropriate.

But that is not the only question at issue here. Michael Nassen Smith and Tafadzwa Tivaringe have problems not only with the assumption that the values Sesanti advocates will assist in the fight for decoloniality and an African renaissance because they are "Afrocentric." They take even more issue with Sesanti's implication that "there is, and has always been, one unique African culture, distinct from European and other cultures to which an Afrocentric academy should attend."[40] These are values, they argue, that are shared by other cultures as well. The desire for the preservation of human life as preference over the accumulation and preservation of wealth, for instance, is not uniquely African. "Such a statement may have been made by Jesus or Lao Tzu."[41]

Smith and Tivaringe do not deny the suppression of African traditions and epistemologies as a fact of history, and that it produces a "normative injunction":

> How are we, as Africans, to rehabilitate indigenous thought in a way that speaks to local histories and particularities while also meeting the concrete challenges that the continent faces in today's hyper-globalised political economy? This is the historic mission of our time.[42]

For our needs today however, they insist, and in order to meet the call of this historic mission, Afro-centrism is not the proper solution. They fear that in doing so, "instead of dismantling the colonial imaginary, Sesanti in fact implicitly supports it."[43] Hence we must be careful of merely "reproducing colonial binaries and Manichean thinking." Instead of an untroubled Afrocentricity, they argue that a "shift of focus or attention is needed, a shift towards a decolonial humanism and an Afro-plurality."[44] Instead of searching after an African purity, we should welcome its diversity, and not unwittingly contribute to colonialism's binaries.

Sesanti does try to avoid the dangers of "a romanticized construction of African culture" against which Erasmus, Smith Nassen, and Tivaringe caution. And that shows his awareness of Biko's self-critical consciousness. The picture that accompanies Sesanti's piece shows him in a T-shirt with Steve Biko's face printed on it. So the

---

38. See Boesak, *Farewell to Innocence*, 142–52.
39. See Boesak, *Pharaohs on Both Sides*, ch. 4.
40. See Smith and Tivaringe, "From Afro-Centrism to De-colonial Humanism," 41–43.
41. Smith and Tivaringe, "From Afro-centrism to De-colonial Humanism," 42.
42. Smith and Tivaringe, "From Afro-centrism to De-colonial Humanism," 41.
43. Smith and Tivaringe, "From Afro-centrism to De-colonial Humanism," 43.
44. Smith and Tivaringe, "From Afro-centrism to De-colonial Humanism," 43.

association is intentional, and it is also detectable in (the spirit of) his choice of words, even though he does not quote Biko directly:

> Against this Eurocentric trajectory, Afrocentric education seeks to rediscover the true history of Africans—the good and the bad, successes and failures—so as to inspire and also to warn Africans against pitfalls. More specifically, it seeks to reclaim those values . . . to sensitise Africans about the importance of not only reclaiming economic power, without which they cannot do much, but also reclaim their ancestral values for educational purposes so as to build not only a human Africa, but a humane world.[45]

I am in agreement with Sesanti when he posits that the aim of all our work should indeed be striving toward that gift of a human face for Africa and the world. And while Sesanti's Bikonian self-critical awareness is clear and highly laudable, it seems to me that if our aim is to remain true to Biko's legacy—perhaps especially in truthfully following the logic of his thinking while confronting the challenges of race, ethnicity, and nationalism as they present themselves in our time—we should think more carefully about the forms our resistance to Eurocentrism should take. Our "historic moment" is a time of still-unconquered imperialism, ongoing colonialism, renewed racism, and the temptations of all sorts of harmful self-preservations—the fertile soil of exclusivism and "othering"—and we would be wise to seriously consider the "shift of focus" Smith and Tivaringe propose. So perhaps the wisdom of an African plurality and a decolonial humanism would be more true to Biko's quest for a human face for the world as we wrestle with his thinking in our times. Smith and Tivaringe write,

> Our continent is home to millions of people of different races, different languages, different belief systems and different traditions. Black, white, Arab, Asian, mixed-race, gay, straight, queer, Christian, Muslim, Hindu, Buddhist, San, Zulu, Maasai . . . Exactly how much of our history and today's human resources are we willing to discard in a stubborn search for Afro-purity?[46]

These two young researchers have opened up points for valuable discussion, and it is exactly what is needed as we continue to explore "the historic mission" in our times. A shift of focus should be firmly on our agenda. Yet one question remains, at least for now: Why are Afro-centricity and Afro-plurality posited as mutually exclusive? And, taking a "de-colonized" humanism seriously, why is indigeneity not a better concept for serving these goals? In South Africa's new, not only racialized, but ethnicized realities and debates, South Africa's first nations, its indigenes, are almost always left out of the equation, and mostly this is an act of political expedience, where the descendants of these indigenous peoples must constantly fight for the right to be "African." Elsewhere

---

45. Smith and Tivaringe, "From Afrocentrism to De-colonial Humanism," 40.
46. Smith and Tivaringe, "From Afrocentrism to De-colonial Humanism," 43.

I have spoken of such deliberate acts of political erasure as "unremembering."[47] Such acts may be politically expedient, but they are not serving the quest for a decolonized humanism. When Biko writes that it is the task of Black Consciousness to correct the lie that "South Africa's history began in 1652,"[48] it is not simply an observation. It is the acceptance of a foundational truth, without which our de-colonized humanism will never be whole. Why can both, as agents of an inclusive indigeneity, not serve the struggle for a de-colonized humanism?

Afro-centricity (as Afro-indigeneity) is, I would suggest, still the most potent expression of resistance against the suppression of African histories, traditions, and epistemologies. In fact, "epistemicide," like genocide, is not at all hyperbole, and the seriousness of this historical situation should not be trivialized under the weight of academic hair-splitting.

Boaventura de Sousa Santos's widely recognized description still stands:

> Epistemicide is the murder of knowledge. Unequal exchanges among cultures always implied the death of the knowledge of the subordinated culture, hence the death of the subordinated groups that possessed it. In the most extreme cases, such as the European expansion, epistemicide was one of the conditions of the genocide. The loss of epistemological confidence that currently afflicts modern science has facilitated the identification of the scope and gravity of the epistemicides perpetrated by hegemonic Eurocentric modernity.[49]

"Euro-centricity" does indeed capture this accurately, and it should remain the focus of these new struggles. Provided that we take the critical and self-critical elements in Black Consciousness seriously, I should think that Afrocentricty and Afro-plurality together as agents of indigeneity, the recovery and rediscovering, the gathering and harnessing of *all* our resources in *all* of their diversities and pluralities, would be a formidable force in the struggle not only for the decolonized African mind, but for a decolonial humanism.

The Politics of Vulgarity

Black Consciousness, Biko insisted, as the search for a human face, is at the heart of a global struggle, "the most positive call to emanate from the black world for a long time."[50] In light of our discussion immediately above, it seems it is time for that call, as a call for the discovery and embrace of our essential humanness and worthiness, to resound again. Slovenian sociologist and philosopher Slavoj Žižek speaks of "public

---

47. See Boesak, *Tenderness of Conscience*, 103–4. See the discussion in ch. 1.
48. See Biko, *I Write What I Like*, 72.
49. Quoted in Paraskeva, *Curriculum*, 2.
50. See Biko, *I Write What I Like*, 101.

vulgarity" rampant on the world stage today.⁵¹ Žižek refers especially to former US president Donald Trump and his vulgar language, the way Trump brags about his sexual assaults on women, his racist talk about Mexicans, Africans, and other people of color, his denigration of vulnerable groups, his homophobia and misogyny, and his justification and encouragement of violent, white supremacies.

As equally guilty as Trump, Žižek says, is Israeli Prime Minister Benyamin Netanyahu. Netanyahu makes much of an unverified exchange between Adolf Hitler and Haj al-Husseini, the grand mufti of Jerusalem, in which, Netanyahu claims—in his constant efforts to demonize Palestinians—that it was al-Husseini who persuaded Hitler to kill the Jews, when Hitler seemed willing only to deport them. Even knowing the depths to which Netanyahu regularly sinks in his verbal denigration of Palestinians, this goes particularly far. But, says Žižek,

> We should be under no illusions about the meaning of statements like those of Netanyahu. They are a clear sign of the regression of our public sphere. Associations and ideas that were till now confined to the obscure underworld of racist obscenity are now gaining a foothold on official discourse.⁵²

This is even more striking when one keeps in mind the way that Trump has mocked "political correctness" and virtually made it the language of the cowardly, those not brave enough to say what they think and believe deep down, a truly perverse inversion of "speaking truth to power." Žižek correctly sees how language breeds, justifies, and legitimizes violence, as in the case of torture encouraged and practiced by the George W. Bush administration:

> The language of vulgarity and brutal violence practiced by the state was made publicly acceptable at the very moment when the public language was rendered politically correct in order to protect victims from symbolic violence. These two phenomena are two sides of the same coin.⁵³

South African black theologian Tinyiko Maluleke has added to the list Trump's despicable characterization of Global South countries as "s-hole countries."⁵⁴

Žižek does not mention former president Barack Obama, but surely Obama's "We tortured some folks"⁵⁵ is as objectionable as Trump's undisguised, intentional "political incorrectness." In just four words, Obama swept all the pain, suffering, and humiliation of the victims aside, all the criminality of it into the dustbin, and all the accountability for it under that all-forgiving rug of American exceptionalism. That cool, casual trivialization of Bush's CIA torture program, and his equally casual dismissal of any chance

---

51. See Žižek, "Return of Public Vulgarity."
52. Žižek, "Return of Public Vulgarity."
53. Žižek, "Return of Public Vulgarity."
54. See Maluleke, "Africans Alienated Inside and Outside."
55. See Gerstein, "Obama: 'We Tortured Some Folks.'"

of prosecution of the guilty should not be overlooked so easily. Coolness is no cover for political vulgarity, as it is no substitute for political integrity.[56]

Concentrating more on Donald Trump here is not only because, as president of the most powerful country in the world, politically, economically, and militarily, at this point in history, he has had by far the loudest megaphone of any other politician in the world. It is what Americans, entirely appropriately, and perhaps not even ironically, call a "bully pulpit." Trump also has an uncanny way of drawing media attention and keeping it on himself. He is a master of media manipulation, though "manipulation," seeing the media's mindless regurgitating of his every word, may hardly be the right term. His daily tweets, however inane, become the headlines of the day. The American Empire, though visibly disintegrating, is like the dragon in the book of Revelation, there a depiction of the Roman Empire. Even though it is on the verge of defeat by Michael and the angels and "going to perdition," its tail still has the power to sweep "a third of the stars of heaven" and throw them down to the earth (Rev 12:4). Even its convulsions of death are acts of terror.[57] One look at the destruction, of its never-ending wars, or that American sanctions are causing in Iran and Venezuela, or its support for the murderous Israeli policies, for instance, not letting up even in the midst of the devastations of the coronavirus, is enough. That other countries, especially those in the European Union, have caved in and followed suit in a kind of helpless, but not guiltless, complicity, is forceful if disheartening testimony to its power still.

So even if he does not mention any of this, Žižek is correct: "Trump is the purest expression of this tendency toward debasement of our [he means the global community's] public life." In agreement with Žižek, I will also argue here that there is much more to this "tendency."

The fact that the US president is backing the worst dictatorships in the world today and is seeking to create some more, as in the repeated but failed coup attempts in Venezuela, is not new. Trump was simply honoring an imperialistic American exceptionalist tradition, the country that has, for well nigh a century, engineered more than seventy regime changes and coup d'etats around the world.[58] In this, Donald Trump was simply being true to an imperialist urge followed mercilessly and relentlessly by US presidents for the last one hundred years, including the two Bushes, Bill Clinton, and Barack Obama.

But more than any occupant of the White House, Trump has used that power to set himself up as a negative "role model" for other leaders in the world, spurring on and blessing the legitimization of narrow, violent, ethnic, exclusivistic nationalisms. Trump's shameless bravado in these matters seems to have great appeal, not only for his political base, but also for his likeminded acolytes around the world. From Rodrigo Duterte's autocratic, gangsterist regime in the Philippines, to Saudi

56. See Jones, "20 Reasons Why Barack Obama Is the Coolest President of All Time."
57. See Boesak, *Comfort and Protest*, ch. 4.
58. See Kinzer, *Overthrow*. See also the excellent work, Blumenthal, *Management of Savagery*.

Arabia's Mohammed bin Salman's youthful but lethal war-mongering and bloodlust. From Hungary's exclusivist, violent Christian nationalism under Viktor Orban to Jair Bolsonaro's corrupt dictatorship in Brazil, whose Minister of Culture, Regina Duarte, blithely minimized the truly horrific years of the country's military dictatorship under whose reign of terror tens of thousands were disappeared and killed: "There has always been torture, [and] humanity has never stopped dying."[59] As I write this, Brazil has become the "hot spot" of the coronavirus in all of South America, and Jair Bolsonaro seems to be out-trumping even Donald Trump in his reckless disregard for human life as his country faces this crisis. Egypt's General Fattah el Sisi, the butcher of Egypt's Arab Spring, which ended the rule of the previous dictator Hosni Mubarak, has more than fulfilled American imperialist desires from Barack Obama to Donald Trump.

Writes journalist Harvey Wasserman in a particularly scathing judgment on the politics of vulgarity:

> Donald Trump is no accident. He is our Imperial Vulture come home to roost. Our Exceptional Karma. The ultimate incineration of a City on a Hill defined by arrogance, brutality, and greed. He has saturated our lives with dictatorship, disease, dementia, depression. But we have no claim to self-pity. Pinochet (Chile), Mobutu (Congo/Zaire), the Greek Junta, the Shah (Iran), Somoza (Nicaragua), Diem/Thieu/Ky (Vietnam), Yeltsin/Putin (Russia), Pol Pot (Cambodia), Lord Jeffrey Amherst (Indigenous America), Salazar (Portugal), Marcos (the Philippines), Alvarado (Honduras), the Duvaliers (Haiti) . . . murderers, thieves, despots, liars, bigots, buffoons, puppets, thugs, butchers, hypocrites, clowns, torturers, mobsters, devils incarnate . . . all installed to serve American corporate interests. They are Trump and he is them. The butchery we've imposed on humankind and the planet has at last come home to roost. Trump is Earth's retaliatory demon, here to ravage the remnants of a cruel, hypocritical, dying empire.[60]

From India's Narendra Modi's equally exclusivist, equally violent Hindu nationalism, to Britain's perfidious Trump clone, Boris Johnson. As if to confirm the last, Trump congratulated Johnson on becoming Britain's Prime Minister, and according to news reports on July 24, 2019, praised Johnson while praising himself: "They like him over there because he is Britain's Trump."[61]

Trump was not wrong, and Britain's Brexit event is as good an illustration as any. Durham University theologian Eve Parker writes,

> Since the Brexit referendum in Britain, racism and race-related hate crimes have risen dramatically, political discourse that is anti-immigrant, racist, xenophobic and Islamophobic has not only become mainstream but has been

---

59. See Sugarman, "America's Cold War Crimes Abroad Are Still Shaping Our World."
60. See Wasserman, "Trump Is No Accident."
61. See "Trump on Johnson: 'They call him Britain's Trump.'"

legitimised by the new Prime Minister, Boris Johnson, and his significant majority following the results of the recent General Election. That came despite the public being aware of his racist, classist, misogynistic, interreligious-intolerant rhetoric, where he has previously compared Muslim women to letter boxes,[62] used racial slurs against black people, argued that Islam has caused the "Muslim world to be literally centuries behind the West."[63] [He] has further argued that single mothers are guilty of "producing a generation of ill-raised, ignorant, aggressive and illegitimate children." Boris Johnson and the current Tory Government in Britain represent a dangerous "Anglosphere" philosophy that is embedded in racism, misogyny, interreligious intolerance, and an Empire ideology.[64]

British black theologian Anthony Reddie has seen this even earlier. His eloquent protest supports her observations as he writes "against the backdrop of Brexit":

> [My] concerns are not with the specifics of whether Britain should remain in or leave the European Union. At the time of writing, Britain is mired in the political paralysis of how to leave the EU and on what terms, indeed if we choose to leave at all. This article offers no opinion on the political matter of remaining or leaving. This ambivalence arises from the belief that whether we do so or not, nothing will change the toxic climate that has been unleashed by the Leave campaign. *Whether Britain leaves or not, a majority of the nation has spoken its mind, in terms of aligning with a toxic, xenophobic fuelled subtext of the Leave campaign that othered visible minorities and created an explicit White-centred discourse around the nature of Britishness and notions of belonging.* The topicality of Brexit will wane but the sense that Britain has been dragged back into the Enoch Powell rhetoric around "Rivers of Blood" will not be dissipated anytime soon.[65]

These violent, and virulent forms of racism, nationalism, and ethnocentrism; the homophobia, transphobia, and patriarchalism; the Islamophobia, religious jingoism, the

---

62. In this same week Islamophobic incidents rose by 375 percent. See Dearden, "Islamophobic incidents rose 375%."

63. Perraudin, "New controversial comments uncovered."

64. See Parker, "'Freedom of Religion' and belonging in Brexit Britain."

65. See Reddie, "Do Black Lives Matter in Post-Brexit Britain?," 2. Emphasis mine. The reference is to Conservative MP Enoch Powell's racist, but nonetheless enormously influential and popular, speech that makes his main theme the "rivers of blood" that will flow if white Britishness is not heeded, honored, and protected. "On the thirtieth anniversary of the speech in 1998," says Reddie, "64% of a Channel 4 studio audience who were brought together to discuss the legacy of his speech believed that Powell was not a racist but a courageous nationalist. In the early part of 2018, there was a contentious proposal to mount a historic blue plaque in Wolverhampton in Enoch Powell's honour as a former distinguished MP for the city. The BBC chose to broadcast the speech in full, citing it of 'historic importance' in the nation's contemporary history, despite the complaints of many black people, who critiqued its incendiary, bombastic rhetoric as deeply problematic and inimical to any helpful sense of community relations in the UK" (2, 3). See also Reddie, *Theologising Brexit*.

endless madness of the endless wars, have taken frightening reality in the vivid prose of Psalm 91. They are "terror of the night, the arrow that flies by day; the pestilence that stalks in darkness, the destruction that wastes by noonday."

I thought about this as I was recalling that great African American scholar, activist, and Pan-Africanist, W. E. B. Du Bois. In 1957, six years before his death, in *The Ordeal of Mansart*, the first part of his still fascinating three-part work, *The Black Flame Trilogy*, Du Bois posed a series of questions that, already challenging in the struggles of his day, would become increasingly so for the times that followed—ours included. He asked:

> How shall integrity face oppression? What shall honesty do in the face of deception? Decency in the face of insult, self-defense before blows? How shall [courage] and accomplishment meet despising, detraction, and lies? What shall virtue do to meet brute force?[66]

These questions, we are discovering, were not only pertinent to the situation in the United States, from where Du Bois was writing and where Dr. Martin Luther King Jr. and the black masses of America answered them so magnificently in the civil rights struggle. Du Bois's voice has been, and is still, calling to us everywhere, in every generation. And this call was answered by the millions in this country who took their faith seriously, who believed that faith can be a force against injustice and imperialism, and who set the example for new generations in the struggles for indivisible justice, undeniable dignity, and inclusive humanity, against the politics of oppression, exploitation, and vulgarity. So with W. E. B. Du Bois in mind, one should think of the politics of vulgarity way beyond Donald Trump's predatory misogyny and lethal racism.

In 2019, Oxfam reported that new billionaires were created every two days between 2017 and 2018, while every day, one thousand people died because of lack of access to basic affordable health care. In its 2020 report, Oxfam states that "economic inequality is out of control." The world's richest 1 percent now have twice as much wealth as 6.9 billion people. Twenty-two men own more than 326 million women in Africa. This represents "a world of extremes," an inequity crisis "that remains unaddressed":

> This great divide is based on a flawed and sexist economic system that values the wealth of the privileged few, mostly men, more than the billions of hours of the most essential work—the unpaid and underpaid care work done by women and girls around the world.[67]

The report argues that this is a political crisis that sounds the death knell for whatever we hope has remained of democracy in the world. "Billionaires are able to buy

---

66. See Du Bois, *Book of Mansart*, iii, 157.

67. See Oxfam, "Time to Care," 10. One shudders to think how the Oxfam 2021 Report will read after the ravages of the COVID-19.

impunity from justice, influence politicians, a pliant media, rig democratic processes, influence elections and public policy to suit their desires."⁶⁸ We should not miss the unstated judgment: it is expressly not for the "common good," a "shared planet," or a "human community." *It is to suit their own desires.* This does not represent only a financial or political crisis for the vast majorities of the world, especially in the Global South, and especially women. It is, the Oxfam Report writers say, "a care crisis."⁶⁹ In other words, a moral crisis. Speaking theologically, Germany's Jürgen Moltmann, thirty years ago, spoke of "a God crisis."⁷⁰ That is what I call the politics of vulgarity.

In 2020, South Africa remains the most unequal society on earth. More than half our population live in utmost poverty. In the meantime, though, for the pampered few, the wealth is piling up. According to a new study released in June 2019 by AfrAsia Bank, Durban, Belito, and Umhlanga in Jacob Zuma's KwaZulu-Natal, with 25 percent, have seen the biggest growth in wealth among South African billionaires over the past decade, a time period which corresponds neatly with the corruption of the Zuma/Gupta years. Meanwhile, some of the richest ones—more than three thousand—live in the Stellenbosch, Paarl, Franschhoek triangle. Right in my backyard, in other words, and amidst the most appalling poverty on the Western Cape wine farms.⁷¹

In a telling investigative piece, *Time Magazine*'s Aryn Baker writes about the lessons the world can learn from South Africa as "worldwide inequality grows." Despite the worldwide euphoria and the iconization of Nelson Mandela, for South Africa's poor, black majority, "very little has changed," Kenny Tokwe from affluent Hout Bay's black informal settlement Imizamo Yethu, tells Baker. This is the most common lament from Black South Africans across the board, despite the proud assertion in 1999 of Prof. Jakes Gerwel, Chairman of Media24, and board member of Naspers, both fabulously wealthy corporates, that South Africa has experienced "a relatively rapid de-racialisation of capital."⁷² This is not the voice of the Kenny Tokwes of the world speaking. This is the voice of South Africa's black, wealthy, privileged elite.

Baker writes in 2019 what most black South Africans have known for the last twenty-five years: "The world's most egregious racial divide has turned into its most extreme economic disparity."⁷³ According to the World Bank 2015 calculations, the top 10 percent (mostly white) owned 70 percent of the nation's wealth, while half the population lives on less than $5 a day. So what is the lesson the world can learn from

---

68. Oxfam, "Time to Care," 16.
69. Oxfam, "Time to Care," 16.
70. Moltmann, *God for a Secular World*, 190.
71. See Afrasia Bank, "2019 South Africa Wealth Report."
72. See Gerwel, "National Reconciliation," 277.
73. Baker, "What South Africa Can Teach Us."

South Africa today? Apparently only one: "In an age of widening divisions between rich and poor South Africa stands out because of its squandered hopes."[74]

And therein, for me, lies the most savage pain of the politics of vulgarity: the squandering of the hopes of the masses who struggled for freedom, who sacrificed endlessly and gave their lives, and who believed in the African National Congress and the trustworthiness of its leaders, including Nelson Mandela. And in this: the blackness of our ruling class, despite their claims upon it when it is expedient, is clearly not enough. Nelson Moldanado-Torres quotes Itumeleng Mosala:

> The black pain of a post-apartheid betrayal is infinitely more painful and dangerous than that of an age when no one had promised freedom to anyone . . . As the Yanks would say, "It is coloniality, stupid!" No need for a doctorate to grasp this. Blackness should be enough![75]

Mosala is not extolling the necessity or virtues of identity politics. In identity politics, blackness, or for that matter femaleness, or queerness, is politics without depth, without commitment, without principles. It expects trust, but does not see that it must be earned through integrity, honesty, and justice. It demands loyalty without the revolutionary reciprocity that makes politics meaningful. One's blackness counts for nothing if it is not identification with the suffering of the black poor, the oppressed, and the left-behind. Blackness, without commitment to the struggle for that radically transformed, egalitarian society Black Consciousness envisioned, is what Black Consciousness derisively called "non-whiteness." It is not only the naked reality of coloniality. It is this subservience to it, the benefiting from it, the revelling in the profiteering from it, that remains colonization's "festering wound," as Vuyani Vellem calls it.[76]

Still, economist Göran Therborn seeks to find a reason for hope. "The advent of democracy," he writes, "came to coincide with a disaster." Yet, even despite the many failures and challenges,

> South Africa [still] constitutes a social laboratory of world significance. It has achieved an almost unique re-foundation of its nation and state. It went from a *conquistador* settler nation and state ruling conquered natives to a (by now) "normal" democratic state, a feat in modern times approximated only by Bolivia, a poorer, but less sharply cloven country.[77]

The question seems to be: Can we as yet break down the skewed and cracked walls and rebuild that egalitarian democracy Biko hoped for upon those foundations laid through centuries of struggle? One thing is clear, however: it has to do a lot more to achieve that human face for its citizens left so far behind.

74. See Baker, "What South Africa Can Teach Us."
75. See Maldonado-Torres, "Ten Theses," 1.
76. See Vellem, "Spirituality of Liberation."
77. Therborn, "Racism," 48, 49.

Throughout 2019, at the US's southern border, parents and children were being separated. Almost half of those have not yet found each other. Babies, toddlers and young children are left to die in those concentration camps the Trump administration called "border facilities." Those children lucky enough to survive are still there, sleeping on concrete floors, not allowed a shower since they have come across the border; no soap, no clean clothes, miserable food. This treatment is brutal by design.[78] Those wanting to help them are turned away at the gates by border guards. A young teacher from Arizona, Scott Warren, has been arrested, charged, and brought to trial where he faces twenty years in prison. His crime? He gave food and water to immigrants wandering through the desert, hoping to reach the US. Indeed: in the US right now, saving lives is a crime. The fact that he was finally acquitted does not change the vulgarity of the politics involved here.[79]

But, and for Christians this is the point, Trump was in power because 81 percent of white Evangelicals in the US voted for him in 2016. He is what white evangelical Christian America wants. People of good will in the United States are struggling, like we are here, to give their country a human face, and Christians, it seems, are in the forefront of trying to keep it on that "far, distant horizon." But these Christians are not committed to peace and justice, to equity, dignity, and an inclusive humanity. They are what African American Judge and pastor Wendell Griffen calls "the hateful faithful."[80]

In June 2019, Franklin Graham, son of the late evangelist Billy Graham and today one of the front leaders and foremost spokespersons for the American white evangelical right, called for a Day of Prayer for President Trump. Graham gave his reasons: the president was under severe attack from enemies of the president and the US, who, by the same token, are also enemies of the faith.[81]

It might be useful to ask who these enemies of Trump and the faithful in the US are. They were, and in a real sense still are, the people who are against the endless wars the US is waging in no fewer than eight Muslim countries as I write; people against his embrace of the murderous regime in Saudi Arabia (also a fundamentalist religious regime) who in 2018 beheaded forty-eight of its citizens, more than half of them charged with nonviolent drug offenses.[82] These are the people against his immigration policies, against the concentration camps along the US southern border. The enemies of the faith are those against sanctions against Venezuela that have taken the lives of more than forty-thousand people since 2017.[83] It is those people who stand in the breach for LGBTQI persons against whom the Trump administration has waged

---

78. See, e.g., Border Action Network, *US-Mexican Border Policy Report*.
79. See Deveraux, "Humanitarian Volunteer Scott Warren Reflects."
80. The title of a forthcoming book by Wendell Griffen.
81. See Morton, "Franklin Graham Calls for a 'Special Day of Prayer' for Trump."
82. See "Saudi Arabia Criticised for 48 Beheadings." Human rights activists fear that these are excuses for punishing persons who oppose the House of Saud.
83. See Third World Resurgence, "U.S. Sanctions Killed over 40,000 Venezuelans since 2017."

a virtual war at every level, those against the propping up of the murderous apartheid regime in Israel and the illegal occupation and deadly colonization of Palestine.

I am not even speaking of the Russians, the Chinese, the Latin Americans, and Mexicans, all those "rapists," "criminals," and "drug dealers" who "invade" the US, and the millions of "bad Muslims," as Mahmood Mamdani calls them,[84] who refuse to bend to America's will, in contrast to the "good Muslims" such as Saudi Arabia's Mohammed Bin Salman. So finally, Christians can rid themselves of that pesky, silly command of Jesus to love our enemies: there are simply too many of them. Who can keep up? As such, they are, as Naomi Klein calls them, "useful enemies,"[85] useful, and indispensable for the purposes of the politics of fear mongering, intimidation, and authoritarianism, but easily dispensable nonetheless.

I have written all the above when there was no sign of a thing called the coronavirus (COVID-19), nor of the chaos it would cause worldwide, nor of the way it would unmask the politics of vulgarity on a global scale such as we are now experiencing as I write. As always, it is now becoming clear, the poor and vulnerable will suffer a double or triple victimization. Journalist Nick Turse writes,

> More than 240,000 people worldwide have already died of COVID-19, and before the pandemic finishes, it could kill hundreds of thousands, even millions, more. But the final toll is destined to be far higher than just those who die of COVID-19. Experts warn that deaths from secondary impacts—poverty, hunger, diseases, and violence exacerbated by the pandemic—may dwarf the number of those who die of the novel coronavirus itself. A new analysis by researchers from King's College London and Australian National University, under the aegis of the United Nations University World Institute for Development Economics Research, for example, warns that the economic contraction caused by COVID-19 could push an additional 500 million people—about 8 percent of the Earth's population—into poverty, reversing 30 years of economic improvement.[86]

There is no more hiding the shameless, stone-cold heart of neoliberal capitalism. It is Naomi Klein's "disaster capitalism" at its worst. The blatant profiteering from the illness, the carelessness of the ill-preparedness for which world leaders like Donald Trump refuse to take responsibility, the endless politicization of the pandemic for selfish political gain. Trump attempted to detract from his own mishandling of the crisis by blaming the WHO and ending US funding to the UN organ, and this remains one of the worst instances of where this is taking us. But even this is topped by the Hitleresque suggestion made by Texas Lt. Governor Dan Patrick that elderly Americans

---

84. See Mamdani, *Good Muslim, Bad Muslim*.
85. See Klein, *Shock Doctrine*, 163ff.
86. Turse, "Exceptionally Dire."

should disregard the risks to their health and their lives and go to work to save the American economy.[87]

And look where that mindless vulgarity has taken the world: an onslaught on democratic principles and civil rights and freedoms of which Hungary, the Philippines, and Malawi are only the most blatant examples. In Israel, the Israeli's make cynical and deadly use of the lockdown to hunt down their political enemies and to push through the annexation of Palestinian land in the West Bank.[88] In Myanmar, the army uses the virus as cover to conclude the genocide of the Rohingyas.[89] Add to that the US's shameless display of unaccountability, exceptionalism, and disdain of international law in its punitive reaction to officers of the International Criminal Court, and Israel's annexation plans regarding the Occupied West Bank. Respected International Law scholar Richard Falk describes those acts as the actions of "rogue states" engaging in "gangster geopolitics."[90]

It is something perhaps even W. E. B. Du Bois did not foresee. Foreign policies characterized by bullying instead of respectful negotiation; forceful capitulation instead of common understanding; enforced submission instead of equal partnership; reckless lawlessness instead of respect for international law. Rabid ethnic and religious nationalism instead of inclusive global security, and xenophobic rage instead of an understanding of our common humanity. Imperialist expansionism instead of peaceful co-existence; destructive, unbridled neoliberal capitalist exploitation instead of planetary security; internationalized thuggery instead of the promotion and protection of human rights, and nationalistic vanity instead of global servanthood. It is a form of international political vandalism. Those questions about honesty, decency, courage, and integrity are now more pressing than ever.

Meanwhile, we will have to grapple with the painful truth that the resilience of religion has proved Harvey Cox wrong and religion is playing a larger, more determining role in public life than our postmodern age has ever seen.[91] Yet the politics of solidarity, decency, and integrity has been swallowed whole by the politics of vulgarity. By overwhelming levels of abusive power, craven cowardice, untamed voraciousness, unrepentant racism, shameless bigotry, and unending violence. And it is backed up by an imperialistic, fundamentalist religion that has turned the revolutionary Savior from Galilee into the fascist Butcher of Nazareth.

It is clear that the world does not yet have that human face. Neither does South Africa. Behind the coronavirus masks we are now required to wear to help save our

---

87. See Sherfinski, "Patrick Suggests He'd Risk Dying to Help Save U.S. Economy."

88. See "Report: Israel Arrested 357 Palestinians in March despite Coronavirus Lockdown."

89. See Hoelzl and Diamond, "Myanmar Military Steps Up Attacks."

90. See Falk, "Gangster Geopolitics." See also Falk, "Rogue States."

91. See Cox, *Secular City*. Twenty-five years later, Cox admitted that he was wrong. In an interview in 1990, Cox acknowledged that "human religiosity is a much more persistent quality . . . Nearly everywhere we look in the world today we witness an unanticipated resurgence of traditional religion." See Cox, "Secular City 25 Years Later," 1025.

lives are hidden the masks that cover infections that will outlast the infections of COVID-19 and that threaten our soul. Behind the arrogant mask of self-satisfied power, behind the smug smiles of greed and instant gratification; behind the self-congratulatory mask of rainbow-nationalism, we hide the grim realities of our immoral and unsustainable inequalities, our poverty, suffering, and abuse, which is the face of the poor, the vulnerable, the women, the girl-children, and the forgotten.

In South Africa, initially at least, the coronavirus crisis was handled fairly well by President Ramaphosa's government, and he himself has acquitted himself of this task with more political responsibility, resolve, and compassion than many other political leaders. Since then, though, as the crisis continues, two things are becoming clear. First, the internal divisions in the ANC and the rather weak leadership from the president are ravaging whatever good intentions there might have been. As so often before, the internal agendas are taking precedence over the interests of the people, especially the poor and vulnerable. Bowing to pressures of nepotism, cronyism, and factionalist loyalties, the ANC has shunned competence, integrity, and leadership. The coronavirus crisis has mercilessly ripped the mask from whatever our need to recover from the Zuma years had tried to hide. The fundamental fault lines we discussed above, preceding the problems we now face, have in fact exacerbated them. Unless these issues are seriously and urgently addressed with no less than a fundamental change in economic policies, political behavior, and moral discernment, the next crisis will find us confronting the same problems, only worse. And calling upon the legacy of Nelson Mandela will not help South Africa deal with these complex issues.[92] The days of belief in "Madiba magic" are firmly over. After we have hopefully won this current battle, we will still be confronted with Jesus's question: "But what will it profit them if they gain the whole world and lose their soul [forfeit their life]?" (Matt 16:28).

Can it be that Wasserman's brutally honest, self-critical reflections can also serve the rest of us, as he asks Americans to "look deep into ourselves"? Americans need, he pleads,

> to excoriate the pain our empire has imposed. The arrogance of our "exceptionalism." The burden of our slave-based misogyny. The injustices of our racism, sexism, ecological destruction, multi-layered bigotries. The wages of our greed. The uselessness of our wars. The absurdity of our military. The blood-sucking death grip of our global corporations. Wrap them all in one big irreverence. Look deep into the ghastly mirror of our merciless inflictions . . . then face who we really have been, and what we must become.[93]

---

92. See Karrim, "Ramaphosa: Mandela's Example Will Help Us Overcome Global Pandemic."
93. Wasserman, "Trump Is No Accident."

The "Envisioned Self"

Finally, we should consider something that Biko references several times.[94] Even though it is crucial, Erasmus, in her discussion of Biko's humanism, does not mention it, but Njabulo Ndebele, in his foreword to the 2017 edition of *I Write What I Like*, does.[95] His is a moving, finely written piece, and he expresses the feelings of many Biko readers, certainly mine, when he writes,

> "The envisioned self"! This expression has lain innocuously between the covers of *I Write What I Like*, Steve Biko's enduring book. I must have read and re-read this expression over the years. But how come I didn't see it? How come my mind didn't take in what my eyes must have seen? Or was it that my mind's eye skipped over the expression each time? Can a reader read unseeingly? I think so.[96]

I think so too, and each re-reading does bring new insights, especially for the topic under discussion here. Biko first mentions this significant phrase several times, and each time the context is crucial.

In the foreword, Ndebele contrasts the idea of (racial) "integration" in the mind of the white liberal to what Biko calls "true integration." There, he says that "the heart of true integration is the provision for each man, each group to rise and attain the envisioned self."[97] The term "integration" has been superseded by the better, and far more comprehensive, term "non-racialism," but the fundamental requirement remains. Attaining the "envisioned self" here means, Biko stresses, that until all sense of false superiority and inferiority, all ingrained sense of white supremacy, all systems and structures of white privilege are broken down and done away with, this cannot happen. We must first attain a "mutual respect for each other" which must be both attitudinal and systemic, which will create space for "complete freedom of self-determination." To be sure, "self-determination" here does not denote a nationalistic project, but rather a humanistic achievement. It emphasizes not nationhood, but rather what we have earlier called "full humanity." Only this, Biko argues, will bring "true integration"; that is, "a genuine fusion of the life-style of the various groups." This, he argued, is not something whites can "give" black people who are suffering "from [an] inferiority complex" because of white racism. It will indeed be the result of black agency, "a very strong build-up of black consciousness such that blacks can learn to assert themselves and stake their rightful claim." So, first, the "envisioned self" cannot be understood apart from black agency, just as it cannot be understood apart from freedom.

But second, clearly the situation Biko sees as ideal—"true"—is something that should be embraced by blacks as well as whites. White racism, white supremacy, and

---

94. Biko, *I Write What I Like*, 53, 74, 101.
95. Ndebele, "The Envisioned Self," vii–xiv.
96. Ndebele, "Envisioned Self," vii.
97. Biko, *I Write What I Like*, 22.

white privilege are all symptomatic of a serious breakdown of white people's humanity. That much we have learned from imperialism, colonialism, apartheid, and their workings. From that dehumanized state whites need to be liberated. This is, as Paulo Freire argued, "the historic obligation of the oppressed,"[98] and what Biko saw as the task of the "selfless revolutionary."[99] But without blacks attaining their "envisioned self," whites will remain in bondage, constantly caught in "a state of frenzy." That is why the revolutionary seeks to "restore faith in life amongst all citizens of this country."[100] In a word, the envisioned self is not simply a *black* self. Neither is it a racial self. It is the restored humanity of all. It is for this reason that I find it hard to follow Erasmus's logic when she contrasts Biko with Fanon on this point:

> Thus, for [Fanon] the path to becoming human lies not in the denial or embrace of "race" but in the recovering of the "human" from its grasp . . . Hence he writes, "I have one right alone: that of demanding human behavior from the other . . . I have no wish to be the victim of the *Fraud* of the black world."[101]

Precisely that demand is at the heart of Black Consciousness, then and now. The whole struggle, as "a quest for true humanity," is a stubborn refusal to cloak oneself in victimhood, staunchly fighting against the "fraud" of the black world. Njabulo Ndebele was exactly right. Holding on the "envisioned self" is "believing in the 'righteousness of its strength.' *Believing in its humanistic goals, it is inclusionary, creating room for all who wish to participate in its emancipatory norms.*"[102]

On page 53, Biko speaks of the "envisaged self" directly in the context of freedom. Here, as we have discussed above, the "envisaged self" is the "free self." The liberation of the mind and the person is paramount. On pages 74 and 101, he speaks again of the "envisioned self," the first in the context of "white racism and Black Consciousness," and the second within the context of his "Quest for True Humanity." In both cases the expression is framed by his famous and enduring adage, "the most potent weapon in the hands of the oppressor is the mind of the oppressed." Liberation of the mind and liberation of the body are inextricable. Only when both are achieved, can one speak of "complete humanness."

Early on, Ndebele shares with the reader that he was struck by this phrase in a re-reading of the 1978 edition, which he received from Fr. Aeldred Stubbs, a "treasured gift of thirty-eight years ago." He also shares Fr. Stubbs's inscription: "With gratitude

---

98. See Freire, *Pedagogy of the Oppressed*. See also the discussion pertinent to this issue in Boesak, *Pharaohs on Both Sides*, ch. 5.

99. "To a revolutionary, State evil is a major evil for out of it flow countless other subsidiary evils that engulf the lives of both the oppressors and the oppressed. The [selfless] revolutionary sees his task, all too often as liberation not only of the oppressed but also of the oppressor." Biko, *I Write What I Like*, 241.

100. Biko, *I Write What I Like*, 241.

101. Erasmus, "'Race' and Its Articulation," 60. Emphasis mine.

102. Ndebele, "Envisioned Self," xii.

& affection, and in hope of better things yet to come."[103] The inscription intimates a meaningful relationship between the two men, so Ndebele's reflection on it a few paragraphs later is not happenstance, nor frivolous or facetious: "If Stubbs' 'better things yet to come' was like the second coming that Christians patiently wait for, Steve Biko's 'envisioned self' was the form of its coming."[104]

The analogy with Christ's second coming however lays a heavy burden on the question that follows: "What could it be in South Africa today that has crystallised the meaning of *'the envisioned self'* with such emergent clarity?" With these words, Ndebele frames "the envisioned self" within an eschatological dimension. He strengthens this by reminding us that "the envisioned self" was "Biko's futuristic concept by which he called for more than just the recovery of a human essence dismembered, distorted, disorientated, and oppressed." Delving even deeper, Ndebele adds another dimension. It also calls "for how that presence could be recovered and remoulded under new historical circumstances spanning more than one hundred and fifty years of a painful yet purposeful effort of seeking to reconstitute it into *a new human being*."[105]

Those last words are the new dimension of "the envisioned self" Ndebele urges us to ponder. Christians know not only about the second coming of Christ, they also know that biblically "being in Christ" constitutes a "new humanity," as the Apostle Paul testifies, "If anyone is in Christ, there is a new creation: everything old has passed away" (2 Cor 5:17). Traditional readings of Paul have confined this text to the spiritual realm, an inward renewal, creating a new person with a new personal relationship to God. Radical Christianity, however, rightly questions this view. American theologian Joel Edward Goza names this understanding one of three foundational religious lies, the first being that "Christians could be in right relationship with God without being in right relationship with the broken and abused of their society." The second lie, "tightly aligned to the first," is that "religion is about the salvation of the soul." In doing this, "Christianity became an increasingly introspective and individualistic thing, oblivious to the world and unable to translate Scripture's social convictions to the world's most basic and earthly needs." The third lie: "Indifference to injustice is no threat to one's intimacy with God."[106]

Since M. M. Thomas of India's immeasurable contribution to liberation theology and the fierce ecumenical debates on Christian participation in revolution that followed, the term "new humanity" has taken on an immensely relevant meaning. Through Thomas's work, the Global South has made an indelible impact on ecumenical thinking, and his thinking became hugely inspirational for liberation theology.[107]

---

103. Ndebele, "Envisioned Self," vii.
104. Ndebele, "Envisioned Self," viii.
105. Ndebele, "Envisioned Self," x. Emphasis mine.
106. See Goza, *America's Unholy Ghosts*, 146.
107. See e.g., Boesak, *Farewell to Innocence*, and the way I leaned on Thomas's work here. For a discussion of Thomas's influence on a generation of liberation theologians, see Rajaiah, *Dalit Humanization*.

In his excellent doctoral dissertation on Thomas, Jeyaraj Rajaiah makes the point that Thomas spoke of "three means toward humanization," that is, toward creating a "new humanity."[108] First, Thomas speaks of "prophetic spirituality" because it calls for transformation of nature, society, and history, and in that process, "one finds self-fulfillment in worldly responsibility." The second means is "conscientization." If people are the subject of history, they should be conscientized of their rights and privileges. The third means to humanization is revolution:

> God, who is the Lord of this world, is also the Lord of the Asian revolution. He is Lord of all the revolutions—political, economic, and social. Christ is here, present, creating, judging, and redeeming (Col 1:15–20).[109]

Thomas's Christ is a living, involved Christ, present in and working through the revolutions for justice, dignity, and freedom everywhere in the world. This Christ is no doctrinal, philosophical, or ideational concept. This Christ, in Thomas's logic, was present in the revolutions in Thomas's time; he is present in our revolution against apartheid and the injustices of its compromises with evil; he is present in the ongoing revolution against the occupation in Palestine, and he is present in the Black Lives Matter revolution now engulfing the United States and the world. Always present, always creating, always judging, and always redeeming. Thomas's Christ is the Christ of the ongoing, global Intifada, as Dabashi calls it. It is the Christ Biko was looking for but could not find in the church. In the revolution, though, Christ is not just "there." Christ is "creating, judging, and redeeming" our earnest but fallible efforts to undo injustice and oppression, and bring justice, dignity, and peace to our world. Christ is there, present, pleading with us not to lose sight of the "essential truth": that the pathos of the Christian in the revolution is not blindly for a Cause, but for justice, dignity, freedom, and humanity. That our revolution is about "the demand of the people for *power as the bearer of dignity* and for significant and *responsible participation in society and social history*."[110] That it is for the creation of a "new humanity."

So Biko's "new humanity," which Ndebele draws upon, has deep and treasured Global South antecedents. An important part of the debate has always centered on the issue whether we are dealing here with an eschatological issue, i.e., something that will be realized only "when Jesus returns," the context within which Ndebele initially places his reflections on this point. Inevitably, such a stance leads to a waiting-upon-Jesus attitude that makes human action in the here and now unnecessary. The world remains as it is while we wait "patiently" for Jesus to return and finally establish the reign of God upon the earth. But Thomas's theology exhorts us to embrace a "prophetic spirituality" that "finds fulfilment in worldly responsibility" here and now.

---

108. Rajaiah, *Dalit Humanization*, 142–45.
109. See Thomas, "Logic of the Christian Mission," 69–74.
110. Thomas and McCaughey, *Christian in the World Struggle*, 19.

Thomas insisted that God is at work in the revolutions for justice and freedom raging across the world in his day. These insights caused a storm within ecumenical circles that would not abate for years. Elsewhere, in agreement with Thomas, I argued the same regarding the continuing global revolutions in our own day.[111] This is how Thomas put it:

> Jesus Christ is also at work in the revolutions as victor over evil powers through His Cross and Resurrection. And His Kingdom and His New Humanity are offered within the revolution as the fulfilment of His promises.[112]

Dutch liberation theologian Bert Ter Schegget grasped this when he writes of politics "as an eschatological sensitivity."[113] For Christians, politics is not determined, confined, and held captive by "the art of the possible." Politics is "the art of expecting the Lord." We engage in politics as if we are—*because* we are—expecting the return of the Lord at any time, in other words, in this life. Therefore, no matter how hard it sometimes seems, we do not give up on, or let go of, the politics of freedom, justice, equity, dignity, and peace, which is the politics of the reign of God. That is what drives us toward the creation of the "new humanity." A new world, as Martin Luther King Jr. would say, does not "roll in on the wheels of inevitability." It is the result of the sacrificial work of those who offer themselves as co-workers with God. It seems though, that Paul is way ahead of us. Paul disabuses us of this notion as he sets the "new humanity" not in the context of a kind of procrastinated eschatology, but within the responsibility of the "new creation" in Christ in this immediate world. It is a "realized eschatology." It is this new creation who, here and now, is called to be an "ambassador for Christ" to whom God has "entrusted the message of reconciliation" (2 Cor 5:19).

In this ongoing struggle, Paul writes, "we do not lose heart," for we know that "it is by God's grace that we are engaged in this ministry" (2 Cor 4:1). Even so, Christians are not deceived: this will not come without pain and sacrifice, and we are not invincible, nor infallible; we are mere "jars of clay." To these jars of clay, however, is entrusted "a treasure" (2 Cor 4:7). One should *hear* the stunned, surprised humility in Paul's words. We do not, because we have no reason to, arrogantly claim power, but rest in the truth that that extraordinary power belongs to God:

> We are afflicted in every way, but not crushed; perplexed but not driven to despair; persecuted, but not forsaken; struck down, but not destroyed; always carrying in the body the death of Jesus, so that the life of Jesus may also be made visible in our bodies. (2 Cor 4:8–10)

This is the "secret" of being human that Ter Schegget argues for. It is another way of understanding Biko's "righteousness of our strength."

---

111. See Boesak, *Farewell to Innocence*; Boesak, *Pharaohs on Both Sides*.
112. Thomas, *Church's Mission and Post-modern Humanism*, 100.
113. See Ter Schegget, *Het Geheim van de Mens*, 131–44.

The "new humanity" is God's instrument to effect true reconciliation in the world. Ndebele evokes South Africa's reconciliation project when he raises a crucial question regarding the "envisioned self," heightening the "burden" we spoke of above. He writes, "Did 1994 become that time?"[114] Is this how we are to understand Stubb's "better things to come"? But even asking the question raises other questions, for 1994 did not bring Stubbs's "better things to come" any closer, and neither did South Africa's reconciliation project, however much our dominant narratives wanted it to be.

I have argued strenuously that South Africans have refused to engage reconciliation as the radical demand for justice, dignity, and equity it is.[115] We have not been willing, or ready, to understand that reconciliation, whether or not we speak politically, if it is to be meaningful, durable and sustainable, should be real, radical, and revolutionary. It is real, and not a cover for political pietism and Christian quietism. It is radical because it is about much more than harmonious personal relationships. It is about the restoration of justice, rights, and human dignity, and not about the protection and preservation of the wealth and power of the already privileged. It is never shallow, but goes to the roots of things. And it is revolutionary because it seeks the transformation of persons, and societies, their systems and structures, their politics and the intentions and workings of their policies. It seeks the transformation of the world. Biblically speaking, it is the ministry through which God is reconciling *the world* unto Godself. Politically speaking, it is the most common-sense strategy toward more justice, more equity, and our desperate need for social cohesion. Therefore it is costly, never cheap.

This understanding has all sorts of radical consequences for the way in which we understand reconciliation. Let me return to Paul in 2 Corinthians 5. In a sense, because we have heard Paul, Christians know that reconciliation is not an "option," as if we can weigh other options, consider the feasibility and the risks, take into account the political possibilities and the economic consequences, make decisions on minimalist versus maximalist approaches, hedging against the shocking demands of the Gospel with calculated, pre-emptive incrementalism, all under the guise of politics as "the art of the possible." Reconciliation is a calling, the very essence of costly discipleship, in which we follow Jesus, called by the same God, exposed to the same risks, led by the same Spirit. It is the immediate calling of the "new creation" in Christ without which the "new humanity" we are striving for is a futility.

In 2 Corinthians 5, Paul tells us that long before we knew it, God was already at work, reconciling the world to Godself in Christ, not counting their transgressions against them. Then God interrupted God's own work, making room for us, entrusting to us the ministry of reconciliation, so that we, having become a new creation and

---

114. Ndebele, "Envisioned Self," xiii.

115. See Boesak, *Tenderness of Conscience*; Boesak, "And Zacchaeus Remained Sitting in the Tree"; Boesak, *Radical Reconciliation*; DeYoung; *Dare We Speak of Hope?*; and Boesak, *Pharaohs on Both Sides*.

urged on by the love of Christ, are now called to be ambassadors of Christ in the work of reconciling the world to God.

We should note two further things: even as we are new in Christ and reconciled to God in Christ, Christ still entreats us, "Be reconciled to God!" That means that to do the work of reconciliation is no easy thing: it calls for daily conversion, daily commitment, and daily obedience, for renewed reconciliation with God, if we are to respond to that calling. It is necessary: for if, in order to reconcile the world with God in his struggles for justice, freedom, and dignity, for the sake of a new humanity and a reconciled world, Jesus had to give up his life, what makes us think that we will get away with anything less than that? The lynching of Jesus, and after him of Malcolm X, Martin Luther King Jr., and Steve Biko in our lifetime, stand as sober reminders.

Second, whereas first God worked without us, now that we have been called to this ministry of reconciliation we have become co-workers with God. For that reason, Paul's proclamation of the ministry of reconciliation does not end with 2 Cor 5:21, as some of us might think; it ends with 2 Cor 6:13. And in truth we are not able to do this work on our own. It is too hard. Once we commit to this work, as servants of God we should be ready for every challenge. That is what Paul explains in 2 Cor 6:4–10.

This, Paul says, is what we face as we engage in the ministry of reconciliation, and Paul does not mince his words: great endurance, afflictions, hardships, calamities, beatings, imprisonments, riots, [unrewarded] labors, sleepless nights, hunger. This is how we endure: by purity, knowledge, kindness, holiness of spirit, genuine love, truthful speech. But we are not alone, because we stand not in our own might but in the power of God, "with the weapons of righteousness for the right hand and for the left" (2 Cor 6:7).

This has nothing to do with the so-called and so-often invoked political realism of the "balance of power" or the tired, convenient political expediencies of the "National Democratic Revolution." Neither has it anything to do with that vacuous excuse for our own moral and political frivolousness we used to call "Madiba magic."

Paul says this because he has learned what reconciliation is and what it is not. Whereas the classic Greek writers in Paul's time used the word reconciliation for peace treaties, political agreements, and interpersonal relationships, they used the word as representatives of the Greek Empire. For the empire, reconciliation always meant to become reconciled with the goals of the empire, the will of the emperor and with what is good for the empire. Reconciliation was the "pacification," in other words, the subjection of weaker nations. It was to make peace with the lies of the empire, to meekly accept the injustices inflicted by the empire on the vanquished, the poor, and the oppressed. Reconciliation was to endure, without protest, the violence of the empire, to remain silent in the face of mendacity, dishonesty, and brutality, in the knowledge that if one did, one would be richly rewarded by the empire's corrupt systems of patronage. So the violent subjugation of nations was naturally seen as an effort to reconcile those "barbarians" with the empire, end the strife caused by their resistance, and celebrate their submission to and assimilation into the empire by accepting the domination the empire imposed. That was reconciliation captured by empire.

The Pauline emphasis on reconciliation, however, comes from his understanding of the life, message, death on a cross, and resurrection of an oppressed, exploited Roman colonial subject named Jesus, from the town of Nazareth in the occupied territory of Galilee. Paul preached a gospel in which every call to reconcile with God meant resistance to empire; a reminder that one cannot call Jesus "Lord" and simultaneously be reconciled with the emperor who considered himself God, son of God, prince of peace, morning star, giver of life, savior of the world. All these titles the early church claimed instead for Jesus, the revolutionary peasant from Galilee, the one who embraced the status of a slave, and as the lowest of the low in Roman society claimed his place as the true Son of God, the true Savior of the world.

For the early church, reconciliation means that there "is no longer Jew or Greek, there is no longer slave or free; there is no longer male and female; for all of you are one in Christ Jesus" (Gal 3:29). That is reconciliation because it demands radical inclusivity, radical justice, and radical equity; and it is real, radical, and revolutionary. For the early church, it meant proclaiming Christ who "disarmed [put to shame] the rulers and authorities [of the empire] and made a public spectacle of them, triumphing over them in it" (Col 2:15). That is reconciliation because it puts earthly powers precisely in their place, reminding them that God alone is God, and as such it is real, radical, and revolutionary.

As a rich, privileged, slave-holding member of Roman society, it is necessary that Philemon, in order not to create dangerous exceptions which undermine the "normal order" of things, keep the slaves in their place, the slave masters secure, and the slave political economy intact, find and severely punish his runaway slave Onesimus. But, according to the Letter to Philemon, as a follower of Jesus, Philemon can no longer reconcile himself to the rules and obligations of Roman society. So he will, Paul writes in his letter to Philemon, welcome Onesimus, no longer as a slave and not only as a brother in Christ, but a *beloved brother in the flesh* (Phil 16). There is no chance of spiritualizing this relationship to an "on Sundays only" affair. With superb, but pressing understatement, Paul assures Philemon that they are "partners" in this quest toward radical equality, even as Paul makes the runaway slave his own partner. Knowing that Philemon is rich and does not need the money, Paul tells him that he will take any expenses for his own account: "I will repay it" (Phil 17–19), even while Paul reminds Philemon that Philemon owes Paul his own life. In what I read as possibly the gentlest piling on of pressure, Paul ends the letter with what can be read as a longing for reunification or as reminder that he will exact some accountability: "Prepare a guest room for me" (Phil 22). Above all, Paul is emphasizing an element that is unmissable for true reconciliation: equality. Once this happens, Philemon can never again "own" Onesimus as a slave; he can only love him as an equal. In doing this, both Philemon and Onesimus are representatives of the new humanity. That is a fundamental reversal of Roman political, societal, and economic rules, and that is reconciliation because it is real, radical, and revolutionary.

This reading and interpretation of the Scriptures had, and has, all sorts of consequences for the way in which we understand reconciliation, politically and otherwise. For Black liberation theology, as it was for M. M. Thomas, the new humanity is the outcome of God's revolutionary activity in the world of which Christians are called to be a part. Christians know that they are not called to "Christianize" the revolution. They are called to work together with those who work towards God's purposes of the humanizing of the world, taking their place not innocuously, but as followers of Jesus Christ, while fully understanding the words of Paul Lehmann,

> The difference between believers and unbelievers is not defined by church membership, or even, in the last analysis, baptism. The difference is defined by imaginative and behavioural sensitivity to what God is doing in the world to make and keep human life human, to achieve . . . the new humanity.[116]

"Another World Is On Her Way"

Zimitri Erasmus's assessment of Biko's humanism is framed within, and by, the study project in which she was involved. The well-endowed Stellenbosch Institute for Advanced Study (STIAS) commenced on several projects under the wide-ranging theme of "Being Human Today." They chose that theme "because race-thinking and racism continue to frame the lives and define the nature of the human condition for most people in the world."[117] The project is meant to have both a scholarly and practical impact, "informing social change by challenging and undermining existing notions of racial difference."[118]

It is within this framework that Erasmus critiques Biko for "celebrating blackness and making it the centre of politics."[119] Fanon, on the other hand, she writes, is "disturbed by the existence of black as a category 'to which one inevitably belongs, whether one desires it or not . . . from a distance, without inquiry, without exchange of a single word.'" To assume, as Biko does, she states, quoting Patrick Ehlen on Fanon with approval, "that racial membership brings peace of mind is to tolerate its misfittings and distortions in exchange for false belonging."[120]

These are all legitimate concerns. By now, however, it should be unnecessary to point out, as I did above, that, first of all, Biko, and that whole Black Consciousness generation, even though we wanted desperately for it to be otherwise, "had to

---

116. Lehmann, *Ethics in a Christian Context*, 117.
117. See Jablonski and Maré, *Effects of Race*, 1.
118. Jablonski and Maré, *Effects of Race*, 2.
119. Erasmus, "'Race' and Its Articulation," 60.
120. Erasmus, "'Race' and Its Articulation," 60.

take cognizance of the fact that ours is far from a normal society."[121] It still is not. Second, for Biko "blackness" was never an end in itself. In apartheid South Africa, it functioned within the "solidarity of blackness" that did not reinforce, but in fact obliterated apartheid's racial and ethnic categories of "Bantu," "colored," and "Indian." As such, politically speaking alone, it was an indispensable instrument of struggle. But it was much more. As a person saddled with a "colored" identity and all that came with that, I personally will never be able to quite express the sense of freedom and sense of belonging I experienced through acceptance of this understanding. The psychological, social, and political power of the discovery of one's own worthiness and personhood was no "false sense of belonging." It is an experience Mandela, coming out of prison after twenty-seven years, and the exiled ANC after thirty years of disconnect with the spiritual and political growth of their own people, would be unable to understand.[122] As it is perhaps difficult for a young "colored" generation suffering under ANC policies permeated with unacknowledged, but nonetheless real, racist notions.

Third, within the apartheid context the restoration of black personhood was essential, what Biko called "the first truth," as bitter and painful as it was to acknowledge. One calls to mind Biko's devastating self-critique of blackness as a condition caused by white racism. Three hundred and fifty years of racism, oppression, and dehumanization have turned the indigenous person into "an empty shell," a "shadow" of their authentic selves, "completely defeated, drowning in [their] own misery, a slave, an ox, bearing the yoke of oppression with sheepish timidity." Black consciousness was the only way to restore that devastated humanity, "to infuse [them] with pride and dignity." But not only that. The black person had also to come to terms with our own complicity in "being misused" and allowing "evil [to] reign supreme in our country."[123] This is not choosing "racial membership" as a "path to humanity." It is, as I have argued above, choosing the path of the restoration of personhood, dignity, and humanity in order to find a "completed humanity."[124]

Fourth, Biko did not assume that racial membership brings peace of mind. The single time Biko speaks directly to the question of peace of mind is when he discusses the task of the selfless revolutionary. There he sees it as the outcome of a struggle for human dignity where whites and blacks exist together in a non-racial society, where race and ethnicity do not count because both the oppressed and the oppressor have been liberated, set free to recognize, and embrace the humanity of the other, and because now, "faith in life has been restored."[125]

121. Biko, *I Write What I Like*, 13. Hence the slogan of the non-racial anti-apartheid sports body, the South African Council on Sports (SACOS), "No normal sports in an abnormal society."

122. See Introduction here, as well as Boesak, *Tenderness of Conscience*, 10–13, where I discuss this issue.

123. Biko, *I Write What I Like*, 30, 31.

124. Biko, *I Write What I Like*, 30–31.

125. Biko, *I Write What I Like*, 241.

The debate about "race" is not new. At the time when the African National Congress was resolutely set on obliterating the legacy of Black Consciousness, Nelson Mandela wrote, "To say that race is a myth and that in our country there are no Africans, Coloureds and Indians, but only words, is to play with words." Then, seemingly not understanding how much like an apartheid apologist he sounded, Mandela continued, "In addition to the colour of their skin and the texture of their hair they differ in historical origins and in their culture and languages . . . race as such exists in the world."[126] Black Consciousness in South Africa, however, despite Mandela's scepticism and harsh critique held to well-tested views developed by black scholars such as renowned African American sociologist and great intellectual hero of our times, C. Eric Lincoln. "Race," he wrote, "is an insidious intruder, a silent partner to every personal relationship." Nonetheless, it is a "cultural fiction":

> An emotional crutch for people whose sense of personal adequacy I threatened. It is the joker in the deck stacked for personal advantage in a game of life where the dealer must always win to break even. But in the world of objective reality, the alleged pure and definable race does not exist . . . If race does not exist in reality, it exists with the force of reality and the consequences of reality in the minds of enough Americans to seriously qualify most orders of relationships between groups and among individuals.[127]

It is perhaps not out of place to remind ourselves that thinking and theorizing about these matters should remain wary of the lures of what Jablonski calls the "academic atmosphere and discourse" that always accompany intellectual endeavours.[128] A quarter century into our democratic transition, South Africans, especially black people, are experiencing the bitter fruits of the post-1994 euphoria about our supposedly "colorblind" society. In the United States, people of color are going through the same trauma after the Obama era. Our struggle for the restoration of our common humanity goes on, but we also understand the continued, if deeply painful, relevance of what Aimé Cesairé called "the singularity of blackness."[129]

The renewed reality and renewed legitimacy and respectability of racism across the globe is, if not absolutely shocking, at least a rude awakening to the realities of human sinfulness. From a disturbing and growing phenomenon at sports events globally,[130] to the right to basic education even today,[131] to the shameful exposure of

---

126. See Mandela, "Whither the Black Consciousness movement?," 21–64.

127. See Lincoln, *Coming through the Fire*, 13, 14.

128. Jablonski and Maré, *Effects of Race*, 3.

129. Cesairé, "Letter to Maurice Thorez," 147.

130. See, e.g., Kilvington, "Racist Abuse at Football Games Is Increasing." Kilvington speaks of the alarming rise of "much more pervasive hate speech" online towards athletes of colour. But he also points to "structural and institutional barriers that prevent black, Asian, and Ethnic Minority groups from enjoying football are just as pervasive."

131. In the United States, equal education rights groups are delighted that a judge ruled in their

it through the crises the coronavirus forces upon us, racism causes destruction and death wherever it rears its head.

Writing about the disproportionate deaths of African Americans through COVID-19, Ibram X. Kendi, director of the Antiracist Research and Policy Center at American University, writes, "America is facing a racial pandemic within the viral pandemic."

> In New York City . . . Latino's make up 34 percent of the known deaths of the coronavirus, higher than their 29 percent share of the city's population. Two small Native American pueblos in New Mexico had higher infections rates than any US county.[132]

Orthopaedic surgeon Kenneth Alleyne concurs:

> Many factors have fueled the racial disparities in COVID-19 outcomes: lower access to health care and higher rates of asthma, diabetes and heart disease. There are social, economic and political reasons for these lopsided outcomes. We call them the "social determinants of health"—a group of nonmedical variables that impact up to 80 percent of health outcomes. These social determinants include access to healthy food, transportation, zip code, health insurance and even mold levels. Most of these are not immediately correctable. New supermarkets with vegetables in communities that are food deserts will not be built tomorrow. The next day we will not narrow education achievement gaps.[133]

Again, the issue is global. Social scientist Keisha-Khan Y. Perry writes,

> Every 23 minutes, in Brazil, a young black between the ages of 15 and 29 is killed. Between 2005 and 2015, 61 percent of the women murdered by the police were black, even though they represent only 24.5 percent of the Brazilian population.[134]

---

favour: schoolchildren in "underserved" communities in Detroit, Michigan, should be allowed equal education. It seems that, unlike the "right to bear arms" equal education is not considered a constitutional right. It bears noting that these "underserved" children are from so-called "black and brown" communities where there is a lack of teachers, where children learn from "out of date text books" and go to schools where sewage from the bathrooms "leak into the hallways." It is food for thought that this is the situation more than sixty years after the 1954 landmark *Brown vs. Board of Education* Supreme Court ruling that outlawed the "separate but equal" principle in education in the United States. See Jurado, "Appeals Court Rules Detroit Students Have a Right to a Basic Education."

132. See Kendi, "Stop Blaming Black People for Dying."

133. See Alleyne, "COVID-19 Is a Perfect Storm for Black Americans." Alleyne continues, "To that long list of traditional social determinants affecting my community, I would like to add one more, with a four-hundred-year context: the African American 'essential worker' designation. In the medical world, as elsewhere, these workers often go unnoticed and too often unnamed. They are the hospital cleaning personnel, the delivery, food service, and warehouse workers, and municipal employees who truly are on the front line. They stand between us and pure social chaos." The vast majority of these are people of color.

134. See Perry, "Land Question," 21.

These are the everyday realities that should inform our intellectual discussions on these matters. Race is a social and political construct, but its devastations play out on real black bodies.

South African psychologist Chabani Manganyi, another participant in the "Race Project," analyzes South Africa's "post-apartheid" racism and the reality of it for the vast majority of its citizens even while still being denied, or ignored, by those in positions of privilege and power, white and black alike. He is acutely aware of South Africa's post-1994 lethal socio-economic disparities and the impact of race upon those. He confesses to being "enchanted by Fanon's profound mistrust of undeserving post-colonial purveyors of both wealth and power such as some of those who suddenly sprung to light in our country since 1994." He concludes,

> It would be nihilism of the worst kind to continue providing credence to the implied inevitability of black inferiority coupled with the varieties of its presumed manifestations in everyday life. When race-based social, economic and educational race-based inequalities become the cardinal point of our focus, the false inevitability of racism is focused on and can be thrown into relief and disrepute. Consequently, when the presumed inferiority of black people takes its rightful place as a false social-psychological legitimation of white superiority by race-conscious whites, the prevailing fiction of never ending white superiority is thrown into relief and disrepute... What history demands from black people themselves is a self-conscious and well-developed determination to interrupt and discredit the presumed inevitability of racial inequality in South Africa and elsewhere.[135]

Whiteness and racism, Manganyi writes, "need to be demystified once for all," so that they "are deprived of the mystique which has sustained them for such a considerable period of time."[136] This, I suggest, is exactly what Biko and Black Consciousness set out to do. That process of demystification is today more relevant and necessary than ever, in South Africa and elsewhere.

Perhaps here Aelred Stubbs's "better things to come" is applicable, not as a world achieved in 1994, but as a call to better understand the meaning of the "distant horizon": as long as it is distant for the poor, the vulnerable, and the excluded, that better world is not yet here. It is a call, Ndebele writes, "to be answered by all South African citizens. But the burden of agency in seeking the answers rests squarely with those once oppressed, who, in the third decade of their freedom, must pursue their 'envisioned self.'"[137] However we may differ on the meaning and the reality of that evasive freedom, the call still stands.

---

135. See Manganyi, "Perspectives on Race and Racism," 29, 30.
136. Manganyi, "Perspectives on Race and Racism," 30.
137. Ndebele, "Envisioned Self," xiii, xiv.

Selfless Revolutionaries

South Africa's Vuyani Vellem has learned from India's M. M. Thomas. He believed firmly in the life-giving hope of African spirituality. For him too, African spirituality was a "prophetic spirituality," a "spirituality of combat" as Thomas also calls it.[138] In the midst of the present darkness, he hears "echoes of fire" because of the vibrancy and resilience of African spirituality. "There is a revival going on," Vellem writes. "An *Imvuselelo*, a throng of singing, dancing, and the preaching masses."[139] It is a hope shared by the struggling masses of the world with a tenacity that is both astonishing and life-giving.

The Oxfam report, even as it sets out the grim realities of our global situation, has caught something of this as it states repeatedly that "a fairer world is possible."[140] But a "fairer" world, that is a safer, more just and equitable, peaceful world, the report also insists throughout, must be "a feminine world."[141] For without women claiming and having their rightful place in the world, without women enjoying their full humanity in an inclusive, indivisibly just human community, this hope remains forlorn. Our human face remains "far, on the distant horizon." Perhaps this understanding turned into practical policies, making the politics of justice, equity, and dignity "habits of the heart"[142] might be Africa's gift to the world, and in so doing fulfil Biko's hope.

As a woman, Arundathi Roy must have understood Biko as well as she understands our global struggle. Our struggle is a struggle "confronting empire," she writes. In this fight, we have already won major victories, and we must claim them. We must find hope and courage in the fruits of our agency and our victories. Every step forward counts.

> We . . . have, each in our way, laid siege to Empire. We may not have stopped it in its tracks yet but we have stripped it down. We have made it drop its mask. We have forced it into the open. It now stands before us on the world's stage in all its brutish, iniquitous nakedness . . . too ugly to behold its own reflection.[143]

In confronting empire, Roy knows we must understand that we cannot enter this fight without the fortitude of our spirituality. We must not only confront empire. We must, amid the clamor of endless wars, the deafening shouts of arrogance, the maddening hubris of indifference, and the cries of pain and suffering, fight for the quiet moments. Vuyani Vellem's *imvuselelo* is that fight which makes it possible for us to create that sacred space of silence that in turn, makes it possible to believe that "Another world is not only possible, she is on her way. On a quiet day, I can hear her breathing."[144]

---

138. See Thomas, "Spirituality of Combat."
139. See Vellem, "Embers from the Zone of Non-Being," 15.
140. Oxfam, "Time to Care," 18–19.
141. The Oxfam Report's entire focus on women and girls and their place in the global economy in order to make it a fairer economy is necessary, justified, and completely convincing.
142. See Bellah et al., *Habits of the Heart*.
143. Roy, "Confronting Empire."
144. Roy, "Confronting Empire."

7

The Need for "a Fighting God"

Black Theology, Black Singularity, and the Essence of Revolutionary Authenticity

"A Fire No Water Could Put Out"

In many ways, it is a blessing that modern Black theology in South Africa did not emerge within the structures of academia. In the United States, James Hal Cone, the father of modern Black theology,[1] wrote his *Black Theology and Black Power* as an

---

1. I distinguish between the Black theology movement of the late 60s onward, starting with the work of James Cone and others, and the early beginnings of Black theology as expressed, for example, in the writings and preaching of the Christian leaders of the eighteenth- and nineteenth-century slave revolts such as Denmark Vesey, Nat Turner, and Sojourner Truth in the United States and Jan Paerl and Cupido Kakkerlak in South Africa. For South Africa, see, e.g., Viljoen, *Jan Paerl*. For the United States, see, e.g., Wilmore, *Black Religion and Black Radicalism*. For an eloquent expression of the early forms of Black theology through her poetry as well as her polemics in the United States by Phyllis Wheatley, see May, *Evangelism and Resistance*, especially the Introduction and chs. 1 and 2. May describes Wheatley as "the first of the African Christian writers to articulate a theology of liberation." May, *Evangelism and Resistance*, 23. This observation takes on added significance in comparison with Jupiter Hammond, her male contemporary and counterpart, whose writings and debates with Wheatley were based on a wholly conservative, what May calls "orthodox Calvinist," perspective basically simply echoing the otherworldly pietism of white theologians' and slave masters' beliefs and interpretation of Scripture. See ch. 2. Equally instructive, as well as intriguing, is the fact that the first sub-Saharan African to study at a European university—Leiden, in the Netherlands—was the erudite and learned Ghanaian Jacobus Elisa Johannes Capitein (1717–47). Capitein gained celebrity status in Europe primarily because of his doctoral dissertation written in Latin, on slavery and Christian liberty as not being opposed to each other. Doubtless, this was the main reason for endearing him to the European Christian and slave-trading establishment. See Prah, *Jacobus Eliza Johannes Capitein*; also Levecq, "Jacobus Capitein: Dutch Calvinist and Black Cosmopolitan." The stark differences with Kimpa Vita can hardly be more pronounced. Capitein's Eurocentric theology, and his vigorous defense of slavery, despite himself—like Wheatley—having been kidnapped and enslaved at the age of eight, were forged in the European academy. Kimpa Vita's liberation theology was born in the vortex

indisputably academic work while already teaching at New York City's famous and prestigious Union Theological Seminary.² Yet, Cone testifies that this work was the culmination of the thinking of a fairly small group of black, radical theological thinkers who emerged from the civil rights movement; in other words, activist theologians from outside the academy. Even though Cone presented his work as an academic, he insists that it does not stem from a seminary or tertiary institution. Rather, it evolved from the Black Church and the black community. Black theology, Cone writes,

> came into being in the context of the struggle of black churches but chiefly identifies with the Civil Rights organizations such as the Southern Christian Leadership Conference (SCLC), the National Conference of Black Churchmen (NCBC), the Interreligious Foundation for Community Organizations (IFCO), and many black caucuses in white churches.³

Equally without doubt, in Africa, the earliest expressions of Black theology, historically, came into being within contexts of roiling revolutionary resistance. Dona Kimpa Vita from the Kongo (1684–1706) was burned at the stake by the Portuguese as a revolutionary resister to colonialist oppression and the imperialist appropriation of the Christian faith by the Roman Catholic Church on July 2, 1706. It is she whose visions depicted Jesus and his mother Mary as African, not as icons for meditative (or syncretistic missionary?) purposes, but as divinely anointed progenitors of struggle, inspiring her to resistance to the foreign powers occupying her country. Hers was, as far as we know, the first explicit Black theology as an African expression of black revolutionary resistance to imperialism. No wonder the present generation of young, African activists acknowledge this Christian young woman as "the mother of the African revolution."⁴ She died a martyr of a revolutionary African faith.⁵

It was Bishop Henry McNeal Turner, fiery theologian from the African Methodist Episcopal Church, who first uttered the words, "God is a Negro."⁶ These words, unapologetically appropriated by James Cone, would throw Cone into a maelstrom of white fear, umbrage, and deeply offended academic dignity when he dared to portray Jesus Christ as the militant Black Messiah in a work that caused such turmoil in white controlled academia, even as it disturbed many in the Black Church itself. *Black Theology and Black Power* remains a brilliant, unrelentingly challenging classic, laying the foundations for Black liberation theology in its present form emphatically, clearly, and systematically.

---

of anti-imperialist struggles for freedom. Almost inevitably, following the rules of patriarchal white power, he became a celebrity. She, on the other hand, was burned at the stake.

2. Cone, *Black Theology and Black Power.*
3. See Cone, *For My People*, 6–7.
4. See Ne Kunda Nlaba's stirring documentary film, *Kimpa Vita.*
5. See Thornton, *Kongolese Saint Anthony.*
6. See Johnson, "God Is a Negro." See also Johnson, *Forgotten Prophet.*

However, in doing so, Cone the academic was teaching at Union Theological Seminary, an institution that at that time had not produced a single black PhD student since its founding in 1836, and those Black theologians of the first hour who worked within the academy as well as within the churches had to battle fiercely to create room for Black theology within the closed, racialized, Euro-centricity of American academia. They eventually did gain some grudgingly conceded space, but it cost years of struggle even today not completely won. As Latinx ethicist Miguel De La Torre testifies, this holds true for other fields as well.[7] Crucially, South African Black theology, in those first vital years, was spared those time- and energy-consuming (some would argue unnecessary) struggles, having the space to allow the debates among ourselves to mature. How else would we have been able to engage in the critical and especially self-critical reflections so crucial for the authenticity of revolutionary activity?[8]

7. Now, decades later, Miguel De La Torre would make the same argument, pointing to the same battle for Latina/o academics and their work, and their struggles for recognition within the still white-controlled academia of the United States. Hispanic scholars, De La Torre writes, are deliberately "kept at bay" within the academy, and not only through hiring practices. "Hispanic ethicists are forced to exhibit academic rigor through the use and application of ethical paradigms that are often incapable of liberating oppressed communities. Consequently the particularity of scholarship emanating from non-Eurocentric communities, as in the case of Latina/o rooted ethical paradigms, poses the risk and danger in the minds of Eurocentric ethicists of negatively impacting the prevailing so-called academic vigor." See De La Torre, "Doing Latina/o Ethics," 5. It appears that the issue is widely problematic. Regarding Communication Studies, and especially Rhetorical Studies, Paula Chakravartty et al., in an article titled "#CommunicationSoWhite," bemoan the absence of black and non-white scholars in publication rates, citation rates, and editorial positions within Communication Studies. "This has negative professional implications both for non-white scholars, in terms of contract renewals, tenure, and promotion, and for the field in general, in terms of visibility of and attention to the knowledge produced." Quoted in Houdek, "Imperative of Race for Rhetorical Studies." Bringing the issue into still clearer focus, Houdek writes, "Rhetorical studies' 'possessive investment in whiteness,' to use George Lipsitz's term, is indeed excessive and extravagant, immoderate and violent—it is outrageous—and the time has come to confront it" (292).

8. See, for instance, the forceful, unadorned way in which Steve Biko speaks of the necessity of Black Consciousness for black people, an issue we discuss in the final section of this chapter. One thinks also of the robust debates between Itumeleng Mosala, Desmond Tutu, and myself on the use (and usefulness) of Scripture for Black liberation theology. These were all indispensable and extraordinarily important debates, waged outside of the control of the white academy, giving us the space and freedom for intellectual honesty in the exchange of ideas without first having to subject ourselves, and our thinking, to the approval or disapproval of white, Eurocentric academic opinion. This does not mean that Black theology in South Africa was spared the full force of the onslaught from white theologians ensconced in their positions of power and academic privilege. Black theology threatened them theologically as much as it threatened the apartheid government politically. Neither does it mean that white theologians would not use these intra-black debates to "pick sides" and attempt to apply their political divide-and-rule tactics in the field of theological discourse. This was the case both during the late 70s and the 80s, as well as in the immediate post-1994 period when Black theology was written off as "passé," since "liberation" had come and we had to concentrate on "post-apartheid" themes such as "democracy," "reconciliation," and "reconstruction." For two brilliant examples against this trend, see Vellem, "Ideology and Spirituality," and Maluleke, "Proposal for a Theology of Reconstruction." As well, Black theology had to fend off the attempts to substitute Black liberation theology for a deeply Western-inspired and -driven "public theology," immediately embraced by white-controlled academia as much more "acceptable" in a context where vigorous critique of the realities of racism,

Birthed into, and within, the heat of struggles for justice, freedom, and dignity, Black theology in South Africa could not but be indelibly shaped, moulded, and infused by those struggles. Being born into the literal flames of struggle in that decisive phase since the early 70s, baptized with fire, and nurtured by the suffering and the joys of fighting for truth, justice, and freedom, endowed South African Black theology with a uniquely fashioned character. But being born into the bosom of resistance brought with it an equally unique responsibility. From its inception, Black theology was held accountable, not so much to the rules and expectations of formal white controlled academia, but to the expectations, sufferings, and hopes of the people. Like American Black theology, South African Black theology is, so to speak, one of a set of historic triplets: Black Consciousness, Black theology, and Black power.[9] That is a configuration that made the personal political and the political theological with an immediacy that was inescapable. Reflecting on that first publication on Black theology in South Africa, black theologians Itumeleng Mosala and Buti Thlagale write,

> The appearance of that book heralded the dawn of a new kind of black militancy: The struggle for the liberation of the oppressed and exploited black people was to be waged at all levels of the social formation. Christianity and the Christian church had up till this time served as the ideological tool for the softening up of black people and as a means by which black culture has been undermined . . . Black people were, as of this time, to draw the liberation struggle to the very centre of capitalist ideology, namely, the Christian theological realm.[10]

To this day, academia in South Africa has not been able to rid itself of the white, male, Euro-centric domination of a meganarrative steeped in traditions, ways of theorizing and thinking, working with entitled assumptions, hopelessly trapped in a history of racist, colonialist, imperialist, apartheid framing, understanding, and interpretation.[11] It is true of academia in general, and theology is no exception. Hence the current battles for decolonization, Africanization, and Africanicity in every sphere and at every level of academia, and these are always linked to continuing struggles for dignity, integrity, and authenticity within academia. In turn, these are inextricably

---

white supremacy and white privilege, black disempowerment and the power of (white) monopoly neoliberal capitalism are considered far too radical to countenance.

9. See the first systematic attempt from South Africa to make these vital connections, Boesak, *Farewell to Innocence*. Notably, Steve Biko's contribution to South Africa's first anthology on Black theology is actually an essay on Black Consciousness; see Biko, *I Write What I Like*, 96–108.

10. See Mosala and Thlagale, *Unquestionable Right to be Free*, 74.

11. See, e.g., Sisanti, "Afrocentric Education," 34–40, and the quite vigorous response by Smith and Tivaringe, "From Afro-Centrism to Decolonial Humanism," 41–43. Also Lebakeng et al., "Epistemicide, Institutional Cultures," 70–87. They write, "Institutions of higher education in South Africa were (and still are) copycats whose primary function was (and still is) to serve and promote colonial Western values" (70). For further discussion, see Heleta, "Decolonisation of Higher Education."

interconnected with actual, daily, broader struggles of still-oppressed, still-marginalized, still-despised, excluded, and threatened communities.

The debates continue to rage on the global stage. MIT historian Craig Wilder argues that in America, the academy was "both beneficiary and defender" of the same social and economic forces that transformed the nation through slavery and colonization, devastating indigenous nations in the process. In fact, Wilder, in an argument that would hold as convincingly for South Africa, makes the case that the American academy "stood beside church and state as the third pillar of a civilization built on bondage."[12]

Staying close to the heart of these actual battles waged by the people is one vital requirement for the debates on Africanicity, de-coloniality, and Africanization not to lose their way, co-opted by the power of the prevailing Euro-centric and Euro-centering forces, hence becoming just another site of capture serving only the interests of the powerful. In the wake of the immediate post-1994 euphoria, when it was hardest, Vuyani Vellem was one of the first, and most consistent, to engage these new realities. In his critique on Villa-Vicencio he wrote,

> Villa-Vicencio proposed the motif of reconstruction as an alternative to liberation and *ipso facto*, Black theology of liberation. It is in this era that Black Theology of liberation was subtly driven to the doldrums, regarded as moribund by some circles in our theological landscape in South Africa.[13]

The first compendium of essays on Black theology in South Africa was produced by black South Africans, not a single one of them in academic positions.[14] They were not even all of them theologians. Take, for example, Steve Biko, whose article is considered by some to be the "best contribution to the book."[15] Every single one of the authors were engaged in the struggle, fighting the might of the apartheid regime every day in any way they could. They were not just thinkers and planners; they were activists and risk-takers for the sake of freedom. Their theology was a response to an ongoing history of genocide, dehumanization, dispossession, oppression, and endless exploitation. It was a theology informed not by dogma, but by the cries and the suffering of the people. It was a theology not entrapped in philosophical speculations, European creedal disputes, and ethical theorizing, but driven by the tenderness of conscience.[16] They were organic theologians, in the words of Antonio Gramsci, "active participants in practical life," as "constructor, organiser, permanent persuader."[17] They

---

12. See Wilder, *Ebony and Ivy*, 11, cited in Grande, "Refusing the University."

13. Vellem, "Ideology and Spirituality," 547.

14. See Moore, *Black Theology*.

15. See the editor's introductory note (from the first, 1978 edition) in Biko, *I Write What I Like*, 96.

16. See Boesak, *Tenderness of Conscience*, especially ch. 7. I borrowed this term from Kuyper, *Six Stone Lectures*, 123, in order to make the point from a black, Afro-centric view.

17. See Gramsci, *Selections*, loc. 141–42.

were listening to the hearts of the people, speaking to the hearts of the people from within the heart of the struggle. That is a gift theology confined to and constrained by academia—even in black institutions—can only yearn for.

That Black liberation theology was called forth not by systematic formulations or the rules of academic acceptability but by the cry for freedom and the call to embodied commitment to the struggle for liberation. By the smell of tear gas, the stripes inflicted by shamboks and the wounds inflicted by bullets; by the unnamable fear in the torture chamber and the indescribable loneliness of the isolation cell in prison. But it was equally shaped by the collective joy of a people knowing what it meant to stand for truth and freedom; by the contagiousness of courage, by the stubborn dreams of freedom that defied both hopelessness and sentimentalized optimism while giving despair no quarter. *That* Black theology was inspired by the power of the people's faith that denied resignation *its* power, and by the incredible resilience that comes from what Biko would call "the righteousness of our strength."[18]

Theirs was a theology born of a living faith, where their worship of God in the sanctuary continued in their worship of God in the streets of struggle. That is what Biko meant when he stated: "No nation can win a battle without faith."[19] One could not call oneself a Black theologian and not be in the forefront of that struggle. The fires of rebellion set by the hopeful, righteous anger of the youthful masses were the external expression of that which kept them close to the flaming heart of that revolution: the fire of righteous strength within themselves. And *that*, as Martin Luther King Jr. rejoiced, was "a fire that no water could put out."[20] That was what kept them real and Black theology authentic.

The Singularity of Blackness

Right from the outset, Black theology, as other expressions of liberation theology, feminist theologies, womanist theology, and more recent queer theology, was defined,

---

18. Biko, *I Write What I Like*, 135–56. Biko uses this powerful expression on 152, but the whole chapter is well worth reading and pondering. For a more detailed, interpretative discussion of this phrase, see Boesak, *Pharaohs on Both Sides*, ch. 4.

19. Biko, *I Write What I Like*, 64.

20. Martin Luther King Jr.'s last, utterly moving speech, delivered on April 3, 1968, the night before his assassination in Memphis, Tennessee, is usually referred to as "The Mountaintop Speech," a reference to King's poignant words with hindsight seen as foreshadowing the possibility of his death. Those eerily prophetic words, "I've been to the mountaintop! Mine eyes have seen the glory of the Lord!" now usually frame reflections on this address, and perhaps rightly so. However, one should not lose sight of the many insights into the radical King in that very same speech, as this marvelous expression indicates. See King, *Radical King*, 265–76. The power of that phrase was evoked in Lebanon's days of revolutionary outrage, when an activist, standing just beyond the force of a water cannon told a journalist: "They have water for the cannons, but there is no water for the people." Al Jazeera *English News Live*, January 18, 2020. He meant, first, water for the people to drink, a critique of the priorities of government, and second, that the powerful force of the water cannon (drinking water weaponized for oppression) cannot stop the people's revolution and the demands for justice.

and understood, as a "contextual" theology. Unlike the claims of universality made by the practitioners of dominant Euro-centric theologies—those "who have the ways and means of making their subjectivity objectivity for everyone else"[21]—it grapples with the existential situations of black, oppressed people engaged in life and death struggles for liberation and justice, refusing to give up their faith in Jesus, their liberator/Messiah. We embraced that black experience in our struggle to embrace the Scriptures[22] and the significance of Jesus of Nazareth, not just for the human story in general, but for the story of black humanity in confrontation with white, Christian, racist domination, exploitation, and oppression in particular.

Black liberation icon and anti-colonialist fighter Aimé Césaire's firm stance in his historic break with the French Communist Party was warmly appropriated by Steve Biko for the purposes of Black Consciousness in South Africa.[23] What Aimé Césaire demanded from us psychologically and politically, we had to embrace theologically as well, that we should "consciously grasp in its full breadth, in this specific moment of our historical evolution, the notion of our particular uniqueness" as black people:

> One fact that is paramount in my eyes is this: we, men of color, at this precise moment in our historical evolution, have come to grasp, in our consciousness, the full breadth of our singularity, and are ready to assume on all levels and in all areas the responsibilities that flow from this coming to consciousness. The singularity of our "situation in the world," which cannot be confused with any other. The singularity of our problems, which cannot be reduced to any other problem. The singularity of our history, constructed out of terrible misfortunes that belong to no one else. The singularity of our culture, which we wish to live in a way that is more and more real.[24]

"Grasping the full breadth" of these realities as one, open to learning and unlearning, "comes to consciousness," means gaining a conscious and deliberate understanding, and making a decision, not only as individuals, but as an oppressed community in

---

21. See De La Torre, "Doing Latina/o Ethics," 5.

22. See, for instance, Cone, *God of the Oppressed*, 28–35. "Thus the black experience *requires* that Scripture be a source for Black Theology," writes Cone. "For it was Scripture that enabled slaves to affirm a view of God that differed radically from that of the slave masters" (29). Emphasis mine. Note that Cone emphasizes the agency of the slaves in their affirmation of God as a God of freedom and justice over and against the appropriation of Scripture as inauthentic use of Scripture by the slave masters for the purposes of oppression and control. Again Cone: "Scripture established limits to white people's use of Jesus Christ as a confirmation of black oppression" (29). As is discussed in Boesak, *Children of the Waters of Meribah*, ch. 1, this is a much-contested issue, but I am in wholehearted agreement with Cone on this.

23. See Biko, *I Write What I Like*, 72.

24. From his 1956 letter to Maurice Thorez, submitting his resignation from the French Communist Party after its failure to show remorse for and condemn the atrocities committed by Stalin, and to admit the deadly existence of antisemitism in "so many countries calling themselves socialist," and its equally disastrous failure to recognize the distinctness of the anti-colonialist struggles of colonized peoples led by the colonized themselves. See Cesairé, "Letter to Maurice Thorez," 147.

resistance; not only politically but socially; not only psychologically but theologically as well. We should, Cesairé insists, grasp "with our full consciousness," not only the meaning and impact of "the terrible misfortunes that belong to no one else," but also the responsibilities *that cannot belong to anyone else*. What he means is the responsibility to understand, analyze, and interpret, to rise up in resistance, to actively engage the historical, social, economic, psychological, and political consequences of these "misfortunes" in full commitment of struggle for the sake of dignity, freedom, justice, and equity. Then we will understand that these "misfortunes" are not incidental, historical happenstance. They are in fact deliberate, calculated acts of violence, indispensable for the successful workings of empire.

However, this "uniqueness," this "peculiarity," is not to be confused with the "uniqueness" whites claimed for themselves as "God's chosen people," a claim made equally eloquently and fervently by English-speaking imperialists and white Afrikaner Calvinists, reflected in the chauvinistic certitude of that tireless imperialist Cecil John Rhodes who spoke of the British as "God's ideal type, his own Anglo-Saxon race."[25] Theirs was a peculiarity that demanded power and privilege at the expense of the humanity and right of existence of others. It is not the uniqueness that claims unique rights which, as a matter of course, obliterate the rights of others—such as the right to sacralized entitlement, dominion, and divinely endorsed impunity. That, in turn, comes with a unique and utterly deadly exceptionalism and innocence, such as we saw in white apartheid South Africa, discussed above, and currently still rampant in white nationalist, imperialist America and, in equal, lethal measure, in the Zionist-Israeli apartheid state.

No, the peculiarity I have in mind following Cesairé and Biko is the singularity of blackness as a *condition* of oppression, exploitation, and subjugation, which, when the oppression is properly understood and oppressed people rise up to claim their dignity and freedom, is turned into a *condition of resistance*. As I have been trying to make clear for some time now, the singularity of blackness signifies the singularity of global oppression.[26] Our growing understanding of globalized systems of oppression and exploitation, and the globalized workings of empire, demand that we understand our struggles as global struggles, wherever imperialism continues to create new victims. It is in this sense that we speak of "global apartheid."[27] It was and is not exclusivist,

---

25. As cited in De Gruchy, *Church Struggle*, 34. While Rhodes's stance was perhaps a more overtly chauvinist, undoubtedly racist, political one, albeit not without strong religious overtones, the "chosenness" claimed by white Afrikaner Calvinists was explicitly based on their systematic, racist interpretation of the Bible, and of the neo-Calvinist doctrines of "election" and "predestination." It was a fundamental cornerstone dogma of the theology of apartheid and their specific, South African brand of "Christian nationalism." In the end, though, no matter the degree of religiosity in the idea, it serves the politics of racist exclusivism, domination, and dispossession. See van Niekerk, "Concept of Chosen People." See also Du Toit, "No Chosen People." For a perspective on the United States on this issue, see, e.g., Stephansen, *Manifest Destiny*.

26. See Boesak, *Dare We Speak of Hope?*; Boesak, *Pharaohs on Both Sides*.

27. See the discussion above, "Full Humanity Requires Freedom."

however. Whites who were ready to accept black leadership and share black aspirations, ready to share the risks of commitment, were invited to join the resistance, thereby "taking upon themselves the condition of blackness" so that the condition of freedom and equality would become the condition of all.[28] "In the final analysis," I said in the keynote address at the launch of the non-racial, non-violent mass political movement, the United Democratic Front in 1983,

> Judgement will be made, not in terms of whiteness or blackness, whatever the ideological content of those words may be today, but in terms of the persistent faithfulness to which we are called in this struggle.[29]

It is the peculiarity of Ubuntu, the constant and deliberate consciousness that my humanity is bound to the humanity of the other, that my humanity is validated by the humanity of the other, that I can only be what I ought to be when the other is what they ought to be. It is the unfettered joy in the spacious longing for oneness and never giving a single quarter to the suffocating clamorings for sameness. It is the responsibility to, as Biko put it, "take cognizance of the deliberateness of God's plan in creating black people black."[30]

It should be clear that for Black liberation theology to remain authentic, it should not only acknowledge, but help to create space for and stand in solidarity with the singularity of women, and women of color in particular; with LGBTQI+ persons and those who are differently gifted, in their struggles for liberation, justice, and dignity in every situation. In this sense, that singularity has an expressly inclusive, expressly global character so that those struggles for human liberation becomes ours. It is a singularity embedded in global, embodied, respectful solidarity, by which I mean a solidarity respectful of organic, indigenous leadership. And while different contexts may call for different strategies and ways of struggle, the *goals* remain inseparable. The quest remains Biko's dream of giving the world "a human face." This understanding seems in the process of crossing borders in all manner of ways. Other disciplines grasp the necessity of this. Kirt H. Wilson writes that

> crossing disciplinary borders should not simply reinforce our own boundaries or "what we already know." Rather, it should prompt us to engage in a

---

28. See Boesak, *Black and Reformed*, 84: "I speak of those whites who have understood their own guilt in the oppression of blacks in terms of corporate responsibility, who have genuinely repented and have been genuinely converted; those whites who have clearly committed themselves to the struggle for liberation and who, through their commitment, have taken upon themselves the *condition* of blackness in South Africa. In a real sense, they bear the marks of Christ. They have learned to identify with what blacks are doing to secure their liberation." I believe the argument stands for allies wanting to join us in global struggles for freedom. It is increasingly relevant, since it is becoming increasingly clear that what is actually at stake, I think, is not simply the liberation of the oppressed worldwide, but the liberation of humankind as well as the liberation of Mother Earth.

29. See Boesak, *Black and Reformed*, 174.

30. Biko, *I Write What I Like*, 53.

continual process of reimagining our responsibilities to intellectual and public communities beyond our own.³¹

Communication and rhetorical studies scholar Matthew Houdek drives the point home in a timely and necessary reminder:

> Outside the academy, the manifold exigencies of race that mark the contemporary conjuncture further emphasize Flores's imperative, too many of which remain unmarked within contemporary rhetorical scholarship. The present moment's (re)new racist, racialized, and colonial intensities certainly warrant collective rebuke, critique, and direct action, from Ferguson to Palestine, Yemen to Myanmar, Puerto Rico to Standing Rock to 1600 Pennsylvania Ave. That much is clear (but still, and with few exceptions, where are the critical rhetoricians?). Yet the more striking the supposed aberrations to the rules of postracial civility become—e.g., white supremacist demonstrations; increased racist assaults; the normalization of Israel's occupation of Gaza and concomitant racialization of the Palestinian people; globally emergent ethno-nationalism; the common sense of state-sanctioned antiblack violence; *rampant "anti-Muslim racism" veiled as Islamophobia* . . . colonial neglect of post-Maria Puerto Rico; inhumane policies that target racialized minorities—the more white liberals, in particular, seem convinced of their own distance from the problem. *And this antiracist posturing that frames racism as the forever elsewhere and the "never us" is particularly troubling given how low the bar has been (re)set for what is considered "racist" or "white supremacist" in the white public imaginary today.*³²

For Africans in America, that singularity had to include their being kidnapped and sold, sometimes by their kinfolk; stolen from the lands of their birth by white Christians, the horrors of the "middle passage," enslavement in new lands by white Christians, and a life of discrimination, exploitation, and dehumanization through a system called "Jim Crow." Today, in my view, it should also include their determination to distinguish themselves from the destructive omnipresence of the American Empire, the ideational enslavement of the romanticized "American dream" and the ideological subservience to American exceptionalism so tragically embraced by Barack Obama.³³

For South African blacks, it had to include invasion and colonization of their lands by white Christians, genocide, enslavement, land theft on a scale in modern history paralleled only by the United States, and, proportionately to that situation,

---

31. Wilson, "Natural and Cosmopolitan Dimensions of Disciplinarity," 295.

32. See Houdek, "Imperative of Race," 295. Emphasis mine. As I write, the fanatic right-wing, armed protests in Michigan against the stay-at-home rules of Governor Whitmer to fight the coronavirus and the Israeli plans for the imminent annexation of the West Bank seem set to confirm Houdek's observations.

33. See Ali, *Obama Syndrome*; see also Boesak, *Dare We Speak of Hope?*; See also Taylor, *From #Black Lives Matter*, especially ch. 5: "Barack Obama: The End of an Illusion."

by the State of Israel.³⁴ It should include the same processes of dehumanization and discrimination through a system called apartheid. It should also, I think, include the new struggle against a sentimentalized "liberation" proclaimed after 1994, and for the restoration of the integrity and authenticity of a hopelessly compromised reconciliation process.

These white Christians brought with them a faith called Christianity, the Christian Scriptures, and sets of beliefs and moral behavior that, so we were told, if we followed these, would bring us eternal salvation. It was made clear to us, however, that for this salvation to occur, we had to follow *their* way of believing, accept *their* ways of interpreting the Scriptures, *their* ideas of God, *their* understanding of Jesus, *their* ways of experiencing the workings of God's Holy Spirit. It did not take us long to understand just how closely our slave masters and their Christian missionaries identified themselves with God, Jesus and the Holy Spirit so that obedience to our earthly masters was seen to be completely, even if completely blasphemously, synonymous with our obedience to God.

We already cited Steve Biko above, "No nation can win a battle without faith." But, Biko went on to say, that battle begins with our refusal to "see God through the eyes of those we are fighting against," those who oppress us in that same God's name.³⁵ For black South Africans, this had to include the fight against the heresies and ravages of something called "the theology of apartheid." Steve Biko then, bringing together struggle and faith in the way he did, and speaking directly to his oppressed people, saw no need for complex academic definitions of Black theology in order to satisfy white academia's requirements. He was not speaking to the academy. He was speaking to his people. For him, Black theology simply, and fundamentally, expressed the black oppressed Christian's need to "describe Christ as a fighting God, not a passive God who allows a lie to rest unchallenged."³⁶

The Need for a Fighting God

At this point, we need perhaps to take a step or two back. When Biko first attempted to define Black theology, he put it thus:

> Black theology seeks to depict Jesus as a fighting God who saw the exchange of Roman money—the oppressor's coinage—in His Father's temple as so sacrilegious that it merited a violent reaction from him—the Son of Man.³⁷

---

34. Strictly speaking, this is also true of Canada, Australia, and New Zealand, all having come into being through British imperialism and colonialism. These countries have done this at such a level of brute force and political manipulation that the realities of settler-colonialism are practically irreversible.

35. Biko, *I Write What I Like*, 64.

36. Biko, *I Write What I Like*, 104.

37. Biko, *I Write What I Like*, 34.

So here, quite deliberately and specifically, Biko points to the revolutionary nature of Jesus's ministry on earth. This is the first image that comes up in his mind when he sees Jesus as a "fighting God." I have engaged with this gospel passage in much greater detail before; here it is necessary only to remind ourselves of the central argument.[38] What Biko is stressing here, I think, is what has been a steadfast conviction in Black theology from the start, namely that Jesus of Nazareth was a revolutionary prophet from Galilee in Roman-occupied Palestine, irrevocably on the side of the poor and oppressed fighting the Roman occupiers as well as their minions, the Jerusalem elites. That does not mean that he was a violent revolutionary. Recognizing the Black Consciousness movement's commitment to a non-violent revolution as Biko explained, that would be a distortion.[39] Rather, it conveys that Jesus was constantly and consistently engaging in what South African radical Christian political leader Albert Luthuli would call "non-violent militant resistance" to the Powers That Be in Jerusalem and in Rome.

According to the gospels, Jesus was "throwing over" the tables of the money changers, "pouring out" their money on the ground, and "driving out" those who were selling and buying (Matt 21:12-13; Mark 11:15-17; Luke 45-46; John 2:13-16). The verbs suggest deep anger. In the Gospel of John, Jesus also made a whip "from cords," and drove "all of them," that is, "both the sheep and the cattle," out of the temple, while he vented his outrage on those engaging in these businesses: "Take these things out of here! Stop making my Father's house a market place!" (John 2:16). At no point, however, do the gospels indicate that he engaged in acts of violence against any person present. And it was not a spontaneous, even improper eruption of emotion as some have sought to argue.[40] It was, in fact, an entirely proper act of revolutionary rejection of the normalization of political and economic thuggery disguised as "religious custom" and "Law." Hence Jesus's scathing words, taken from the prophet Jeremiah, "den of robbers."

Here, the "den of robbers" is not so much the place where they *hide the loot*, as the place where the robbers *seek refuge*. Jesus's anger is not for nothing: the elites and the keepers of the Law rob the poor and oppressed *in the name of God,* and then they

---

38. See Boesak, *Children of the Waters of Meribah,* 145–46.

39. See Biko, *I Write What I Like,* 168: "Now the line that [the Black People's Convention] adopts is to explore as much as possible non-violent means within the country, *and that is why we exist . . .* even though there are [many] people who have despaired of the efficacy of non-violence as a method." Emphasis mine. And on 169: "I don't believe for a moment that we are going to willingly drop our belief in the non-violent stance—as of now." Biko pointed out that he "could not predict the future." But in that future, the United Democratic Front reclaimed the militant, nonviolent traditions espoused by Albert Luthuli and the Black Consciousness movement, and for the most part, despite incredible provocations, held steadfast to it.

40. See among others Van Aarde, *Fatherless in Galilee,* 78. However, even though Van Aarde calls Jesus's action an "emotional outburst," he does argue that this act was so offensive, so revolutionary that it might have "led to Jesus' death on the cross."

use the temple as refuge from the anger of the people and the wrath of God, as if the temple, and the God of the temple, will provide cover for their misdeeds.

In referring to Jesus's actions in the temple compound that day, Biko would, I think, be in full agreement with black theologian Obery Hendricks:

> This is not a temper tantrum. No, this was no spontaneous eruption of emotion . . . The Temple was the center of Israel's economy, its central bank and treasury, the depository of immense wealth. Indeed so much of the activity of the Jerusalem Temple hinged upon buying and selling and various modes of exchange that it is no exaggeration to say that in a real sense the Temple was fundamentally an economic institution.[41]

The point is that Jesus is a revolutionary who goes to the temple "as a place of opposition, not to sacrifice but to disrupt."[42] Here Jesus attacks not the temple as place of worship, but the temple as *the center of economic power* where the poor is squeezed for all they have in the name of God, but for the benefit of the temple elites and the rich and powerful (Mark 12:41–44). Jesus's going to the temple that day was not a simple, random act. He was going there for a purpose, and that purpose was to make a revolutionary point about God, the temple, the powerful, and the customs, rules, and traditions that kept the people captive, subjugated, and submissive.

Moreover, the cleansing of the temple falls within the context of Jesus's triumphal entry into Jerusalem, as a direct, oppositional, revolutionary counter-act to the entry of the Roman Governor and his troops, a "pre-arranged counter-procession,"[43] causing "turmoil" in the city and havoc in the temple.

Black theology has no reason to disagree with William Herzog II when he writes of Jesus's parables as "subversive speech":

> If [Jesus] had been the kind of teacher popularly portrayed in the North American church, a master of the inner life, teaching the importance of spirituality and a private relationship with God, he would have been supported by the Romans as part of their rural pacification program. That was exactly the kind of religion the Romans wanted peasants to have. Any beliefs that encouraged magic, passivity before fate, and withdrawal from the world of politics and economics into a spiritual or inner realm would have met with official approval. Had Jesus' parables indulged in apocalyptic speculation or threatened the end of the world, he would have been watched, but left alone. The Eastern Empire had its share of astrologers and visionaries. Had he merely proclaimed any or all of the themes ascribed to him by Joachim Jeremias, he would have inspired arguments but not malice. Had he anticipated narrativity and metaphoricity, he would have been remarkable but not crucified. Narrativity and

---

41. See Hendricks, *Politics of Jesus*, 113, 114.
42. See Boesak, *Children of the Waters of Meribah*, 145.
43. See Borg and Crossan, *Last Week*, 3–5; also Boesak, *Children of the Waters of Meribah*, 143–45.

metaphoricity were not capital crimes in the Roman Empire, and the one thing about Jesus that can be known with certainty was that he was executed as an enemy of the state and the Temple. He was crucified between two "social bandits" (*lestes*) on the charge of subversion because he claimed to be "king of the Jews."[44]

Consequently, we believe Obery Hendricks to be quite correct in the clarity of this observation:

> To say that Jesus was a political revolutionary is to say that the message he proclaimed not only called for change in individual hearts but also demanded sweeping and comprehensive change in political, social, and economic structures in his setting in life: colonized Israel. It means that if Jesus had his way, the Roman Empire and the ruling elites among his own people either would no longer have held their positions of power, or if they did, would have had to conduct themselves very, very differently. It means that his ministry was to radically change the distribution of authority, power, goods and resources, so all people—particularly the little people, or "the least of these," as Jesus called them—might have lives free of political oppression, enforced hunger and poverty, and undue insecurity.[45]

That is what Black theology means in its search for Jesus as a fighting God.

Not Allowing the Lie to Rest Unchallenged

Black theology's Black Messiah is a fighting God who would not let the lie "rest unchallenged," says Biko in his expansion of his definition. Since all oppression begins with lies, the revolution of this fighting God begins with exposing, challenging, and overcoming the lie. It is for this reason that Jesus's confrontation with the tempter, the "father of all lies" (John 8:44), is placed so early in the Synoptic Gospels (Matt 4:1–11; Mark 1:12–13).[46] In Luke (4:1–13), it comes even before the scene in the temple where Jesus announces his manifesto (4:18–19). Three times, Jesus denounces the father of lies. No, it is not true that food security for oneself, excluding everyone else, is the key to life. And no, it is not true that God is available to our every foolish whim—that is a vainglorious presumption that reeks of arrogance and obsession with power. And no, it is not in your power to "give" me "all the kingdoms of the world." The powers of this world are illegitimate, driven by violence, greed, and desires for domination and destruction. They are already doomed to perdition. God is the true Ruler of this world,

---

44. See Herzog, *Parables as Subversive Speech*, 27. This is surely as applicable to the African church and the Christian church elsewhere.

45. Hendricks, *Politics of Jesus*, 5. On Jesus as social and political revolutionary, see Horsley, *Jesus and Empire*, 103.

46. For a more detailed discussion of this, see Boesak, *Children of the Waters of Meribah*, 136–37.

I am God's anointed, God's reign is at hand, and all flesh, rich and poor, enslaved and free, despised and exalted, shall see it together.

However, exposing and challenging the lie in order to find, and stand for the truth that shall make us free, calls for the engagement of struggle. Our theology, therefore, would be a theology for the struggle, our spirituality a spirituality of struggle.[47] It is the spirituality that allows us to bow our knees in fear and trembling before God so that we do not ever have to bow or tremble before any earthly power.

For Black liberation theology on both sides of the ocean, we were clear on who should define that struggle. Said Albert Luthuli, "The struggle would be for freedom, justice and human dignity and there could be no substitute: we are bent on liberation."[48] And again, "Our struggle is a struggle and not a game."[49] On both sides of the ocean we also agreed that since power concedes nothing without a demand, it would mean confrontation at the risk of freedom and life. And yet again, as we learned from Frederick Douglass:

> If there is no struggle, there is no progress. Those who profess to favor freedom and yet deprecate agitation are men who want crops without plowing up the ground; they want rain without thunder and lightning. They want the ocean without the awful roar of its many waters. The struggle may be a moral one, or it may be a physical one, and it may be both moral and physical, but it must be a struggle. Power concedes nothing without a demand. It never did and it never will . . . The limits of tyrants are prescribed by the endurance of those whom they oppress.[50]

Luthuli was as sober and left us with no illusions:

> We shall not win our freedom except at the cost of great suffering, and we must be prepared to accept it. Much African blood has already been spilt, and assuredly more will be . . . We do not desire to shed the blood of the white man; but we should have no illusion about the price he will exact in African blood before we are admitted to citizenship in our own country.[51]

Getting clarity on these vital issues was indispensable for Black theology as we stood on the threshold of that decisive, life-changing era. These are the truths we need to stand on and fight against the mendacity, the obfuscation, and the illusionist ideologies that are the oppressor's stock in trade and whose end goal is making us believe that struggle is not necessary, or plausible, or "Christian."

At the heart of Black theology is the firm conviction that Jesus of Nazareth belonged historically in a situation of oppression, that he was a member of an oppressed

---

47. See Boesak, *Tenderness of Conscience*, ch. 7.
48. Luthuli, *Let My People Go!*, 147.
49. Luthuli, *Let My People Go!*, 124.
50. See Douglass, "If There Is No Struggle."
51. Luthuli, *Let My People Go!*, 148.

people, living in occupied Palestine, and that he came to set his people free (Luke 4:16–18). Right from the start we grappled with the question: What would it look like if we understood the true revolutionary nature of these words and took them seriously not just for our spiritual comfort or physical survival, but for our decision not to accept the condition of oppression and dehumanization forced upon us? To prophetically imagine a different world *and enact* it?[52]

It is thus within this context we must understand Biko's declaration that Black theology seeks Jesus as "a fighting God, not a passive God who allows a lie to rest unchallenged." We are here not speaking of the life-preserving lie that Biko cautions elsewhere Black theology should not treat as a mortal sin such as the lies to the police of an illegitimate state enforcing oppressive laws when one has forgotten or lost one's Pass book. Nor should it count as a lie when a mother refuses to tell the truth to Security Police when another mother's son is hiding in her house, even though she is endangering her and her family's lives for the sake of saving the life of another. Those are life-preserving "lies" like the lies told to the Nazi's by extraordinarily courageous resisters who kept Jews in hiding in their homes during the horrors of the Nazi reign. Those persons are rightly called "righteous." Those life-preserving "lies" should not be called "lies" at all. These are truths that should be kept from being revealed to oppressive, murderous regimes whose systemic, inherent mendacity does not deserve a truth they will only use for the purposes of undeserved death.

Neither are we speaking of the "expedient lie" politicians tell for some short-term nefarious purpose. Journalist and prophetic social critic Chris Hedges speaks of the expedient lie as "the falsehoods and half-truths uttered by politicians such as Bill Clinton [on NAFTA], George W. Bush [on Iraq] and Barack Obama [on the Pacific Trade Agreement]."[53] These lies (like the astonishing flow of lies from Donald Trump's mouth, one supposes[54]) were "common political lies . . . a form of manipulation." Chris Hedges has a point. However, we should keep in mind that the lies about the nonexistent Weapons of Mass Destruction told by George W. Bush and Tony Blair to justify their invasion of Iraq while that invasion was in fact about imperial lust and ambition, expansion of spheres of power and the purposes of neoliberal capitalism: robbing Iraq of its oil reserves. Those were unabashed expressions of imperial arrogance, greed, and lawlessness. Even though, as Hedges correctly observes, these lies served a particular moment of "cover-up" and need no repetition after having served

---

52. See Brueggemann, *Prophetic Imagination*, xxi.

53. See Hedges, "Permanent Lie."

54. On *The Washington Post* "Fact Checker," Glenn Kessler, Salvador Rizzo, and Meg Kelly have reported that Donald Trump had told 30,573 lies over the course of his four-year term in office. See Kessler et al., "Trump's false or misleading claims total 30,573 over four years." One might be stunned by the sheer volume of lies, or Trump's apparent confidence that he could get away with it; or one might be worried by the pathological nature they betray. But it is always imperative to remember how much each of these lies served not only to justify Trump's actions but the consequences these lies have on the most vulnerable in the US, and in societies across the world, and on a daily basis.

their purpose (for those politicians), we should keep in mind that all of these lies have lasting, and devastating, consequences.

Now, so many years later, says Hedges, one does not find either Blair or Bush going around the world still telling those lies of justification. They are more likely to simply remain silent about them, ignoring those lies, hoping the world would forget.[55] The truly vulgar truth, though, is that these powerful men from powerful Western countries, all of them white apart from Barack Obama, will not be held accountable as the war criminals they are. The world might not totally forget, but the world is quite willing to look the other way, its eyes fixed on the next African dictator and war criminal they can haul before the International Criminal Court. That willful neglect of seeking justice for the millions who died and are still suffering as a result of those initial lies continues to enable those liars and their lies. Tony Blair's power allows him to dictate the meaning of "regret" and "apology." The opinion of the people of Iraq, just as their suffering, does not count. Only it now goes far beyond Bush or Blair. Seeing these things through the eyes of the Global South, and more particularly through the eyes of the millions who died in Iraq, Afghanistan, Syria, Somalia, and now Yemen, these lies should also fall into Hedges's category of the "permanent lie."

The "permanent lie," Chris Hedges argues, is the lie not told as political expediency, to cover the true reasons for a momentary justification of the essentially unjustifiable, just until the world can "move on." The permanent lie is different because it is perpetrated "even in the face of overwhelming evidence that discredits it." It is "irrational," writes Hedges. "The permanent lie is the apotheosis of totalitarianism." Hedges is primarily, and understandably, concerned with the situation in the United States and its reigning political class, especially in what has become known as "the era of Trump" where they, i.e., the ruling elites, "no longer play by any rules."[56]

Hedges is not wrong, and it is wise to keep in mind his long, unblemished record of anti-imperialist wisdom and discernment of the issues that really matter. It is also wise to remember that as long as the United States of America remains the violent, beating heart of global empire, Trump's lies, irrationality, and neo-fascist totalitarianism, eagerly imitated by politically powerful acolytes around the globe, even after his

---

55. George Bush may have remained prudently silent since he stepped out of public life, but as recently as 2016, Tony Blair was still justifying his actions and political morality. After publication of the Chilcot Inquiry's very critical report on the invasion of Iraq, Blair vigorously rejected the findings. "I express sorrow, regret, and apology" he said, but apparently only for "some mistakes made in the planning." As with apartheid's F. W. De Klerk, it is only the execution of the plans that has failed. The plans themselves are not morally wrong. It is then a matter of practical mistakes, not of a deeply morally reprehensible policy. As it turns out, Blair, the powerful white politician from the powerful Western country, the UK, preserves for himself the right to define the meaning of "regret" and "apology." By the end of his response, "Blair had delivered a defiant justification of his reasons for taking the UK to war," wrote the *Guardian*. The self-assured arrogance is stunning: "I did not mislead this country, there were no lies, there was no deceit." See Mason et al., "Tony Blair." In other words, the lies do go on, as permanentized as is the endless misery engulfing the Iraqi people.

56. Hedges, "Permanent Lie."

departure as US president, continue to spell disaster for the rest of the politically and economically vulnerable world on an almost daily basis. However, our responsibility goes deeper. Again looking through Global South eyes, as colonized and re-colonized peoples under imperial domination, we would have to ask: What rules? What are these rules that the empire "no longer" plays by? The empire's rules have always been the rules that benefited the empire, guaranteed its domination, trivialized its savagery, justified its crimes, maximized its profits, normalized its mendacity, sacralized its violence. For us, Hedges's "no longer" has no meaning. We have lived, and are even now living caught up in the actualities and the consequences of the permanent lie. Imperialist totalitarianism, as imperialist terrorism, has been with us for far too long.

So, following the lead of Aimé Césaire, we stand by the singularity of oppressed, colonized, and re-colonized peoples under constant imperial attack. For us, the permanent lie is told as an eternal inversion of the truth, as justification not of one moment of political crisis for the powerful, but rooted in, inextricable from, and indispensable for the permanent justification of permanent imperial structures of domination and subjugation. It is the insidious, pernicious, pervasive lie presented as scientific fact, historical "inevitabilities," philosophical self-evident conclusions, and theological indisputabilities parading as divine truth, intended to sacralize permanent systems of oppression and exploitation. It is the lie we see in the workings of colonialism, "post-colonial" realities we now call "coloniality," re-colonization and perpetual imperialism. Permanent mendacity is the empire's lifeblood.[57]

True to himself, however, Chris Hedges does not believe we should give up. There is a remedy for this situation, he believes. We must resist, he says, "we must pit power against power."[58] That is exactly what Black Consciousness, Black power, and Black theology set out to do. From the beginning, we recognized that all oppressions begin with the permanent lie rooted in power.

What lies? I will take some time considering some of them. About black people and white people, beginning with those fundamental, foundational lies we were expected to believe about ourselves, forced upon our minds, drilled into our consciousness, and seared into our flesh.

The lie that whiteness was the epitome of goodness, civility, and rightness, and that blackness was darkness in body, in mind, in spirit, and in soul; less worthy, less trustworthy, less deserving, less human—*that lie*. The lie perpetrated by respected European scholars, scientists, theologians, and philosophers held in the highest regard as the uppermost echelons of European scholarship. So naturally, we hear the philosopher Georg Wilhelm Friedrich Hegel from his lofty heights, his dark, intellectualized

---

57. See Boesak, *Dare We Speak of Hope?*, 55–65; and Boesak, *Children of the Waters of Meribah*, 27. One of the most recent, screaming examples probably is the Trump administration's justifications of its assassination of Iran's General Qassem Suleimani uncritically echoed by the vast majority of the US mainstream media; see Shupak, "Stop the War."

58. Hedges, "Permanent Lie."

racism, and unfathomable *Abendland* arrogance, pronouncing his judgements of us from thousands of miles away:

> If you want to understand [the Negro] rightly, you must abstract all elements of respect and morality and sensitivity [for] there is nothing remotely humanized in the Negro's character... Africa proper, as far as history goes back, has remained for all purposes of connection with the rest of the world, shut up. It is... that land of childhood, which, lying beyond the days of self-conscious history, is enveloped in the dark mantle of Night[59]

That lie.

No wonder American theologian Joel Goza calls Europe and its Renaissance philosophers "the original crime scene where... America's ideologies were first crafted, and where we can begin to understand our ongoing addiction to racist ideas, institutions and ways of life."[60]

The lies about history—that South Africa's history began in 1652 and that the Dutch colonizers found here a *terra nullius*, an empty land, making it clear that those who had lived here for thousands of years did not count, because it was inconceivable that "savages" could be counted as people with a right to existence or life or land.

That the Europeans who came to South Africa were sent by God to settle a savage, untamed land in a dark continent and bring the light of the gospel to heathen who knew nothing about God—*that lie.*

Those lies about the Bible—that it justified colonization, land theft, oppression, genocide, slavery, exploitation, and apartheid, and sanctified and sacralized white supremacy.

About apartheid—that it was God's will, that it was the only "Christian" solution to South Africa's "race problem"—a problem which they—not God, and not us—created; and that the people who created the problem also had the right to prescribe to blacks the solution to the problem.

---

59. Hegel, *Philosophy of History*, cited in Magubane, "African Renaissance," 24, 25. Recently, Joel Edward Goza has published a fascinating analysis of the ideational roots of American racism. Goza makes us not only understand the current racist realities of the United States of America, but also where these come from, and how they have been solidified by practical political engineering, intellectual, scientific and philosophical endeavor, and religious manipulation. Goza's analysis of America's most beloved and revered philosophers Thomas Hobbes, John Locke, and (the later interpretations of) Adam Smith is careful and relentless. He convincingly shows how the "enlightened thinking" of these philosophers is exposed "through the work taking place in the bodies of Africans and Indians" then and still today. His take on Darwin is instructive: "Though Darwin is two centuries away, the very title of his masterpiece displays the racialized edge of scientific rationality. Though we know his masterpiece under the title *The Origins of Species*, Darwin originally did not; for he entitled the book *On the Origins of Species by Means of Natural Selection, or by Means of Preservation of Favoured Races in the Struggle for Life* (1859)." Goza concludes, "The theory of evolution was part of the project of articulating the origins of white superiority." Goza, *America's Unholy Ghosts*, 43.

60. Goza, *America's Unholy Ghosts*, 29.

I am speaking of the lie perpetrated by apartheid church leaders such as the Dutch Reformed Church's Dr. Andries Treurnicht, that most vigorous proponent of sacralized whiteness, apartheid, and the theology that came to bear its name:

> I know of no policy as moral, as responsible to Scripture, as the policy of separate development... If the... Christian Afrikaner can be convinced that there are no principles or biblical foundations for this policy of separate development, it is but a step to the conviction that it is unchristian or immoral.[61]

Or his equally implacable colleague, Dr. Koot Vorster:

> Our only guide is the Bible. Our policy and outlook on life are based on the Bible. We firmly believe the way we interpret it is right. We will not budge one inch from our interpretation [in order] to satisfy anyone in South Africa or abroad... We are right and will continue to follow the way the Bible teaches.[62]

In making apartheid God's will, they conferred upon that evil system salvific qualities, as if not God's love, grace, and power through Jesus Christ was our salvation but apartheid, which means racial separation, white superiority, white supremacy, and white *Baasskap—that lie.*

About God—that God is a willful, unashamed, white, racist, insatiable robber of land and life; a slaveholding, misogynistic, mendacious, patriarchal, homophobic, genocidal, infanticidal maniac—*that lie.*[63]

That that God has a chosen people, white people, to whom God has given the right to rule and oppress together with the right to impunity, so that whatever they did was eternally excusable on earth and unreservedly forgivable in heaven—*that lie.*

The lie that in order to love Jesus and be his followers, black people must revere white people, obey them, call them *"Baas"* and *"Miesies,"* and never complain because that would be ungrateful and therefore unchristian. That, in order to be acceptable to and loved by God, we were obliged to bend to oppression, humiliation and dehumanization as our God-willed and irrevocable earthly condition.

The lie that we were compelled to embrace slavery and be grateful for it because it is ultimately for our benefit. So argued, among many others, the early nineteenth-century Dutch Reformed Church missionary Rev. M. C. Vos, in his passionate plea to slave owners to allow their slaves to receive religious instruction. The enslaved, he wrote, might have been happy with their "dear families" in the lands from which they were stolen; but if, however, they are taught "that the things which seem unbearable to us are the will of God for our good," they will make for better slaves. Indeed, if they had not been brought to this "Christian country" and made slaves, they never

---

61. A. P. Treurnicht, *Credo van 'n Afrikaner*, cited in Villa-Vicencio, "All-Pervading Heresy," 59–60.

62. *Sunday Times*, November 8, 1970, cited in Villia-Vicencio, "All-Pervading Heresy," 59.

63. Adapted from new atheist Richard Dawkins's famous description of what he called "the God of the Old Testament"; see Dawkins, *God Delusion*, 51.

would have heard of "the saving grace of our Lord Jesus Christ, and on dying would be lost forever."[64]

That unqualified exceptionalism and eternal innocence are divinely ordained, gifted by God to the empire and its ruling classes, justification for what Joel Goza calls "the final political and the final religious lie" namely that "justice is retributive rather than restorative . . . and that indifference to injustice is no threat to one's intimacy with God."[65]

Those lies.

That a society built on the foundations of invasion, racism, slavery, land theft, the genocide and dehumanization of the indigenes, and the decimation of black personhood should be acceptable to oppressed people, and not in need of profound, relentless, revolutionary challenge and transformation.

The lie that in order to survive in the world of white power, white supremacy, and white privilege, we must embrace internalized revilement and perpetual psychological trauma by despising ourselves, our culture, our history, and strive toward whiteness, or as close to whiteness as we could get, or be allowed to get, in an eternal quest of becoming "civilized," and gaining white people's approval.[66] The irony in

---

64. See Rev. Vos's argument to slave owners to allow their slaves to receive religious instruction in Boesak, *Farewell to Innocence*, 83–84, there discussed as a prime example of religion in the service of ideology. Upon hearing this, Vos writes, the slave owner exclaimed, "Why have I not been told this before?" He immediately agreed to allow his slaves religious instruction. But see also B. A. Zuiddam of South Africa's North West University's recent, vigorous defence of Vos's pure Christian motivations: "M.C. Vos, A Remarkable Story!" Note that Zuiddam's first task, as prioritized in the Abstract already, is to prove Vos's whiteness. He stresses that "there is no genealogical warrant to treat Vos as something else than a White, European minister and writer." So with the purity of Vos's white, European, racial credentials settled, Zuiddam then argues for the purity of his Christian credentials: "The real motivation for Vos's missionary endeavours was not racial, but spiritual." Foremost in Vos's mind, Zuiddam contends, was "the promotion of the Gospel [among the enslaved] and knowledge of the Scriptures [by the enslaved]." For Vos, as glowingly approved by Zuiddam almost two full centuries later, slavery was not an issue at all, since the benefits of getting to know Christ were so great. It goes without saying that slave-holding America had similar views on slavery and the benefits of religious instruction, of which the work of Charles Colcock Jones (1804–63), *Religious Instruction of the Negroes,* is arguably one of the best examples. Beginning with "[The Negroes] are the most dependent of all people upon us for the word of life," he goes on to stipulate the benefits accrued from religious instruction. Even though the "pecuniary benefits of Masters" is high on his list of six, the most important benefit is for the enslaved: "The souls of our servants would be saved . . ." Readers can find these documents at https://docsouth.unc.edu. Theologian Joel Goza makes the same point when he quotes English philosopher John Locke, as Locke argues for the beneficial value of Poor Houses for children of the poor, lower classes "above the age of three." Locke recommends that they be "soundly whipped" if their enthusiasm for work failed to meet the expectations of their overseers. Locke—the "father of liberalism," as Goza calls him—wrote, "By this means the mother will be eased of a great part of her trouble in looking after and providing for them at home, and so be at the more liberty to work; the children will be kept in much better order, be better provided for, and from infancy be inured to work." See Goza, *America's Unholy Ghosts*, 96.

65. Goza, *America's Unholy Ghosts*, 106.

66. See Frantz Fanon's unsurpassed treatment of these questions in his classic *Black Skin, White Masks*. One gets an idea of the relevance of Fanon's thinking as it is embraced by students in South

this is unbearable, since however much blacks would become "civilized," they would never become white people's equal. No wonder Adam Small would scathingly call this "white nihilism." "We do not exist for white people," Small wrote. "We exist!"[67]

The lie that courts of law set up by white Christian invaders are sacred spaces of civilization, even if those laws are made and enacted for the sole purpose of justifying the vilest acts of white supremacy, from decriminalizing willful murder and racial bigotry to criminalizing interracial love, a law prompting black South African poet Adam Small's riveting and still-haunting question: "Whose law? God's law? Man's law? Devil's law?"[68]

The lies that make white, racist judges the sole, respected, and unquestionable arbiters of the law, even when they declare that a black person "has no rights a white man is bound to respect," as pronounced by US Supreme Court Chief Justice Roger Taney in 1857.[69] Or, for that matter, that land theft, because it is "legalized" by an act of

---

Africa's 2015 #RhodesMustFall protests and the way the protests were reported by mainstream media. Nicola Bidwell's analysis is highly instructive: "'A feeling of inferiority?' asks Frantz Fanon, in his essay 'The Fact of Blackness.' 'No,' he says, 'a feeling of nonexistence.' Recently, South African students protesting for #Rhodes Must Fall joined a succession of liberation movements referencing Fanon over the past 50 years. Among many creative acts, students wore placards that read 'recognize me.' Mainstream media reported protests at formerly exclusively white universities most extensively; they also tended to portray protesting students at majority black universities as prone to violence—woeful evidence of Fanon's contemporary significance to race identity politics in education. His relevance to HCI, specifically, is simply illustrated by image searches using Google.com.na. Only two of the first 50 people in photos returned for 'person using computer' are black unless the special filter category 'black' is used. There is no filter for 'white,' but there are categories for 'work,' 'office,' 'icon,' and so on. Indeed, the black man is an 'object in the midst of other objects,' 'black in relation to the white man,' Fanon writes, and 'has no ontological resistance.' (Searches for 'person with computer' using one of the languages in the country where I live, 'nakulongifa okomputa,' do not yet yield any image results.)" See Bidwell, "Black Skin, White Masks."

67. See Small, "Blackness versus Nihilism."

68. Small, "What abou' de lô?" ("What About the Law?"), a shatteringly poignant poem about an interracial couple whose love for each other ran afoul of South Africa's racial laws and who finally committed suicide rather than being kept apart by those laws, a not uncommon situation in apartheid South Africa.

69. The consequences of that infamous "Dred Scott decision," argues Harvard University historian Walter Johnson, are impacting African Americans to this day and are an excellent example of yet another element of "the permanent lie." Johnson writes, "When Dred Scott filed his case in the Missouri Courts in 1846, he was on good legal footing . . ." The principal issue at stake, however, was not the strength of his legal argument, but the question of whether Dred Scott had any right to sue in the first place. That right, the court found, was "the sole prerogative of the citizens of the United States, and Scott, being black, was not one." In the view of the Court, he was "of an inferior order and altogether unfit to associate with the white race, either in social or political relations, and so far inferior that they had no rights which the white man was bound to respect." Johnson calls it "ten of the most notorious words in the history of the United States." Arguably, the next thirteen words would prove just as devastating, and today resounds in the manifold ways of modern slavery: "That the negro might justly and rightfully be reduced to slavery *for his benefit*." Most pertinent to our discussion though, is Johnson's conclusion: "More than a century after the Dred Scott decision argued that black people lived in Missouri by the grace of white people," Johnson writes in 2017, "we are seeing the outline of an actually existing police state." See Johnson, "No Rights Which the White Man Is Bound to Respect."

an unrepresentative, illegitimate, minority white parliament, has both historical, legal and moral authority, and that black people, in order to be considered "law-abiding" should accept those immoral "legal" positions and their devastating consequences regarding black landlessness for instance without question.

The lie that being a good Christian means believing that fighting against oppression and exploitation is futile, impossible, and sinful, for rebellion against the white power structure is *ipso facto* rebellion against God. Accepting the fact that while embracing apartheid might make you a good Christian, it will never make you a citizen in the country of your birth. Simultaneously, however, racism's logic makes the point moot: a good black Christian did not need citizenship on earth, because white people will provide all that black people need, and in any case, blacks are not deemed responsible enough to have it. *Their* citizenship, after all, is not on earth but in heaven. Only white people needed both. *Those lies.*

The fact that Western, Euro-centric theology presents itself as universal, its presuppositions as self-evident truths, and its assumptions as unassailable scientific facts, is the result of objective study, inevitable social Darwinism, and divine entitlement, and not embedded in white supremacy, white power, and white privilege.

That is why we need a fighting God: to not let these lies rest unchallenged.

However, exposing the lie means struggle, for we understood that power is never given up voluntarily by the oppressor. Rather—as we have learned from Frederick Douglass, Martin Luther King Jr., and Albert John Mvumbi Luthuli—it has to be wrenched from their hands. Power concedes nothing without a demand *and it never will*; but the limits of tyrants are prescribed by the endurance of those whom they oppress.

Pretending that a struggle was not necessary, or that there was no struggle already going on, was a lie. So was pretending that fighting oppression was not a duty for those who believed in a just, compassionate God.

So with Black Consciousness, Black theology, and Black power and our belief in Jesus as a fighting God, the prophetic church in South Africa, by the grace of God, was able to carve for itself a role of great honor in the struggle for freedom and justice. The young generation of the 1976 revolution and of the multi-generational, multi-racial, multi-faith masses in the campaigns of defiance and resistance of the 1980s made "ungovernability" *the* political reality for the apartheid regime. We won the decisive battle for international political solidarity in terms of boycotts, divestment, and sanctions. And the ultimate persuasive argument was not so much our words, but our convictions, our willingness to suffer, the readiness to die for what we believed in. Not our rhetorical agility, but our blood on the walls and floors of apartheid's prisons and torture chambers and on the streets of the nation. That is what Biko called "the righteousness of our strength."

We dismantled the barricades of Christianized, international white solidarity, overcame the ideologically inspired theological resistance to declare apartheid a sin and its theological justification a heresy, thereby destroying South African white Christianity's pseudo-innocence and apartheid's pretense of political morality. We stormed the gates of official apartheid a final time, and won. We had learned to become what Steve Biko called a generation of "selfless revolutionaries."[70]

"Not a Theology of Absolutes"

Finally, we must consider something else Biko added to his understanding of Black theology, and it is, in my view, of crucial importance. Black theology, he writes, "does not claim to be a theology of absolutes."[71] As far as I can tell, Biko is the only one to describe Black theology thus.

Let us unpack this a bit. First, on the face of it, Biko's words sound somewhat obvious. After all, Black liberation theology is, by its very nature, an *ecumenical* theology. Denominationalism would play no role except where denominations were regarded as particular sites of struggle. Denominationalism was, as was apartheid's racial categorizations, seen as part of the "divide-and-rule" strategies of the ruling classes. "What divided white South African Christians, and conversely what united blacks and whites *in Christ*, however significant both might have been, was never significant enough to break the bonds of common white interests."[72]

But even as far back as 1883, S. N. Mvambo had perceived that white solidarity is not hindered by either language, ethnicity, or denominational affiliation:

> In fighting for national rights, we must fight together. Although they look as if they belong to different churches, the white people are solidly united when it comes to matters of this nature. We blacks think that these churches are hostile to one another, and in that way, we lose our political rights.[73]

Second, we now understand much better, despite its enormous impact on the history of the church and the world, how the Protestant Reformation was, as far as the oppressed and colonized people of the world were concerned, subjected to the realities of empire.[74] Understanding all this also meant that Black theology was not

---

70. Biko, *I Write What I Like*, 241. The fact that that revolution has been hijacked by the exiles-dominated African National Congress and turned into a neo-imperialistic tool for the re-colonization of a democratic South Africa is a tragedy discussed elsewhere, see, e.g., Bond, *Elite Transition*; Terreblanche, *Lost in Translation*; Boesak, *Pharaohs on Both Sides*. The judgment of South Africa's younger generation is blunt and brutal: "The ANC of first century Jerusalem (the religious establishment) was folding under pressure exerted by the Roman powers because they'd never had the moral backbone to resist plundering their own people alongside their oppressors." See Khumalo, *You Have to Be Gay*, 271.

71. Biko, *I Write What I Like*, 104.

72. See Boesak, *Tenderness of Conscience*, 138–39.

73. Quoted in De Gruchy, *Church Struggle in South Africa*, 51.

74. It was Helmut Gollwitzer whose observations in this regard sparked new understandings of this issue in Black theological debates. "For the white confessors of the faith," Gollwitzer wrote in part, "regardless of their particular Christian hue, the people of colour were all destined for bondage;

hampered by the battles around creeds and dogmas, the throne-and-altar wars that so besieged and besmirched European Christendom. Neither could we be bothered to spend too much time on those all-consuming arguments about Transubstantiation and Consubstantiation; or about election, predestination, or white neo-Calvinism's beloved TULIP dogma that gave rise to such bitter strife.[75] Certainly not while all these doctrinal battles made no difference whatsoever to the life situations of the indigenous peoples these same white Christians oppressed, enslaved, and killed. James Cone spoke for all of us:

> While not diminishing the importance of Luther's theological concern, I am sure that if he had been born a black slave, his first question would not have been whether Jesus was present at the Lord's Table, but whether he was really present at the slave's cabin, whether slaves could expect Jesus to be with them as they tried to survive the cotton field, the whip, and the pistol.[76]

Third, one could not have "black solidarity" and "the community of the black oppressed" as Black Consciousness demanded in the political arena, and have a denominationally splintered theological arena. So the Roman Catholics Simangaliso Mkhatshwa and Buti Thlegale worked in close partnership and solidarity with the Lutheran Manas Buthelezi, the Congregationalist Bonganjalo Goba, the Methodists Seth Mokitimi and Elliot Mgojo, and myself, a Reformed minister, to name just a few of that first generation. The contribution of each was considered vital to the whole. Denomination politics was not on their minds. The politics of freedom was.

One must keep in mind as well that Black liberation theology in South Africa is an *African* expression of Black theology. In that sense, shunning absolutes was essential. In an enlightening conversation at a conference I attended in 2018, black theologian Rothney Tshaka during the Q&A reminded us that for Africans, the truth is like the majestic Baobab tree. "It requires many arms, linked together, to encircle it." Moreover, Black theology in South Africa, while holding onto its relationship with Black theology in North America, had no wish to separate itself completely from African

---

'oneness in Christ' might pertain to heaven, but certainly not on this earth." See Gollwitzer, "Why Black Theology?," 155. The essay originally appeared as a chapter in Gollwitzer, *Die Kapitalistische Revolution*. For a detailed discussion on this issue, see Boesak, *Children of the Waters of Meribah*, ch. 1, especially 1–8.

75. Formulated amidst fierce debates and dissensions, leading to the expulsion of some at the Reformed Synod of Dordt (1618–19), and even the beheading of one Johan Vanoldenbarneveldt sometime later, TULIP is an acronym for humanity's "Total depravity," God's "Unconditional election," Christ's "Limited atonement," God's "Irresistible grace" and God's "Preservation of the Saints." Black liberation theologians from the Reformed tradition totally ignored white Calvinists' obsessions with these matters especially since it is highly contested whether these are originally from Calvin anyway. Their concern was to discover John Calvin's bold and entirely persuasive theology of social justice, which instead they saw as the essence of Calvin's theology and the Reformed tradition; see, e.g. Boesak, *Black and Reformed*, especially ch. 9, and *Kairos, Crisis, and Global Apartheid*, ch. 1. See also Boesak, *Tenderness of Conscience*, ch. 7.

76. See Cone, *God of the Oppressed*, 13.

Theology, even though it must be said that the relationship was not always an easy one. It is true that the older, more conservative generation of African theologians had some trouble with Black theology: its proud use of the term "Black," its unabashed political engagement and belief in political resistance to structures of oppressive power, and its critical stance to some aspects of African culture. Desmond Tutu has endeavored to engage with these issues.[77] But, as South African theologian Rothney Tshaka has recently pointed out, and illustrating the continuing relevance of the debate, the questions of liberation and inculturation need not be mutually exclusive, in fact, they are two sides of the same coin, neatly bridging the gap between the older and younger generations on this issue.[78]

Fourth, even more importantly though, not being a theology of absolutes means that Black theology is a *living* theology, not a closed system of sacralized, dogmatized ideologies. It is a theology critical of systems of oppression and capable of self-critique. Black theology is as unsparing in its critique of the black situation as the result of systems of white power as it is of black Christianity; of white racism and white capitalist exploitation as it is of white Christianity. By the same token, however, it is as critical of black people's complicity in their own oppression. I consider this a crucial point, for authentic revolutionary understanding recognizes the paralyzing dangers of the entitlements induced by oppression: self-destructive self-pity, self-righteous victimhood, and self-deluding innocence. Hence Biko's brutal honesty about black people as he speaks about "the first truth, as bitter as it may seem," quoted earlier in this work. It is an essential element of Black Consciousness. Here we consider these words again, now within the context of its importance for Black theology:

> Reduced to an obliging shell, [the Black person] looks with awe at the white power structure and accepts what he regards as the inevitable "position." Deep inside his anger mounts at the accumulating insult, but he vents it in the wrong direction—on his fellow man in the township, on the property of black people. No longer does he trust leadership, *for the 1963 mass arrests were blameable on bungling by the leadership, nor is there any to trust.* In the privacy of his toilet his face twists in silent condemnation of white society but brightens up

---

77. See Engdahl, "Black Atlantic as Reversal." See also Tutu, "Black Theology/African Theology," 483–491. The tensions, already reflected in the title Tutu gave his contribution, were not completely overcome. John Mbiti, for instance, continued to view Black theology as a specifically American phenomenon, a consequence of enslavement in America and a judgement on American Christianity. It had nothing to do with Africa, its ongoing state of neo-colonization, the continent's enforced submission to American imperialism, the oppression and exploitation of its peoples by ruthless leaders, and certainly not as a call to radical engagement by African theologians; see Mbiti, "An African Views American Black Theology," 477–82. For many of us it was clear that Mbiti never really understood, or accepted, Black theology, and his condescension did not help: "I understood the reason for their bitterness, their anger and their hatred, all of which comes through in their Black Theology." See Mbiti, "An African Views Black Theology," 481. In 2013, at a conference at the University of the Western Cape, I shared the speaker's stage with John Mbiti, and the tensions were still palpable.

78. See Tshaka, "How Can a Conquered People Sing Praises?"

in sheepish obedience as he comes out hurrying in response to his master's impatient call . . . His heart yearns for the comfort of white society and makes him blame himself for not having been "educated" enough to warrant such luxury. Celebrated achievements by whites in the field of science—which he understands only hazily—serve to make him rather convinced of the futility of resistance and to throw away any hopes that change may ever come. *All in all, the black man has become a shell, a shadow of a man, completely defeated, drowning in his own misery; a slave, an ox bearing the yoke of oppression with sheepish timidity.*[79]

"This *is* the first truth," Biko writes with emphasis. This "is what we have to acknowledge before we can start on any programme designed to change the status quo." As with his blistering critique of the Black Church, where Biko accuses us of "conniving" with a colonized Christianity in keeping Christianity "the ideal religion for the subjugation of our people" and of an "appallingly irrelevant interpretation of the Scriptures,"[80] Biko understood that when liberation is at stake, this is the kind of honest, self-critical understanding that is required. Without this, a revolution has no integrity, no authenticity, and no genuine hope to offer. This is, I contend, what Biko means by a theology that does not embrace absolutes. It is simultaneously the embodiment of the truth so desperately needed, even if sometimes desperately evaded, through which Biko brings wholeness to his understanding of Black theology. As challenging as these may be for black people to embrace, as devastating are they for the permanent imperial lie.

Fifth, Black theology is a theology capable of evolving, with an openness to embrace changing situations. It is open to the necessity of learning and unlearning, to hear and to respond to the voices of oppressed and suppressed communities and persons, even, and especially, those long suppressed in our own midst. It is a theology of

---

79. Biko, *I Write What I Like*, 31–32. Emphasis mine. I would not employ Biko's male exclusivist language today, but it is an important pointer to those matters Black theology, and similarly black political discourse, has to acknowledge and unlearn, and to the necessity of the openness of a non-absolutist theology I am speaking about.

80. Biko, *I Write What I Like*, 58–65. From one point of view, one may read the title of Biko's book as some sassy, even taunting, thumbing-of-the-nose at the white power structures: writing what he liked even when he was banned by the apartheid regime and prohibited from writing anything for publication, albeit under the pseudonym *Frank Talk*. As political commentary on apartheid racism and its manifestations, it is devastatingly critical. It is indeed what African Americans would call "sass." It is more than "back talk." Sass, writes Womanist theologian Mitzi Smith, means, "We might at any time resist our oppressor . . . but we might not survive." Smith, "Race, Gender, and the Politics of 'Sass,'" 99. As we have also seen in Biko's engagement with Judge Boshoff in the BPC/SASO trial, Biko is risking his life by laughing in the face of the mightiest government on the continent. But within this context it becomes clear that Biko knew what risks he was taking. As self-critique directed at black folks, it was even more devastating: How dare he speak in such a way to a people already crushed by oppression, vilification, and self-doubt, and so much in need of sympathy and uncritical affirmation! How hard would it be for us blacks to really accept "this first truth," and how much easier to ignore it and reject Biko, his philosophy, and his revolution? Still, he understood God's word to Ezekiel: "Whether they hear or refuse to hear (for they are a rebellious house), they shall know that there has been a prophet among them" (Ezek 2:5).

freedom. Inasmuch as Black theology fights for the freedom of the oppressed, it claims the right of freedom for itself. I would suggest that without the right to self-liberating freedom, the fight for the freedom of the oppressed, and the oppressor, would not even be possible.

As a theology of freedom in the sense of both Luke 4:16–18 and Paul's letter to the Galatians (5:1) and not of absolutes, Black theology clings to the fundamental message of these scriptural passages. Black theology sets itself resolutely against all new forms of enslavement. It firmly asserts that it has the freedom to learn the wider understandings of liberation: freedom for *all* captives, including those held in the captivity of gender-based injustices and inequalities. It insists on the liberation of *all* the oppressed, including those oppressed by the hatreds of bigotry, homophobia, hetero-patriarchy, and transphobia. The healing of all *those* broken-hearted; those hearts broken not only by a hard-hearted society, but by African cultural distortions totally void of the Ubuntu we proclaim; not simply by a hypocritical church in general, but by a hetero-patriarchal, hetero-normative Black Church in particular.

But there is more. In the new and exciting debates raging about Africanization, coloniality, and decolonization Black theology has to be ready to firmly take its stand and make its contribution. In my most recent work, I have made the argument as follows.[81]

The struggles for authentic Africanity are firmly rooted within the struggles inspired by Black Consciousness. Our insights formed during those struggles are hugely relevant today. Tshaka confirms this when he writes, "Colonialism had as one of its objectives the goal of conquering Africa and relegating her people to the status of being sub-humans." As Black Consciousness knew, postulated, and advocated, it was not only about our territory and its resources, it was also about our humanity. I will continue to plead for two major things here: one, that these struggles be seen as struggles against empire and continuing imperial dominance in Africa by empire. Not only must the colonial and apartheid baggage be engaged, these must be engaged as the result of projects inextricable from the imperialist venture that even today has still not ended. This is the irrevocable context for these endeavors today.

That also means that Africanity, as Tshaka maintains, and as I have argued above, "refers to the spatiality, specificity, temporality, and particularity" of the African conquered in the unjust wars of colonisation" while it also emphasizes, as relentlessly as it can, African agency in the ongoing, determined struggles of Africans to embrace their full humanity, gain their entire liberation, dignity, and the power to self-realization and self-determination, free from the shackles of imperialist imposition.

The second matter is as important. This struggle must, from the very beginning, include women as equal partners, recognize women's agency, and accept women's leadership and unique contribution. If this is not the case, our Africanity cannot be authentic, our Africanness can never be whole, and our processes of Africanization and decoloniality will remain flat and static. Like a sun that sits on the horizon but

---

81. See Boesak, *Children of the Waters of Meribah*, 153–54.

never rises, it will promise a new, brighter day, but remain chained to the darker impulses of a night that never really let go.

Finally, if the particularity of blackness is as central to Black theology as we have argued, it must mean that the particularity of queerness in a crushingly violent homophobic, transphobic world, and the singularity of being a woman in a patriarchal world of injustice and gender-based violence, and the uniqueness of differently abled persons in a deplorably indifferent world, must be as central to Black theology today. A theology that shuns absolutes will repent of our own patriarchy, homophobia, transphobia, and racism, of our own excess of love for neoliberal capitalism even while paying lip service to the God of the poor and the destitute.

Understanding South Africa today—not just its unrepented racism, but also its unacknowledged ethnocentrisms; not just the burdens from its apartheid past but also the anguish from its re-colonized present; not just the poverty created by white greed and exploitation, but also the unconscionable social and economic inequalities created by black greed and indifference—means understanding the need for Black liberation theology's Jesus as a fighting God.

If we dare to have the honesty, integrity, and decency to acknowledge and accept the flaming critique of South Africa's younger generation, we would hear Siya Kumalo and in hearing him embrace Biko again, and this time much more intimately:

> The ruling party's claim to South Africa's loyalty is that the ANC of J.L. Dube, S. Makgatho, R. Mahabane, created to liberate black people, actually did. This isn't true: on the contrary, they signed a deal with the Romans of our day . . . it is *not* true that the negotiated settlement was the liberation those sacrifices [made by the people] had always looked forward to. The resultant Constitution is *not* the Freedom Charter.[82]

Now that the need for a Black theology of liberation is once again rising in South Africa, we would also know that the need is not for a Black theology that seeks appeasement with the empire and accommodation with the ruling classes, even, and especially if those ruling classes are "our own people." Siya Khumalo calls the Jerusalem elites of Jesus's day "the ANC of first century Jerusalem" because "they never had the moral backbone to resist plundering their own people alongside their oppressors."[83]

Harsh judgment, indeed—at least as brutally honest as Biko tried to teach us all to be. If for the young Siya Kumaloses of this world, "our own people" have become the Jerusalem elites, collaborating with the present-day Roman Empire in the oppression and plundering of their own people, then what Black theology needs to do is to find and present that Jesus who is a fighting God, the one who will not let the lie rest unchallenged, and who will not rest until the people are free and the temple is no longer a den of thieves.

---

82. Khumalo, *You Have to Be Gay*, 273.
83. Khumalo, *You Have to Be Gay*, 271.

8

When Tomorrow Is Yesterday

Black Theology, Black Consciousness, and Our Incomplete Revolution

"Yesterday Is a Foreign Country"

In chapter 2, we re-engaged with then-Deputy President Thabo Mbeki's idea of an "African Renaissance." In this final chapter, we have reason to revisit that idea and reflect on it from a different perspective. Back in 1998, when Thabo Mbeki announced his grand vision for the "African Renaissance," he harked back to words from a group of young Afrikaners he had been in discussion with. He found those words inspiring. "Yesterday is a foreign country," they told him. "Tomorrow belongs to us!"[1] Many of us joined the Deputy President in his enthusiasm. After all, it was promising: young Afrikaners wanting to make the apartheid past "foreign," claiming a morrow of non-racial democracy, justice, and equality for all South Africans. In those euphoric days, most of us wanted desperately for the country to succeed, and it sounded as if at last there was a generation of young Afrikaners who wanted it too. It sounded like a kind of "all-hands-on-deck" call that gave us hope.

---

1. See Boesak, *Tenderness of Conscience*, 1, 2. In his opening address to the African Renaissance Conference, Mbeki spoke in tones of high optimism of the sentiments expressed. "They spoke of how our country's transition to democracy had brought them their own freedom; of how their acceptance of themselves as equal citizens with their black compatriots defined apartheid South Africa and its legacy as foreign to themselves, of how South Africa, reborn, constitutes their own heritage." See "Statement by Deputy President Mbeki at the African Renaissance Conference." Journalist Allister Sparks's *Tomorrow Is Another Country* is a word play on this phrase. A passionate white liberal defense of the elite pact between the ANC and the apartheid government, it is an excellent example of the dominant narrative about the heroism and political wisdom of F. W. De Klerk and the "chemistry" between De Klerk and Nelson Mandela, and the triumphs of the secret talks between 1985 and 1989. For a concise overview of the relationship between Thabo Mbeki and the Afrikaners as reflected in the development of the secret talks and beyond, see Brits, "Mbeki and the Afrikaners," 33–69.

It is more than ironic though, seeing how that young generation, now a powerful and privileged older generation twenty-five years later, have remained in the seats of economic power long enough for us to see how much that "tomorrow" really does belong to them.[2] In light of the continued economic disempowerment and impoverishment of the vast majority of South Africa's people, those words now sound more like an exclusivist war cry or a confident neo-colonialist claim than inspirational support for genuine transformation. Apart from the small black elite, thanks to the secret deals and the elite pacts made with the African National Congress exile leadership with Thabo Mbeki strongly taking the lead, for those masses, that "tomorrow" has remained painfully and devastatingly elusive.[3] It seems hindsight can also be a painful reminder of a lack of insight. Our present contexts in South Africa prompt a re-thinking of those words, which we will endeavor to do with the help of Steve Biko.

In an all-important interview, which the editors of *I Write What I Like* place, as far as could be determined, between 1969 and 1972, Steve Biko, with clear prophetic insight, said this:

> I think there is no running away from the fact that now in South Africa there is such an ill distribution of wealth that any form of political freedom which does not touch on the proper distribution of wealth, will be meaningless. The whites have locked up within a small minority the greater proportion of the country's wealth. If we have a mere change of face of those in governing positions, what is likely to happen is that black people will continue to be poor, and you will see a few blacks filtering through into the so-called bourgeoisie. *Our society will be run almost as of yesterday.* So for meaningful change to appear there should be an attempt at reorganizing the whole economic pattern and economic policies.[4]

Note that Biko's critique here is of South Africa's economic policies and what he calls "the *whole economic pattern.*" That critique was not just of aspects of what some today call "predatory capitalism," as if capitalism as a system is inherently good, but has a few wayward tendencies. It is much more, I think, if only a fleeting reference in this interview, a critique and rejection of the very nature of neoliberal capitalism, no more brutally exposed in these times than by the ravages of the coronavirus. It is Naomi Klein's exposé of "disaster capitalism" multiplied one-hundred fold.[5] And what is be-

---

2. In 2017, by far the largest portion of wealth in the country and among the top 10 percent was still in the hands of whites. See Anwar, "White People in South Africa." And so it would remain. In 2020, among the six richest billionaires in the country, only one—Patrice Motsepe—is black; see Bronkhorst, "These Are the 6 Richest People in South Africa."

3. See for this e.g., Terreblanche, *Lost in Transformation*; Bond, *Elite Transition*.

4. See Biko, *I Write What I Like*, 169.

5. See Klein, *Shock Doctrine*. Among the now already countless examples of profiteering from the crisis, putting essential workers' lives at risk by not providing adequate protection, and shameless price gouging of essential goods, one of the most hideous is the Hitleresque suggestion by Texas Lt. Governor Dan Patrick. Older Americans, he says, should disregard the virus, their safety and desire

ing exposed is not its "weaknesses" but the absolute inevitabilities of its workings and its innate anti-humanness.

Of course, Biko knew that the essence of our revolution was not only gaining power in order to affect the social and economic transformation the country so badly needed. He knew it was about much more. Hence his insistent reach for something greater, and deeper, and in a sense infinitely more essential.

> We have set out on a quest for true humanity, and somewhere on the distant horizon we can see the glittering prize. Let us march forth with courage and determination, drawing from our common plight . . . and our brotherhood [and sisterhood]. In time we shall be in a position to bestow upon South Africa the greatest gift possible—a more human face.[6]

However, Black Consciousness understood also that a revolution is not simply for oneself. Biko found satisfaction in the fact that "the black people of the world . . . have at last established a solid base for meaningful cooperation around themselves in the larger battle of the Third World against the rich nations."[7] Today that is truer than ever before. The interconnectedness of the world, the global nature of the war against the poor, the internationalized reality of capitalist corporatist power, the very nature of empire and its military omnipresence, the global spread of the politics of vulgarity discussed in chapter 6, make a self-centered revolution a futile one. All this speaks to the reality and necessity of the connectivity of global nature of struggles for justice, freedom, and dignity, and all of these underscore what Martin Luther King Jr. called our "inescapable network of mutuality," our "single garment of destiny."[8]

Today, as the Black Lives Matter movement captivates, in truly unprecedented fashion, the attention, support, and solidarity of similar movements across the world, a timely reminder comes from Palestine. Sam Bahour, born in Youngstown, Ohio, but now living in Palestine, writes, "BLM is a movement that specifically aims to

---

for life, and risk their lives for the sake of the American economy. "Let's get back to work. Let's go back to living. Don't sacrifice the country. Don't do that," he said on television, a call that has now been taken up by numerous American political figures and corporate representatives. In cruel irony, Patrick invites them to "go back to living" while he knows he is inviting them to their possible death. It is, fundamentally, a call for older Americans to offer themselves as sacrifice on the altar of "the Market" because their lives, like the lives of the poor and vulnerable everywhere, are expendable, useful only if they can serve the economy. Calling on those Americans not to "sacrifice the country," he orders them to sacrifice their lives. The cruelty is all the more shameless since a rich, privileged, powerful person like the Lt. Governor knows he can avail himself of the medical care that is routinely excluding the poor, and so save himself should he become ill. See Sherfinski, "Texas Lt. Gov. Dan Patrick." No wonder South African theologian Ernst Conradie argues that "market-based consumerism may well amount to idolatry." See his "To Cover the Many Sins of Galamsey Mining." The quote is on 122, but see especially the section headed, "Mine, Mine, Mine, Jesus is Mine! Ideology, Idolatry, and Heresy."

6. Biko, *I Write What I Like*, 108.

7. Biko, *I Write What I Like*, 78.

8. In his last sermon before his death, given in the Episcopal National Cathedral in Washington, DC. See King, "Remaining Awake," 269.

'eradicate white supremacy and build local power to intervene in violence inflicted on Black communities by the state and vigilantes.' A noble cause indeed, but not one detached from a broader array of interrelated issues."[9] Echoing Martin Luther King Jr. from almost fifty years earlier, Bahour goes on to remind his American comrades that America's problems are deeply systemic, deeply structural, and deeply pervasive. He enumerates the areas that need thorough and permanent transformation, making the point we have made so often and will keep on making: that of America's present position of power and its ability to inflict terrible harm upon the rest of the world:

> From Palestine, and I assume from every corner of the globe, the oppressed around the world are watching, as we engage in our struggles for freedom. We are not merely observers; we have as much to benefit from fixing America as every American citizen. For it is America's narrow military-industrial-congressional complex interests that have wrought havoc across the world and prohibited other countries to be held accountable for their actions. A better America means a better world. A corrected America means less death and destruction from Minneapolis to Caracas to Bethlehem.[10]

Consequently, speaking of the role and contribution of Africa to what I have elsewhere called the "ubuntufication of the world," Biko writes, expanding his lens from South Africa to the whole world, as is right and proper:

> We believe that in the long run, the special contribution to the world by Africa will be in this field of human relationships. The great powers of the world may have done wonders in giving the world an industrial and military look, but the great gift still has to come from Africa—giving the world a more human face.[11]

For those of us who were part of the Black Consciousness movement, it is strangely satisfying, but simultaneously strangely disturbing, and for some of us truly heart breaking to see how right Biko was, how prophetic his wisdom, how relevant his insights are for South Africa today. But even as we heard him, we knew he was right. Our generation had heard and understood Ghana's Kwame Nkrumah well, who taught us that political freedom without economic freedom, by which he meant control over our social and economic resources and the decisions about them for the good of the people, is no more than neo-colonialism. Nkrumah was as consummate a politician as he was a wise mentor, a truly organic leader with a formidable intellect who set his knowledge to work for the sake of the people of Africa. "The essence of neo-colonialism," he taught us,

---

9. See Bahour, "America's Intifada Must Dig Deeper."
10. See Bahour, "America's Intifada Must Dig Deeper."
11. Biko, *I Write What I Like*, 51.

> is that the State which is subject to it is, in theory, independent, and has all the outward trappings of international sovereignty. In reality, its economic system and thus its political policy is directed from outside.[12]

However, Nkrumah also saw very early that the neo-colonialist grip on Africa was broad and comprehensive, as we are increasingly discovering today. Their methods, he warned, are "subtle and varied." Nkrumah elaborates, "They operate not only in the economic field, but also in the political, religious, ideological, and cultural spheres."[13] The political maneuverings of the rich North should be understood in a wider context, he knew, and dissected through the lens of the Global South in order to truly understand the impact of these actions on Africa and other countries of the Global South. He understood what US President Eisenhower was talking about when, in his famous last address to the American people, he warned America against the danger of "the Military-Industrial Complex." Nkrumah looked with Global South eyes. Lurking behind all this, Nkrumah saw,

> are the extended tentacles of the Wall Street octopus. And its suction cups and muscular strength are provided by a phenomenon dubbed "The Invisible Government" arising from Wall Street's connections with the Pentagon and various intelligence services.[14]

Looking at and understanding the devastating history of US interventions, coup d'etats, and regime-change wars across the Global South—from the assassination of democratically elected leaders who refused to do the bidding of the US to the endless wars for endless profits we are witnessing today, killing Global South citizens by the millions—one would be utterly foolish, blind, or willful not to see the truth of this statement. Furthermore, considering the truly astounding role US media have been playing, in what Noam Chomsky and Edward Herman, in their masterful and still unsurpassed treatise on the real workings of the modern mainstream media as "defender of the dominant classes," called "manufacturing consent"[15]—before, but especially after 9/11—it is perhaps more appropriate to speak of the Military-Industrial-Financial-Media-Intelligence Complex. None of it happened without a carefully calculated and coordinated plan executed by the powerful network of organizations, agencies, and institutions Nkrumah pointed us to, and which make the American Empire commit such deadly crimes against humanity (not to mention its war crimes) on such a regular basis. That this behavior caused dangerous "blowback" for the US, as international

---

12. Nkrumah, *Neo-Colonialism*, 1.

13. Nkrumah, *Neo-Colonialism*, 1. Of course, I speak here of the Nkrumah of the 1950s and early 60s, before he became so fatally obsessed with power and self-aggrandizement that he, like so many promising African leaders, forgot what he stood for and why his people loved and followed him.

14. Nkrumah, *Neo-Colonialism*, 1.

15. See Herman and Chomsky, *Manufacturing Consent*.

politics scholar Chalmers Johnson rightly saw,[16] is doubtless true. But, as the endless wars of terror on terror make clear, "blowback" did not stop the U S hunger for global power and the lust for the spread of white, monopolist, acquisitive neoliberal capitalism with the threat of military devastation at its core.[17]

But perhaps that implacable, early twentieth-century American hero of truth-speaking, the late Major General Smedley Darlington Butler of the US Marines, one of the exceedingly few military officers to speak out so courageously about the real motivations behind war, today more shamelessly paraded than ever before, said it best. "War is a racket," he wrote. "It has always been. It is possibly the oldest, easily the most profitable, surely the most vicious. It is the only one in which the profits are reckoned in dollars and the losses in lives." Smedley Butler makes it plain, proving Nkrumah's point at every turn:

> I spent 33 years and four months in active military service and during that period, I spent most of my time as a high class muscle man for Big Business, for Wall Street and the bankers. In short, I was a racketeer, a gangster for capitalism. I helped make Mexico and especially Tampico safe for American oil interests in 1914. I helped make Haiti and Cuba a decent place for the National City Bank boys to collect revenues in. I helped in the raping of half a dozen Central American republics for the benefit of Wall Street. I helped purify Nicaragua for the International Banking House of Brown Brothers in 1902–1912. I brought light to the Dominican Republic for the American sugar interests in 1916. I helped make Honduras right for the American fruit companies in 1903. In China in 1927, I helped see to it that Standard Oil went on its way unmolested. Looking back on it, I might have given Al Capone a few hints. The best he could do was to operate his racket in three districts. I operated on three continents.[18]

The deliberate, yet chillingly casual[19] turning of targeted sanctions, boycotts and divestment from an instrument of nonviolent pressure on an oppressive, racist government committing a crime against humanity (apartheid South Africa), into a weapon of mass destruction (Iraq under Bill Clinton; Iran and Russia under Obama; Iran, North Korea, and Venezuela under Donald Trump) is only the open face of this

---

16. See Johnson, *Blowback*.

17. For one of the most comprehensive and exhaustive analyses of this, see Kinzer, *Overthrow*. See also the excellent work, Blumenthal, *Management of Savagery*.

18. See Butler, *War Is a Racket*, xii–xiii.

19. One calls to mind the way Clinton's secretary of state, Madeleine Albright, pooh-poohed the question on national television whether the 500,00 deaths in Iraq, the majority of them children, as a result of US sanctions, and more than the number of children killed in the bombing of Hiroshima, were "worth it." "Oh, it's worth it," she responded so coolly that that remark now characterizes Ms. Albright in the minds of millions in the Global South, as she herself characterizes the essence of American Empire. See "Madeleine Albright: The deaths of 500,000 Iraqi children was worth it," YouTube video, posted by postpanic3, May 2014, youtube.com/watch?v=bntsfiAXMEE.

terrifying phenomenon. The economic warfare against the poor, so essential to the neo-colonialist project and the survival of empire, goes on at much more subtle levels as Kwame Nkrumah prophetically understood, even though this particular phenomenon emerged after his time, as the neo-colonialist project waxed in lethal sophistication. Self-confessed "economic hitman" John Perkins explains:

> Economic hit men (EHMs) are highly paid professionals who cheat countries around the globe out of trillions of dollars. They funnel money from the World Bank, the U.S. Agency for International Development (USAID), and other foreign "aid" organizations into the coffers of huge corporations and the pockets of a few wealthy families who control the planet's natural resources. Their tools include fraudulent financial reports, rigged elections, payoffs, extortion, sex, and murder. They play a game as old as empire, but one that has taken on new and terrifying dimensions during this time of globalization. I should know; I was an EHM.[20]

American economist Michael Hudson, in discussing capitalism's "free market theory," puts it yet another way. He calls it "the first premise of the free market theory."

> You cannot have a free market unless you are willing to assassinate everyone who opposes you. Unless you can have a regime change for any country that does not follow the free market. All of Roman history is this: the fifth, fourth, third, second and first century B.C.[E.], every single activist of debt cancellation, of land redistribution, of democracy, was killed.[21]

These are all witnesses to the truth so boldly spoken by this African prophet. And for the new generation, grappling with the all-important matters of Africanness, Africanity, neo-colonialism, coloniality, de-colonization, and empire, the call to listen and learn from him could not be more urgent, if only to make us understand that the new struggles have deeper roots than sometimes admitted to.

The globalization research project of the Evangelisch Reformierte Kirche in Germany and the Uniting Reformed Church in Southern Africa, of which I was privileged to be a part, has offered a helpful definition of empire, since then widely accepted in ecumenical discourse on these matters:

> We speak of *empire*, because we discern a coming together of economic, cultural, political and military power in our world today, that constitutes a reality and a spirit of lordless domination, created by humankind, yet enslaving simultaneously; an all-encompassing global reality serving, protecting and defending the interests of powerful corporations, nations, elites and privileged people, while imperiously excluding, even sacrificing humanity and exploiting creation; a pervasive spirit of destructive self-interest, even greed—the

---

20. See Perkins, *New Confessions of an Economic Hitman*, xi. See also his Introduction in Hiatt, *Game as Old as Empire*.

21. See Hudson, "Resisting Empire."

worship of money, goods and possessions; the gospel of consumerism, proclaimed through powerful propaganda and religiously justified, believed and followed; the colonization of consciousness, values and notions of human life by the imperial logic; a spirit lacking compassionate justice and showing contemptuous disregard for the gifts of creation and the household of life.[22]

I prefer this definition of empire because it describes a much more complex, interrelated, and comprehensive structure of global power than the usual understanding of empire as global neoliberal capitalism in tandem with (US) global military power. Michael Hudson, for example, demotes even military power in order to make his point. To an extent, as the United States, wielding its immense power through economic sanctions—currently at least thirty countries—has repeatedly demonstrated,[23] Hudson is not wrong. However, the exclusive emphasis on financial control and economic power—i.e., capitalism—tends to exclude the other, rather crucial aspects of ongoing global hegemony and imperial power, what we now call "coloniality":

> The precondition for any country looking for global dominance, or to create an empire, is the balance of payments and the ability to dominate and control the world's monetary system. Ultimately, money is even more of a lever than military force, as we are seeing today . . . American hegemony enables the United States to stop any country from growing by pulling out the connections of its financial system. Dollarization has enabled the United States to run balance of payments deficits without any limits at all.[24]

As such, the definition offered by the Globalization Project goes even further than Ramón Grosfoguel, that intrepid exponent of the decolonial revolution does here, even though his understanding is absolutely spot on.

> To call the present world-system "capitalist" is, to say the least, misleading. Given the hegemonic Eurocentric "common sense," the moment we use the word "capitalism," people immediately think that we are talking about the "economy." However, "capitalism" is only one of the multiple entangled constellations of colonial power matrix of what I called, at the risk of sounding ridiculous, "Capitalist/Patriarchal Western-centric/Christian-centric Modern/Colonial World-System." Capitalism is an important constellation of power, but not the sole one. Given its entanglement with other power relations, destroying the capitalist aspects of the world-system would not be enough to destroy the present world-system. To transform this world-system it is crucial to destroy the historical-structural heterogenous totality called

---

22. See Boesak et al., *Dreaming a Different World*, 2. For further, detailed discussion of this definition of empire, see Boesak, *Dare We Speak of Hope?*, 5ff.

23. See Elmerraji, "Countries Sanctioned by the US." Elmerajji writes, in agreement with Hudson, "Military might is nothing compared to the repercussions that economic and trade sanctions from the US can bring."

24. Hudson, "De-Dollarization."

the "colonial power matrix" of the "world-system" with its multiple forms of power hierarchies.[25]

So the militant, nonviolent revolution I have been speaking of throughout this work must, as I have argued, itself have this all-comprehensive quality and character. "It requires," writes Grosfuegel, "a broader transformation of the sexual, gender, spiritual, epistemic, economic, political, linguistic, aesthetic, pedagogical and racial hierarchies of the 'modern/colonial western-centric Christian-centric capitalist/patriarchal world-system.'"[26]

In light of this discussion, perhaps Kwame Nkrumah spoke too soon of "the last stages of imperialism." With what we now know of the workings of the American Empire, its relentless economic, political, and military grip on the throats of the most vulnerable in the world, with "the colonial power matrix" such an accurate characterization, it is clear that Kwame Nkrumah had it right. At the heart of the empire is not only a fire-spewing dragon, though that image is also frighteningly, and despairingly, fitting. We now have another image to contend with and to keep in mind as we confront empire: an octopus with its tentacles and suction cups and brute strength. If ever there was a "tomorrow" for Global South citizens and for the prey of empire everywhere, it is not yet.

Almost as of Yesterday

After twenty-five years of democracy, South Africans now know for certain that a black face in office, rather than a white one, as Biko had foreseen, does not guarantee justice and rights for our people. Our experience now teaches us that a black face in office does not guarantee economic opportunity, economic security, and economic dignity for our youth. After twenty-five years, we know that what we have is not the democracy we thought we were fighting for, but in fact the fruits of what University of KwaZulu Natal economist Patrick Bond called an "Elite transition from apartheid to neoliberalism."[27] It is what the late, greatly lamented Sampie Terreblanche of Stellenbosch University bluntly called "the elite conspiracy" between the African National Congress and the white political and economic establishment.[28] In painful lesson after painful lesson, we have learned that a democratic society is not necessarily a liberated one. So indeed we have today what Biko referred to as "the few blacks filtering through into the so-called bourgeoisie" while the vast majority of our people remained mired in the misery of continuing impoverishment.

---

25. See Grosfuegel, "Decolonizing Postcolonial Studies."
26. Grosfuegel, "Decolonizing Postcolonial Studies."
27. See Bond, *Elite Transition.*
28. See Terreblanche, *Lost in Transformation.*

"South Africa is still the most economically unequal country in the world," writes economist Göran Therborn.[29] That means that overall economic inequality has remained the same as during the last decades of apartheid, while "between-race" inequality among the rich has declined, and the white-black gap of median earnings has increased. "Post-apartheid economic inequality has been driven by increasing gains at the top."[30] But Therborn makes another point. Not only is this the present situation. The problem lies deeper, even in the planning of the present government's focus on "categorical elite equalization and may keep overall equality out of the view and concern." That means that ongoing inequalities *are built into* the future economic planning of government.

> A telling illustration of the latter is the National Planning Commission objective, that in 2030 the country should have an economic inequality (Gini) coefficient of 0,6, meaning that *in 2030 South Africa should continue to be the world's most unequal country* (perhaps together with Namibia). The poorest 40 percent of the population were graciously to be conceded 10 percent of the national income.[31]

We should be clear. This is by design. Just after 1994, the ANC was able to convince even some critical observers that it really had no choice; it was virtually being blackmailed by the West, the World Bank, and the IMF.[32] Even if it was true then, and I have never been entirely convinced, it certainly is not now. South Africa's new, small, black aristocracy, who have made such disastrous, if immensely profitable common cause with the old white capitalist class, have done so even though they knew that the heart of that system is endless greed, endless exploitation, endless carelessness, endless compassionlessness without which neoliberal capitalism cannot survive. Hence we should not be at all surprised at what we see today: the bottomless corruption, the shameless cronyism, nepotism, and cadre-favoritism, all sustained by a deliberate disdain for the poor and the vulnerable. It means that government policies are designed to maintain the chasm between rich and poor, to throw up the barricades that protect the wealthy and keep the poor outside the walls of coddled privilege. If inequality is built into the system, it is unavoidable in perpetuity, or at least as long as the present system lasts. It also means that tinkering with the system and calling it "reforms" should be unacceptable. What is required is total eradication of that system replacing it with a more just and equitable alternative.

---

29. See Therborn, "Racism, Existential Inequality," 47.
30. Therborn, "Racism, Existential Inequality," 47.
31. Therborn, "Racism, Existential Inequality," 46. Emphasis mine.
32. See Klein, *Shock Doctrine*. Her chapter based on her interview with ANC economic experts is called "Democracy Born in Chains: South Africa's Constructed Freedom."

At this point, the tomorrow that millions have struggled, sacrificed, and died for, is hardly different from the yesterday we rose up against. And it is for all these reasons that we speak of an incomplete revolution.

Speaking the words in our first quotation from Biko in 1977, just months after Soweto's children began to change history, Biko knew that the revolution had started. That generation soon realized that to call what was happening in Soweto a "protest" was inadequate. We began to understand that there are times when, in the words of Black poet and philosopher Adam Small, protest can be "a form of begging." We stopped calling it a "rebellion," or even an "uprising" as some did. We called it a revolution,[33] because we understood that what began in Soweto and would morph into the United Democratic Front was a revolution of the people but uniquely led by the youth. We understood that Soweto was not so much a *place* but a *condition*; a condition of oppression, exploitation, and marginalization, a condition of outrage, anger and despair; and that it was our duty to turn that into a condition of consciousness, of decision, and of resistance.

Again turning to Hamid Dabashi, we understood the Black Consciousness revolution in two ways. First, in the sense of recognizing what Iranian scholar Hamid Dabashi years later would give words to when he discusses the Arab Spring:[34] "What we are witnessing is a revolution against domestic tyranny and globalized disempowerment alike, now jointly challenged beyond the entrapment of postcolonial ideologies." It is no longer to be understood in the Marxian sense, as a single cataclysmic event.[35] These revolutions, including the revolution that ended formal and legal apartheid in South Africa, have not yet run their course. What we are witnessing in the Arab and Muslim world, in Palestine, Chile, and South Africa is "the unfolding of an open-ended revolt, the conjugation of a new revolutionary language and practice, predicated on a reading of reality that is an *opera aperta*—an 'open work' . . . a self-propelling hermeneutics that mobilizes a constellation of suggestions yet to be fully assayed."[36]

---

33. Steve Biko's intimate friend, spiritual guide, and struggle comrade, Fr. Aeldred Stubbs, had it right when he tells of his return from England to Soweto, and his presence in Soweto on June 16, "when the killings of students . . . marked yet another irreversible step on the road to freedom. Returning to Johannesburg on July 1 one could only find words in W. B. Yeats to describe the revolution in the atmosphere: 'All, all is utterly changed . . . / A terrible beauty is born . . .'" See Stubbs, "Martyr of Hope: A Personal Memoir," in Biko, *I Write What I Like*, 175–244. The quote is on 219.

34. See Dabashi, *Arab Spring*, 2, 3.

35. See Dabashi, *Arab Spring*, 5, 6: "Revolution in the sense of a radical and sudden shift of political power with an accompanying social and economic restructuring of society—one defiant class violently and conclusively overcoming another—is not what we are witnessing here, or not quite yet. There is a deep-rooted economic and social malaise in all these societies. . . No single angle of vision—economic, social, political, or cultural—would reveal the totality (and yet inconclusive disposition) of these massive social uprisings. Instead of denying these insurgencies the term 'revolution,' we are now forced to reconsider the concept and understand it anew . . . The longer these revolutions take to unfold, the more enduring, grassroots-based, and definitive will be their emotive, symbolic, and institutional consequences."

36. See Dabashi, *Arab Spring*, 230. See also Boesak, *Kairos, Crisis, and Global Apartheid*, 19–20.

It is something new, still unfolding and open to the future. As we have seen, Dabashi calls that "delayed defiance."

It is not delayed in the sense of postponement, I think, but rather in the sense of alert political judgement and strategic engagement. It is a kind of revolutionary vigilance. It will unfold in phases, always cognizant of the endless abilities of existing power structures and realities to adapt and mutate, to adopt new strategies, to offer meaningless reforms as response to pressure, to co-opt and bribe, to neutralize and eliminate. "Significant in the new revolutions," Dabashi writes, "is the acute awareness that this is resistance against imperial power and might in all their global manifestations." One might consider it, Dabashi says, "a Palestinian intifada going global."[37]

That is exactly what we have seen since Soweto and the United Democratic Front, and now in the "delayed defiance" of countries such as Sudan, Algeria, Chile, Tunisia, and Haiti. We are seeing it again in Hong Kong, in the internationalized manifestations of the Black Lives Matter movement, and it is always present in Palestine. In South Africa, this revolution is such a delayed defiance, taking new shape in the new post-1994 situation.

Secondly, we understood that a genuine revolution was about fundamentally addressing and transforming systems of injustice, exploitation, and oppression into structures and systems of justice and dignity. We gradually came to understand that the issue was not just race, but also class. Over and above that, moreover, our understanding was shaped by what Martin Luther King Jr. called "a revolution of values."[38] The new revolutionary generation, King believed, will look at situations of oppression, injustice, exploitation, and exclusion, and will say, "This is not just." They will not only see this and say it; they will join the revolution of "the shirtless and barefoot" people, Fanon's "wretched of the earth" to create the "beloved community." For such "selfless revolutionaries" as Biko called them, people would be over profits, justice would be inclusive and compassionate, dignity would be irreplaceable. For them, martyrdom would not be sought, but sacrifices, if called for, would be gladly made, for we had heard Albert Luthuli: "The road to freedom is via the Cross."[39]

They would not ask what the people *need*, because they know that if we only work with what people needed, it is the powerful that determine and define those needs, as well as how, when, and to what measure to respond to them. They would rather ask what the people *deserved*. For if we ask what the people *deserve*, it is not their needs but their rights, not their needs, but their dignity, not their needs, but their full humanity that mattered, and that is what would determine our response. People need houses, but people *deserve* decent homes. People *need* to be paid for their work, but they *deserve* a decent, living wage. Children *need* schooling, but they *deserve* the kind of education that would equip them for the challenges of the modern world, to

---

37. Dabashi, *Arab Spring*, 6.
38. See King, "Beyond Vietnam," 215.
39. Luthuli, *Let My People Go!*, 239.

see, understand, and use the opportunities that a proper education brings. If we work with people's needs, we keep them needy, dependent, and powerless. But they know that, in the words of the 1966 statement by the National Committee of Negro Churchmen in the United States, "powerlessness breeds a race of beggars,"[40] and empowering people means letting the people make clear what they deserve.

That is why in the Black Consciousness movement, we did not merely speak of our ideal of a "non-racial, non-sexist, open democracy" as the slogan went. Our ideal was an open, nonracial, nonsexist, responsible, responsive, *and egalitarian* democracy.[41] The omission of that crucial word ("egalitarian") in the current slogan and understanding of what is called South Africa's "National Democratic Revolution" is not accidental.

Our revolution of values kept us keenly aware of the oppression of our people, but did not embitter us so that we created space even for our oppressors to join the struggle for freedom. We took Paulo Freire seriously when he reminded us of the "historic obligation of the oppressed: to free the oppressed as well as the oppressor."[42] So we built the United Democratic Front that crossed all barriers of race, class, color, culture, and religion. It became the largest, nonviolent, militant, nonracial movement in the history of our struggle.

Back in 1998, when we already knew about the corruption that dogged the arms deal scandal, the moral, political, and socio-economic consequences of which are haunting us today still, Thabo Mbeki spoke a truth that was perhaps more prophetic than he knew, more brutally honest than he had meant to, leaving the ANC, and all the rest of us, no avenue of blame or escape:

> The thieves and their accomplices, the givers of the bribes and the recipients are as African as you and I. We are the corrupter and the harlot who act together to demean our Continent and ourselves.[43]

What South Africa is going through at the moment is beyond disheartening. The Zondo Commission[44] is not only lifting the veil on the kind of corruption the depths

---

40. The statement appeared as an advertisement in *The New York Times*, July 31, 1966. See episcopalarchives.org/church-awakens/files/original/58857a3c. Coming as it did three years before the publication of James Cone's groundbreaking work, *Black Theology and Black Power*, the importance of this statement within the context of those times can hardly be overstated. It certainly set the context for Cone's work and it permanently and irrevocably changed the debates on Black power, power, and powerlessness within church and society and had immediate impact on black politics globally and on the ecumenical discourse on these matters. Biko appropriates a key phrase from this statement, "Powerlessness breeds a race of beggars"; see Biko, *I Write What I Like*, 86.

41. See Biko, *I Write What I Like*, 170.

42. See Freire, *Pedagogy of the Oppressed*. See the discussion within the present South African context in Boesak, *Pharaohs on Both Sides*, ch. 5.

43. See Mbeki, "African Renaissance Statement of Deputy President Thabo Mbeki."

44. The Zondo Commission, appointed by President Cyril Ramaphosa and presided over by Judge Raymond Zindo, is a commission of inquiry into state corruption, what is called "state capture" in South Africa.

of which we could not begin to imagine, it is also ripping into our soul in ways we were never prepared for. As a company, Bosassa may have changed its name,[45] but the very word has now indelibly and unforgettably entered the lexicon of global scandals. Bosassa is the symbol of what happens when an organization forgets that nobility may be inherited, but trustworthiness has to be earned, and sacrifice has to be respected. That arrogance and hubris are never good substitutes for the integrity, decency, and honesty that calls forth the love of the people. Bosassa is the weeds that grow on the grave of the nobility of our struggle.

I should perhaps pause here to make clear that I do not mean an "incomplete revolution" to be the opposite of a "perfect" revolution. I do not agree with orthodox neo-Calvinism's idea that "total depravity" is the eternal human condition, but I do believe in humanity's sinful *condition*. For me, as a Christian, that means that unless we surrender to Christ and the redemptive power of the Holy Spirit, we will remain prisoners of that condition. To recall our earlier discussion: Black theology fully understands the Apostle Paul's desperate cry as he reflects on "the sin that dwells within me," that drives him to ignore the "good I want to do" and rather drives him to do the evil he does not want to do. "Oh wretched man that I am! Who shall rescue me from this body of death?" (Rom 7:19, 20, 24). Human beings' tendencies towards selfishness, self-centeredness, and self-delusion, the blindness that cannot see the self-destruction in how the elevation of self-interest endangers the common good, make the "perfect revolution" as impossible as the "perfect world."

However, Christians who consider themselves followers of Jesus of Nazareth, and empowered by God's Holy Spirit know that we are called, in the words of the Belhar Confession, "to stand where God stands," namely *with* the poor, the defenseless, the oppressed and the disinherited, and *against* any form of injustice, because that is what Jesus came to do. So we shall not stop striving and working towards that world of love, justice, equality and peace, that world, in the words of the prophet Isaiah, where "justice and peace shall embrace." German theologian Jürgen Moltmann saw it well:

> As a social concept, equality means justice. As a humanitarian concept, equality means solidarity. As a Christian concept, equality means love. Either we shall create a world of social justice, human solidarity and Christian love, or this world will perish through the oppression of people by people, through a-social egotism, and through the destruction of the future in the interest of short-term, present-day profits.[46]

---

45. It is now called African Global Operations. As a private company it was the recipient of countless lucrative contracts, tenders and deals through which, many witnesses have alleged, many politicians, top civil servants and cabinet ministers benefited and fraudulently enriched themselves. As of this writing, the work of the commission continues, and one would have to wait and see whether any criminal actions will follow.

46. See Moltmann, *God for a Secular Society*, 130–131.

Brazilian liberation theologian Rubem Alves is correct when he states, "What drives us is not the belief in the possibility of a perfect society, but rather the belief in the non-necessity of this imperfect order."[47] It is the absolute dissatisfaction with our situation perpetually being "almost as of yesterday." It is a dissatisfaction fueled by righteous anger because we know that it is the incompleteness in which the powerful and privileged prosper, but the poor and the oppressed, the defenseless and the vulnerable, the weak and the powerless are cast aside and left behind. It is the continual striving toward wholeness, the openness to learning and unlearning, towards a more whole becoming, perhaps what Biko meant when he talked about our striving towards our "envisioned self."[48]

South Africa has surpassed Brazil and is now the country with the deepest social and economic inequality on earth. The rich/poor gap is now wider than in the days of apartheid. That means the future of our country, all our people, especially our youth, is captured by yesterday. For them, there might be no tomorrow. Young South Africans know this and their judgement is relentless: "From this perspective," says Siya Kumalo, "the new South Africa is old South Africa 2.0, or as Conrad Koch describes the New South Africa's economy, 'apartheid without the guilt.'"[49] That is concisely, and precisely put. "Even 26 years into democracy," writes Unisa scholar Boitumelo Senokoane in an article dealing with the effects of the coronavirus on the poor in South Africa, "we remain unready to govern." After all, he says,

> governance in the context of poverty involves abolishment of poverty, or at least its reduction. The rich continue to get richer while the poor continue to be poor . . . Poverty is a scandal . . . Poverty destroys the soul.[50]

Senokoane utters a dire warning when he quotes eighteenth-century French philosopher Jean Jacques Rousseau: "When the people have nothing to eat, they will eat the rich." Even though he adds a qualifier by saying that this is not his wish, the warning nonetheless stands.

The Jerusalem of Jesus's Day

What, through the work of various commissions of inquiry is being revealed as the real "state of the nation," are the consequences of untrammeled greed and a deep-seated corruption at every level of government and in the private sphere; the abysmal mismanagement of precious state resources, to say nothing of the waste of even more precious human resources. The callousness of officials whom we had elected and in whom we had invested our power to govern. The disdain with which our democratic

---

47. Cited in Bonino, *Toward a Christian Political Ethics*, 90.
48. Biko, *I Write What I Like*, 53, 74, 101.
49. Khumalo, *You Have to Be Gay*, 215–16.
50. See Senokoane, "Poor Are Cut Off from Economic Activity."

dreams and ideals have been treated is matched only by the disdain with which the hopes of the poor, the aspirations of our children and the sacrifices of our people have been treated by those in power. The very word "Bosassa" is now much more than just the symbol of the myriad ways in which we have lost our direction.

But even more than that: what we have witnessed during the month of September 2019 has powerfully focused our minds on the tragic truth that if we even believe in Ubuntu we are a people seriously in need of Ubuntu. The waves of xenophobic violence and criminal vigilantism exposed not just the inadequacies of our intelligence and police services. It also exposed the dysfunctionality of our politics and the inefficaciousness of our politicians. As a caller on an afternoon radio program put it, it shows how impossible we have made it for ourselves, for how can government gather proper intelligence about lurking dangers such as these when all intelligence energy is spent on spying on each other, of watching factions, of plotting against each other, of covering up their own misdeeds while plotting to expose those of the enemy within, abandoning the interests of the nation for the self-destructive self-interests of factionalism?

So in one, single week we were reminded how close we always are to the horrific temptations of 2008: our people necklacing our brothers and sisters from other countries, as they did in Kathlehong to thirty-five-year-old Isaac Sithole. His murderers left his burnt-out body in the street for his widow to weep over while leaving us wondering how we could ever have had the nerve to defend necklacing as an instrument of liberation, how we could have ever made peace with violence as a method of political blackmail, as we did in the early 1990s. Can we ever close that door, now that we have opened it?

Since 1994, we have rubbed our Ubuntu-ness in Africa's face. We have preened and basked in the admiration of the world because we were the ones who knew what "reconciliation" meant. We deemed ourselves fit to teach other nations from Rwanda to Ireland to Serbia how it worked and how they should follow our example. We have so much to learn still, and the first seems to be a lesson in humility. The second is to learn to embrace the painful healing of honest self-critical reflection as necessary for our growth toward our envisioned self, for our ability to give South Africa and the world a human face.

But even more: the spate of unspeakable violence unleashed upon young girls and women has stunned the country, shaken our complacency, drowned us in shame. Just after August, it almost looks as if there are men who want to show their anger that we should even dare to have such a thing as Women's Month, calling attention to gender injustices, gender inequality, and gender-based violence, while calling into question the kind of manhood they seem murderously bent on preserving. It is as if they are determined to spit in the face of women, daring them to fight back. But in spitting in the face of women, they are spitting in the face of the country and all our people. They are spitting in the face of God. So besides all else, it has huge moral dimensions.

Politically too, that September's gender-based violence has brought us to yet another point of decision. What kind of people are we? After all, gender-based violence has been a daily occurrence in our communities for ages. And it was, and still is, aided and abetted by too many churches and their ideologized theologies of baptized bigotry, sacralized patriarchalism, and sanctified homophobia. It is also aided and abetted by our complacency, our silence, and our infinite ability to fail the very basics of our own constitutional righteousness.

This is a moment we, the people of South Africa, cannot walk away from. Our righteous outrage must outdo, outdistance, and outrun the toxic, destructive anger of those men. At the very least, we must not only come to understand the fear of women; we must come to match the anger of women. As men, we must also understand that that fear is for *us*, that that anger is directed toward *us*. It is not the women who must prove themselves not fearful or innocent; it is men who must prove themselves not dangerous, not predatory, not guilty. If we cannot do this, as a people we will have forfeited the right to claim to be a people striving toward reconciled community; as a nation, we will have forfeited the right to raise our voice or cast our vote in international forums on human rights. As a country, we would rightly be branded not a "rainbow place of hope," but a vacuous space for meaningless sloganeering, mindless pietistic prattle, and mindboggling hypocrisy.

Inasmuch as we have failed to make South Africa a safe place for girl children and women, we have failed to make South Africa a safe place for democracy, for integrity, dignity, and decency. Those are the signs of an incomplete revolution.

In our country gender-based violence is a pandemic. In 2013, when news of the horrific rapes in India spread shock, nausea, and anger across the world, in the same time span South African women had been brutalized by men in the same horrific crime: *nine-thousand rapes in seven weeks*, including the torture, horrifying rape *with a steel pipe*, and murder of seventeen-year-old Anene Booysen. South African men rape seventy-five-year old grandmothers as well as three-year-old children. September has seen the killing that has caused the Uyinene hashtag to go viral and sweep the nation. And that is right. But that young UCT student was not the only one to suffer violence in that same week. The boxing champion Leighandre Jegels disappeared and was killed, and so were at least five other young girls, one only twelve years old. In that same week, a man in Athlone, just around the corner from where I live, raped a one-year-old baby. In our schools, our daughters are subjected to sexual violence on a scale that is shocking. As a country, we should ponder and respond to the question: If we men are not shamed into action by that statistic, what on earth will it take?

As I write this, the coronavirus is raging across the earth, threatening the total structure of the global capitalist systems, exposing the incompetence of governments who constantly brag how "great" they are, taking human lives by the hundreds. The virus has brought forth calls for human solidarity, for consideration of others, for forging bonds of togetherness even though "social distancing" is now part of the modes of survival.

Once again, however, it emerges that the feelings of shared vulnerability do not include women. University of San Francisco scholar Rebecca Gordon's question has quickly become a reality. Writing on the coronavirus and its impact on especially women, she asks, "Are you safer outside risking coronavirus, or inside with a bored, angry male partner?"[51] Almost immediately, we hear from China, the country where the virus first took hold, that gender-based violence has risen alarmingly, that the lockdown of neighborhoods and sometimes whole cities have made violence against women and children easier. An anti-domestic violence organization reports that gender-based violence cases are triple those for the same month in 2019. "According to our statistics, 90% of the (recent) causes of violence are related to the COVID-19 epidemic."[52] Even in a crisis of these proportions, the women and the children must bear a double burden, laid upon them not by God or circumstances, but by men.

The United Nations now speaks of the exponential growth of gender-based violence with the rise of COVID-19 as a "shadow pandemic":

> UNHCR, the United Nations' refugee agency, notes that even before the COVID-19 pandemic, an estimated one in three women had experienced physical or sexual abuse. Confinement, lockdowns, and quarantines coupled with deteriorating socioeconomic conditions have now created a perfect storm. "These factors significantly increase the risks of intimate partner violence, with refugees, internally displaced and stateless persons among the most vulnerable," according to the agency. But the "shadow pandemic" of violence against girls and women extends far beyond refugees and displaced war victims, with reports of domestic violence having increased by 30% in France, while calls to help lines have jumped 30% in Cyprus and 33% in Singapore.[53]

I discuss the question of South Africa and our LGBTQI community elsewhere,[54] but here it is appropriate to comment on the contradictions that strain South African society. The Constitution guarantees equal rights and equal protection under the law for LGBTQI persons, but it seems that as a society we are drifting further and further away from the ethos of Ubuntu our Constitution aspires to and which South Africans almost routinely claim as essential to our world view and way of life.[55]

"Our voting majority is homophobic," laments Siya Kumalo, and it is exacerbated by an African religious and political leadership who have allowed themselves to be bamboozled and bribed by the American Christian Right who bring with them

   51. Gordon, "Future May Be Feminine, but the Pandemic Is Patriarchal."
   52. See Zhang Wanqing, "Domestic Violence Cases Surge." On Saturday, March 3, SABC evening news reported the same rise in domestic violence for South Africa.
   53. See Turse, "'Exceptionally Dire.'"
   54. See Boesak, *Kairos, Crisis, and Global Apartheid*, ch. 4.
   55. See the discussion in Boesak, *Pharaohs on Both Sides*, ch. 4.

> An anti-gay craze that subverts democracy by centering accountability around anti-gay, anti-feminist principles that prop up patriarchal leaders who otherwise don't have a political leg to stand on.[56]

As a result, this young, gay, Christian activist has no confidence in politicians who "expediently vacillate on gay rights depending on the political climate." It is a vacillation that "counterfeits the balancing act needed by events outside people's bedrooms like economic upheavals, evolving treaties and climate change." They are all fundamentally untrustworthy, because

> like typical politicians, they'll all shift toward acceptance at the first sign that homophobia is costing them votes because politics is easy and gay lives are more dispensable than the paper their apology statements will be printed on.[57]

Meanwhile, the assaults on LGBTQI persons continue to rise. Khumalo argues, and who can really gainsay him,

> When "othering" and discrimination are normal, dictators rise on the back of scapegoating. It's how Hitler did it . . . When they surrender scapegoats on the altar of . . . homophobia they open the collective up for violation . . . We are "state captured" by actual enemies, becoming the Jerusalem of Jesus' day. We open our coffers and hand over our own for crucifixion until there is practically no one left for foreign empires to decimate.[58]

Hence, what follows should come as no surprise. In 2011, since the murder and alleged gang rape of a lesbian activist, Noxolo Nogwaza, in Kwa Thema, Erkuhuleni, human rights activists have warned of an "epidemic" of brutal homophobic attacks in South Africa. Noxolo was a victim of a seemingly particularly South African hate crime called "corrective rape." It is an increasingly common crime, through which gangs of young men, often Christians, rape lesbians in order to "turn" them straight, or to "cure" them of their "deviant" sexual orientation. Noxolo's head was disfigured through stoning, indeed suggesting a religious motivation (and justification), and she was stabbed several times with glass from broken beer bottles.[59] But here is the true vulgarity of this situation: four years later, in 2015, her killers are still free. By 2015, at least eighteen LGBTQI persons (as far as we know) have since been murdered. Homophobia and transphobia remain so prevalent throughout South African society, writes human rights activist Tracy Doig, that LGBTQI people "don't even recognize taunts and insults as a form of violence against them."[60]

56. See Khumalo, *You Have to Be Gay*, 263–64.
57. Khumalo, *You Have to Be Gay*, 264.
58. Khumalo, *You Have to Be Gay*, 261, 262.
59. See Smith, "South Africa gay rights activists warn of homophobic attacks after murder."
60. See Doig, "Four Years Later." In Cape Town, the case of the killers of a young lesbian woman, Zoliswa Nkonyane from Khayelistha township, took six years to bring convictions, after the case had been postponed forty times.

Unless LGBTQI persons find complete, equal, and unconditional acceptance, unless women and children experience our country, its public spaces, private spaces, and places of worship as places of safety; and as long as our police services and court system act as if the lives of LGBTQI persons do not matter and their deaths do not diminish us as a people; and as long as we make "othering" our instinctive body armor, we will have an incomplete revolution. South African politicians speak proudly of our "National Democratic Revolution." But what kind of revolution is it that remind LGBTQI persons, women, young people, and the poor of "Jerusalem in Jesus's day"?

Seduced by Rainbow-nationism

As I write, the country is convulsing with anger at former president F. W. De Klerk, who, in an interview with the South African Broadcasting Corporation, made the statement that apartheid might well have been wrong, but it was not, as people claimed, a "crime against humanity." De Klerk, somewhat stunned by the angry backlash, ultimately succumbed to the pressure and issued a patently non-heartfelt apology, "an attempt," reported the BBC, "to calm a fortnight of increasingly furious debate" a full two weeks later.[61]

"At first," reports the BBC, "South Africa seemed to shrug" until the opening of Parliament and the EFF's Julius Malema's outburst on the floor. To the surprise of some, I shared De Klerk's surprise at the angry reaction of so many, overwhelmingly black South Africans. Here is my reasoning. Right from the start, right after he received the Nobel Peace Prize along with Nelson Mandela, F. W. De Klerk had refused to offer more than a qualified apology for apartheid. I am not even mentioning asking forgiveness from South Africa's oppressed people for the crime against humanity whites had perpetrated against the indigenous peoples of this land for over three-hundred-and-fifty years. So this latest episode should have come as no surprise. In part, this is pure, plain, and simple white arrogance; in part, it is denial; in part, it is that incessant need to take on the cloak of victimhood because it is the surest form of self-defense, and the best bulwark against genuine change and transformation.

But it is also we, the oppressed people of South Africa, who had told ourselves that true reconciliation is too costly, too high a bar to set. In consequence, we offered white South Africans a cheap reconciliation: one without contrition, without remorse, without repentance, without justice, without restoration. We accepted the colonialist view of the land question, and hid those ugly realities within the most prized outcome of the negotiated settlement: the Constitution. Then we sacralized the Constitution by embedding it in the language of reconciliation, Ubuntu, and human rights, thereby making the issue of stolen land and the restoration of that land an almost untouchable matter.[62] If it were not for the sometimes-irreverent insistence of a new revolutionary

---

61. See "FW de Klerk and the South African row over apartheid and crimes against humanity."
62. So, again not surprisingly, we let it slide when in 2017 (on Sikita Makwetla's SABC radio

generation, we would not now have those crucial debates about the land, our historic dispossession, and our right to reclaim it. So why are we surprised at F. W. De Klerk? De Klerk is the one who should be surprised at our reaction to his latest—and only his latest—outrage since he has been saying this for a long time. We gave him permission by offering a reconciliation that was far more sensitive to the desires of white South Africans, and to the agreements reached in those pre-negotiation secret talks, than to the historical, spiritual, economic, and political claims of Black oppressed people.

So let me summarize my argument.[63] I believe that unless reconciliation is radical, real, and revolutionary, it is not true reconciliation. As I understand biblical reconciliation, it is not possible without:

- Acknowledging the alienation and the reasons for it that now calls for reconciliation;
- Confronting the evil of the past and present, including the evil within ourselves that refuses to acknowledge the evil of the past and present because it benefits us;
- Remorse and repentance;
- Forgiveness being asked for given;
- Justice;
- Finally, reconciliation, which is possible only among equals.

Since 2005, in several publications, I have discussed some or other aspect of reconciliation. I have paid special attention to De Klerk and his continued justifications of apartheid, stating that apartheid was not morally reprehensible, because it was a policy with good intentions for black people. I have also worked explicitly with the story of Zacchaeus, one of Rome's chief tax collectors in the province of Galilee in the

---

afternoon show, December 21, 2017), Omri van Zyl, CEO of Agri South Africa, argued that land restitution is "not a moral issue. It is an economic issue, because a farm is an economic unit." In doing so, he neatly separates "the land" from agri-business, as well as the colonial-era theft of land from historical reality. The argument also ignores the deliberate "legitimizing" of that land theft through successive acts of a fraudulent parliament built on racialist exclusion, disempowerment, and silencing. So now, seen only as a "farm," an economic enterprise and nothing more, "the land" about which whites, especially Afrikaners, have always waxed so lyrically as being part of their "Boer" identity, becomes nothing more than "a farm" as economic entity, detached from any notions of belonging and emotional rootedness. He also separates it from any moral responsibility, including the responsibility for restitution. That means that blacks have no claim on the land historically, in the sense of identity, or rootedness, or belonging. Now downgraded to mere romanticism, these are no longer valid notions of human existence so central to African life. This is as clearly an apartheid, "for blacks only" argument as one can get. It is an act of complete and total alienation and renewed dispossession, which, if allowed to stand, offers no recourse or recompense, except a helpless kind of remembering in the African mind, which is nothing but spiritual and political surrender. For whites, it's the opposite. See the strong romantic, ethno-patriotic, militant lyrics of Anton Myburgh's song, well-loved among Afrikaans-speaking whites, "Die Boer en Sy Roer" ("The Farmer and His Gun").

63. See Boesak, *Tenderness of Conscience*, ch. 4; Boesak, *Running with Horses*; Boesak, *Pharaohs on Both Sides*, especially chs. 4, 5, 6.

Gospel of Luke, and how important that story is for understanding reconciliation, not merely for those who take the Bible seriously, but because the story's implications for *political reconciliation* are so vital.

Zacchaeus, the biblical story tells us, not only received his rewards from the Roman authorities for collecting taxes, but also a percentage of whatever his agents collected. If tax collectors in general were hated by the people, Zacchaeus, as chief tax collector, was hated most of all. I believe that Zacchaeus chose that tree to wait for Jesus, not so much because he was short in stature, but because being in a tree was the safest spot for him given how much he was hated by that hostile crowd, and because of his total alienation from the people. In response to Jesus's announcement of sharing a meal with Zacchaeus and his family, this reviled man, shows us what true reconciliation is. I draw ten lessons from this story in illustration of what I mean by radical, real, and revolutionary reconciliation.

First, Zacchaeus acknowledged his personal complicity in and benefit from a system of oppressing others. Zacchaeus did not try and defend himself by arguing that he had to make a living, that this was merely his job, or that he had a family to look after. He knew that he unjustly benefited from systematized oppression and suffering.

Second, reconciliation requires both acknowledgement of guilt and remorse for that oppression. It also requires acknowledging that the victim has a right to restitution. It has nothing to do with my magnanimity, it is all about justice. It is acknowledging my victim's pain as a result of what I have done and making it right with acts of justice.

Third, reconciliation is not merely spiritual, it calls for reparation and restitution—real and tangible gains for the victims of oppression. Pledging to give half of his possessions to the poor and pay back four fold whatever he had stolen was not a symbolic gesture. It was an act of reparation and restitution required in order to make repentance result in justice, rather than merely an assuagement of guilt. Without restitution, reconciliation is not possible.

Fourth, Zacchaeus shows that there can be no reconciliation without equality. By divesting himself of half of his wealth and restoring four times whatever he had stolen from what remained Zacchaeus removed himself from the exclusive club of the wealthy in Jericho and became a man of the people.

Fifth, repentance and reconciliation involves more than restoring our broken relationships with God. It is also about restoring broken relationships with others, those whom we have damaged with our arrogance, greed, violence, and lust for power and domination.

Sixth, Zacchaeus did not treat this moment as just between him and Jesus, just as his sin was not just between him and God. Unlike David, in Psalm 51:4, "Against you, and you alone have I sinned" omitting his sins against Bathsheba and Uriah, treating them as not worthy of his repentance and remorse, Zacchaeus publicly acknowledged his sin against the people he had victimized, robbed, and oppressed. He backed his remorse by his public expression and commitment to restoration with those he had harmed by his sin.

Seventh, uncovering the sin, showing remorse, making restitution, and restoring relationships with deeds of compassionate justice makes clear that then, and only then, is reconciliation complete, right, sustainable, and radical, because it becomes transformational. That is its salvific power.

Eighth, genuine reconciliation not only results in personal salvation but brings salvation for Zacchaeus *and his house*. Not only Zacchaeus, but also his children benefited from the wealth generated by systemic oppression. So not only Zacchaeus, but also his children were released from the curse of generational guilt and shame that comes with exploitative, systematic oppressive relationships.

Ninth, repentance and reconciliation impelled Zacchaeus to confront his life of self-aggrandizement as a functionary of Roman imperialism and convert to a value system focused on divine justice rather than on imperial dictates and personal perks. This is what Martin Luther King Jr. meant when he spoke of the need for a "a radical revolution of values."

Tenth, genuine reconciliation produces a new identity. Reconciliation changed Zacchaeus from being a hated "chief tax collector" to being a "son of Abraham." Reconciliation not only changes the way we feel. It transforms us into agents of God's love, God's justice, and God's reconciliation. It changes the way we live. So is reconciliation an option? No, it is not an option, it is a reality without which the church cannot be the Church of Jesus Christ and the world cannot be God's world. And it is real, because it is radical and revolutionary; it is radical and revolutionary, because it is the gospel.

I argued then that the main problem with South Africa's reconciliation process is that we have left Zacchaeus "sitting in the tree." In other words, we have learnt nothing from him. We have shunned this biblical model of radical reconciliation as "excessive spiritualization," setting the bar too high, running toward a cheap, shallow reconciliation for fear of "pathologizing the nation" with unrealistic demands.[64] In 2012, after his infamous interview with CNN's Christiane Amanpour, Elna Boesak wrote an article responding to De Klerk's refusal to acknowledge the criminal nature of apartheid. There are things, she told De Klerk, that might be forgiveable, but they are never excusable.[65] In other words, ask for forgiveness, but don't try to offer excuses for apartheid.

If De Klerk took reconciliation seriously, he would have worked assiduously to make sure all these things were in place and he would have given leadership to whites to do the same. But he did not then and he does not now. He refuses to acknowledge

---

64. See my engagement with Jakes Gerwel, who raises the issue of "pathologizing the nation," in Boesak, *Tenderness of Conscience*, ch. 4.

65. See E. Boesak, "Time for Apartheid's Truth to Be Spoken." Boesak sounds a warning more valid today than ever: "A nation lost in the storm raging in the wilderness between alienation and reconciliation, will not survive."

that apartheid was an unbelievably cruel, oppressive, and exploitative system and a crime against humanity. He refuses to repent, to show any kind of remorse. He is not interested in dismantling the systems of power and privilege he helped to maintain and benefited from. Therefore, he cannot bring himself, even now, to help South Africa build new structures of justice that would give dignity to our people and redress the wrongs of the past. Perhaps the deepest truth, and I cannot stress that enough, is that De Klerk refuses reconciliation because he cannot bring himself to see black people as his equals. But again, we have known this for a long time now.

In that CNN interview I referred to above, De Klerk once again publicly defended apartheid, the Bantustans, the apartheid legal system, and the apartheid courts which found Mandela guilty of treason.[66]

On Amanpour's insistent questioning, De Klerk refused to acknowledge that apartheid was morally wrong and that he has anything to apologize for. Recalling what he did present as an apology, De Klerk went on to say, "What I haven't apologized for is the original concept of seeking to bring justice to all South Africans through the concept of nation states." This, he admits, "failed." He advances three reasons:

a. because whites wanted to keep too much land for themselves;
b. because whites and blacks became economically integrated; and
c. because the majority of blacks said that "this is not how we want our rights."

Asked twice whether he thought apartheid was morally repugnant, De Klerk responded, "I can only say in a qualified way. Inasmuch as it trampled human rights it was, and remains, morally reprehensible." But originally, in its pure form, De Klerk insists, apartheid was not wrong; it was simply "seeking to bring justice to all South Africans." Note that "qualified" and the "inasmuch as." In reality in De Klerk's view, that "inasmuch" was not very much at all, certainly not if he regards it excusable. In 2012, there was no outrage, no waves of national indignation, no sense of wounded expectations.

In the CNN interview, De Klerk speaks as if the problem was "white people wanting too much land," not at all giving a thought to what was the heart of colonialism and apartheid: dispossession, land theft, disenfranchisement, genocide, and brutal oppression. In De Klerk's view, the fact that apartheid was well-meant but did not "work" makes its failure a matter of mere practicalities, at most perhaps a political miscalculation; not because it was morally repugnant, socially perverted, and politically unsustainable, let alone sinful and evil. Once having set such a bad example for whites in South Africa, holding up apartheid as morally acceptable, but practically hampered, it became his mantra: "Apartheid would have worked, if . . ." This is why so

---

66. Burke, "Under Fire, South Africa's former president repudiates apartheid." Clearly Mr. Burke's understanding of "repudiation" is not the same as mine. What is clear here, in my view, is not De Klerk's willingness to repudiate apartheid, even under pressure, but rather his refusal to repudiate apartheid as morally reprehensible and a crime against humanity.

many have lost hope in our reconciliation process. His is not the language of reconciliation. It is the language of deception, justification, and mortification.

In the February 2020 SABC interview, De Klerk simply reiterates what he has stated as his firm beliefs since 1994. So one would have to ask the question: Why the outrage? De Klerk has been saying this, encouraging white South Africans to feel this way, for as long as we can remember. But the point is: seduced by our ideology of rainbow-nationism, we allowed him to. We gave him permission to think that way and say it out loud. We offered white people forgiveness that they saw no need or reason to ask for. So it's not just white arrogance and unrepented racism that are to blame. *We* must take responsibility for the De Klerks of this world. It is black leadership who invited him to parliament. *We* gave him honor and respect, even when we already heard him say these things. We know better. We cannot plead innocence.

More than forty years ago, and following James Baldwin, I made the point that in these matters it is the innocence which constitutes the crime.[67] So the ultimate question becomes: Which crime weighs more? The crime of denying the crime or the crime of enabling, protecting, and elevating the criminal? The truth South Africa has tried to run away from for twenty-five years is this: unless we do speak truth to ourselves in this matter, we cannot speak truth to the likes of De Klerk. Until we do, we are not the rainbow nation we imagine ourselves to be, but rather the nation "lost in the raging storms in the wilderness between alienation and reconciliation." Unless we embrace this truth, our outrage and protests will be no more than another form of begging.

Tomorrow's Children

Christians in the struggle see social justice as the "essential truth of the struggle." They find themselves "in the grip of this truth *and cannot but witness to it*" wrote India's M. M. Thomas.[68] Being in the grip of that essential truth is embracing the restlessness that longs for a different world, a new humanity, a recreated tomorrow. This is the heart of it: Christians choose to join the struggle because they join God in God's struggle for justice and dignity, for the humanization of the world. It is embracing the restlessness that longs for a different world, a new humanity, a recreated tomorrow.

It is Dietrich Bonhoeffer's stubborn, provocative, defiant hope as he writes from the prison that he would not leave alive:

> There are people who regard it as frivolous, and some Christians think it impious for anyone to hope and prepare for a better future. They think that the meaning of present events is chaos, disorder, and catastrophe; and in resignation or pious escapism they surrender all responsibility for reconstruction and

---

67. See "Introduction" in Boesak, *Farewell to Innocence*.
68. See Thomas and McCaughey, *Christian in the World Struggle*, 39, 40.

for future generations. It may be that the day of judgment will dawn tomorrow; in that case, we shall gladly stop working for a better future. But not before.[69]

It means, paraphrasing Brazilian liberation theologian Rubem Alves, having the imagination and creativity to work for the rebirth of the future, a rebirth of the dreams, ideals and hopes others have abandoned or sold out, but too many had believed in, fought for, sacrificed for, given their lives for. It means stubbornly clinging to the possibility of making that hopeful, just, and peaceable tomorrow a reality. That, Alves says, frees us from the shackles and enslavements of yesterday and makes each one of us, as the hopeful title of his book proclaims, "tomorrow's child."

Despite the pain of disappointments, disillusionments, bewilderments, and betrayals, the revolution of values retains its grip. So Alves writes,

> If ours is not the harvest season, it may well be a time for sowing . . . In spite of—and because—our tall trees have been cut down, our air polluted with fear, and our soil turned into a heap of refuse, a new seed must be planted: the seed of our highest hope.[70]

In a first writing, I came to this point on April 4, 2020, fifty-two years since Martin Luther King Jr.'s murder. Now it is just a few months later, and the United States is burning from coast to coast. The anger at the continuous lynching of black people at the hands of the police, the continuing smugness of white power, white supremacy, and white privilege, the continuous perversion of justice as killers in uniform are either not prosecuted or set free by racists courts will no longer be denied. The continuous pseudo-innocence of whites who are more upset about the claims of racism than about cold-blooded murder can no longer be borne. The state-sanctioned violence, aided and abetted by a racist, neo-fascist in the White House, will no longer be countenanced. Where this will end, no one knows. But American racism has sown the wind; is the whirlwind upon us? Again, James Baldwin comes to mind:

> Everything now, we must assume, is in our hands; we have no right to assume otherwise. If we—and now I mean the relatively conscious whites and the relatively conscious blacks, who must, like lovers, insist on, or create, the consciousness of the others—do not falter in our duty now, we may be able, handful that we are, to end the racial nightmare, and achieve our country, and change the history of the world. If we do not now dare everything, the fulfillment of that prophecy, re-created from the Bible in song by a slave, is upon us: *God gave Noah the rainbow sign, No more water, the fire next time.*[71]

The global battle for dignity, freedom and justice now might very well be that fire Baldwin foresaw. But precisely because it is a fire, we ourselves will not emerge from

---

69. See Bonhoeffer, *Letters and Papers from Prison*, 15.
70. Alves, *Tomorrow's Child*, 197.
71. Baldwin, *Fire Next Time*, 105–106.

it unscathed. Martin King knew that, and so did Steve Biko. As the imperialist establishment wakes up to the fact that this revolution is a revolution of the people's awakening, they know that brutal force alone won't do it for them anymore. We should remember Nkrumah's warning, that imperialism's methods are "subtle and varied." So are the temptations. Co-option is a tried and tested method. We shall have to be wary, not only of politicians, but also of corporations who can, and will, offer us much more than a mere thirty pieces of silver. It is therefore no surprise at all to read how corporations in America are trying to buy their way into the heart of the revolution in order to dilute, distract, and control it. Writes *Jacobin's* Tom Gilpin:

> As they nimbly co-opted the language of the protests, corporate leaders offered up "solutions" to structural *racism that won't diminish managerial control or redistribute power in the workplace, meaning their proposals won't promote actual structural change of any sort*. With a few well-publicized contributions and some new rounds of diversity training, business elites hope to emerge from the present crisis with their privilege, and their profits, intact.

Gilpin illustrates:

> "We do not tolerate inequity, injustice or racism," McDonald's announced, with CEO Joe Erlinger insisting, "when any member of our McFamily hurts, we all hurt." To address this "hurt," McDonald's announced it will donate $1 million to the NAACP and the National Urban League and promised "tangible goals related to diversity." Many corporations made similar commitments. Amazon said it will give $10 million to "organizations supporting justice and equity," and Walmart pledged $100 million over five years to create "a new entity aimed at promoting economic opportunity and healthier living."[72]

But such contributions, publicized with much fanfare, Gilpin points out, in fact are chump change to these immensely powerful corporations. For Walmart, $100 million over the next five years represents less than 1/250 of one percent of the nearly $3 trillion in income it expects to rake in during that period. Put another way, its gift would translate to a mere $13 extra a year, for the next five years, to each Walmart employee in the United States. Enough has already been written about Amazon boss Jeff Bezos's insane wealth. Gilpin goes on,

> Yet Walmart, Amazon, and McDonald's don't pay livable wages. Benefits, when offered at all, are paltry (the lack of paid sick leave has become especially visible in COVID times). Schedules are unpredictable and job security tenuous. Working conditions are onerous. How much do black lives matter to America's leading corporations? Not enough to put any real money on the table.[73]

72. See Gilpin, "Corporations Are Claiming 'Black Lives Matter.'" Emphasis mine.
73. Gilpin, "Corporations Are Claiming 'Black Lives Matter.'"

What is really is necessary is not these "gifts" that simply serve to bolster the corporations' image and strengthen their efforts to exert control over the movement, if not to buy it outright. What they should do, and what the revolution should insist on, to begin with, is living wages, proper benefits, proper working conditions, and above all the right to unionize.

What is needed are not incremental changes or tinkered reforms to a capitalist system that is in fact not capable of reform. More, enough, or "real" money on the table will not do it. We need "a whole new system," Biko insisted, a whole new way of thinking about economics and our economic structures and policies, in order to create a nonracial, nonsexist, open, responsive, *egalitarian* democracy. The struggle is not just against white supremacy, white privilege, and racism. In this struggle the black, wealthy elites who owe their positions of privilege to the very racist systems they ostensibly rail against, are not our allies. And they, like their white partners, will fight to the death to keep it that way. From what I can see, for these privileged black elites, the revolution is indeed televised, as they sit, dispensing admonitions and exhortations from behind the microphone and in front of the cameras. They are not there in the streets to hear the abuse, to feel the blows, to see the guns up close, to run from tear gas and smoke bombs; dodge chemical grenades and police vehicles driven straight into the crowd. For them the revolution still is a photo op after the bleeding stops. The cycles of subjection Willie Lynch represents are all integral to the cycles of power, privilege, patriarchy, and profit. The establishment knows that; otherwise, the fire would not be necessary. It is for these reasons that Martin Luther King Jr. repeatedly, warned that "the next phase" would be much, much harder. The opposition would be fierce, relentless, and unspeakably violent. Let us be under no illusion that the fire would come only from us.

So perhaps it is fitting that we end with words from a man who has been through the flood and the fire, whose eyes have seen the tears, and the suffering and the blood. As they have seen the coming of the glory of the Lord. A man who, whether marching in the streets, speaking inspiration and courage into his people, or prophesying truth to the powers of this world; whether walking through the valley of death or standing on his mountaintop, truly was "tomorrow's child." The night before his death, he was giving his last address to the striking sanitation workers in Memphis, Tennessee, and their crowd of supporters, calling on the people not to get distracted, to keep those minds set on freedom. He focused on what mattered:

> Let's keep the issues where they are. The issue is justice . . . There are thirteen hundred of God's children here suffering, sometimes going hungry, going through dark and dreary nights wondering how this thing is going to come out. That's the issue . . . For when people get caught up with that which is right and they are willing to sacrifice for it, there is no stopping point short of victory.[74]

---

74. See King, *Radical King*, 265–76.

Martin Luther King Jr. was right, and this generation would be wise to heed him. The issues are still freedom, justice, dignity, equality, but the "thirteen hundred of God's children" in Memphis have now grown to millions across the world. They are oppressed, hungry, neglected, despised, excluded. Their lives do not matter. The dangers and threats are not metaphorical. The hunger they suffer is literal, devastating, and not only in places like refugee camps everywhere, or in war-torn Yemen, in Africa, and Latin America, but also in Europe, Britain, and the United States.[75] And it is like nothing we have ever seen before.[76] They are robbed in ways too numerous to mention by a system that is merciless in its exploitation and demonically masterful in its manipulation of disasters for profit. They are, infinitely more than the privileged in powerful and protected places, exposed to a pandemic unprecedented in our lifetime, and that in vast, shattering disproportions. They, more than anyone, know that the glib truism that the coronavirus pandemic is "an equalizer" is a cruel myth. The rich profit from it,[77] they are thrown the crumbs from the table. They die in grossly disproportionate numbers. They are "going through dark and dreary nights wondering how this thing is going to work out."[78] But they are in the streets in their global millions, marching, demanding, sacrificing; their eye on an entirely different, fundamentally transformed future of revolutionary hope, turning those dark dreary nights into bright beacons of hope. They refuse to be victims of scandalous political opportunism, of so-called leaders who are more concerned about obeisance to their wealthy, corporate donors than about the lives of the people. Adam Small need not fear: their protest is decidedly not a form of begging. They are demanding a fundamental transformation of societies across the world.

On the streets today are no longer just the thirteen hundred Memphis sanitation workers, although all on those streets would identify with their cause—they are interracial, inter-generational, inter-gender, interfaith, international crowds all "caught up with that which is right."[79] They are not facing the Memphis Police Department; they are confronting a national, militarized police transformed into an occupying force, complete with chemical grenades, smoke bombs, and tear gas; military assault rifles, military vehicles, and helicopters, brought over from the battlefields of Iraq and

---

75. Oxfam reports that 121 million people, or 12,000 people per day, could die from hunger linked to COVID-19 by the end of 2020. That is potentially more than could die from the disease. See Oxfam, "The Hunger Virus."

76. "The world has never faced a hunger emergency like this. It could double the number of people facing acute hunger to 265 million by the end of this year." See Dahir, "'Instead of Coronavirus, the Hunger Will Kill Us.'"

77. See Lerner, "Big Pharma Prepares to Profit." "As the new coronavirus spreads illness, death, and catastrophe around the world, virtually no economic sector has been spared from harm. Yet, amid the mayhem from the global pandemic, one industry is not only surviving, it is profiting handsomely." This is not even taking into account the way the "rescue packages" are benefiting big business and the bank over ordinary citizens and small businesses.

78. King, "I've Been to the Mountaintop," 268.

79. King, "I've Been to the Mountaintop," 268.

Afghanistan. They are no longer facing only dogs, water cannons, and policemen with "ordinary" rifles. They are facing white supremacists, using ordinary vehicles weaponized for murder, charging into protesting crowds with the intention to kill, with police in official police cars setting the example. It is the KKK without the hoods.[80] Their aim is not to change Mayor Henry Loeb's mind. It is not even to change a president's mind. Their aim is to bring down empire and all its workings. The sacrifices they are making are testimony to the world of their courage and determination.

It is Albert Luthuli's nonviolent militancy, Martin Luther King Jr.'s revolution of values, and Steve Biko's gifting of the human face come to life. So indeed, if they keep the focus where the issues are, "there is no stopping point short of victory."

---

80. See Johnson, "KKK in the PD." See also Philimon, "Police Departments Have 400-Year History of Anti-black Racism."

Bibliography

"The Accra Confession." In *Accra 2004: That All May Have Life in Fullness; World Alliance of Reformed Churches 24th General Council Proceedings*, 153–60. Geneva: WARC, 2005.

Adam, Heribert. "The Nazis of Africa: Apartheid as Holocaust." *Canadian Journal of African Studies/Revue Canadiens des Études Africaines* 31 (1997) 364–70.

African Monitor Poverty Report. Cape Town: African Monitor, 2010.

"Saudi Arabia Criticised for 48 Beheadings in Four Months of 2018." *The Guardian*, April 26, 2018.

Alexander, Michelle. *The New Jim Crow: Mass Incarceration in the Age of Colorblindness*. New York: New Press, 2010.

Ali, Tariq. *The Obama Syndrome: Surrender at Home, War Abroad*. London: Verso, 2010.

Allen, James. *Without Sanctuary: Lynching Photography in America*. Santa Fe: Twin Palms, 2000.

Alleyne, Kenneth. "How Covid-19 Is a Perfect Storm for Black Americans." *The Washington Post*, April 27, 2020.

Alves, Rubem. *Tomorrow's Child: Imagination, Creativity, and the Rebirth of Culture*. New York: Harper & Row, 1972.

Anwar, Mohammed Amir. "White People in South Africa Still Hold the Lion's Share of All Forms of Capital." *The Conversation*, February 27, 2017.

"Apartheid as Kerklike Beleid, I." *Die Kerkbode*, September 22, 1948.

Araújo, Marta, and Silvia Rodriguez Maesa, eds. *Eurocentrism, Racism, and Knowledge*. London: Palgrave Macmillan, 2015

Asmal, Kader, Louise Asmal, and Ronald Suresh Roberts. *Reconciliation through Truth: A Reckoning of Apartheid's Criminalised Governance*. Cape Town: David Philip, 1996.

Baderoon, Gabeba. "Remembering Slavery in South Africa." *Africa Is a Country*, December 7, 2014. https://www.africasacountry.com/2014/12/remembering-slavery-in-south-africa.

Bahour, Sam. "America's Intifada Must Dig Deeper." *Counterpunch*, June 19, 2020.

Baker, Aryn. "What South Africa Can Teach Us as Worldwide Inequality Grows." *Time Magazine*, May 2, 2019.

Baker, Mike. "Washington State County Declares Writing 'Black Lives Matter' in Chalk a Crime." *The New York Times*, July 17, 2020.

Baldwin, James. *The Fire Next Time*. New York: Dial, 1963.

Baldwin, Lewis V. "Martin Luther King Jr., a 'Coalition of Conscience,' and Freedom in South Africa." In *Freedom's Distant Shores: American Protestants and Post-colonial Alliances with Africa*, edited by R. Drew Smith, 53–82. Waco: Baylor University Press, 2006.

———. *Toward the Beloved Community: Martin Luther King Jr. and South Africa*. Cleveland: Pilgrim, 2019.

Baldwin, Lewis, V., and Rufus Burrow Jr., eds. *The Domestication of Martin Luther King Jr.: Clarence B. Jones, Right-Wing Conservatism, and the Manipulation of the King Legacy*. Eugene, OR: Cascade, 2013.

Baptist, Edward E. *The Half Has Never Been Told: Slavery and the Making of American Capitalism*. New York: Basic, 2016.

Barth, Karl. *The Doctrine of the Word of God*. Vol. 1.2, *Church Dogmatics*. New York: Bloomsbury, 2004.

———. *The Epistle to the Romans*. Translated by Edwyn C. Hoskyns. Oxford: Oxford University Press, 1968.

Bates, Stephen. "The Hidden Holocaust." *The Guardian*, May 12, 1999.

Bates, Thomas R. "Gramsci and the Theory of Hegemony." *Journal of the History of Ideas* 36 (1975) 351–66.

Battalora, Jacqueline. "Whiteness: The Workings of an Ideology in American Society and Culture." In *Gender, Ethnicity and Religion: Views from the Other Side*, edited by Rosemary Radford Ruether, 3–23. Minneapolis: Fortress, 2002.

"Battle of Cuito Cuanavale 1988." *South African History Online*, May 30, 2011. sahistory.org.za/article/battle-cuito-cuanavale-1988.

Bay, Mia. *To Tell the Truth Freely: The Life of Ida B. Wells*. New York: Hill & Wang, 2009.

Bell, Terry, and Dumisa Buhle Ntsebeza. *Unfinished Business: South Africa, Apartheid and Truth*. Cape Town: RedWorks, 2001.

Bellah, Robert N., et al. *Habits of the Heart: Individualism and Commitment in American Life*. Berkeley: University of California Press, 1985.

Bevins, Vincent. *The Jakarta Method: America's Anti-communist Crusade and the Mass Murder Program That Shaped Our World*. New York: PublicAffairs, 2020.

Bidwell, Nicola. "Black Skin, White Masks." *UPSpace Institutional Repository*, May 2016. http://hdl.handle.net/2263/57383.

Biko, Stephen Bantu. *I Write What I Like*. 40th anniversary ed. Edited by Aelred Stubbs. Johannesburg: Picador Africa, 2017.

Blumenthal, Max. *The Management of Savagery: How America's Security State Fueled ISIS and the Rise of Donald Trump*. London: Verso, 2019.

Boesak, Allan Aubrey. "And Zacchaeus Remained in the Tree: Justice and the Truth and Reconciliation Commission." *Verbum et Ecclesia* 29 (2008) 636–54.

———. *Black and Reformed: Apartheid, Liberation, and the Calvinist Tradition*. Maryknoll, NY: Orbis, 1984.

———. *Children of the Waters of Meribah: Black Liberation Theology, the Miriamic Tradition, and the Challenges of 21st Century Empire*. Eugene, OR: Cascade, 2019.

———. *Comfort and Protest: The Apocalypse from a South African Perspective*. 1984. Reprinted, Eugene, OR: Wipf & Stock, 2015.

———. *Coming In Out of the Wilderness: A Comparative Study of the Ethics of Martin Luther King Jr. and Malcolm X*. Kampen: J. H. Kok, 1974.

———. *Dare We Speak of Hope?: Searching for a Language of Hope in Faith and Politics*. Grand Rapids: Eerdmans, 2014

———. *Die Vlug van Gods Verbeelding: Bybelverhale van die Onderkant*. Stellenbosch: Sun, 2005.

———. *Farewell to Innocence: A Socio-ethical Study on Black Theology and Black Power.* Maryknoll, NY: Orbis, 1977.

———. *The Finger of God: Sermons on Faith and Responsibility.* Maryknoll, NY: Orbis, 1982.

———. *Kairos, Crisis, and Global Apartheid: The Challenge to Prophetic Resistance.* New York: Palgrave Macmillan, 2015.

———. *Pharaohs on Both Sides of the Blood-Red Waters: Prophetic Critique on Empire; Resistance, Justice, and the Power of the Hopeful Sizwe—a Transatlantic Conversation.* Eugene, OR: Cascade, 2017.

———. *Running with Horses: Reflections of an Accidental Politician.* Cape Town: JoHo!, 2009.

———. *The Tenderness of Conscience: African Renaissance and the Spirituality of Politics.* Stellenbosch: Sun, 2005

———. "Theological Reflections on Empire." In *Globalisation: The Politics of Empire, Justice and the Life of Faith*, edited by Allan Boesak and Len Hansen, 59–72. Beyers Naudé Centre Series on Public Theology 4. Stellenbosch: Sun, 2009.

———. "To Stand Where God Stands: Reflections on the Confession of Belhar." *Studio Historiae Ecclesiasticae* 34, no. 1 (July 2008) 163–67.

Boesak, Allan Aubrey, and Curtiss Paul DeYoung. *Radical Reconciliation: Beyond Political Pietism and Christian Quietism.* Maryknoll, NY: Orbis, 2012.

Boesak, Allan Aubrey, and Charles Villa-Vicencio, eds. *When Prayer Makes News.* Philadelphia: Westminster, 1986.

Boesak, Allan Aubrey, Johann Weusmann, and Charles Amjad-Ali, eds. *Dreaming a Different World: Globalisation and Justice for Humanity and the Earth.* Stellenbosch: Sun, 2010.

Boesak, Elna. "Alienation, Reconciliation and the Rubicon Between." Paper read at the Transformation in Highly Diverse Societies Colloquium, University of the Free State, Bloemfontein, November 25, 2009.

———. "Time for Apartheid's Truth to Be Spoken." *Sunday Independent*, May 21, 2012. iol.co.za/sundayindependent/time-for-apartheids-truth-to-be-spoken-1301002.

Bond, Patrick. *Against Global Apartheid: South Africa Meets the World Bank, IMF, and International Finance.* 2nd ed. London: Zed, 2004.

———. *Elite Transition: From Apartheid to Neoliberalism in South Africa.* Pietermaritzburg: University of Kwa Zulu-Natal Press, 2005.

———. "Is the Reform Really Working?" *The South Atlantic Quarterly* 103 (2004) 817–39.

Bonhoeffer, Dietrich. *Ecumenical, Academic, and Pastoral Work, 1931–32.* Edited by Victoria J. Barnett, Marks S. Brocker, and Michael B. Lukens. Translated by Anne Schmidt-Lange et al. Dietrich Bonhoeffer Works 11. Minneapolis: Fortress, 2012.

———. *Ethics.* Edited by Clifford J. Green. Translated by Reinhard Krauss, Charles C. West, and Douglas W. Stott. Dietrich Bonhoeffer Works 6. Minneapolis: Fortress, 2005.

———. *Letters and Papers from Prison.* Edited by Eberhard Bethge. New York: Simon & Schuster, 1997.

Border Action Network. *US-Mexican Border Policy Report.* El Paso: Border Network for Human Rights, 2008.

Borg, Marcus, and John Dominic Crossan. *The Last Week: The Day-by-Day Account of Jesus' Final Week in Jerusalem.* San Francisco: HarperSanFrancisco, 2006.

Botha, D. P. "Church and Kingdom in South Africa: Dutch Reformed Perspective." In *Your Kingdom Come: Daily Meditations and Group Reflections*, edited by Margaret Nash, 64–84. Johannesburg: SACC, 1980.

Breitman, George, ed. *The Last Year of Malcolm X: The Evolution of a Revolutionary*. New York: Pathfinder, 1967.

Brown, Deneen L. "Remembering 'Red Summer,' when white mobs massacred Blacks from Tulsa to D.C." *National Geographic Magazine*, June 19, 2020. https://www.nationalgeographic.com/history/2020/06/remembering-red-summer-white-mobs-massacred-blacks-tulsa-dc/.

Bright, John. *A History of Ancient Israel*. 3rd ed. Louisville: Westminster John Knox, 2000.

Brits, J. P. "Mbeki and the Afrikaners." *Historia* 53 (2008) 33–69.

Bronkhorst, Quinton. "These Are the 6 Richest People in South Africa." *BusinessTech*, February 27, 2020.

Brueggemann, Walter. *1 & 2 Kings*. Smyth & Helwys Bible Commentary. Macon: Smyth & Helwys, 2000.

———. *The Prophetic Imagination*. Minneapolis: Fortress, 2001.

Burke, Samuel. "Under fire, South Africa's former president repudiates apartheid." *CNN*, May 17, 2012. https://www.cnn.com/2012/05/16/world/africa/south-africa-de-klerk.

Butler, Smedley Darlington. *War Is a Racket: The Antiwar Classic by America's Most Decorated Soldier*. New York: Skyhorse, 2016.

Calland, Richard. *Anatomy of South Africa: Who Holds the Power?*. Cape Town: Zebra, 2006.

Calvin, John. *Commentaries*. 22 vols. Translated and edited by John King et al. Grand Rapids: Baker, 1981.

———. *Institutes of the Christian Religion*. Translated by Henry Beveridge. 1846. Reprinted, Grand Rapids: Eerdmans, 1989.

———. *Opera 45*. Edited by Johann-Wilhelm Baum and Eduard Wilhelm Eugen Reuss. Schwetschke: Brunsvigal, 1863.

Cannon, Katie Geneva. *Katie's Canon: Womanism and the Soul of the Black Community*. New York: Continuum, 1995.

Carter, Warren. *Matthew and Empire: Initial Explorations*. Harrisburg, PA: Trinity, 2000.

Cesairé, Aimé. "Letter to Maurice Thorez." Translated by Chike Jeffers. *Social Text* 28 (2010) 145–52.

"Challenge to the Church: A Theological Comment on the Political Crisis in South Africa." The Kairos Document (1985). *South African History Online*, June 1, 2012. http://www.sahistory.org.za/archive/challenge-church-theological-comment-political-crisis-south-africa-kairos-document-1985.

Chávez, Aida. "Louisville Police Left Body in the Street." *The Intercept*, June 1, 2020.

"Chinese Imperialism—A New Force in Africa." *Internationalist Communist Tendency*, January 9, 2008. http://www.leftcom.org/en/articles/2008-09-01/chinese-imperialism-a-new-force-in-africa.

Churchwell, Sarah. "American Fascism: It Has Happened Here." *The New York Review of Books*, June 22, 2020.

———. *Behold, America: The Entangled History of "America First" and "the American Dream."* London: Bloomsbury, 2018.

Claassens, Aninka. "Mandela didn't sell out, post-94 ANC did." *Mail & Guardian*, August 8, 2018. https://mg.co.za/article/2018-08-08-mandela-didnt-sell-out-post-94-anc-did/.

Clarke, Sathianathan, Deenabandhu Manchala, and Philip Vinod Peacock, eds. *Dalit Theology in the Twenty-First Century: Discordant Voices, Discerning Pathways*. New Delhi: Oxford University Press, 2010.

Clingan, Ralph Garlin. *Against Cheap Grace: A Study in the Hermeneutics of Adam Clayton Powell, 1865–1953, in His Intellectual Context*. New York: Peter Lang, 2002.

Cloete, G. D. *Hemelse solidariteit: 'n weg in die relasie tussen christologie en soteriologie in die Vierde Evangelie*. Kampen: J. H. Kok, 1980.

Cone, James H. *Black Theology and Black Power*. New York: Seabury, 1969.

———. *The Cross and the Lynching Tree*. Maryknoll, NY: Orbis, 2015.

———. *For My People: Black Theology and the Black Church*. Maryknoll, NY: Orbis, 1984.

———. *God of the Oppressed*. Maryknoll, NY: Orbis, 1997.

———. *Martin & Malcolm & America: A Dream or a Nightmare?*. Maryknoll, NY: Orbis, 1991.

———. *The Spirituals and the Blues: An Interpretation*. Maryknoll, NY: Orbis, 1972.

"Confession of Belhar." *Dutch Reformed Mission Church in South Africa*, September 1986. https://www.pcusa.org/site_media/media/uploads/theologyandworship/pdfs/belhar.pdf.

Conradie, Ernst. "To Cover the Many Sins of Galamsey Mining." *Missionalia* 46 (2018) 109–30.

Couper, Scott. *Albert Luthuli: Bound by Faith*. Pietermaritzburg: University of KwaZulu-Natal Press, 2010.

Cox, Harvey. *The Secular City: Secularization and Urbanization in Theological Perspective*. Princeton: Princeton University Press, 1965.

———. "The Secular City 25 Years Later." *The Christian Century* (November 7, 1990) 1025–29.

Crawford-Browne, Terry. *Eye on the Money*. Cape Town: Penguin, 2011.

Cromhout, M. "Die Vermyding van Etniese Spanning en Konflik in Suid Afrika: Wat kan Paulus se ervaring ons leer?" *HTS Teologiese Studies/Theological Studies* 67 (2011). https://doi.org/10.4102/hts.v67i1.782.

"Cuba Comes to Italy's Aid." *teleSUR English*, March 22, 2020. https://www.telesurenglish.net/news/Cuba-Comes-to-Italys-Aid-by-Sending-Team-of-Doctors-and-Nurses-20200322-0004.html.

Dabashi, Hamid. *The Arab Spring: The End of Colonialism*. London: Zed, 2012.

Dahir, Abdi Latif. "'Instead of Coronavirus, the Hunger Will Kill Us.' A Global Food Crisis Looms." *The New York Times*, April 22, 2020.

Daniels, David D. "'Doing All the Good We Can': The Political Witness of African American Holiness and Pentecostal Churches in the Post-Civil Rights Era." In *New Day Begun: African American Churches and Civic Culture in Post-Civil Rights America*, edited by R. Drew Smith, 164–82. Durham: Duke University Press, 2003.

Davis, Mike. "The Coronavirus Crisis Is a Monster Fueled by Capitalism." *In These Times*, March 20, 2020. https://inthesetimes.com/article/coronavirus-crisis-capitalism-COVID-19-monster-mike-davis.

Dawkins, Richard. *The God Delusion*. New York: Mariner, 2008.

De Gruchy, John W. "Bonhoeffer, Nelson Mandela, and the Dilemma of Violent Resistance in Retrospect." *Stellenbosch Theological Journal* 2 (2016) 43–60.

———. *The Church Struggle in South Africa*. Grand Rapids: Eerdmans, 1979.

———. *Reconciliation: Restoring Justice*. Cape Town: D. Philip, 2002.

De Gruchy, John W., and Charles Villa-Vicencio, eds. *Apartheid Is a Heresy*. Cape Town: D. Philip, 1983.

Bibliography

De Gruy, Joy. *Post Traumatic Slave Syndrome: America's Legacy of Enduring Injury and Healing*. New York: HarperCollins, 2017.

De Kiewiet, C. W. *The Imperial Factor in South Africa: A Study in Politics and Economics*. Cambridge: Cambridge University Press, 1937.

De Klerk, F. W. *The Last Trek—a New Beginning: The Autobiography*. London: Palgrave Macmillan, 1999.

De Kock, Victor. *Those in Bondage: An Account of the Life of the Slave at the Cape in the Days of the Dutch East India Company*. London: George Allen, 1950.

De Lange, Johnny. "The Historical Context, Legal Origins and Philosophical Foundations of the South African Truth and Reconciliation Commission." In *Looking Back, Reaching Forward*, edited by Charles Villa-Vicencio and Wilhelm Verwoerd, 14–31. Cape Town: University of Cape Town Press, 2000.

De La Torre, Miguel. "Doing Latina/o Ethics from the Margins of Empire: Liberating the Colonized Mind." *Journal of the Society of Christian Ethics* 33 (2013) 3–20.

Dearden, Lizzie. "Islamophobic incidents rose 375% after Boris Johnson compared Muslim women to 'letterboxes', figures show." *Independent*, September 2, 2019. https://www.independent.co.uk/news/uk/home-news/boris-johnson-muslim-women-letterboxes-burqa-islamphobia-rise-a9088476.html.

Desmond, Cosmas. *The Discarded People: An Account of African Settlement*. Johannesburg: Christian Institute of South Africa, 1971.

Deveraux, Ryan. "Humanitarian Volunteer Scott Warren Reflects on the Borderlands and Two Years of Government Persecution." *The Intercept*, November 23, 2019.

DeYoung, Curtiss Paul. *Living Faith: How Faith Inspires Social Justice*. Minneapolis: Fortress, 2007.

Doig, Tracy. "Four Years Later, Noxolo Nogwaza's Killers Are Still Free." *Mail & Guardian*, April 24, 2015.

Douglas, Kelly Brown. *Stand Your Ground: Black Bodies and the Justice of God*. Maryknoll, NY: Orbis, 2015.

Douglass, Frederick. "If There Is No Struggle, There Is No Progress." 1857. BlackPast.org, January 25, 2007. https://www.blackpast.org/african-american-history/1857-frederick-douglass-if-there-no-struggle-there-no-progress/.

———. *My Bondage and My Freedom*. New York: Miller, Orton & Mulligan, 1855.

———. *Narrative of the Life of Frederick Douglass: An American Slave*. 1845. Reprinted, Cambridge: Cambridge University Press, 2011.

Du Bois, W. E. B. *The Book of Mansart*. 3 vols. New York: Mainstream, 1957.

———. *Dusk of Dawn: An Essay toward an Autobiography of a Race Concept*. In *Writings*, edited by Nathan Huggins, 549–802. New York: Library of America, 1986.

Dunbar-Ortiz, Roxanne. *An Indigenous People's History of the United States*. Boston: Beacon, 2014.

———. *Loaded: A Disarming History of the Second Amendment*. San Francisco: City Lights Open Media, 2018.

Du Toit, André. "No Chosen People: The Myth of the Calvinist Origins of Afrikaner Nationalism and Racial Ideology." *The American Historical Review* 88 (1983) 920–52.

Dyson, Michael Eric. *I May Not Get There with You: The True Martin Luther King Jr*. New York: Touchstone, 2000.

Elmerraji, Jonas. "Countries Sanctioned by the US and Why." *Investopedia*, February 1, 2020.

Elphick, Richard. "Evangelical Missions and Racial 'Equalization' in South Africa, 1890–1914." In *Converting Colonialism: Visions and Realities in Mission History, 1706–1914*, edited by Dana L. Robert, 112–33. Grand Rapids: Eerdmans, 2008.

Emerson, Michael O., and George Yancey. *Transcending Racial Barriers: Toward a Mutual Obligations Approach*. New York: Oxford University Press, 2011.

Engdahl, Hans. "The Black Atlantic as Reversal: A Reappraisal of African and Black Theologies." *HTS Teologiese Studies/Theological Studies* 73 (2017). https://doi.org/10.4102/hts.v73i3.4618.

Enklaar, Ido H. *Life and Work of Dr. J. Th. van der Kemp, 1747–1811: Missionary Pioneer and Protagonist of Racial Equality in South Africa*. Cape Town: A. A. Balkema, 1988.

Erasmus, Zimitri. "'Race' and Its Articulation of the Human." In *The Effects of Race*, edited by Nina G. Jablonski and Gerhard Maré, 53–68. Stellenbosch: Sun, 2018.

Esack, Farid. *Qur'an, Liberation and Pluralism: An Islamic Perspective of Interreligious Solidarity against Oppression*. Oxford: OneWorld, 2000.

Evans, Zachary. "Susan Rice Blames 'Foreign Actors' for Stirring George Floyd Protests: 'Right Out of the Russian Playbook.'" *National Review*, June 1, 2020.

Ezroura, Mohamed. "Englishness, Postcoloniality, and Epistemicide: The Mission of English and the Moroccan University." Lecture presented at Moroccan V. University, Rabat, Morocco, 2019. academia.edu/38022167/Englishness_The_Mission_of_English_and_the_Moroccan_University?email_work_card.

Falk, Richard. "Gangster Geopolitics and Israel's Annexation Plans." *Al Jazeera*, May 13, 2020.

———. *The Great Terror War*. New York: Olive Branch, 2003.

———. "Rogue States Sanction the International Criminal Court." *Global Justice in the 21st Century* (blog), June 26, 2020. https://richardfalk.wordpress.com/2020/06/26/rogue-states-sanction-the-international-criminal-court/.

Fanon, Frantz. *The Wretched of the Earth*. Translated by Constance Farrington. New York: Grove Weidenfeld, 1963.

Finkelman, Paul. "Three-Fifths Clause: Why Its Taint Persists." *The Root*, February 26, 2013. https://www.theroot.com/three-fifths-clause-why-its-taint-persists-1790895387.

Foner, Philip S., ed. *Frederick Douglass: Selected Speeches and Writings*. Chicago: Lawrence Hill, 1999.

Ford, Paul Robeson. "Black People Have the Right to Defend Themselves by the Same Means Their White Counterparts Do." *Baptist News Global*, May 27, 2020.

Fortin, Jacey, and Allyson Waller. "87 Face Felony Charges After Protesting Breonna Taylor's Death." *The New York Times*, July 15, 2020. https://www.nytimes.com/2020/07/15/us/protesters-arrested-breonna-taylor-kentucky.html.

Freire, Paulo. *Pedagogy of the Oppressed*. New York: Penguin, 1972.

"FW de Klerk and the South African row over apartheid and crimes against humanity." *BBC*, February 18, 2020. https://www.bbc.com/news/world-africa-51532829.

Gaum, Laurie, and Frits Gaum. *Praat verby grense*. Cape Town: Umuzi, 2010.

Gerstein, Josh. "Obama: 'We Tortured Some Folks.'" *Politico*, August 1, 2014. https://www.politico.com/story/2014/08/john-brennan-torture-cia-109654.

Gerwel, Jakes. "National Reconciliation: Holy Grail or Secular Pact?" In *Looking Back, Reaching Forward*, edited by Charles Villa-Vicencio and Wilhelm Verwoerd, 277–86. Cape Town: University of Cape Town Press, 2000.

Giliomee, Hermann Buhr, and Bernard Mbenga. *New History of South Africa*. Cape Town: Tafelberg, 2007.

Gilpin, Toni. "Corporations Are Claiming 'Black Lives Matter.' That Would Be News to Their Workers." *Jacobin*, June 14, 2020.

Gollwitzer, Helmut. *Die Kapitalistische Revolution*. Munich: Kaiser, 1974.

———. *The Way to Life: Sermons in a Time of World Crisis*. London: T&T Clark, 1981.

———. "Why Black Theology?" In *Black Theology: A Documentary History, 1966-1979*, edited by Gayraud S. Wilmore and James H. Cone, 1:152-73. Maryknoll, NY: Orbis, 1993.

Gonaver, Wendy. *The Peculiar Institution and the Making of Modern Psychiatry, 1840-1880*. Chapel Hill: University of North Carolina Press, 2018.

Gordon, Rebecca. "The Future May Be Feminine, but the Pandemic Is Patriarchal." *TomDispatch*, March 31, 2020. readersupportednews.org/opinion2/277-75/62150-focus-the-future-may-be-feminine-but-the-pademic-is-patriarchal.

Goza, Joel Edward. *America's Unholy Ghosts: The Racist Roots of Our Faith and Politics*. Eugene, OR: Cascade, 2019.

Gqola, P. D. "Contradictory Locations: Black Women and the Discourse of the Black Consciousness Movement in South Africa." *Meridian* 2.1 (2001) 130-152

Gramsci, Antonio. *Selections from the Prison Notebooks*. Edited and translated by Quentin Hoare and Geoffrey Nowell Smith. London: Lawrence and Wishart, 1971. Ebook.

Grande, Sandy. "Refusing the University." In *Toward What Justice? Describing Diverse Dreams of Justice in Education*, edited by Eve Tuck and K. Wayne Yang, 47-65. London: Routledge, 2018.

Graybill, Lyn S. *Truth and Reconciliation in South Africa: Miracle or Model?* Boulder, CO: Lynne Rienner, 2002.

Greenwald, Glenn. "MLK's Vehement Condemnations of US Militarism Are More Relevant than Ever." *The Guardian*, January 21, 2013.

Griffen, Wendell. "A 'Monument' to Black People Massacred 100 Year Ago in Arkansas Reeks of the Hypocrisy Jesus Condemned." *Baptist Global News*, August 22, 2019.

———. "We Are Cursed." *Baptist News Global*, April 20, 2020.

Griffen, Wendell, and Lauri Umansky. "Want to Truly Memorialize a 100-Year-Old Race Massacre? Let the People See the Truth." *Baptist News Global*, October 8, 2019.

Grosfoguel, Ramón. "Decolonizing Postcolonial Studies and Paradigms of Political Economy: Transmodernity, Decolonial Thinking, and Global Coloniality." *Transmodernity: Journal of Peripheral Cultural Production of the Luso-Hispanic World* 1 (2011). http://escholarship.org/uc/item/21k6t3fq.

Guha, Ramachandra. "Churchill, the Greatest Briton, Hated Gandhi, the Greatest Indian." *Atlantic*, April 6, 2019.

Hansen, Len, ed. *The Legacy of Beyers Naudé*. Stellenbosch: Sun Media, 2005.

Hedges, Chris. "The Permanent Lie, Our Deadliest Threat." *Truthdig*, December 17, 2017.

———. *Wages of Rebellion: The Moral Imperative of Revolt*. New York: Nation Books, 2015.

Heering, H. J. *Ethiek der voorlopigheid*. Kampen: Kok, 1972.

Heleta, S. "Decolonisation of Higher Education: Dismantling Epistemic Violence and Eurocentrism in South Africa." *Transformation in Higher Education* 1 (2016) 1-8.

Hendricks, Obery M., Jr. *The Politics of Jesus: Rediscovering the True Revolutionary Nature of Jesus' Teachings and How They Have Been Corrupted*. New York: Doubleday, 2006.

Herman, Edward S., and Noam Chomsky. *Manufacturing Consent: The Political Economy of the Mass Media*. New York: Pantheon, 1988.

Herzog, William R. *Jesus, Justice, and the Reign of God: A Ministry of Liberation*. Louisville: Westminster John Knox, 2000.

———. *Parables as Subversive Speech: Jesus as Pedagogue of the Oppressed*. Louisville: Westminster John Knox, 1994.

Hiatt, Steven, ed. *A Game as Old as Empire: The Secret World of Economic Hitmen and the Web of Global Corruption*. San Francisco: Berrett-Koehler, 2007.

Hochschild, Adam. *King Leopold's Ghost: A Story of Greed, Terror, and Heroism in Colonial Africa*. Boston: Houghton Mifflin, 1998.

Hoelzl, Verena, and Cape Diamond. "Myanmar Military Steps Up Attacks as Coronavirus Spreads." *Al Jazeera*, April 16, 2020.

"Hong Kong children's shop told to remove protester statue." *BBC*, June 18, 2020. https://www.bbc.com/news/world-asia-china-53097979.

Horsley, Richard A., ed. *In the Shadow of Empire: Reclaiming the Bible as a History of Faithful Resistance*. Louisville: Westminster John Knox, 2008.

———. *Jesus and Empire: The Kingdom of God and the New Disorder*. Minneapolis: Fortress, 2003.

———. *Jesus and the Powers: Conflict, Covenant, and the Hope of the Poor*. Minneapolis: Fortress, 2011.

———, ed. *Paul and Empire: Religion and Power in Roman Imperial Society*. Harrisburg, PA: Trinity Press International, 1997.

———, ed. *Paul and Politics: Ekklesia, Israel, Imperium, Interpretation; Essays in Honor of Krister Stendahl*. Harrisburg, PA: Trinity Press International, 2000.

Houdek, Matthew. "The Imperative of Race for Rhetorical Studies: Toward Divesting from Disciplinary and Institutionalized Whiteness." *Communication and Critical Studies* 13 (2018) 292–99.

Huddleston, Trevor. *Naught for Your Comfort*. Glasgow: Collins, 1956.

Hudson, Michael. "De-Dollarization: Toward the End of the US Monetary Hegemony." YouTube.com/watch?v=h45Bovld7Vk.

———. "Resisting Empire." YouTube.com/watch?v=xluStDQp9yE, November 15, 2019.

Hughes, Langston. *The Collected Poems of Langston Hughes*. Edited by Arnold Rampersad and David Roessel. New York: Vintage, 1995.

Human Rights Watch. *Broken People: Caste Violence against India's "Untouchables."* March 1, 1999. https://www.hrw.org/report/1999/03/01/broken-people.

Jablonski, Nina, and Gerhard Maré, eds. *The Effects of Race*. Stellenbosch: Sun, 2018.

Jones, Charles Colcock. *The Religious Instruction of the Negroes in the United States*. Savannah, GA: Thomas Purse, 1842.

Jones, Clarence B. *Behind the Dream: The Making of the Speech That Transformed a Nation*. New York: St. Martin's, 2011.

Jones, Clarence B., and Joel Engel. *What Would Martin Say?* New York: HarperCollins, 2008.

Johnson, André E. *The Forgotten Prophet: Bishop Henry McNeal Turner and the African American Prophetic Tradition*. Lanham, MD: Lexington, 2012.

———. "God Is a Negro: The (Rhetorical) Black Theology of Bishop Henry McNeal Turner." *Black Theology* 13 (2015) 29–40.

Jones, Stephen. "20 Reasons Why Barack Obama Is the Coolest President of All Time." *The Mirror*, January 20, 2017. https://www.mirror.co.uk/news/world-news/why-barack-obama-coolest-president-9185880.

Johnson, Chalmers. *Blowback: The Costs and Consequences of American Empire*. New York: Henry Holt, 2000.

Johnson, Krista. "Liberal or Liberation Framework? The Contradictions of ANC Rule in South Africa." *Journal of Contemporary African Studies* 21 (2003) 321–28.

Johnson, Vida B. "KKK in the PD: White Supremacist Police and What to Do about It." *Lewis and Clark Law Review* 23 (2019) 205–61.

Johnson, Walter. "No Rights Which the White Man Is Bound to Respect." *Boston Review: A Political and Literary Forum*, September 27, 2017.

———. *Soul by Soul: Life Inside the Antebellum Slave Market*. Cambridge: Harvard University Press, 1999.

Jurado, Joe. "Appeals Court Rules Detroit Students Have a Right to a Basic Education." *The Root*, April 26, 2020. https://www.theroot.com/appeals-court-rules-detroit-students-have-a-right-to-a-1843045725.

JS and Promise Li. "The Hong Kong Movement Must Stand with Black Lives Matter." *Hong Kong Times*, June 7, 2020.

Kahl, Brigitte. *Galatians Re-imagined, Reading with the Eyes of the Vanquished*. Minneapolis: Fortress, 2014.

Karis, Thomas, and Gwendolen M. Carter, eds. *From Protest to Challenge: A Documentary History of African Politics in South Africa, 1882–1964*. 6 vols. Stanford: Stanford University Press, 1972–2010.

Karrim, Azarrah. "Ramaphosa: Mandela's Example Will Help Us Overcome Global Pandemic." July 18, 2020. https://www.news24.com/news24/southafrica/news/ramaphosa-mandelas-example-will-help-us-overcome-global-pandemic-20200718.

Keevy, Ilze. "African Philosophical Values and Constitutionalism: A Feminist Perspective on *Ubuntu* as a Constitutional Value." LLD diss., University of the Free State, 2008.

———. *African Philosophical Values and Constitutionalism: A Feminist Perspective on Ubuntu as a Constitutional Value*. Bloemfontein: University of the Free State, 2008.

Keller, Jared. "Inside America's Auschwitz." *Smithsonian Magazine*, April 4, 2016. https://www.smithsonianmag.com/history/inside-americas-auschwitz-180958647/.

Kelly, Geffrey B., and F. Burton Nelson, eds. *A Testament to Freedom: The Essential Writings of Dietrich Bonhoeffer*. San Francisco: HarperSanFrancisco, 1990.

Kendi, Ibram X. "Stop Blaming Black People for Dying of the Coronavirus." *The Atlantic*, April 14, 2020.

Kennedy, Geoffrey Studdert. *After War, Is Faith Possible? The Life and Message of Geoffrey "Woodbine Willie" Studdert Kennedy*. Edited by Kerry Walters. Eugene, OR: Cascade, 2008.

Kennedy, John F. "Address on the First Anniversary of the Alliance for Progress." *American Presidency Project*, March 13, 1962. https://www.presidency.ucsb.edu/documents/address-the-first-anniversary-the-alliance-for-progress.

Kessler, Glenn, Salvador Rizzo, and Megyn Kelly. "Trump's false or misleading claims total 30,573 over four years." *The Washington Post*, January 24, 2021. https://www.washingtonpost.com/politics/2021/01/24/trumps-false-or-misleading-claims-total-30573-over-four-years/.

Khumalo, Siya. *You Have to Be Gay to Know God*. Cape Town: Kwela, 2018.

Kilvington, Daniel. "Racist Abuse at Football Games Is Increasing, Home Office Says, but the Sport's Race Problem Goes Much Deeper." *The Conversation*, October 9, 2019.

Kimpa Vita: The Mother of the African Revolution. Directed by Ne Kunda Nlaba. London: Labson Bizizi-Cine Kongo, 2016.

King, Martin Luther, Jr. "Beyond Vietnam: A Time to Break Silence." In *The Radical King*, edited by Cornel West, 201–17. Boston: Beacon, 2015.

———. *"In a Single Garment of Destiny": A Global Vision of Justice*. Edited by Lewis V. Baldwin. Boston: Beacon, 2013. Kindle.

———. "I've Been to the Mountaintop." In *The Radical King*, edited by Cornel West, 265–76. Boston: Beacon, 2015.

———. "Let My People Go." In *The Radical King*, edited by Cornel West, 107–12. Boston: Beacon, 2015.

———. "Letter from a Birmingham Jail." In *The Radical King*, edited by Cornel West, 127–46. Boston: Beacon, 2015.

———. *The Radical King*. Edited by Cornel West. Boston: Beacon, 2015.

———. "Remaining Awake through a Great Revolution." In *A Testament of Hope: The Essential Writings of Martin Luther King Jr.*, edited by James Melvin Washington, 268–78. San Francisco: Harper & Row, 1986.

———. *Strength to Love*. New York: Harper & Row, 1963.

———. *The Trumpet of Conscience*. New York: Harper & Row, 1967.

———. *Where Do We Go from Here: Chaos or Community?* New York: Harper & Row, 1967.

———. *Why We Can't Wait*. New York: Harper & Row, 1963.

Kinghorn, J., ed. *Die N. G. Kerk en Apartheid*. Johannesburg: Palgrave Macmillan, 1986.

Kinzer, Stephen. *Overthrow: America's Century of Regime Change from Hawai'i to Iraq*. New York: Henry Holt, 2006.

Klein, Naomi. "Capitalism Killed Our Climate Momentum, Not Human Nature." *The Intercept*, August 3, 2018.

———. *The Shock Doctrine: The Rise of Disaster Capitalism*. New York: Henry Holt: 2007.

Krabill, Ron. "Symbiosis: Mass Media and the Truth and Reconciliation Commission of South Africa." *Media, Culture & Society* 23 (2001) 567–85.

Kuyper, Abraham. *Six Stone Lectures*. Grand Rapids, Eerdmans, 1931.

Landler, Mark. "In an English City, an Early Benefactor Is Now 'a Toxic Brand.'" *New York Times*, June 14, 2020. https://www.nytimes.com/2020/06/14/world/europe/Bristol-Colston-statue-slavery.html.

Lebakeng, Nase, et al. "Epistemicide, Institutional Cultures and the Imperative for the Africanisation of Universities in South Africa." *Alternation* 13 (2006) 70–87.

Lehmann, Paul. *Ethics in a Christian Context*. New York: Harper & Row, 1963.

Lerner, Sharon. "Big Pharma Prepares to Profit from the Coronavirus." *The Intercept*, March 13, 2020.

Levecq, Christine. "Jacobus Capitein: Dutch Calvinist and Black Cosmopolitan." *Research in African Literatures* 44 (2013) 145–66.

Lincoln, C. Eric. *Coming Through the Fire: Surviving Race and Place in America*. Durham: Duke University Press, 1996.

Lodge, Tom. *Black Politics in South Africa since 1945*. Johannesburg: Ravan, 1994.

Lombard, R. T. J. *Die Nederduitse Gereformeerde Kerke en Rassepolitiek*. Pretoria: NG Kerkboekhandel, 1981.

Lopez, Davina C. *The Apostle to the Conquered: Re-imagining Paul's Mission*. Minneapolis: Fortress, 2008.

Lovaas, Scott. "Manufacturing Consent in Democratic South Africa: Application of the Propaganda Model." PhD diss., University of the Witwatersrand, 2008.

Luthuli, Albert. *Let My People Go! The Autobiography of Albert Luthuli*. Cape Town: Tafelberg/Mafube, 2006.

Lynch, Willie. *The Willie Lynch Letter and the Making of a Slave by Willie Lynch*. South Carolina: CreateSpace, 2014.

Lyttleton, Joseph. "The Black Lives Matter and Hong Kong protesters share methods and a cause, but fail to unite." *Millennial Source*, June 25, 2020.

Machemer, Theresa. "Christopher Columbus Statues Beheaded, Pulled Down across America." *Smithsonian Magazine*, June 12, 2020.

Maeso, Silvia Rodríguez, and Marta Araújo. "Eurocentrism, Political Struggles and the Entrenched *Will-to-Ignorance*: An Introduction." In *Eurocentrism, Racism and Knowledge*, edited by Marta Araújo and Silvia Maeso, 1–22. New York: Palgrave Macmillan, 2015.

Magona, Sindiwe. *Mother to Mother*. Boston: Beacon, 1998.

Magubane, Bernard. "The African Renaissance in Historical Perspective." In *African Renaissance: The New Struggle*, edited by M. W. Makgoba, 10–36. Cape Town: Mafube & Tafelberg, 1999.

Maharaj, Mac, ed. *Reflections in Prison*. Cape Town: Zebra Press and the Robben Island Museum, 2001.

Malcolm X. *The End of White Supremacy: Four Speeches by Malcolm X*. Edited by Imam Benjamin Karim. New York: Arcade, 1971.

———. *Malcolm X Speaks: Selected Speeches and Statements*. Edited by George Breitman. New York: Merit, 1967.

Maldonado-Torres, Nelson. "Outline of Ten Theses on Coloniality and Decoloniality." http://caribbeanstudiesassociation.org/docs/Maldonado-Torres_Outline_Ten_Theses-10.23.16.pdf.

Maluleke, Tinyiko. "Africans Alienated Inside and Outside: *Yinde Lendlela*." *Journal of Theology for Southern Africa* 162–63 (2019) 137–56.

———. "Can Lions and Rabbits Reconcile?" *Ecumenical Review* 53 (2001) 190–201.

———. "May the Black God Stand Please!: Biko's Challenge to Religion." In *Biko Lives! Contesting the Legacies of Steve Biko*, edited by Andile Mngxitama, Amanda Alexander, and Nigel C. Gibson, 115–26. New York: Palgrave Macmillan, 2008.

———. "The Proposal for a Theology of Reconstruction: A Critical Appraisal." *Missionalia* 22 (1994) 245–58.

———. "Reflections and Resources: The Elusive Public of Public Theology; a Response to William Storar." *International Journal of Public Theology* 5 (2011) 79–89.

———. "Truth, National Unity, and Reconciliation in South Africa: Aspects of an Emerging Agenda." *Missionalia* 25 (1997) 245–58.

Mamdani, Mahmood. *Good Muslim, Bad Muslim: America, the Cold War, and the Roots of Terrorism*. New York: Doubleday, 2004.

———. "Reconciliation without Justice." *Southern African Review of Books* 46 (November/December 1996).

———. *When Victims Become Killers: Colonialism, Nativism, and the Genocide in Rwanda*. Princeton: Princeton University Press, 2001.

"Mamie Till: More Than a Mother." *National Center for Civil and Human Rights* (blog). https://www.civilandhumanrights.org/mamie-till/.

Mandela, Nelson. "Address by President Nelson Mandela at the Opening of Parliament, 5 February 1999." www.gov.za/address-president-nelson-mandela-opening-parliament-5-february-1999.

———. "Address by President Nelson Mandela in Special Debate on Report of Truth and Reconciliation Commission, Cape Town." *Nelson Mandela Foundation*, September 10, 2004. http://www.mandela.gov.za/mandela_speeches/1999/990225_trc.htm.

———. "Address to a Rally in Cape Town on His Release from Prison (February 11, 1990)." In *Great Speeches of the Twentieth Century*, edited by Janet Baine Kopito, 193–97. London: Preface, 2008.

———. "The Fifth Steve Biko Memorial Lecture." September 10, 2004, University of Cape Town.

———. "I Am Prepared to Die." *Nelson Mandela Foundation*, April 20, 2011. http://db.nelsonmandela.org/speeches/pub_view.asp?pg=item&ItemID=NMS010&txtstr=prepared%20to%20die.

———. "Whither the Black Consciousness Movement? An Assessment." In *Reflections in Prison*, edited by Mac Maharaj, 21–64. Cape Town: Zebra Press and the Robben Island Museum, 2001.

———. "5th Steve Biko Lecture by Nelson Mandela, Cape Town." *Nelson Mandela Foundation*, September 10, 2004. http://www.mandela.gov.za/mandela_speeches/2004/040910_biko.htm.

Manganyi, Chabani. "Perspectives on Race and Racism." In *The Effects of Race*, edited by Nina G. Jablonski and Gerhard Maré, 11–34. Stellenbosch: Sun, 2018.

Mangcu, Xolela. *Biko: A Biography*. Cape Town: Tafelberg, 2017.

———. *To the Brink: The State of Democracy in South Africa*. Scottsville: University of KwaZulu-Natal Press, 2008.

Mangu, Andre Mbata B. "Democracy, African Intellectuals, and African Renaissance." *International Journal of African Renaissance Studies* 1.1 (2006) 147–63.

Mason, Rowena, Anushka Asthana, and Heather Stewart. "Tony Blair: 'I express more sorrow, regret and apology than you can ever believe.'" *The Guardian*, July 6, 2016. https://www.theguardian.com/uk-news/2016/jul/06/tony-blair-deliberately-exaggerated-threat-from-iraq-chilcot-report-war-inquiry.

Matsuda, Mari J., et al., eds. *Words That Wound: Critical Race Theory, Assaultive Speech, and the First Amendment*. Boulder, CO: Westview, 1993.

Maxwell, Lida, and Sonali Chakravarti. "Chelsea Manning Against the Grand Jury." *Jacobin*, June 10, 2019.

May, Cedric. *Evangelism and Resistance in the Black Atlantic, 1760–1835*. Athens: University of Georgia Press, 2008.

Mbeki, Thabo. *Africa: The Time Has Come; Selected Speeches*. Cape Town: Tafelberg/Mafube, 1998.

———. "The African Renaissance Conference Statement by Deputy President Thabo Mbeki." Galagher Estate, SABC, September 14, 1998.

Mbiti, John. "An African Views American Black Theology." In *Black Theology: A Documentary History*, edited by Gayraud S. Wilmore and James H. Cone, 1:477–82. Maryknoll, NY: Orbis, 1979.

McGee, Paula. *Brand® New Theology: The Walmartization of T. D. Jakes and the New Black Church*. Maryknoll, NY: Orbis, 2016.

Mellet, Patric Tariq. *The Lie of 1652: A Decolonised History of Land*. Cape Town: Tafelberg, 2020.

"Report: Israel Arrested 357 Palestinians in March despite Coronavirus Lockdown." *Middle East Monitor*, April 17, 2020. https://www.middleeastmonitor.com/20200417-report-israel-arrested-357-palestinians-in-march-despite-coronavirus-lockdown/.

Mieder, Wolfgang. *"Making a Way Out of No Way": Martin Luther King's Sermonic Proverbial Rhetoric*. New York: Peter Lang, 2010.

Miguez Bonino, José. *Towards a Christian Political Ethics*. Philadelphia: Fortress, 1983.

Mngxitama, Andile, Amanda Alexander, and Nigel C. Gibson, eds. *Biko Lives! Contesting the Legacies of Steve Biko*. New York: Palgrave Macmillan, 2008.

Mofokeng, Takatso. *The Crucified among the Cross-Bearers: Towards a Black Christology*. Kampen: Kok, 1983.

Moltmann, Jürgen. *God for a Secular World: The Relevance of Theology*. Minneapolis: Fortress, 1999.

Moore, Basil, ed. *Black Theology: The South African Voice*. London: C. Hurst, 1973.

Morton, Victor. "Franklin Graham Calls for a 'Special Day of Prayer' for Trump: 'This Is a Critical Time for America.'" *The Washington Times*, May 27, 2019.

Mosala, Itumeleng J., and Buti Thlagale. *The Unquestionable Right to Be Free: Essays in Black Theology*. Johannesburg: Skotaville, 1986.

Mothlabi, M., ed. *Essays on Black Theology*. Johannesburg: Ravan, 1972.

Mphahlele, Eskia. *ES'KIA: Education, African Humanism & Culture, Social Consciousness, Literary Appreciation*. Johannesburg: Kwela, 2002.

Myburgh, Anton. "Die Boer En Sy Roer." musixmatch.com/lyrics/Anton-Myburgh/Boer-En-Sy_Roer.

National Committee of Negro Churchmen. "Position Statement in Support of Black Power." July 31, 1966. https://episcopalarchives.org/church-awakens/items/show/183.

Naudé, C. F. Beyers. *My Decision*. Johannesburg: The Christian Institute, 1963.

———. *My Land van Hoop*. Cape Town: Human & Rousseau, 1995.

———. "Steve Biko: The Man and His Message." In *The Legacy of Beyers Naudé*, edited by Len Hansen, 77–80. Stellenbosch: Sun, 2005.

Naudé, Beyers, and Dorothee Sölle. *Hope for Faith: A Conversation*. Grand Rapids: Eerdmans, 1986.

Naudé, Piet J. *Neither Calendar nor Clock: Perspectives on the Belhar Confession*. Grand Rapids: Eerdmans, 2011.

Ndebele, Njabulo S. "The Envisioned Self." Foreword to Steve Biko, *I Write What I Like*, vii–xiv. Johannesburg: Picador Africa, 2017.

Nkrumah, Kwame. *Neo-colonialism: The Last Stage of Imperialism*. London: Thomas Nelson, 1965.

"Obama's War on Whistleblowers Leaves Administration Insiders Unscathed." *The Guardian*, March 16, 2015. https://www.theguardian.com/us-news/2015/mar/16/whistleblowers-double-standard-obama-david-petraeus-chelsea-manning.

Oxfam. "The Hunger Virus: How COVID-19 Is Fuelling Hunger in a Hungry World." July 9, 2020. https://www.oxfam.org/en/research/hunger-virus-how-covid-19-fuelling-hunger-hungry-world.

———. "Time to Care: Unpaid and Underpaid Care Work and the Global Inequality Crisis." Oxfam Briefing Paper, January 2020. https://oxfamilibrary.openrepository.com/bitstream/handle/10546/620928/bp-time-to-care-inequality-200120-en.pdf.

Paraskeva, João, ed. *The Curriculum: Whose Internationalization?* New York: Peter Lang, 2016.

Parker, Eve. "'Freedom of Religion' and Belonging in Brexit Britain: Towards an Intersectional, Interreligious Theology of the Freedom of Religion." Paper presented at the World Communion of Reformed Churches' consultation on Freedom of Religion, Hattersheim am Main, Germany, February 2020.

Petrequin, Samuel. "Belgian king expresses regret for violence in colonial rule." *Star-Tribune*, June 30, 2020.

Perkins, John. *The New Confessions of an Economic Hitman*. San Francisco: Berrett-Koehler, 2016.

Perraudin, Frances. "New controversial comments uncovered in historical Boris Johnson articles." *The Guardian*, December 9, 2019. https://www.theguardian.com/politics/2019/dec/09/new-controversial-comments-uncovered-in-historical-boris-johnson-articles.

Perry, Keisha-Khan Y. "The Land Question." In *Race and Capitalism: Global Territories, Transnational Histories*, edited by Ananya Roy, 19–23. Los Angeles: Institute on Inequality and Democracy, UCLA Luskin School of Public Affairs, 2017.

Philimon, Wenei. "Not Just George Floyd: Police Departments Have 400-Year History of Anti-black Racism." *USA Today*, June 7, 2020.

Pierce, Charles. "This Was a Fascist Rally Down To its Bones." *Esquire*, July 18, 2019.

Pillay, Pravina, and Thayabaran Pillay. "South African Intellectuals Drive towards Attainment of African Renaissance Goal in Africa." *African Renaissance* 15.1 (April 2018) 45–56.

Prah, Kwesi Kwaa. *Jacobus Eliza Johannes Capitein, 1717–1747: A Critical Study of an Eighteenth-Century African*. Trenton, NJ: African World, 1992.

Rajaiah, Jeyaraj. *Dalit Humanization: A Quest Based on M. M. Thomas' Theology of Salvation and Humanization*. Delhi: SPCK, 2017.

Ramphele, Mamphela. *Laying Ghosts to Rest: Dilemmas of the Transformation in South Africa*. Cape Town: Tafelberg, 2008.

Reddie, Anthony G. "Do Black Lives Matter in Post-Brexit Britain?" *Studies in Christian Ethics* 32 (2019) 387–401.

———. *Theologising Brexit: A Liberationist and Postcolonial Critique*. New York: Routledge, 2019.

Rodney, Walter. *How Europe Underdeveloped Africa*. London: Boglo-L'Ouverture, 1972.

Rothuizen, G. *Primus Usus Legis: Studie over het burgerlijk gebruik van de wet*. Kampen: Kok, 1966.

Roy, Arundathi. "Confronting Empire." *The Nation*, February 20, 2003.

Sacks, Jonathan. *The Dignity of Difference: How to Avoid the Clash of Civilizations*. New York: Continuum, 2005.

Sales, Jane. *The Planting of the Churches in South Africa*. Grand Rapids: Eerdmans, 1971.

Seme, Pixley ka Isaka. "The Regeneration of Africa." In Vol. 1, *The African Abroad, or, His Evolution in Western Civilization: Tracing His Development Under Caucasian Milieu*, by William Henry Ferris, 436–39. New York: Tuttle, Morehouse & Taylor, 1913.

Senokoane, Boitumelo. "The Poor Are Cut Off from Economic Activity." *The Star* (South Africa), April 24, 2020. https://www.pressreader.com/south-africa/the-star-south-africa-late-edition/20200424/281981789735892.

Sesanti, Simphiwe. "Afrocentric Education for an African Renaissance: Philosophical Underpinnings." *New Agenda: South African Journal of Social and Economic Policy* 62 (2016) 34–40.

Sherfinski, David. "Texas Lt. Gov. Dan Patrick Suggests He'd Risk Dying to Help Save U.S. Economy." *The Washington Post*, March 24, 2020.

Shupak, Greg. "Stop the War. Stop US Empire." *Jacobin*, January 8, 2020.
Small, Adam. "Blackness versus Nihilism: Black Racism Rejected." In *Black Theology: The South African Voice*, edited by Basil Moore, 11–16. Baarn: Ten Have, 1975.
Smit, Dirk J. *Essays in Public Theology: Collected Essays* 1. Edited by Ernst M. Conradie. Stellenbosch: Sun, 2007.
———. "What Does 'Public' Mean? Questions with a View to Public Theology." In *Christian in Public: Aims, Methodologies and Issues in Public Theology*, edited by Len Hansen, 11–14. Stellenbosch: African Sun Media, 2007.
Smith, David. "South Africa gay rights activists warn of homophobic attacks after murder." *The Guardian*, May 3, 2011. https://www.theguardian.com/world/2011/may/03/south-africa-homophobic-attacks.
Smith, Michael Nassen, and Tafadzwa Tivaringe. "From Afro-centrism to Decolonial Humanism and Afro-plurality: A Response to Simphiwe Sesanti." *New Agenda: South African Journal of Social and Economic Policy* 62 (2016) 41–43.
Smith, Mitzi. "Race, Gender, and the Politics of 'Sass': Reading Mark 7:24–30 through a Womanist Lens of Intersectionality and Inter(con)textuality." In *Womanist Interpretations of the Bible: Expanding the Discourse*, edited by Gay L. Byron and Vanessa Lovelace, 95–112. Atlanta: SBL, 2016.
Smith, R. Drew, ed. *Freedom's Distant Shores: American Protestants and Post-colonial Alliances with Africa*. Waco, TX: Baylor University Press, 2006.
———, ed. *New Day Begun: African American Churches in Post-Civil Rights America*. Durham: Duke University Press, 2003.
Sparks, Allister. *Tomorrow Is Another Country*. Chicago: University of Chicago Press, 1995.
Stephansen, Anders, *Manifest Destiny: American Expansion and the Empire of Right*. New York: Hill & Wang, 1996.
Stern, Mark Joseph. "Trump Wants to Strip House Seats from States under Three-fifths Clause." *Slate*, July 22, 2020.
Sue, Donald W., et al. "Racial Micro-aggressions in Everyday Life: Implications for Clinical Practice." *American Psychologist* 62 (2007) 271–86.
Sugarman, Jacob. "America's Cold War Crimes Abroad Are Still Shaping Our World." *Jacobin*, May 19, 2020.
Taylor, Keeanga-Yamahtta. *From #BlackLivesMatter to Black Liberation*. Chicago: Haymarket, 2016.
———. "How Do We Change America?" *The New Yorker*, June 15, 2020.
Terreblanche, Sampie. *Lost in Transformation: South Africa's Search for a New Future since 1986*. Johannesburg: KMM Review, 2012.
Ter Schegget, G. H. *De Andere Mogelijkheid*. Baarn: Ten Have, 1973.
———. *Het Geheim van de Mens*. Baarn: Ten Have, 1972.
Therborn, Göran. "Racism, Existential Inequality and Problems of Categorical Equalisation: Reflections on the South African Experience." In *The Effects of Race*, edited by Nina Jablonski and Gerhard Maré, 35–52. Stellenbosch: Sun, 2018.
Thomas, M. M. *The Church's Mission and Post-modern Humanism: A Collection of Essays and Talks, 1992–1996*. Delhi: SPCK, 1996.
———. "Issues Concerning the Life and Work of the Church in a Revolutionary World." In *Unity of Mankind*, edited by A. H. van den Heuvel, 89–98. Geneva: WCC, 1969.
———. "The Logic of the Christian Mission." *The Pilgrim* 3 (1959) 69–74.
———. "A Spirituality of Combat." *Princeton Theological Bulletin* 5 (1984) 144–46.

Thomas, M. M., and J. D. McCaughey. *The Christian in the World Struggle*. A Grey Book of the World Student Christian Federation. Geneva: WSCF, 1951.

Thornton, John Kelly. *The Kongolese Saint Anthony: Dona Beatriz Kimpa Vita and The Antonian Movement, 1684–1706*. Cambridge: Cambridge University Press, 1998.

"Trump on Johnson: 'They call him Britain Trump.'" *BBC News*, July 23, 2019. https://www.bbc.com/news/av/world-us-canada-49090804.

Tshaka, Rothney. "How Can a Conquered People Sing Praises of Their History and Culture? Africanisation as the Integration of Inculturation and Liberation." *Black Theology: An International Journal* 14 (2016) 91–106.

Tuchman, Barbara. *The March of Folly: From Troy to Vietnam*. London: Abacus, 1986.

Turse, Nick. "'Exceptionally Dire': Secondary Impacts of Covid-19 Could Increase Global Poverty and Hunger." *The Intercept*, May 4, 2020.

Tutu, Desmond. "Black Theology/African Theology: Soul Mates or Antagonists?" In *Black Theology: A Documentary History*, edited by Gayraud S. Wilmore and James H. Cone, 483–91. Maryknoll, NY: Orbis, 1979.

———. *A Voice in the Wilderness*. Johannesburg: Ravan, 1984.

"The 2019 South Africa Wealth Report Describes Wealth at Home as Moderate." *Afrasia Bank*. June 27, 2019. https://www.afrasiabank.com/en/about/newsroom/news/2019/the-2019-south-africa-wealth-report-describes-growth-at-home-as-moderate.

"U.S. Sanctions Killed over 40,000 Venezuelans since 2017." *Third World Resurgence* 337–38 (January/February 2019) 25.

Van Aarde, Andries. *Fatherless in Galilee: Jesus as Child of God*. Harrisburg, PA: Trinity Press International, 2001.

———. *Jesus, Paul, and Matthew*. Vol. 2, *To and from Jerusalem*. Cambridge: Cambridge Scholars, 2020.

Van Niekerk, Brimadevi. "The Concept of Chosen People in the Construction and Maintenance of Jewish Identity." *HTS Teologies Studies/Theological Studies* 74, Art. #4947 (2018). https://doi.org/10.4102/hts.v74i3.4947.

Vellem, Vuyani. "Embers from the Zone of Non-Being." Unpublished paper, Council on World Mission DARE conference, Bangkok, May 2017.

———. "Ideology and Spirituality: A Critique of Villa-Vicencio's Project of Reconstruction." *Scriptura, an International Journal of Bible, Religion, and Theology in Southern Africa* 105 (2010) 547–58.

———. "Spirituality of Liberation: A Conversation with African Religiosity." *HTS Teologiese Studies/Theological Studies* 70, Art. #2752 (2014). http://dx.doi.org/10.4102/hts.v70i1.2752.

Verdoolaege, Annelies. "Media Representations of the South African Truth and Reconciliation Commission and Their Commitment to Reconciliation." *Journal of African Cultural Studies* 17 (2005) 181–99.

Viljoen, Russel. *Jan Paerl: A Khoikhoi in Cape Colonial Society, 1761–1851*. Leiden: Brill, 2006.

Villa-Vicencio, Charles. "An All-Pervading Heresy: Racism and the 'English-Speaking Churches.'" In *Apartheid Is a Heresy*, edited by John W. De Gruchy and Charles Villa-Vicencio, 59–74. Cape Town: D. Philip, 1983.

———. *Trapped in Apartheid: A Socio-theological History of the English-Speaking Churches*. Maryknoll, NY: Orbis, 1988.

———. *Walk with Us and Listen: Political Reconciliation in Africa*. Cape Town: University of Cape Town Press, 2000.

Villa-Vicencio, Charles, and Wilhelm Verwoerd, eds. *Looking Back, Reaching Forward*. Cape Town: University of Cape Town Press, 2000.

Waldrep, Christopher, ed. *Lynching in America: A History in Documents*. New York: New York University Press, 2006.

Wasserman, Harvey. "Trump Is No Accident." *Counterpunch*, June 3, 2020.

Weber, Max. *Economy and Society: An Outline of Interpretive Sociology*. New York: Bedminster, 1968.

Wells-Barnett, Ida B. *On Lynchings*. 1892. Reprint, Mineola, NY: Dover, 2014.

West, Cornel, ed. "The Radical King We Don't Know." In *The Radical King*, edited by Cornel West, ix–xvi. Boston: Beacon, 2015.

———. "Ta-Nehisi Coates Is the Neoliberal Face of the Black Freedom Struggle." *The Guardina*, December 17, 2017. https://www.theguardian.com/commentisfree/2017/dec/17/ta-nehisi-coates-neoliberal-black-struggle-cornel-west.

West, Gerald O. "People's Theology, Prophetic Theology, and Public Theology in Post-Liberation South Africa." http://www.academia.edu/7263452.

West, Traci C. "Gay Rights and the Misuse of Martin." In *The Domestication of Martin Luther King Jr.: Clarence B. Jones, Right-Wing Conservatism, and the Manipulation of the King Legacy*, edited by Lewis V. Baldwin and Rufus Burrow Jr., 141–56. Eugene, OR: Cascade, 2015.

"What Is Public Theology?" *Centre for Theology and Public Issues*. https://www.otago.ac.nz/ctpi/what/

Wicomb, Zoë. "Shame and Identity: The Case of the Coloured in South Africa." In *Writing South Africa: Literature, Apartheid and Democracy, 1970–1995*, edited by Derek Attridge and Rosemary Jolly, 91–107. Cambridge: Cambridge University Press, 1998.

Wilder, Craig. *Ebony and Ivy: Race, Slavery, and the Troubled History of America's Universities*. New York: Bloomsbury, 2014.

Williams, Reggie L. *Bonhoeffer's Black Jesus: Harlem Renaissance Theology and an Ethic of Resistance*. Waco, TX: Baylor University Press, 2014.

Wilmore, Gayraud S. *Black Religion and Black Radicalism: An Interpretation of the Religious History of African Americans*. Maryknoll, NY: Orbis, 2006.

Wilmore, Gayraud S., and James H. Cone, eds. *Black Theology: A Documentary History*. Vol. 1. Maryknoll, NY: Orbis, 1979.

Wilson, Kirt H. "The Natural and Cosmopolitan Dimensions of Disciplinarity: Reconsidering the Origins of Communication Studies." *Quarterly Journal of Speech* 101 (2015) 244–57.

Wise, Tim. "Whites Swim in Racial Privilege." In Tim Wise, *Speaking Treason Fluently: Anti-Racist Reflections from an Angry White Male*. Berkeley, CA: Soft Skull, 2008.

Wolterstorff, Nicholas. *Hearing the Call: Liturgy, Justice, Church, and World*. Edited by Mark R. Gornik and Gregory Thompson. Grand Rapids: Eerdmans, 2011.

Wood, Amy Louise. *Lynching and Spectacle: Witnessing Racial Violence in America, 1890–1940*. Chapel Hill: University of North Carolina Press, 2009.

Woodson, Carter G. *The Mis-Education of the Negro*. 1933. Reprint, Trenton, NJ: Africa World, 1998.

Wright, Richard. *The Color Curtain: A Report on the Bandung Conference*. Jackson: University of Mississippi Press, 1995.

Young, Josiah Ulysses. *No Difference in the Fare: Dietrich Bonhoeffer and the Problem of Racism*. Grand Rapids: Eerdmans, 1998.

Zhang Wanqing. "Domestic Violence Cases Surge During COVID-19 Epidemic." *Sixth Tone*, March 2, 2020. https://www.sixthtone.com/news/1005253/domestice-violence-cases-surge-during-covid-19-epidemic.

Zimmermann, Jens. "Bonhoeffer and Nonviolence." *Theologica Wratislawavensia* 11 (2016) 198–211.

Žižek, Slavoj. "The Return of Public Vulgarity." *Newsweek*, December 2, 2016. newsweek.com/return-public-vulgarity-425691.

Zuiddam, B. A. "M. C. Vos, A Remarkable Story! (1759–1824) in the light of his times," *In die Skriflig, In Luce Verbi*, 46 (2), art. #56, 12 pages. DOI:10.4102/ids.v46:2.56.

Index

#AllLivesMatter, 171
#BlackLivesMatter, 171
#BlueLivesMatter, 171
#RhodesMustFall, 35, 52, 246
#Uyinene, 270
16th Street Baptist Church Bombing, 157
1788 Khoi Uprising, the, 132
1820 Missouri Compromise, the, 193n27
1850 Fugitive Slave Act, the, 193
1854 Kansas-Nebraska Act, the, 193
1857 Dred Scott US Supreme Court decision, the, 193, 194, 246
1913 Land Act, 137, 152
1919 Chicago Riot, the, 94
1919 Elaine Race Massacre, the, 49, 50, 51, 157
1919 Red Summer, the, 49, 157,
1921 Tulsa Massacre, the, 157
1935 Harlem Riot, the, 94
1936 Land Act, 137, 152
1956 Women's' March, the, 73, 144
1956–1961 Treason Trial, the, 162
1959 Potato Boycott, the, 161
1960 Cottesloe Declaration, the, 135, 137, 138, 154
1960 Sharpeville Massacre, the, 134, 135, 137, 138, 139, 140, 157, 160, 162, 163, 172
1968 Message to the People of South Africa, 135, 141, 154
1976 Soweto Uprising, the, 45, 62, 113, 143, 144, 148, 174, 264, 265
1982 Belhar Confession, the, 76
1983 South African constitution, 1985 Kairos Document, the, 76
1985 Theological Rationale for the Day of Prayer, the, 76
2002 World Summit for Sustainable Development, 157
2012 Rugby World Cup, 149
2012 Marikana Massacre, 163
2020 Democratic Primary Race, 182
2020 United States Presidential Race, 71

Abdurahman, Abdullah, 73
Abyssinian Baptist Church, 68, 69
Accra Confession, the, 150
Adams College, 136, 137
Adoniram, 83
AfrAsia Bank, 205
African Global Operations, 267
African Methodist Episcopal Church, the, 131, 226
African National Congress (ANC), the, 7, 8, 9, 12, 16, 17, 18, 19, 28, 47, 67, 78, 79, 80, 88, 102, 112, 128, 134, 135, 137, 139, 141, 149, 157, 162, 163, 175, 176, 206, 210, 220, 221, 248, 253, 254, 255, 262, 263, 266,
African Renaissance, 77, 78, 79, 80, 197, 254
Africom, 34
Afrikaner Broederbond, 88
Agri South Africa, 274
Ahishar, 83
Al Jazeera, 39, 230
Al Jazeera English, The Stream, 39
Albright, Madeleine, 259
Al-Husseini, Haj, 200
Allah, 57
Allen Temple Baptist Church, 162
Alleyne, Kenneth, 222
Alliance of Black Reformed Christians of Southern Africa (ABRECSA), the, 76
Alvarado (Honduras), 202
Alves, Rubem, 268, 279
Amanpour, Christiane, 276, 277
Amazon, 280
American Committee on Africa, the, 158

INDEX

Amherst, Jeffrey, 202
Amos, the Book of, 23, 56
Antiracist Research and Policy Center, the, 222
Arab Spring, the, 5, 32, 202, 264
Araújo, Marta, 42, 43
Arbery, Armaud, 94, 169
Ashera, 32
Ashur, 30, 32, 38
Ashurbanipal, 30, 31, 33
Asmal, Kader, 15, 17
Assange, Julian, 59
Australian National University, 208

Baal, 32
Baard, Francis, 73
Baderoon, Gabeba, 28, 29
Bahour, Sam, 256, 257
Baker, Aryn, 205
Baker, Ella, 73
Baker, Mike, 3
Baldwin, James, 20, 40, 64, 92, 100, 119, 125, 178, 278, 279
Baldwin, Lewis V., 145, 156, 158
Ball, Krystal, 48
Bandung Conference, the, 4
Bantustan Policy, the, 137, 138, 141, 142, 143, 146, 277
Barth, Karl, 23
Bates, Stephen, 38
Bates, Thomas, 25
Bathsheba, 275
Beck, Glenn, 180
Belgian Network for Black Lives, 39
Bezos, Jeff, 280
Biden, Joe, 71, 181, 182
Biko, Nkosinathi, 25
Biko, Steven Bantu, 1, 2, 4, 8, 9, 10, 12, 20, 21, 22, 24, 25, 26, 27, 32, 42, 43, 45, 46, 51, 52, 53, 54, 55, 56, 57, 58, 59, 60, 61, 67, 73, 75, 81, 89, 93, 94, 98, 100, 101, 102, 103, 104, 106, 108, 109, 110, 112, 113, 114, 115, 116, 119, 120, 124,126, 129, 133, 135, 137, 143, 144, 150, 151, 159, 160, 164, 166, 168, 170, 173, 177, 178, 185, 187, 188, 189, 190, 194, 195, 196, 197, 198, 199, 206, 211, 212, 213, 214, 215, 217, 219, 220, 223, 224, 227, 229, 230, 231, 232, 233, 235, 236, 238, 240, 247, 248, 250, 251, 253, 255, 256, 257, 262, 263, 264, 266, 280, 281, 283
Bin Salman, Mohammed, 202, 208
Black Church, 43, 44, 63, 66, 68, 69, 78, 109, 110, 116, 126, 144, 145, 146, 156, 162, 226, 251, 252

Black Consciousness, 4, 5, 7, 8, 9, 20, 21, 24, 25, 26, 27, 37, 42, 43, 45, 46, 47, 65, 66, 72, 77, 79, 88, 92, 99, 102, 103, 104, 106, 109, 110, 111, 112, 113, 114, 115, 116, 117, 118, 119, 120, 121, 123, 135, 138, 143, 146, 155, 159, 160, 164, 166, 187, 190, 199, 206, 211, 212, 219, 220, 221, 223, 227, 228, 231, 236, 242, 247, 249, 250, 2252, 256, 257, 264, 266
Black Liberation Theology, 4, 6, 21, 24, 26, 42, 66, 116, 126, 132, 143, 159, 187, 188, 191, 219, 226, 227, 230, 233, 239, 248, 249
Black Lives Matter (BLM) 3, 5, 6, 31, 32, 33, 35, 39, 79, 214, 256, 265
Black Sash, the, 7
Black Theology, 4, 7, 27, 60, 63, 65, 66, 90, 109, 110, 112, 115, 116, 124, 126, 155, 160, 225, 226, 227, 228, 229, 230, 231, 235, 236, 237, 238, 239, 240, 242, 247, 248, 249, 250, 251, 252, 253, 266, 267
Blair, Tony, 240, 241
Boesak, Elna, 119, 276
Boezak, Hendrik, 132
Bolsonaro, Jair, 202
Bond, Patrick, 157, 262
Bonhoeffer, Dietrich, 63, 67, 68, 69, 85, 176, 177, 185, 278
Booysen, Anene, 270
Boraine, Alex, 11
Bosassa, 267, 269
Botha, D. P., 160, 161
Botha, Louis, 36
BPC/SASO trial, 1976-1977 45
Brexit Referendum, the, 202, 203
British Broadcasting Corporation (BBC), the, 203, 273
Brown Douglas, Kelly, 61, 93, 94, 95, 190, 191
Brown, Michael, 31
Buitendag, Johan, 128
Bunyan, John, 56
Burke, Samuel, 277
Burrow, Rufus, 180
Bush, George W., 48, 49, 180, 183, 200, 201, 240, 241, 259
Buthelezi, Manas, 249
Butler, Smedley Darlington, 259

Caesar, 101
Calata, James, 132
Calhoun, John, 33
Calvin, John, 72, 73, 74, 83, 90, 107, 108, 111, 148, 184, 193, 194, 195, 249
Cameron, Daniel, 37

Cannon, Katie, 30, 71
Cape Argus Newspaper, The, 149
Capitein, Jacobus Elisa Johannes, 225
Capone, Al, 259
Castle, Stephen, 36
Central intelligence Agency (CIA), the, 200
Centre for Theology and Public Issues, the, 81
Césairé, Aimé, 119, 159, 205, 221, 231, 232, 242
Channel, 4 203
Charles, Ray, 183
Charter of Alliance of Black Reformed Christians of Southern Africa, the, 146
Chauvin, Derek, 52
Chicago Theological Seminary, 45
Chickeeduck, 33
Chikane, Frank, 76, 129, 162
Chilcot Inquiry, the, 241
Chirenje, J., Mutero, 131
Chomsky, Noam, 9, 10, 71, 258
Christian Institute of South Africa, 128, 135
Churchill, Winston, 33,
Churchwell, Sarah, 93, 94
Clingan, Ralph G., 67, 69
Clinton, Bill, 201, 240, 259
CNN, 48, 277
Coates, Ta-Nehisi, 71
Colenso, John, 130
Colston, Edward, 33, 52
Columbus, Christopher, 33
Cone, James Hal, 4, 52, 63, 65, 66, 67, 74, 76, 77, 78, 93, 115, 159, 191, 225, 226, 227, 231, 249, 266
Congregational Church, the, 132
Conradie, Ernst, 256
Consumer Financial Protection Bureau, 48
Corinthians, Paul's Letter(s) to the, 16, 101, 213, 215, 216, 217
Coronavirus (COVID-19) 208, 210, 222, 255, 271, 280, 282
Cory Methodist Church, 181
Couper, Scott, 134, 136, 137
Cox, Harvey, 209
Cullen, Countee, 68

Dabashi, Hamid, 5, 6, 32, 214, 264, 265
Darwin, Charles, 243
David, 275
Davis, Mike, 60
Dawkins, Richard, 21, 22
De Bruin, Sophie, 73
De Gruchy, John, 13, 130, 177
De Klerk, F. W., 12, 241, 254, 273, 274, 246, 277, 278
De La Quelerie, Maria, 36

De La Torre, Miguel, 41, 42, 43, 44, 45, 227
De Lange, Johnny, 14
De Sousa Santos, Boaventura, 199
Declaration of Conscience, the, 159
Defiance Campaign, the, 27, 132, 134, 156, 159, 160, 161
Dehaene, Jean-Luc, 38
Democratic Alliance (DA), the, 118
Desmond, Cosmas, 135, 137
Dexter Avenue Baptist Church, 156
Dhai, Ames, 20
Die Kerkbode, 161
Diem/Thieu/Ky (Vietnam) 202
District Six, Cape Town, 153
Doig, Tracy, 272
Donne, John, 158
Douglass, Frederick, 22, 23, 85, 159, 162, 166, 186, 195, 239, 297
Dreyer, Yolanda, 128
Du Bois, W. E. B., 73, 204, 209
Duarte, Regina, 202
Dube, John L., 132, 253
Dunbar-Ortiz, Roxanne, 40
Dutch Reformed Church(es), the, 66, 70, 74, 75, 76, 113, 124, 128, 133, 135, 153, 160, 161, 163, 175, 189, 244
Dutch Reformed Mission Church, the, 128, 137, 146, 152
Duterte, Rodrigo, 201
Duvaliers (Haiti), The, 202
Dwane, James, 131
Dyson, Michael Eric, 180

Eastern Cape Herald Newspaper, The, 104
Economic Freedom Fighters (EFF), the, 273
Ehlen, Patrick, 219
Eisenhower, Dwight David, 258
El Sisi, Fattah, 202
Elmerajji, M., 260
Elphick, Richard, 131
Elsie's River, Cape Town, 172
Emerson, Barbara, 38
Emerson, Michael O., 149
Enjeti, Saagar, 48
Episcopal National Cathedral, 256
Epistemicide, 55, 140, 152, 199, 228
Erasmus, Zimitri, 187, 219
Erlinger, Joe, 280
Esquire magazine, 86
Ethiopian movement, 131
European Union (EU), the, 38, 60, 201, 203
Evangelisch Reformierte Kirche, 260
Evaton, Johannesburg, 134
Ezroura, Mohamed, 87

Index

Falk, Richard, 21, 209
Fanon, Frantz, 4, 5, 29, 63, 64, 72, 90, 91, 92, 97, 99, 105, 106, 114, 159, 180, 187, 212, 219, 223, 246
Fernandez, Leonardo, 59, 60
Finkelman, Paul, 193
Floyd, George, 3, 19, 31, 32, 38, 52, 94, 95, 121, 170, 171
Ford, Paul Robeson, 170, 173, 174
Fortin, Jacey, 37
Fortuin, Bernard, 172
Fox News, 48, 180
Freedom Charter, the, 20, 80, 142, 143, 253
Freire, Paulo, 53, 168, 212, 266

Galatians, Paul's Letter to the, 101, 102, 218, 252
Gandhi, Mahatma, 2, 33, 158
Garnet, Henry Highland, 150, 166, 195
Gaum, Frits, 142
GEAR (Growth, Employment, and Redistribution) 18
Genocide of Rohingyas, the, 209
German Bundesliga, 52
Gerwel, Jakes, 13, 120, 205
Gibson, Douglas, 118
Gilpin, Tom, 280
Global South, the, 2, 28, 31, 60, 85, 121, 151, 181, 200, 205, 213, 214, 241, 242, 258, 259, 262
Goba, Bonganjalo, 249
Gollwitzer, Helmut, 86, 248
Gordon, Rebecca, 271
Goza, Joel Edward, 96, 97, 213, 243, 245
Graham, Billy, 207
Graham, Franklin, 207
Gramsci, Antonio, 25, 63, 70, 71, 72, 73, 84, 229
Gray, Freddie, 37
Greek Junta, 202
Griffen, Wendell, 49, 50, 51, 52, 86, 207,
Grosfoguel, Ramón, 26
Group Areas Act, the, 152, 153
Guardian, The, 38, 241
Guevara, Che, 178
Guptas, the, 78, 205

Habakkuk, the Book of, 7, 55, 83, 139
Habermas, Jürgen, 82
Harlem Renaissance, 68, 70, 191
Hedges, Chris, 240, 241, 242
Hegel, Georg Wilhelm Friedrich, 242
Hendricks, Obery M, 237, 238
Herman, Edward, 9, 10, 71, 258
Herzog, William, 237

Hill, Rising, The, 48
Hitler, Adolf, 33, 67, 69, 176, 177, 207, 189, 190, 200, 208, 255, 272
Hobbes, Thomas, 227, 243
Hochschild, Adam, 38, 39, 40, 41
Hose, Sam, 74
Houdek, Matthew, 227, 234
House of Saud, the, 207
Huddleston, Trevor, 128, 133, 137, 141
Hudson, Michael, 260, 261
Hughes, Langston, 68
Hurley, Denis, 142

Institute for Race Relations, the, 142
Institute of Contextual Theology, the, 146
International Banking House of Brown Brothers, 259
International Criminal Court, the, 49, 209, 241,
International Monetary Fund (IMF), the, 34, 263
Interreligious Foundation for Community Organizations (IFCO), the, 226

Jablonski, Nina G., 221
Jackson, Andrew, 33
Jackson, Jesse, 143
Jackson, Joseph H., 162
Jacobin Magazine, 280
Janssens, Jan Willem, 130
Jefferson, Thomas, 56
Jegels, Leighandre, 270
Jeremiah, the prophet, 23, 31, 236
Jim Crow Law(s) 52, 92, 234
John, Gospel of, 24, 111, 190, 236, 238
Johnson, Boris, 36, 202, 203
Johnson, Chalmers, 259
Johnson, Walter, 194, 246
Jones, Charles Colcock, 245
Jones, Clarence B., 180
Jones, Scipio Africanus, 50
Joseph, Helen, 73
Josiah, King, 30, 31, 32, 33, 39,
Judge Boshoff, 45, 46, 251

Kakkerlak, Cupido, 132, 225
Kariuki, Josiah Mwangi, 46
Kaunda, Kenneth, 188
Keevy, Ilze, 70
Kelly, Meg, 240
Kendi, Ibram X., 222
Kennedy, Geoffrey Studdert, 107
Kennedy, John F., 176
Kenyatta, Jomo, 46
Kessler, Glenn, 240
Khumalo, Siya, 192, 253, 272

King Jr, Martin Luther, 4, 6, 25, 26, 27, 30, 32, 49, 52, 55, 60, 63, 64, 73, 78, 79, 85, 100, 117, 127, 136, 153, 154, 155, 156, 157, 158, 159, 162, 163, 165, 166, 167, 168, 169, 171, 173, 174, 176, 178, 179, 180, 181, 182, 183, 184, 185, 186, 195, 204, 215, 217, 230, 247, 256, 257, 265, 276, 279, 280, 281, 282, 283
King Leopold II of Belgium, 37, 39, 41, 189
King Phillippe of Belgium, 40
King, Rodney, 52
King's College London, 208
Kingsolver, Barbara, 40, 41
Klein, Naomi, 84, 208, 255
Koch, Conrad, 268
Kruger, Jimmy, 170
Ku Klux Klan (KKK), the, 171
Kulinski, Kyle, 48, 49
Khumalo, Siya, 253, 268, 271
Langa, Cape Town, 134, 160, 190

Lao Tzu, 197
Le Grange, Louis, 179
Lee, Robert E., 33
Lehmann, Paul, 219
Lincoln University, 157
Lincoln, Abraham, 56, 179
Lincoln, C., Eric, 221
Lipsitz, George, 227
Liuzzo, Viola, 73
Loader, James Alfred, 128
Locke, John, 243, 245
Lodge, Tom, 132
Loeb, Henry, 283
London Missionary Society (LMS), the, 129
Lovaas, Scott, 10
Luke, Gospel of, 31, 105, 106, 107, 127, 236, 238, 240, 252
Luther, Martin, 56
Lutheran Church(es), the, 129
Luthuli, Albert John Mvumbe, 4, 6, 60, 67, 73, 74, 75, 79, 132, 133, 134, 135, 136, 137, 139, 140, 141, 144, 150, 154, 155, 156, 157, 159, 160, 161, 162, 163, 164, 168, 169, 173, 174, 175, 177, 178, 186, 195, 236, 239, 247, 265, 283

Maeso, Silvia Rodriguez, 42, 43
Magona, Sindiwe, 189
Mahabane, R., 253
Makgatho, S., 253
Malcolm X, 4, 56, 63, 78, 166, 180, 181, 217
Malema, Julius, 273
Maluleke, Tinyiko, 11, 17, 21, 82, 200

Mamdani, Mahmood, 15, 18, 19, 189, 208
Mandela, Nelson, 7, 8, 9, 12, 13, 16, 17, 18, 19, 36, 46, 60, 102, 123, 134, 141, 161, 162, 168, 169, 173, 174, 175, 176, 177, 178, 181, 205, 206, 210, 221, 254, 273, 277
Manganyi, Chabani, 223
Mangcu, Xolela, 119
Manning, Chelsea, 58
Mao Tse Tung, 174
Marcos (the Philippines), 202
Martin, Trayvon, 31, 61, 93, 191
Mark, Gospel of, 24, 111, 190, 236, 238
Matthew, Gospel of, 24, 95, 105, 128, 174, 175, 193, 210, 236, 238
Mbeki, Thabo, 7, 10, 15, 16, 76, 77, 78, 80, 157, 254, 255, 266
Mbiti, John, 250
Mboya, Tom, 46
McAtee, David, 37
McDonald's, 280
Mellet, Patric Tariq, 88
Mgojo, Elliot, 249
Miriam, 72
Mkhatshwa, Simangaliso, 249
MNSBC, 48
Mobutu (Congo/Zaire), 202
Modi, Narendra, 202
Mokitimi, Seth, 249
Mokone, Mangena, 131
Moldanado-Torres, Nelson, 206
Moloch, 98
Moltmann, Jürgen, 205, 267
Mosala, Itumeleng, 206, 227, 228,
Motsepe, Patrice, 255
Mountaintop Speech, the, 230
Moyers, Bill, 31
Mubarak, Hosni, 202
Muhammad, Elijah, 57
Mvambo, S. N., 248
Myburgh, Anton, 274

National Association for the Advancement of Colored People (NAACP), the, 280
National Baptist Convention, the, 162
National City Bank, the, 259
National Committee of Negro Churchmen, the, 159, 266
National Conference of Black Churchmen, the, 226
National Council of Black Churchmen, the, 112
National Party, the, 12, 132, 138, 161
National Planning Commission, the, 263
National Union for the Total Independence of Angola (UNITA), the, 176

National Union of South African Students, the, 7
National Urban League, the, 280
Naudé, Beyers, 57, 128, 135, 140, 141, 153, 154, 184, 185
Ndebele, Njabulo, 53, 59, 211, 212, 213, 214, 216
Ndugane, Njonkongkulu, 148
Neal, Claude, 94
Nehru, Jawaharlal, 158
Nel, Hendrik Christoffel (Colonel) 175
Netanyahu, Benyamin, 200
Netherdutch Reformed Church of Africa, the, 128
New Partnership for African Development (NEPAD), the, 10,
New York Times, The, 266
Ngoyi, Lilian, 73
Nkonyane, Zoliswa, 272
Nkrumah, Kwame, 257, 258, 259, 260, 262, 280
Nogwaza, Noxolo, 272
Nolan, Albert, 76
Non-Aligned Movement, 4
North Atlantic Treaty Organization (NATO), the, 38, 86
North West University, 245
Ntsikana, John, 132

Obama, Barack, 31, 34, 58, 180, 181, 182, 200, 201, 202, 234, 240, 241
Odinga, Oginga, 46
Onesimus, 218
Oosterwyk, Rudy, 19
Oppenheimer, Harry, 163
Oxfam, 86, 204, 205, 224, 282

Paerl, Jan, 131, 144, 225
Palestine, 19, 24, 35, 151, 153, 191, 200, 208, 209, 214, 234, 236, 240, 256, 257, 264, 265
Pan-African Congress (PAC), the, 134
Parker, Eve, 202
Parks, Rosa, 73
Patrick, Dan, 208, 255, 256
Patriot Act, the, 49
Paul, the Apostle, 56, 99, 100, 101, 102, 109, 124, 177, 213, 215, 216, 217, 218, 252, 267
Perez, Fabio, 3
Perkins, John, 260
Perry, Keisha-Khan Y., 222
Peter, the Apostle, 57, 136, 174
Pharaoh, 75
Philemon, Paul's Letter to, 101, 218
Philippians, Paul's Letter to the, 101
Pierce, Charles, 86
Pinochet (Chile), 202
Plaatjie, Sol, 73, 132, 144
Plaatjies, George, 128
Pol Pot (Cambodia), 202
Pope Leo X, 83
Powell Sr., Adam Clayton, 68
Powell, Enoch, 203
Pro Veritate, 135, 154
Progressive National Baptist Convention, 162

Rajaiah, Jeyaraj, 214
Ramaphosa, Cyril, 78, 210
Ramphele, Mamphela, 115
Reagan, Ronald, 180
Reconstruction and Development Programme (RDP), the, 17, 18
Reddie, Anthony, 203
Reed, Dreasjon, 169
Reeves, Richard Ambrose, 161
Rhodes, Cecil John, 35, 36, 232
Rice, Susan, 171
Rivonia Trials, the, 134, 162
Rizzo, Salvador, 240
Roberts, Deotis, 4
Rodney, Walter, 63
Roman Catholic Church, the, 70, 135, 226,
Romans, Paul's Letter to the, 23, 99, 101, 267
Rose, McHale, 169
Rothuizen, Gerard, 62, 63
Roy, Arundathi, 224
Russell, David, 52, 53, 57, 125
Rwandan Holocaust, the, 54, 189, 269

Salazar (Portugal), 202
Samuel DeWitt Proctor Conference, 94
Sanders, Bernie, 71
Sartre, Jean Paul, 63, 72
Savimbi, Jonas, 176
Schlebusch, Alwyn, 75
Seme, Pixley ka Isaka, 32, 77, 79, 81, 132,
September, 11 2001 (9/11) 21, 49
Sesanti, Simphiwe, 196, 197, 198
Shah (Iran), the, 202
Shelly, Mary, 86
Sheppard, William, 39
Shepstone, Theophilus, 130
Sisulu, Walter, 158
Sithole, Isaac, 269
Small, Adam, 37, 89, 110, 246, 264, 282
Smit, Dirkie, 82
Smith, Adam, 243
Smith, J., Alfred, 162

Smith, Michael Nassen, 197
Smith, Mitzi, 251
Smithsonian Magazine, 95
Sobukwe, Robert, 162
Solomon, King, 82
Somoza (Nicaragua), 202
Sophiatown, Johannesburg, 153
South African Broadcasting Corporation (SABC), the, 273, 273
South African Council of Churches (SACC), the, 43, 75
Southern Christian Leadership Conference (SCLC), the, 100, 162, 226
Sparks, Allister, 254
Standard Oil, 259
Standing Rock resistance, the, 6, 183, 234
Star Newspaper, The, 104
Stellenbosch Institute for Advanced Study (STIAS) 219
Stellenbosch University, 262
Stern, Mark Joseph, 193
Steve Biko Center for Bioethics, University of the Witwatersrand, 20
Stubbs, Aeldred, 12, 52, 53, 60, 126, 212, 213, 216, 223, 264
Stuurman, Klaas, 132
Suleimani, Qassem, 242
Sylvester, Henry, 73
Synod of Dordt, the, 249

Tambo, Oliver, 135
Taylor, Breonna, 37, 94, 169,
Taylor, Keeanga Yamahtta, 31, 94, 173
TeleSur (English) 59
Ter Schegget, Bert, 76, 192, 215
Ter Schegget, G. H., 58, 192, 215
Terreblanche, Sampie, 79, 120, 262
Thembu Church, the, 131
Theological University of the Reformed Churches, 62
Therborn Göran, 206
Theron, Izak, 128
Thessalonians, Paul's Letter to the, 101
Thlagale, Buti, 228
Thomas, M. M., 2, 4, 6, 7, 25, 33, 213, 214, 215, 219, 224, 243, 278
Thorez, Maurice, 231
Three-Fifths Clause, the, 166, 193
Tile, Nehemia, 131
Till Mobley, Mamie, 78
Till, Emmett, 78
Time Magazine, 205
Tivaringe, Tafadzwa, 197, 198
Tokwe, Kenny, 205

Transvaal Indian Congress (TIC), the, 43
Treurnicht, Andries P., 189, 244
Tri-Cameral Parliament
Trump, Donald, 31, 32, 35, 37, 48, 49, 71, 84, 86, 87, 93, 181,193, 200, 201, 202, 204, 207, 208, 240, 241, 242, 259
Truth and Reconciliation Commission (TRC), the South African, 10, 11, 12, 13, 14, 17, 18, 104, 118
Truth, Sojourner, 225
Tsafendas, Dimitri, 46
Tshaka, Rothney, 249, 250, 252
Tuchman, Barbara, 83
Turner, Henry McNeal, 131, 226
Turner, Nat, 225
Turse, Nick, 208
Tutu, Desmond, 11, 12, 13, 26, 81, 172, 227, 250
Twain, Mark, 39

U.S., Agency for International Development (USAID), the, 260
Ubuntu, 14, 54, 115, 116, 120, 122, 143, 157, 189, 196, 197, 233, 252, 269, 271, 273
Ubuntufication, 6, 122, 168, 178, 257
Umansky, Lauri, 51
Umkhonto we Sizwe, 134, 139, 178
UNHCR, the UN Refugee Agency, 271
Union of South Africa
Union Theological Seminary, 63, 226, 227
United Democratic Front (UDF), the, 7, 20, 43, 48, 134, 138, 148, 193, 233, 236, 264, 265, 266
United Nations (UN), the, 59, 94, 208, 289
United Nations University World Institute for Development Economics Research, 208
Uniting Reformed Church, 260
University of Cape Town (UCT) 270
University of San Francisco, 271
University of South Africa (UNISA) 196, 269
University of the Western Cape, 174, 250
Uriah, 275
US Congress, 96

Van Aarde, Andries Gideon, 128
Van der Kemp, Johannes, 130
Van Eck, Ernest, 128
Van Riebeeck, Jan, 36
Van Riebeeck, Maria, 36
Van Winkle, Rip, 155, 165
Van Zyl, 274
Vanoldenbarneveldt, Johan, 249
Vellem, Vuyani, 206, 224, 229
Verdoolaege, Annelies, 10
Verwoerd, Hendrik F., 46, 161, 177

Index

Vesey, Denmark, 225
Villa-Vicencio, Charles, 118, 129, 130, 131, 133, 189, 229
Vita, Dona Kimpa, 225, 226
Vorster, Koot, 244
Vos, M. C., 244, 255

Wall Street, 71, 157, 258, 259
Waller, Allyson, 37
Walmart, 280
Warren, Scott, 207
Washington Post, The, 240
Wasserman, Harvey, 202, 210
West, Cornel, 71, 119, 168
Wheatley, Phyllis, 225
White, Dale, 154
Wicomb Zoë, 28, 29
WikiLeaks, 58, 59
Wilder, Craig, 229
Williams, George Washington
Williams, Reggie, 67, 69
Williams, Stephanie Collingwood, 39
Willie Lynch Letter, the, 95, 96, 97, 98, 299
Wilmore, Gayraud S., 63, 66, 67, 131, 132, 162, 225
Wilson, Kirt H., 233

Wilson, Richard, 14
Woodson, Carter, 66
World Alliance of Reformed Churches (WARC), the, 76
World Bank, the, 205, 260, 263
World Council of Churches (WCC), the, 59, 135, 148, 154
World Health Organization (WHO), the, 59, 86
Wrankmore, Bernie, 128
Wright Jr., Jeremiah A., 49, 63
Wright, Richard, 5

Yahweh, 33, 83, 127
Yancey, George, 149
Yeltsin/Putin (Russia), 202

Zacchaeus, 107, 274, 275, 276
Zikode, S'bu, 73
Zindo, Raymond, 266
Žižek, Slavoj, 199, 200, 201
Zondo Commission, the, 266
Zuiddam, B. A., 245
Zulu, Alpheus, 4
Zuma, Jacob, 78, 80, 205, 210

www.ingramcontent.com/pod-product-compliance
Lightning Source LLC
Chambersburg PA
CBHW080758300426

44114CB00020B/2753